The Price
of
POWER

Books & Things Publishing, LLC
4410 Brookfield Corporate Dr. #220149
Chantilly, VA 20153

THE PRICE OF POWER
Text copyright © 2025 Gigi Smith
Cover design by Butter Bird Design
Design and format by Books & Things Publishing, LLC
First Edition August 2025
ISBN 978-1-962140-35-5
Library of Congress Control Number: 2025914276

To schedule author events and order in bulk, visit
www.booksandthingspublishing.com.

Help support the author by leaving a review.

I dedicate this book to my friends, Brianna, Shani, Megan, Mike, Marcie Jo, Cass, and Alexis, whose love keeps me both soft and great! And to my mama, Tonya, who always knew this day would come, I love you and miss you every day! We in here, gang!! On hood.

CONTENTS

PROLOGUE

A Mother's Warmth, A Father's Shadow

Lacy was only six years old when her mother, Amanda, died in what her father called a "tragic accident." But those brief six years were filled with warmth and love, moments that would forever stand in stark contrast to the coldness that followed.

Amanda Jacobs was everything Richard Jacobs, her father, was not—soft, nurturing, and endlessly patient. She had a way of making Lacy feel special, as if she were the most important person in the world. Lacy's favorite memories were of the times she spent in the kitchen with her mother, perched on the counter as Amanda baked pies, cookies, and cakes. The kitchen was always filled with the sweet scent of vanilla and cinnamon, and Amanda's voice, humming You Are My Sunshine softly, would wrap around Lacy like a warm blanket.

When Lacy was sad or scared, Amanda would scoop her up into her arms, holding her close and singing lullabies that seemed to make all the bad feelings go away. Lacy would nestle her head against her mother's chest, feeling the steady rhythm of her heartbeat and the softness of her embrace.

But all of that changed when Amanda died. Suddenly, the warmth and comfort that had defined Lacy's world were gone, replaced by the strict, unyielding presence of her father and the stern governess, Hilda, who took over her care.

Hilda was a tall, imposing woman with graying hair pulled back into a tight bun. She dressed in somber, unadorned clothing, and her expression was perpetually stern. Hilda was efficient, ensuring that Lacy's days were filled with lessons, chores, and strict routines, but there was no warmth in her care. She rarely smiled, and the few words she spoke were clipped and to the point.

"Sit up straight, Miss Lacy," Hilda would say as Lacy worked on her lessons, her tone brooking no argument. "A proper young lady does not slouch."

Lacy learned quickly that tears and protests were useless. Hilda was not like her mother; she did not comfort or console. Instead, she enforced the rules with an iron hand, ensuring that Lacy grew up to be the perfect daughter her father demanded.

One day, the late afternoon sun cast a warm golden light over the sprawling Jacobs estate, its rays filtering through the tall oaks that bordered the property. The garden, meticulously tended to by a small army of gardeners, bloomed with a riot of colors—roses, tulips, and lilies swaying gently in the summer breeze. But the estate's beauty did little to comfort young Lacy Jacobs, who sat alone on the edge of a marble fountain, her small fingers trailing idly through the cool water.

At just eight years old, Lacy was a delicate, ethereal child, with large, expressive eyes that seemed to take in the world with a mixture of wonder and caution. Her dark hair, neatly braided by Hilda, who rarely let her out of sight, framed a face that had not yet lost its baby fat. She wore a white dress, pristine and pressed, that her father insisted she always wear when she was outside. Lacy's mother had once chosen her clothes and had once been the one to braid her hair, but those days were now distant, faded like the edges of a well-worn photograph.

Lacy sighed, her breath forming little ripples on the water's surface. She couldn't remember much about her mother—just fleeting images, like the scent of lavender that used to cling to her dresses or the soft lullabies she would sing at bedtime. Her mother's death had been sudden, or at least that's what Lacy was told. A tragic accident, her father said. Lacy had learned not to ask too many questions.

Her father, Richard Jacobs, was a man of towering presence, both in stature and reputation. He was feared and respected in equal measure, his name whispered in circles that Lacy was too young to understand. To the world, he was a successful businessman and a pillar of the community. But to Lacy, he was something else entirely—a figure of both admiration and fear, a man who could control the world around him with a mere word or a glance.

Today, as the sun dipped lower in the sky, casting long shadows across the garden, Lacy's solitude was interrupted by the sound of heavy footsteps on the cobblestone path. She looked up to see her father approaching, his broad shoulders framed by the fading light. Richard Jacobs was a man who carried power with him like a second skin. His hair, dark and meticulously combed, had begun to show streaks of gray, but his eyes were as sharp as ever, cold and calculating.

"Lacy," he called out, his voice deep and resonant, a sound that commanded attention. "Come here, sweetheart."

Lacy quickly stood up, smoothing down her dress as she approached him. Her father rarely came to the garden; his domain was the grand office inside the mansion, a place Lacy had only ever seen from the doorway.

"Yes, Daddy?" she asked, her voice small and tentative.

Richard smiled, but it didn't reach his eyes. He held out his hand, and Lacy hesitantly took it. His skin was warm, the grip firm but not painful. Together, they walked toward the mansion, the gravel crunching under their feet.

As they entered the house, the air changed, growing cooler and more still. The scent of polished wood and rich leather filled Lacy's nostrils, mixed with the faintest trace of her father's cologne— something expensive and foreign. The mansion was vast, its corridors lined with portraits of ancestors who seemed to watch Lacy as she passed. It always made her feel small, as though the weight of history pressed down on her tiny shoulders.

Richard led her to his office, a room that seemed to pulse with a life of its own. The walls were lined with bookshelves, filled with leather-bound volumes that smelled of age and wisdom. A large oak desk dominated the space, its surface covered with papers, files, and a chessboard, the pieces mid-game. The windows, draped in heavy curtains, allowed only slivers of the dying light to enter, casting eerie patterns on the Persian rug.

Richard motioned for Lacy to sit in a chair opposite his desk. She did so, her legs dangling off the edge, her feet not quite touching the floor. Richard settled into his leather chair with a sigh, his eyes drifting over the chessboard. He picked up the queen, turning the piece over in his hand, his expression thoughtful.

"Do you know why I've brought you here, Lacy?" he asked, his tone gentle, almost fatherly.

Lacy shook her head, her heart fluttering with a mix of curiosity and apprehension. "No, Daddy."

Richard leaned forward, his eyes locking onto hers. "I want to teach you something important. Something your mother would have wanted you to know."

At the mention of her mother, Lacy's breath caught in her throat. She nodded, eager to learn anything that could bring her closer to the memory of the woman she had lost.

Richard set the queen back on the board and gestured to the pieces. "This," he said, "is a game called chess. Have you ever played before?"

Lacy shook her head again, wide-eyed. "No, Daddy."

Richard smiled faintly. "It's a game of strategy, of power. Every piece has its role, its place on the board. But the most important piece—the one that holds the true power—is the queen. She can move in any direction, as far as she wants. She controls the board. Without her, the king is defenseless."

Lacy listened intently, her eyes following her father's hand as it moved the pieces around the board. "So, the queen is the strongest?" she asked, a note of awe in her voice.

Richard nodded, his gaze darkening as he looked at the queen in his hand. "Yes, Lacy. The queen is the strongest. And you must learn to be like her—strong, untouchable. You must always protect yourself and never let anyone take your power away."

Lacy's brow furrowed as she tried to grasp the weight of his words. "But, Daddy, what about the king? Isn't he important, too?"

Richard's expression hardened slightly, a shadow passing over his features. "The king is only as powerful as the queen allows him to be. Remember that, Lacy."

Before Lacy could ask more questions, the phone on Richard's desk rang, its sharp tone cutting through the quiet room. Richard held up a hand to silence her, then picked up the receiver.

"Yes?" His voice was cold, businesslike. As he listened, his expression became even more inscrutable. "I see. No, it must be taken care of immediately. No loose ends. Do you understand?"

Lacy watched, her heart pounding in her chest, as her father's demeanor shifted. His tone, though controlled, carried an undercurrent of menace that sent a shiver down her spine. She didn't understand the words, not fully, but she could sense the danger in them.

"Good," Richard said, finally. "Make sure it's done."

He hung up the phone with a decisive click and turned back to Lacy, his face softening into a forced smile. "Sometimes, Lacy," he said, his voice smooth again, "we have to make difficult decisions to protect what's ours. Do you understand?"

Lacy nodded slowly, though she wasn't sure she did. She felt a strange mix of fear and admiration for her father, a man who seemed to hold the world in his hands.

Richard reached across the desk, picking up the queen and placing it gently into Lacy's small palm. "This is for you," he said. "A reminder of what you must become."

Lacy looked down at the chess piece, its smooth, cool surface resting in her hand. She felt the weight of it, both physically and metaphorically, even if she couldn't yet understand its full significance.

"Thank you, Daddy," she whispered, her voice barely audible.

Richard stood, signaling that their conversation was over. "Remember, Lacy," he said as he escorted her to the door, "power is the most valuable thing you can possess. Never forget that."

As Lacy walked back through the mansion's long corridors, the queen clutched tightly in her hand, the shadows seemed to grow longer, darker. The house, once a place of security and comfort, now felt different—more imposing, more suffocating. The weight of her father's words and the eerie silence that followed them pressed down on her small frame.

As she passed a portrait of her mother in the hallway, Lacy paused, staring up at the image of the woman she barely remembered. Her mother's eyes seemed to follow her, a silent witness to the conversation that had just taken place. For a fleeting moment, Lacy thought she smelled lavender, the scent of her mother's perfume, but it vanished as quickly as it came, leaving her with only the cold reality of her father's world.

Lacy continued to her room, the chess piece still gripped in her hand and, with each step she took, the innocence that had once defined her began to fade, replaced by the lessons of power and control that her father had so carefully, so ruthlessly, begun to teach.

CHAPTER 1

Now, at thirty-four, Lacy had become the woman her father always wanted—ambitious, successful, and powerful. But beneath the polished exterior, the same soft heart her mother had nurtured still beat strong. Standing at 5'9", Lacy was a striking Black woman with long, luxurious black hair that, when left natural, cascaded in bouncy curls that perfectly framed her somewhat rounded face, highlighting her full lips and beautiful Nubian nose. Her kind eyes, often alight with intelligence and quick wit, softened the formidable aura she projected in her professional life. Years of running and yoga had sculpted her body into a curvy yet athletic form, exuding both strength and grace. Though she cherished her natural curls, Lacy often wore her hair straightened, pulled back in a low bun or ponytail, a style that complemented her polished, commanding presence.

Lacy Jacobs stepped into her campaign headquarters and was immediately met with a whirlwind of activity. Phones were ringing, staffers were huddled in intense discussions, and the hum of dozens of conversations filled the air. The view of the city was breathtaking, a constant reminder of the power she wielded in the heart of the smaller metropolis of Richmond. The open floor plan allowed Lacy to see almost everyone at once—a sea of determined faces working toward a common goal: her victory. The walls were lined with posters of her campaign slogans, charts tracking her progress, and a large countdown clock reminding everyone of how many days were left until the election.

Chloe, Lacy's personal assistant, was the first to spot her. A petite woman in her late twenties, Chloe had a sharp eye for detail and an even sharper mind. Her blonde hair was always neatly styled, and while her clothes were not designer, they were impeccably chosen and pressed, reflecting her dedication to professionalism. Chloe made her way through the busy office, a tablet in one hand and a coffee cup in the other, weaving through the chaos with practiced ease.

"Morning, Lacy," Chloe greeted her, offering a warm smile as she handed over the coffee. "I've got your schedule for the day."

"Thanks, Chloe," Lacy replied, taking the coffee with a nod of appreciation. The familiar bitterness of the brew was a comforting reminder of the routine she thrived in.

Just then, Paige, the campaign manager, approached with a confident stride. Paige was a striking woman, her dark skin glowing under the office's fluorescent lights. She was impeccably dressed in a tailored suit that exuded both power and sophistication. Paige was one of the most sought-after campaign managers in the country, known for her strategic brilliance and unflinching resolve. Like Lacy, Paige had grown up in a world where power and money were both a gift and a burden, and the two shared a mutual respect that went beyond mere professionalism.

"Lacy, we need to go over the latest polling data," Paige said, her voice calm but commanding. "There's a slight dip in support among younger voters. We need to address it, and I've got some ideas."

Lacy nodded, gesturing for them to walk toward her office as they spoke. "Let's go over it now. I want to make sure we're hitting all the right notes in the next speech."

As they walked, Chloe fell into step beside them, quickly briefing Lacy on the other tasks for the day. "You've got a donor call in about an hour, then a meeting with the communications team to finalize the messaging for the new ads. After that, we'll head to the statehouse for your committee hearing."

Lacy's office was the epitome of modern elegance—marble floors, minimalist furniture, and a carefully curated collection of art that adorned the walls. But what stood out most was the paperweight on her desk: a queen chess piece, larger than life, its smooth, polished surface reflecting the light. It was a gift from her father, a constant reminder of the lessons he had instilled in her since childhood.

Paige chimed in, "And don't forget the debate prep this afternoon. We need to make sure you're ready. Also, watch out for Whitmore. He's going to be gunning for you, and it isn't good press."

Lacy gave a small, determined smile. "Deep breaths, ladies, we got this."

The trio reached Lacy's office, a glass-walled room that offered a view of the entire campaign floor. Inside, the space was decorated with minimalistic yet luxurious touches—plush chairs, sleek desks, and a few personal mementos that reminded Lacy of her journey. She sat behind her desk, Chloe and Paige standing on either side as they dove into the details of the campaign.

After an hour of strategizing, Lacy was prepared for the day ahead. As she stepped out of her office and headed to the conference room for her call, the energy of the headquarters buzzed around her, but Lacy felt centered, focused. She was ready to face whatever challenges the day would bring.

Later that day, the hum of activity in Lacy Jacobs' campaign headquarters was at its peak when Paige rushed into Lacy's office, her expression uncharacteristically tense. Lacy looked up from her desk, where she had been reviewing the latest polling data, and immediately sensed that something was wrong.

"What's going on?" Lacy asked, setting down the tablet and giving Paige her full attention.

Paige, always poised, took a deep breath before replying. "We've got a situation. The local news station just ran a segment claiming that one of our key donors, Harrison Industries, is under investigation for environmental violations. It's blowing up on social media, and our opponents are already starting to spin it as proof that you're in bed with corrupt corporations."

Lacy's eyes narrowed slightly, but she remained calm. Harrison Industries was a smaller manufacturing company that produced raw materials for various industries. They weren't one of her father's companies, which gave her some distance, but their support was still important. "How credible is the report?"

"It's based on a preliminary investigation," Paige said, her tone measured but urgent. "Nothing conclusive, but it's enough to cause a stir. If we don't handle this quickly, it could snowball."

Lacy nodded, already shifting into crisis management mode. "Get me the communications team on a conference call in five minutes. I want a full breakdown of the situation and a draft of our official statement ready by the time I'm done with my meetings. Also, get someone to pull up everything we know about Harrison Industries' environmental practices. We need to see if there's any merit to this."

Paige immediately started typing notes into her tablet, but before she could leave, Lacy added, "And get me the contact for Harrison's CEO. I want to speak with him directly."

Paige raised an eyebrow, impressed by Lacy's quick thinking, but not surprised. "On it," she said before hurrying out of the office.

Five minutes later, Lacy was on the phone with her communications team, her voice steady and authoritative as she directed the conversation.

"We need to get ahead of this," Lacy said. "First, we release a statement expressing our commitment to environmental responsibility and our willingness to cooperate with any investigation. But we don't throw Harrison under the bus—not yet. Emphasize that the investigation is ongoing, and we'll monitor the situation closely."

"Understood, Senator," replied Jason, her communications director. "I'll have the draft ready for your approval within the hour."

"Good," Lacy replied. "And start pushing out some positive stories to counterbalance this. Highlight our clean energy initiatives and partnerships with environmental groups. I want the public to see that our campaign stands for sustainability."

After the call ended, Lacy leaned back in her chair, considering her next move. Just then, Paige returned with a folder containing Harrison Industries' environmental track record.

"Here's everything we have on Harrison," Paige said, handing over the documents. "And the CEO, Grant Harrison, is expecting your call."

Lacy skimmed through the documents quickly, her mind already piecing together a strategy. "They had a leak a few years back, but they patched it quickly and paid the fines. It looks like when they knew there was a problem, they fixed it."

Paige smiled, recognizing the steely resolve in Lacy's voice. "How shall we proceed?"

Lacy's eyes met Paige's, a determined glint in them. "I'm going to make sure it was just a one-time thing and if there is something he is hiding, he better tell me now or face the full force of a Senate investigation once I'm governor. He knows which option will be better for his business."

Paige chuckled, shaking her head in admiration. "And here I thought my job was to handle the tough stuff. What do you even need me for, Lacy?"

Lacy grinned, the tension of the moment lifting slightly. "To keep me from getting too full of myself, Paige. Thank you for always making it easy."

Paige laughed, the lighthearted exchange a welcome reprieve from the stress of the situation. "You've got it, boss."

Lacy dialed Grant Harrison's number, her expression turning serious once more. As she listened to the phone ring, she knew that by the end of this call, Harrison Industries would either be on the right side of the environmental debate or be left in the dust. And in the process, she would not only save her campaign but also prove that power could be wielded for good.

By the time she hung up, she had secured Harrison's cooperation. They agreed to issue a joint statement promising transparency and a renewed commitment to environmental standards. The crisis was averted before it could escalate.

Paige reentered Lacy's office just as she finished the call. "Is it fixed?" Paige asked, already knowing the answer.

Lacy chuckled, a rare moment of lightness breaking through the stress of the day. "It's fixed. We make a good team."

"Damn right we do," Paige replied, her tone both appreciative and proud.

With the crisis behind them, Lacy turned her attention back to the campaign, more determined than ever to stay ahead of the game. She knew there would be more fires to put out, more challenges to face, but with Paige by her side and her own unwavering resolve, she was ready for whatever came next, including a meeting at the state house with Senator Whitmore.

****

The statehouse was a different kind of battlefield, one where the weapons were words and the casualties were reputations. The historic building stood tall and imposing, its stone columns and intricate architecture symbolizing the weight and tradition of the legislative process. Inside, the grand halls echoed with the voices of lawmakers, staffers, and lobbyists, all hustling to push their agendas forward. The air was thick with the scent of polished wood and old leather, a tangible reminder of the history and power contained within these walls. Lacy Jacobs moved through the building with purpose, her heels clicking against the polished marble floors as she headed toward the committee room.

As she approached the heavy oak doors of the committee room, she took a deep breath, straightened her posture, and pushed them open with deliberate grace. The room was already filled with state senators and delegates seated around a large, oval-shaped, mahogany table. The walls were adorned with portraits of past legislators, their stern gazes watching over the proceedings like silent judges.

All eyes turned to her as she entered, the low murmur of conversation dwindling to a hush. Lacy maintained her composure, offering a polite nod to the assembled lawmakers as she moved toward her seat. She could feel the weight of their gazes, some appraising, others scrutinizing, but she refused to let it unsettle her.

At the head of the table sat Speaker Harold Whitmore, his presence as commanding as ever. He was a man in his late sixties, with a shock of silver hair and piercing blue eyes that had seen decades of political maneuvering. Dressed in a crisp navy suit and a striped tie that screamed old-school democrat conservatism, Whitmore embodied the traditionalist faction of their party—a faction that often clashed with Lacy's more progressive ideals.

As she took her seat, Whitmore cleared his throat loudly, making a show of checking his watch before fixing her with a cold, condescending stare.

"Glad you could join us, Senator Jacobs," Whitmore drawled, his voice dripping with sarcasm. "I trust your schedule isn't too burdened to spare some time for the state's business."

A few quiet chuckles echoed around the room, and Lacy felt a flush of irritation rise in her cheeks. But years of political experience had taught her to mask her emotions behind a veneer of cool professionalism. She met Whitmore's gaze evenly, offering a composed smile that didn't quite reach her eyes.

"My apologies for the delay, Mr. Speaker," she replied smoothly. "I was securing a key endorsement that will significantly advance our state's clean energy goals. I believe that qualifies as state business, wouldn't you agree?"

A brief flicker of annoyance crossed Whitmore's face, but he quickly concealed it, his expression settling back into stony indifference.

"Well, let's hope it was worth the wait," he retorted before turning his attention back to the agenda. "Now, as I was saying, today's committee meeting will address the proposed budget reallocations for infrastructure development."

As the meeting commenced, Lacy opened her binder, revealing a neatly organized stack of documents annotated with her notes and highlighted sections. She listened attentively as various committee members presented their reports and arguments, her mind already formulating responses and counterpoints.

The first item on the agenda was a proposal to divert funds from renewable energy projects to traditional infrastructure repairs—a move that Whitmore and his allies were pushing hard. Lacy knew this was a direct challenge to her platform, an attempt to undermine her commitment to progressive policies by framing them as fiscally irresponsible.

After a few minutes of spirited discussion, Whitmore looked around the table before settling his gaze back on Lacy.

"Senator Jacobs, since you've been so vocal about environmental issues, perhaps you'd care to explain how you intend to fund these expensive renewable energy projects without neglecting our crumbling roads and bridges," he said, his tone laced with skepticism.

Lacy sat up a little straighter, feeling the eyes of her colleagues settle on her once more. She welcomed the challenge; this was her arena, and she was prepared.

"Thank you, Mr. Speaker," she began, her voice clear and confident. "I believe we can achieve a balanced approach that addresses both our immediate infrastructure needs and our long-term sustainability goals. By leveraging public-private partnerships and federal grants specifically earmarked for renewable energy, we can fund green initiatives without sacrificing essential repairs. Moreover, investing in renewable energy now will save the state money in the long run through reduced energy costs and job creation in emerging sectors."

She paused, letting her words sink in before continuing. "It's not a matter of choosing one over the other but finding innovative solutions that serve multiple purposes. I have outlined several such proposals in the documents I've provided, which include detailed budget analyses and projected fiscal impacts."

Whitmore's expression remained impassive, but Lacy didn't miss the slight tightening of his jaw—a telltale sign that she had struck a nerve.

"Interesting theory, Senator," he replied, his voice tinged with condescension. "But theories don't fill potholes or repair aging bridges. Our constituents expect tangible results, not lofty ideals."

Then, with a poised yet sharp undertone, Lacy said, "Mr. Speaker, you're right. Theories do not fill potholes; however, nor does funneling money into buddies at the police departments while consistently voting against city revitalization projects for new and existing infrastructures, such as potholes and bridge maintenance. Does it?" She stared directly at Senator Whitmore. Let's focus on how our citizens' tax money will be responsibly allocated. Roads and bridges will be prioritized, but we will also ensure that any surplus, grant money, or discretionary funds we secure are invested in creating a safer and cleaner future."

Her eyes swept over the room, locking back onto Whitmore's. "That's how we balance addressing the needs of today with our unwavering dedication to the future of our constituents."

A few nods of agreement came from other members around the table, emboldening Lacy further. Senator Dianna Lopez, a respected figure known for her balanced views, chimed in. "I have reviewed Senator Jacobs' proposals, and I find them both practical and forward-thinking. Perhaps we should consider forming a subcommittee to explore these options in more detail."

Whitmore's eyes flickered toward Senator Lopez, a hint of frustration evident in his gaze. It was clear that he hadn't anticipated others siding with Lacy so openly.

"Very well," he conceded reluctantly. "We'll table that suggestion for now and move on to the next item."

The meeting continued, covering various topics from education reform to healthcare funding. Throughout, Lacy remained actively engaged, articulating her points with clarity and poise. Whitmore attempted to undermine her contributions several times, interrupting her or dismissing her ideas as impractical. But Lacy held her ground, countering his criticisms with facts and measured arguments that left little room for rebuttal.

Each exchange between them was a subtle duel, words and glances serving as weapons in their ongoing battle for influence. The tension was palpable, not just between Lacy and Whitmore but among the other committee members who were increasingly drawn into their ideological tug-of-war.

At one point, during a heated debate over healthcare allocations, Whitmore's facade cracked slightly.

"Perhaps if Senator Jacobs spent less time chasing social media headlines and more time understanding the practicalities of governance, we wouldn't be wasting time on proposals that have no chance of passing," he snapped, his frustration evident.

Lacy felt a surge of indignation but forced herself to remain calm. She took a deep breath before responding, her voice steady and composed.

"Mr. Speaker, understanding the practicalities of governance means recognizing the needs of all our constituents, not just those who fit within certain people's narrow view. Innovative policies may seem challenging at first, but that's how progress is made. Dismissing new ideas without proper consideration does a disservice to the people we claim to represent."

A murmur of agreement rippled through the room, and Whitmore's face flushed slightly, his eyes narrowing as he regarded her. It was clear that he was unaccustomed to being challenged so directly, especially by someone he considered his junior both in age and experience.

The remainder of the meeting proceeded with less overt hostility, though the undercurrent of tension remained. By the time the session adjourned, Lacy felt both exhausted and invigorated. She had held her own against Whitmore's attempts to belittle her, and more importantly, she had managed to sway several committee members to consider her proposals seriously.

As the other lawmakers filtered out, collecting their papers and exchanging quiet conversations, Whitmore approached Lacy, his expression a mask of strained cordiality.

"That's the second time this week you've been late, Lacy," he said, his tone low but sharp, using her first name in a pointedly familiar way that bordered on disrespect. "If you want to be taken seriously as a candidate for governor, you need to show a little more respect for this office."

Lacy met his gaze steadily, her eyes reflecting a mixture of resolve and controlled irritation. She chose her words carefully, ensuring her response was both respectful and assertive.

"I appreciate your concern, Mr. Speaker, and I will strive for better punctuality in the future. However, I believe respect for this office is also demonstrated through our commitment to thoughtful, forward-looking policies that serve all our constituents. Today's discussions were productive, and I look forward to continuing this important work."

Whitmore's lips thinned even more into a hard line, his eyes flashing with barely concealed anger at her subtle rebuke. He took a step closer, lowering his voice further.

"Listen here, young lady," he hissed, the veneer of politeness slipping away. "I've been in this game a lot longer than you, and I know how things work. Ambition is all well and good, but don't overstep your bounds. This state doesn't need reckless idealism for a spoiled little daddy's girl; it needs steady, experienced leadership."

Lacy felt a spark of anger flare within her, but she kept her composure, refusing to be intimidated.

Lacy could feel the adrenaline coursing through her veins as Whitmore leaned in, his breath hot with barely contained contempt. The dismissive use of her first name stung, and with the jab about her father and their relationship, her heartbeat quickened, pounding in her ears. Her jaw tightened, and she could feel the heat rising in her chest, the pulse of anger spreading through her body. It was a sensation she had been taught to control, to channel into the poised, composed demeanor that politics demanded. But this time, she decided to drop the mask.

With a steely gaze, she met Whitmore's eyes, her voice dropping to a low, dangerous register. "All that experience, and you still lost the nomination," she began, her tone razor-sharp. "I wonder if it's because you reek of outdated ideas, three failed marriages, and a lifetime of bureaucracy. You're a relic, Harold, and I work tirelessly every day to put you and everything you represent in a museum where relics of the past belong."

She took a deliberate step closer, her eyes narrowing as she continued. "With all due respect—and believe me, that's very little— you need to understand something: The people elected me to lead. Now, you can get on the Lacy train, or you can find out exactly what happens when you're standing in its way." She smiled sinisterly.

Lacy grabbed her bag, the tension in her body suddenly releasing as a wave of triumph washed over her. She flashed Whitmore a cool, dismissive smile. "Have a good day, Mr. Speaker." Without waiting for a response, she turned and walked away, her steps firm and unhurried, leaving him standing in the empty room.

As she exited the committee room, the rush of adrenaline slowly ebbed, replaced by an exhilarating sense of power. Her head was held high, her shoulders back, and she felt as if she were walking on air. The thrill of standing up for herself, of dropping the diplomatic veneer and letting her true strength shine through, filled her with pride. She didn't like being that woman—her father's daughter, a force to be reckoned with—but, oh, did she love shutting him down.

Behind her, Whitmore's seething gaze burned into her back, but the satisfaction of putting him in his place made the moment all the sweeter.

As Lacy strode down the hallway, Chloe was there, waiting as always, tablet in hand, and a knowing smirk on her face. "Nicely done," she murmured, falling into step beside Lacy. "I think you gave Whitmore a run for his money today. He looked like he was going to burst a blood vessel."

Lacy chuckled, the tension in her shoulders easing slightly. "That wasn't the plan, but I won't pretend I didn't enjoy it."

Chloe laughed, her eyes sparkling with amusement. "Well, remind me to send flowers to his blood pressure medicine." She swiped through her tablet, then glanced at Lacy with a mock-serious expression. "But, speaking of Whitmore, your legislative assistant, Lena just called. Apparently, Whitmore's Chief of Staff is saying he's considering moving to censure you for being late to the committee meetings twice this week. He's trying to make a scene of it."

Lacy's eyes narrowed. "Of course he is. Whitmore can't handle being challenged, so he's throwing a tantrum in the form of a censure. Classic move."

Chloe nodded, her expression all business. "What do you want to do?"

Lacy stopped in her tracks, a flash of determination in her eyes. "I've got a plan. If Whitmore wants to play this game, we'll play it smarter. I'll draft a statement to preempt the censure—something that puts him on the defensive, makes it look like he's targeting me personally because I'm pushing for reforms he doesn't like. We'll frame it as him being afraid of change, afraid of progress."

Chloe listened intently, taking quick notes on her tablet. "Got it. I'll get the communications team ready to draft that statement as soon as you have the main points."

Lacy nodded, then suddenly glanced at her calendar app on her phone. Her brow furrowed for a moment, and then she let out a sigh. "Wait—tomorrow's my day off, isn't it? I scheduled that weeks ago."

Chloe looked up with a bemused smile. "Yes, you did. And you told me not to let you talk me into letting you work. Remember?"

Lacy exhaled, momentarily thrown. "Yes. Buttttttt……with Whitmore pulling this, maybe I should—"

Chloe cut her off, shaking her head firmly. "No. You're taking the day off, Lacy. We put these days on your calendar for a reason. And you know you're no good to us if you're running on empty. We can handle Whitmore's little bitch fit. Lena and I have it covered."

Lacy sighed but relented. "Fine, you're right. But make sure Lena knows the plan. She needs to get our allies on the committee to speak up in my defense and to emphasize Whitmore's desperation. Make it clear he's threatened by the changes we're pushing for."

"Already on it," Chloe replied, jotting down more notes. "I'll get Lena up to speed and have her coordinate with the committee members. We'll make Whitmore regret even thinking about censure. Oh hey, just a reminder—Lorenzo's has a case of that wine you and your dad like," she said casually. "Since, you know, Thursday night is dinner with your dad."

Lacy rolled her eyes playfully. "A case? Sounds about right. It'd take at least that much to make dinner with him fun."

Chloe laughed. "Come on, maybe this time will be different."

"Maybe," Lacy replied, her tone just a little too flat to be convincing.

Chloe chuckled, giving her a sympathetic look. "Look, tomorrow's your day off. Don't stress about it. Let the team handle Whitmore—

we're already on it. You just relax, enjoy your day, and focus on something other than politics for a change."

Lacy sighed but smiled, appreciating Chloe's support. "Alright, alright. I'll try. Thanks, Chloe."

"Any time," Chloe replied. "Just don't forget to grab that wine. You know, just in case," she added with a wink.

Lacy laughed. "Trust me, I won't. Thanks."

As they stepped out into the crisp evening air, Lacy took a deep breath, feeling a bit of the day's tension ease. The sun was dipping below the skyline, casting warm, golden hues over the city she loved. She turned to Chloe with renewed determination. "Alright, let's make sure we're ready for whatever Whitmore throws at us. And get that statement drafted."

Lacy chuckled, heading toward the car. For a moment, she allowed herself to relax, to let the tension of the day fade away. Tomorrow, she would take her day off, recharge, and come back ready to fight again. With Chloe and her team in her corner, she knew they were more than ready to take on whatever challenges came next.

Lacy stopped by Lorenzo's on her way home, picking up three bottles of the Cabernet she and her dad both liked—enough to get through dinner and maybe even soften the edges of their inevitable tension. Back home, she reheated some leftovers, savoring the quiet comfort of a simple meal, then took a hot shower to wash away the day's tension. Just as she was toweling off, her phone buzzed with a text from Chloe: "Good news: Whitmore can't censure you for being late. Worst he can do is tweet about it, and we've got that covered if he does." Lacy smiled and replied, "Thanks, Chloe. You're the best." Feeling reassured, she let herself relax. Tomorrow was her day off, and for once, she felt ready to enjoy it without any lingering worries. After responding to Chloe's reassuring text, Lacy set her phone aside, feeling a bit of the day's tension ease. She curled up on the couch with a blanket for a moment, letting the quiet of the evening settle around her, the familiar comfort of her home wrapping her in its embrace.

With a deep breath, she allowed herself to unwind, her worries slowly fading into the background. Realizing she'd feel better in the comfort of her own bed, she got up, turned off the lights, and slipped beneath the soft cream-colored duvet, the cool sheets soothing against her skin. Tomorrow would be her day off—a day she had planned and forgotten, but now seemed more needed than ever. As she drifted off to sleep, the hum of the city outside her window faded into a distant murmur, her body finally relaxing into the warmth of her bed, ready to greet the next day with a clearer mind.

When morning came, the light filtered gently through the curtains, waking her naturally. Lacy stretched, feeling the tension in her muscles release as she took a deep breath. She slid out of bed, her bare feet sinking into the soft rug, and made her way toward the living room. As she walked, the cool hardwood floors felt grounding beneath her, guiding her toward the sunlit space. She paused by the large floor-to-ceiling windows, watching as the golden light poured in, bathing the room in a warm, inviting glow. The city below was just beginning to stir, but here, in her quiet sanctuary, everything felt still, tranquil. She stood there for a moment, letting the sunlight wrap around her, the simple beauty of the morning filling her with a sense of calm she hadn't realized she needed.

The living room was dominated by a large, low-profile sectional in a soft gray, complemented by a glass coffee table with sharp, clean edges. The walls were a soothing shade of off-white, adorned with abstract art pieces that spoke to her refined taste. The polished hardwood floors gleamed under the soft light from carefully placed modern lamps, creating an atmosphere of quiet sophistication.

However, amidst the sleek modernity of her surroundings, a few personal items hinted at the layers beneath Lacy's composed exterior. On a small side table near the window, nestled between a tall vase of fresh lilies and a stack of political biographies, was a weathered photograph, its edges frayed with age. The picture, encased in a simple silver frame, showed her mother, Amanda, beaming with pride as she held a newborn Lacy in her arms. The joy in Amanda's eyes was palpable, a stark contrast to the stern, controlled presence Lacy had grown accustomed to in her own life.

Beside that treasured photo was another, more mysterious image—one Lacy often found herself staring at during moments of quiet reflection. The photograph was torn, missing its top half, and it showed only her mother's arm entwined with that of a man she did not recognize. It was the only other picture of her mother that her father had ever given her, and Lacy often wondered about the man's identity and the circumstances behind the torn photo. The image was a puzzle piece from a past that had always felt just out of reach, a reminder of the life her mother had before it was cut tragically short.

Elsewhere in the apartment, other small, personal touches contrasted with the minimalist design. A shelf in the corner held a collection of Lacy's favorite cookbooks, their well-worn spines a testament to her love of baking—a passion inherited from her mother. A delicate porcelain figurine of a ballerina, a gift from her mother on her fifth birthday, stood proudly next to a modern sculpture, its elegant lines echoing the grace of the dancer.

In the bedroom, a plush cream-colored duvet covered the king-sized bed, its soft texture inviting after long days filled with campaign meetings and public appearances. On the nightstand, a simple lamp with a sleek, modern design sat next to a small, faded music box that played a lullaby Amanda used to sing to her. The box was another relic of her childhood, its chipped paint and scratched surface evidence of to the many nights Lacy had wound it up, seeking comfort in its familiar tune.

Today was one of her rare off days, a day she had set aside for herself to unwind and recharge. The campaign was in full swing, but Lacy had learned the importance of taking time to care for herself, even in the midst of chaos. As she moved through her apartment, the contrast between the modern decor and the few cherished personal items served as a constant reminder of the duality within her—a woman who had mastered the art of power and control, yet still clung to the tender memories of a softer, more innocent time.

She started her morning with a yoga session in her sunlit living room, the gentle stretches and poses helping her to center herself and clear her mind. As she flowed from one position to the next, Lacy felt the tension of the past week slowly unwind from her body. The familiar creak of the hardwood floor beneath her as she moved, the warmth of the sunlight filtering through the tall windows, and the rhythmic sound of her own breath created a sanctuary where she could truly let go.

With each deep inhale, Lacy visualized the stress and expectations melting away, her muscles softening, her mind quieting. The burdens she carried—her father's relentless demands, the pressure of the campaign, the carefully maintained facade of perfection—seemed to lift, if only for a little while. The yoga mat beneath her feet was the only place where she felt truly untethered, free from the world outside.

As she moved into a deep forward fold, the stretch released the last bit of tension in her lower back, and she allowed her thoughts to drift. She thought of her mother's gentle voice, always reminding her to find her center before making any decisions. "Clear your mind, Lacy," Amanda used to say, her hands warm as they smoothed over Lacy's young shoulders. "When your mind and heart are at peace, you'll know which way to go." It was a reminder that no matter how much the world demanded of her, she was still in control of her own path. And today, her path was one of peace.

After yoga, Lacy made her way to the kitchen, the transition from her practice to her routine feeling seamless and natural. The kitchen, with its sleek marble countertops and state-of-the-art appliances, was a space where Lacy could lose herself in the simplicity of creation. As she measured out the flour and sugar, she felt a sense of grounding— her fingers working deftly, almost instinctively, as she mixed the batter for blueberry muffins.

The act of baking was a ritual for her, one that always brought a sense of comfort and connection. As she folded the plump, juicy blueberries into the batter, she found herself humming a tune her mother used to sing, the melody soft and sweet on her lips. Each swirl of the wooden spoon felt like a dance, the rhythm of her movements syncing with the steady beat of her heart. The kitchen filled with the warm, inviting scent of vanilla and fresh berries, wrapping around Lacy like a hug. This was another lesson from her mother—finding moments of peace in the simplest of tasks, using them as a way to clear the mind and open the heart.

Once the muffins were in the oven, Lacy sat down at her kitchen table with a cup of herbal tea and her journal. She often used her journal as a way to process her thoughts and emotions, a habit she had picked up during her time in Europe. Today, she wrote about her plans for the future, her hopes for the campaign, and the memories of her mother that had been on her mind lately.

Lacy found herself lost in thought, reflecting on the path that had led her to where she was today. Lacy took a slow sip of her herbal tea, savoring the soothing warmth as she let the steam rise and curl around her face. She set the cup down carefully, its gentle clink against the saucer the only sound in the stillness of the kitchen.

She opened her journal, the pages thick and slightly worn from years of use, and picked up her pen. For a moment, she simply stared at the blank page, letting her thoughts settle. The phone, already set to "Do Not Disturb," buzzed faintly on the counter, but she ignored it. This was her time—a sacred space she had carved out to reconnect with herself, away from the endless demands and expectations.

Finally, she began to write:

Sometimes I wonder if I've strayed too far from the path I set out on. Europe feels like a distant memory, but the lessons I learned there still anchor me when the world gets too loud. I can still hear Mama's voice reminding me to find my center, to listen to my heart. I wish she were here now—I could use her wisdom more than ever.

The campaign is gaining momentum, but I feel like I'm playing a role that isn't mine. Dad's influence is always there, and while I know he's proud of the woman I've become, I'm not sure I am. I keep thinking about the community center project, the people who will benefit from it. That feels like my work, but even then, Dad's voice is in my ear telling me it's all part of a larger game.

I've been thinking about Mama a lot lately. Maybe it's the stress, or maybe I'm realizing how much of her I've lost over the years. She believed in love and kindness, in strength that didn't have to be hard or cold. I want to find that kind of strength in myself, but every day feels like a battle.

Maybe this campaign is about more than just winning—it's about finding my own voice, my own path. I hope I'm strong enough to listen to it.

Lacy.

She paused, her pen hovering above the page, then set it down with a sigh. The smell of the muffins grew richer, signaling they were almost done. She allowed herself a small smile, feeling a little lighter. After taking the muffins out of the oven to cool, Lacy set a pot on the stove for a slow-cooked dinner, savoring the soothing rhythm of preparing a meal. The warmth of the kitchen and the gentle hum of the stove eased her mind, and before long, she felt her eyelids grow heavy. With a satisfied sigh, she settled onto the couch, letting herself drift into a nap as the afternoon light streamed through the windows.

Lacy awoke from what felt like the best nap she'd had in weeks. The warmth of the late afternoon sun filtered through the sheer curtains of her living room, casting a golden hue over the space. She stretched luxuriously on the plush couch, feeling the last traces of sleep fade away. The air was filled with the rich, mouthwatering aroma of the stew simmering on the stove—a hearty blend of tender beef, carrots, onions, and potatoes, seasoned to perfection with rosemary, thyme, and a hint of red wine.

As she slowly sat up, a satisfied smile spread across her face. The apartment was quiet, save for the occasional bubble of the stew and the distant hum of traffic outside. It was the kind of peaceful solitude she rarely had the chance to savor, and she intended to enjoy every moment of it.

Reaching for her phone, Lacy opened her favorite music app and started playing Megan Thee Stallion Radio. The room instantly came alive with the infectious beats of hip-hop, the bass vibrating through the hardwood floors, sending energy thrumming through her veins. Lacy couldn't help but laugh, the sound bright and carefree, as the music took hold of her.

She kicked off her slippers, feeling the coolness of the floor beneath her feet, and began to move. At first, her steps were slow and deliberate, her hips swaying gently in time with the music. But as the rhythm built, so did her movements, becoming more animated, more expressive. Lacy spun around, her long, straightened hair flowing behind her as she let the music guide her. She started to twerk playfully, laughing at herself as she caught her reflection in the window. There was no one here to judge, no public eye scrutinizing her every move— just her, the music, and the joy of being completely free.

The savory scent of the stew filled the air, mingling with the faint sweetness of the vanilla candle burning on the counter. The aroma wrapped around her like a comforting embrace, grounding her in the moment as she danced and swayed around the kitchen. Her senses were fully alive—the feel of her muscles moving, the pulse of the music, the warm, inviting smells, and the rich taste of life itself.

She grabbed a wooden spoon and gave the stew a quick stir, tasting the broth and letting the flavors dance on her tongue. Perfect. It was rich and savory, the kind of meal that nourished not just the body but the soul—a dish that took time and care, just like the way she was tending to herself in this rare moment of solitude.

With the music still softly playing in the background, Lacy grabbed her copy of Ida B. Wells' biography from the coffee table. The cover was slightly worn from repeated readings, a testament to how often she returned to the story of a woman whose strength, courage, and tenacity had always inspired her. She settled into her favorite armchair, the one that fit her body just right, and opened the book to the marked page. The soft leather cradled her as she turned the pages, the smell of aged paper and ink mingling with the aroma of the simmering stew.

As she read, the rhythmic flow of the music continued to play in the background, punctuated by the occasional sizzle and bubble from the pot on the stove. Megan Thee Stallion's voice, full of confidence and unapologetic power, provided a fitting soundtrack to the life story of Ida B. Wells, a woman who had refused to back down in the face of injustice.

Lacy felt a deep connection to both women—one from history, the other from the present. They were both examples of what it meant to be strong, to carve out a place in the world on your own terms. They reminded her of the strength that came not from force or power, but from a deep, unwavering commitment to one's truth.

She couldn't help but think of her mother, the way she had embodied that same kind of quiet strength. As she read about Ida's battles for justice, Lacy felt a renewed sense of purpose—an affirmation that the path she was on, no matter how challenging, was one worth walking.

Time seemed to slow down as she lost herself in the book, the music, and the comforting scents around her. It was as if the apartment had become a cocoon, a space where she could shed the weight of the world and simply be herself—Lacy, the woman with a soft heart, a kind spirit, and a strength that came from love, not power.

Hours passed in this blissful state, the stew slowly thickening and deepening in flavor as it cooked on the stove. Eventually, as the sun began to set and the last rays of daylight filtered through the windows, Lacy put down the book and stood up. She moved to the kitchen, turning off the stove and ladling the stew into a bowl. The rich, comforting aroma filled her senses as she took the first bite, savoring the depth of flavor that had developed over the hours.

As she enjoyed her meal, the music still playing softly in the background, Lacy felt a deep sense of contentment. She knew that tomorrow would bring new challenges, new battles to fight, but for now, she allowed herself to simply be. She was reminded, in these quiet moments, of who she truly was—a woman shaped by love, driven by purpose, and grounded in the strength that had been passed down to her through generations.

And as the night continued on, Lacy knew that no matter how far she rose in the political arena, she would always carry a piece of this peace, this joy, and this love with her. It was her mother's legacy, Ida's example, and Megan's anthem all wrapped into one—a reminder that she was not just a queen in her father's game, but a woman with her own story to tell, her own power to wield.

After finishing her meal and cleaning up the kitchen, Lacy decided it was time to unwind even further. She headed to her bathroom and turned on the shower, letting the water run hot as she gathered her things. The bathroom quickly filled with steam, the air thick with the scent of eucalyptus from the shower tablets she loved so much. She stepped under the hot spray, sighing in pleasure as the water cascaded over her. She lathered her skin with her favorite lavender-scented body wash, the soothing fragrance mixing with the steam and enveloping her in a cloud of calm.

After her shower, Lacy wrapped herself in a plush towel and made her way to the bedroom. She slipped into a short silk nightie in a deep emerald hue, the smooth fabric clinging softly to her curves. A matching robe fell loosely around her frame, its whispering touch cool against her warmed skin. Cozy slippers cushioned her steps as she began her nightly routine.

She laid out tomorrow's outfit with practiced precision—a tailored navy suit, sharp and confident. Her gold watch and simple stud earrings rested neatly on the dresser, ready to complete the look. After scanning the notes she had prepared earlier, she nodded to herself. The campaign would demand her full focus, and she was determined to be ready.

Finally, she slipped into bed, the cool sheets soothing her as she nestled under the comforting weight of the blankets. Picking up the remote, she scrolled through TV options, torn between something new and something familiar. Familiar won. Grey's Anatomy's opening theme filled the room, and a wave of nostalgia swept over her.

She let the familiar faces of Meredith and Cristina draw her in, their drama and camaraderie like a balm for her weary mind. The dialogue played softly, blending with her thoughts as her eyelids grew heavy.

Before long, the steady hum of the TV and the warmth of her bed lulled her to sleep. The glow of the screen cast gentle shadows, the voices fading into a soothing backdrop. For a moment, the weight of tomorrow disappeared, replaced by the peaceful embrace of now.

Tomorrow would bring newness in many forms, but for now, Lacy was enveloped in a world where she could simply be—a world where the weight of expectations and the pressures of politics melted away, leaving only the warmth of the covers, the soft light of the TV, and the comforting embrace of sleep.

CHAPTER 2

The ramshackle house creaked with every gust of wind that pushed through the cracked windowpanes. The walls, once painted white, were now a sickly yellow, stained with age and neglect. In the corner of the small living room, a threadbare sofa slumped under the weight of time and the family's troubles. A single bulb hung from the ceiling, casting a dim, flickering light that barely illuminated the room.

Seven-year-old Richard Jacobs sat on the edge of that sofa, his small hands clenched into tight fists. His heart pounded in his chest, each beat reverberating in his ears as he listened to the harsh, slurred voice of his father, Gerald Jacobs, tearing through the thin walls.

"You useless bitch! You think you can just sit around while I'm out bustin' my ass?" Gerald's voice was thick with alcohol, each word laced with venom. He was a tall, imposing man, his frame hardened from years of factory work and manual labor, but softened by the booze that now consumed him.

Richard's mother, Dorothy, stood in the kitchen doorway, her hands trembling as she clutched the hem of her faded dress. She was a slight woman, her once-vibrant eyes now dull with fear and exhaustion. Her dark skin, a rich brown that had once glowed with life, now seemed ashen under the weight of the years and the burdens she bore.

"Gerald, please, I—" Dorothy's voice quivered as she tried to reason with him, but she didn't get far.

"Shut up!" Gerald roared, slamming his fist down on the flimsy table, sending a half-empty bottle of whiskey crashing to the floor. "Don't talk back to me!"

Richard's body tensed as he watched his father advance on his mother, his large hand raised as if to strike her. A surge of anger and desperation welled up inside the boy, pushing him off the sofa and into the fray.

"Stop it!" Richard shouted, his voice high-pitched and filled with a courage he didn't quite feel. He darted between his parents, his small body a barrier between his father's rage and his mother's fear.

Gerald's bloodshot eyes snapped to his son, and for a moment, there was a stunned silence. Then, his face twisted into a sneer.

"You think you can protect her, boy?" Gerald's voice dripped with contempt as he grabbed Richard by the collar, lifting him off the ground effortlessly. "You're just as weak as she is. Love makes you weak."

Richard struggled in his father's grip, his feet kicking helplessly in the air. "I'm not weak! I love Mama, and you can't hurt her!"

Gerald's sneer deepened as he looked at his son, seeing in him the same defiance he had long since beaten out of Dorothy. Without warning, he flung Richard across the room. The boy hit the wall with a sickening thud and crumpled to the floor, pain radiating through his small frame. Dorothy cried out, rushing to her son's side, but Gerald was there first, pulling her back by her hair.

Richard's vision blurred with tears, but he could still see the terror in his mother's eyes, could still hear her pleading for Gerald to stop. But Gerald didn't stop. He was a man consumed by his own demons, and that night, those demons took over completely. He turned on Richard with a savage fury, fists flying as he pummeled the boy, screaming all the while about weakness, about how love made a man vulnerable.

Richard's world was a haze of pain and fear, but somewhere deep inside, a seed was planted. A seed of determination. He would grow stronger. He would never let himself be weak again. And most of all, he would find a way to get his mother away from this monster.

****

It didn't happen overnight. The years passed, and Richard learned to be careful, to be cunning. He did what he could to make money, whether it was running errands for the neighborhood hustlers or acting as a lookout for the local drug dealers. He watched, he learned, and he saved every penny he earned.

By the time Richard was fifteen, he had become a fixture in the streets. He had grown taller, stronger, and his once round face had sharpened with the edge of hard-earned wisdom. His mother had noticed the changes in him, the way his eyes no longer held the innocence they once did, but she never asked where the money came from when Richard handed it to her in small, carefully folded bills. She was just grateful to have enough to keep food on the table.

One night, Richard came home to find his mother sitting at the small kitchen table, the only place in the house that still felt somewhat warm. The air was thick with the scent of fried chicken, a rare treat she had prepared as a celebration.

"Richie," she said softly as he entered, using the pet name she had called him since he was a boy. "You're home late."

Richard shrugged, pulling a wad of cash from his pocket and placing it on the table in front of her. "I've been working…… But look….. We've got enough now, Mama. We can leave."

Dorothy's eyes widened, her hand trembling as she reached out to touch the money. It was more than she had ever seen in one place. But with the money came the weight of reality, and fear clouded her eyes. "Richie, I don't know if we should…"

"We have to," Richard insisted, his voice firm. "We can't stay here anymore. Don't worry mama, I'll take care of you, I promise."

Before Dorothy could respond, the front door creaked open, and the sound of heavy, stumbling footsteps echoed through the small house. Richard's heart sank as his father's shadow loomed in the doorway, his presence filling the room with the harsh smell of alcohol and stale sweat.

"What's all this?" Gerald slurred, his eyes narrowing as they fell on the money. "Where'd you get that, boy?"

Richard stood his ground, his fists clenched at his sides. "It's none of your business. We're leaving, and you can't stop us."

Gerald's face twisted into a drunken sneer as he lunged for the money. "The hell you are! That's my money. You live in my house!!"

But Richard was faster. He grabbed the money before his father could reach it, shoving it into his pocket. Gerald's face flushed with anger, and he swung his fist at Richard, but this time, Richard was ready. He ducked under the blow and, with a strength he had gained from years of fighting to survive, he struck back. His fist connected with his father's jaw, the impact sending the older man stumbling back.

Dorothy cried out, her hands flying to her mouth as she watched in horror. "Richie, stop!"

But Richard couldn't stop. He wouldn't. He had waited too long for this moment, had endured too much. He hit Gerald again, harder this time, knocking him to the floor. Gerald groaned, trying to push himself up, but Richard was on him, pinning him down.

"You're not taking anything from us anymore," Richard spat, his voice cold and hard. "We're leaving, and you're never going to hurt us again, you drunk piece of shit!!!"

Gerald looked up at his son, and for the first time, there was fear in his eyes. "Go on, then," he muttered, his voice thick with bitterness. "Leave before I kill you both."

Richard didn't need to be told twice. He grabbed his mother's hand, pulling her away from the broken man on the floor. Dorothy hesitated for a moment, her eyes filled with tears, but when she looked at her son—really looked at him—she saw the strength and determination that had grown in him, the fierce love that drove him to protect her. She nodded, squeezing his hand tightly.

She whispered, her voice trembling. "We'll go."

They left that night, taking only what they could carry. Richard led his mother to a small, rundown hotel on the outskirts of the city, a place where other families lived long-term, scraping by on what little they had. It wasn't much, but it was safe, and it was theirs.

Richard continued to hustle, his determination to provide for his mother driving him to take on more dangerous jobs. He started stealing cars, learning the ins and outs of the trade, and soon he was making more money than he ever had before. He saved every cent, and by the time he was sixteen, he had enough to put a down payment on a small house for him and his mother.

The day they moved in was one of the happiest days of Dorothy's life. She wore a new dress, a soft blue that brought out the warmth in her brown skin, and for the first time in years, she smiled—a real, genuine smile that reached her eyes.

Richard watched her as she unpacked their few belongings, his heart swelling with pride. He had done this. He had given his mother a home, a place where she could finally be safe and happy.

One evening, Richard came home late, the sun already setting as he walked through the door of their small house. The smell of his mother's cooking greeted him, a comforting scent that made the house feel like home. But as he stepped into the kitchen, he froze.

There, sitting at the table, was Gerald Jacobs, with a sickly smile on his face.

"Hey there, Richie," Gerald slurred, his words slow and deliberate. "Look at you. Doing well for yourself, huh?"

Richard's stomach churned as he took in the sight of his father, the man he had worked so hard to escape. The stench of alcohol hung heavy in the air, mixing with the savory aroma of the food on the stove, creating a nauseating contrast.

Dorothy stood by the counter, her hands trembling as she stirred a pot of stew. When she saw Richard, her eyes filled with tears, and she looked away, unable to meet his gaze.

"What the hell are you doing here?" Richard demanded, his voice cold and unforgiving.

Gerald took a swig from the cup of water, his eyes glassy as he looked up at his son. "I'm here to talk, that's all. We're family, aren't we? I see you're doing well, and I figured it's time we...patched things up."

"Get out," Richard said, his voice low and dangerous. "You're not welcome here."

"Now, don't be like that," Gerald replied, trying to sound soothing, but the desperation in his voice was clear. "I know I wasn't the best father, but I'm still your old man. And look at your mama here—she wants us to be a family again, don't you, Dorothy?"

Dorothy's hands tightened on the spoon she was holding, her knuckles turning white. "Richie," she whispered, her voice pleading. "He's trying...he's trying to be better. Maybe we could give him a chance."

Richard's heart twisted in his chest. He could see the hope in his mother's eyes, the longing for the family they never had, the family she still believed could exist. But he knew better. He knew the man sitting at their table was a parasite, a leech who would suck them dry and leave them with nothing.

"No," Richard said firmly, his voice leaving no room for argument. "He's not staying. He's not coming back into our lives, Mama. He will destroy everything we've built."

"Richie, please," Dorothy begged, tears spilling down her cheeks. "I just want...I just want us to be a family again. I want you to have a father. I want...I want my man in my life."

Richard's hands curled into fists, the anger boiling inside him threatening to spill over. He couldn't believe what he was hearing.

After everything his father had done, after all the pain and suffering he had caused, his mother was willing to let him back in?

"No, Mama," Richard said, his voice shaking with fury. "He's not coming back. And if you can't see that, then you're just as blind as he is."

Dorothy flinched at his words, her tears flowing freely now. "Richie, I'm sorry...I'm sorry..."

But Richard was done listening. He turned to Gerald, his eyes blazing with hatred. "You have two seconds to get out of this house, or I swear to God, I'll shoot you dead."

Gerald's smile faltered, fear flickering in his eyes as he saw the cold determination in his son's face. He nodded slowly, pushing himself to his feet. "Alright, alright...I'll go. But just remember, boy, I'm still your father."

"Not anymore," Richard spat as his father shuffled past him, the smell of whiskey and sweat lingering in the air.

As Gerald left the house, the door closing behind him with a soft click, Richard turned to his mother, his heart heavy with anger and disappointment. "I'm not letting him back in, Mama. I'm not."

Dorothy nodded, wiping her tears with the back of her hand. "I'm sorry, Richie. I just...I just wanted to believe..."

Richard's expression softened slightly, his heart aching at the sight of his mother's sorrow. "I know, Mama. But he's not going to change. And I'm not going to let him ruin what we have."

That night, Richard couldn't sleep. He lay in bed, staring at the ceiling, his mind racing. He knew his father. He knew that Gerald wouldn't just walk away. He'd come back, and when he did, he'd take everything from them. Richard couldn't let that happen. He wouldn't.

The next day, Richard made a decision. It was a decision that weighed heavily on his soul, one that he knew would change him forever. But it was the only way to protect his mother, to protect the life they had built together.

He waited until nightfall, until the streets were quiet and the city was asleep. Then, he made his way to his father's house, a rundown shack on the edge of town. The air was thick with the smell of garbage and decay, the stench clinging to his nostrils as he approached the front door.

Richard's heart pounded in his chest as he pushed the door open, the rusty hinges creaking in protest. The house was dark, save for the dim light of a single lamp in the living room. Gerald was there, slumped in a chair, a bottle of whiskey in one hand and a cigarette in the other. His eyes were half-closed, his head lolling to the side as he muttered to himself.

Richard stepped inside, his footsteps silent on the worn floorboards. He pulled the gun from his pocket, the cold metal heavy in his hand. His breath came in shallow, steady bursts as he approached his father, his heart pounding louder and louder in his ears.

"Richie..." Gerald slurred, not even noticing the gun in his son's hand. "You come to...come to talk?"

Richard didn't answer. He raised the gun, his finger hovering over the trigger, his mind racing with memories of all the pain, all the suffering, all the nights he had watched his mother cry herself to sleep. All because of this man.

"I'm sorry, Mama," Richard whispered, his voice trembling and eyes filling with tears as he squeezed the trigger.

The gunshot echoed through the small house, a deafening roar that seemed to shake the very walls. Gerald jerked in his chair, his eyes widening in shock as the bullet tore through his chest. The cigarette fell from his lips, landing on the floor with a soft hiss. Blood oozed from the wound, staining his shirt a dark crimson.

Richard watched as his father's body slumped forward, the life draining from his eyes. The room fell into a heavy silence, broken only by the sound of Richard's ragged breathing and the soft crackle of the dying cigarette.

He stood there for what felt like hours, the gun still clutched in his hand, his mind numb. The reality of what he had done slowly began to sink in, the weight of it pressing down on him, threatening to crush him. But as he stared at his father's lifeless body, a strange sense of relief washed over him. It was over. The man who had haunted his nightmares, who had made his life a living hell, was gone. And Richard had done what needed to be done.

Back to the Present

The memory of the gunshot echoed in Richard's mind, the sound snapping him back to the present. The hot water continued to pound against his back, the steam swirling around him like a thick fog. He blinked, realizing he had been standing under the showerhead for far too long, lost in the dark memories of his past.

With a deep breath, Richard turned off the water, the sudden silence almost deafening. He stepped out of the shower, the cool air hitting his wet skin, sending a shiver down his spine. He grabbed a towel and dried himself off, his movements slow and deliberate, as if trying to shake off the lingering shadows of the past.

The darkness was over. Gerald Jacobs was dead, and Richard had built a life that no one could take from him. He had power, wealth, and control—everything he had ever wanted. And tonight, he had dinner with Lacy, the one person who mattered most to him now.

The thought of Lacy brought a small smile to his lips. She was everything he had ever hoped for—strong, ambitious, and determined to make her mark on the world. Even if she didn't always understand him, even if their relationship was strained at times, Richard was proud of her. And tonight, he would enjoy their time together, even if Lacy didn't feel the same.

As he dressed in his usual tailored suit, Richard pushed the dark memories aside. The day awaited, and with it, the responsibilities and challenges that came with being Richard Jacobs. But tonight, for a few hours at least, he could set all of that aside and simply be a father having dinner with his daughter. And that, for Richard, was enough.

The day passed in a blur of meetings and phone calls, Richard's mind always a step ahead as he maneuvered through the intricacies of his empire. He was a man who thrived on control, on knowing every detail of the world around him. But even in the midst of his business dealings, his thoughts often drifted to Lacy. She was everything to him, the one bright spot in his otherwise dark world.

As evening approached, Richard found himself looking forward to dinner. He knew Lacy would be distant, as she always was, but it didn't matter. Just having her there, sharing a meal with her, was enough to remind him that despite everything, she was still his daughter.

The dining room was elegantly set, the table adorned with fine china, crystal glasses, and a bottle of Richard's favorite red wine breathing in the center. The meal was a carefully prepared affair—roast duck with a side of truffle mashed potatoes and sautéed asparagus. The kind of dinner that would impress even the most discerning palate.

Lacy arrived right on time, as she always did. She was dressed impeccably in a tailored black dress that subtly highlighted her curvaceous, athletic frame. Her long, straightened hair was pulled back into a low bun, and her makeup was flawless—elegant yet understated. But despite her polished appearance, there was a distance in her eyes, a guardedness that Richard had come to expect.

"Lacy," Richard greeted her warmly, standing to kiss her cheek as she entered the room. "You look beautiful."

"Thank you, Dad," Lacy replied, her voice polite but lacking enthusiasm. She took her seat across from him, her movements measured and controlled, every inch the poised politician she had become. Yet beneath the surface, a flicker of something else lingered—an unease she couldn't quite shake.

They began the meal in silence, the clinking of silverware the only sound in the room. Richard watched Lacy closely, searching for an opening, a way to connect with her. But she remained focused on her plate, her expression unreadable, her thoughts elsewhere.

As he studied her, memories of Amanda surfaced—her laughter, her warmth, the way she could light up a room just by being in it. Amanda had been the bridge between them once, her love for Lacy softening Richard's stern edges, making him the father he had once hoped to be. But with Amanda gone, that bridge had crumbled, leaving behind a chasm of unspoken words and unresolved tensions.

After a few moments, Richard decided to break the silence. He knew he had to tread carefully. "How are things with Brent?"

Lacy's fork paused midway to her mouth, the question catching her off guard. A slight tension crept into her shoulders, but she quickly recovered, placing the fork back down on her plate with deliberate grace. "We're fine," she replied, her tone curt, clearly uninterested in discussing her relationship.

Richard felt a pang of disappointment, his hopes for a genuine conversation slipping away. He had introduced Lacy to Brent at one of his business parties, thinking they would be a good match. Brent was well-mannered, ambitious, and came from a respectable family. But the way Lacy responded now told him that things were not as perfect as he had hoped.

He tried to hide his disappointment with a sip of wine, the rich taste doing little to soothe the growing tension between them. He had always struggled to connect with Lacy after Amanda's death, his attempts to guide her often coming across as controlling rather than caring. But he couldn't help it—he had lost Amanda, and he wasn't going to lose Lacy too.

Sensing that Lacy was shutting down, Richard decided to shift the conversation. "How's the campaign going? I've heard good things."

Lacy glanced up at him, her expression softening slightly at the mention of her work. The campaign was something she could talk about, something that didn't touch on the more complicated aspects of their relationship. "The campaign is going well. We've got about 7 months to go, but the support is strong. I'm confident we're on the right track."

Richard smiled, feeling a swell of pride. "I'm very proud of you, Lacy. You've come a long way."

Lacy nodded, a small, genuine smile tugging at her lips. "Thank you, Dad." There was a warmth in her voice that hadn't been there before, a glimmer of the connection Richard so desperately wanted.

For a moment, the tension eased, and they fell into a more comfortable rhythm. They spoke of politics, business, and the state of the world, carefully avoiding any topics that might lead to conflict. Richard even tried to inject some humor into the conversation, reminiscing about some of the more absurd moments from his early days in business. Lacy responded with polite laughter, the sound light but lacking the genuine mirth Richard remembered from her younger years.

As the meal came to an end, Richard poured them both another glass of wine, savoring the last few moments of the evening. He knew that Lacy wasn't as excited about these dinners as he was, but he appreciated that she made the effort. It was her way of showing that she still cared, even if she didn't say it outright.

Richard noticed Lacy seemed a little more relaxed than earlier, and he decided to test the waters. "So, I hear Speaker Whitmore is still giving you trouble."

Lacy rolled her eyes, a slight smirk pulling at the corners of her lips. "You could say that. He's been extra grumpy lately—seems to have made it his mission to keep me on my toes. You'd think he'd have more pressing matters than trying to trip me up at every turn."

Richard chuckled, the sound low and almost conspiratorial. "Whitmore's been around forever. He's like an old bulldog—mean, stubborn, and doesn't know when to quit. But he's harmless."

"Harmless, maybe. But I'd rather not have him snapping at my heels all the time," Lacy replied, her smirk widening. "Still, I'm hoping I can get him on board with some of my proposals. He might be stubborn, but even he can't ignore the writing on the wall forever."

Richard leaned back in his chair, a knowing look in his eyes. "Don't worry about Whitmore. Trust me, he'll come around."

Lacy raised an eyebrow, her skepticism clear. "You really think so?"

Richard nodded, a small smile playing on his lips. "I've seen his type a hundred times; he'll fall in line or get whacked on the nose with the newspaper."

Lacy couldn't help but laugh softly at that, the image of Speaker Whitmore as a grumpy, defeated old bulldog brightening her mood. "I hope you're right, Dad. It would make things a lot easier."

"I am right," Richard said confidently. "Just trust me on this one."

Lacy's smile lingered as she took another sip of wine, feeling a rare moment of camaraderie with her father. The tension between them hadn't completely disappeared, but this brief exchange had helped to ease some of it, reminding Lacy that there were still things they could connect over, even if only for a moment.

When it was time to leave, they stood and embraced. Richard held her a little longer than usual, his arms encircling her in a way that was both protective and desperate. He kissed her forehead, a gesture that was more habit than anything else, but one that still held the weight of his love for her.

"Take care of yourself, Lacy," he said softly, his voice tinged with an unspoken plea for her to stay close.

"I will, Dad," Lacy replied, her voice equally soft. But as she pulled away, the distance returned, settling between them like a wall neither could breach.

They parted ways, Richard watching as Lacy walked out of the dining room, her heels clicking against the polished floors with a measured rhythm. He knew she was still distant, still holding something back, but he also knew that these dinners were the one thing that kept them connected. And for Richard, that was enough—for now.

As he returned to his office, Richard allowed himself a moment of reflection. He had lost Amanda all those years ago, and the pain of that loss still lingered, a dull ache in his chest. But he still had Lacy. And no matter what happened, he would do whatever it took to keep her close, to protect her from the harsh realities of the world, even if it meant pushing her away in the process.

He sat down at his desk, the soft light of the lamp casting shadows across the room. The silence was heavy, filled with the memories of a past that Richard couldn't quite escape. But tonight, for a few hours at least, he had been a father sharing a meal with his daughter. And that, for Richard, was enough to keep the darkness at bay.

But as he stared at the empty glass of wine in front of him, the flicker of pride he had felt earlier began to fade, replaced by the nagging fear that Lacy was slipping further and further away. He had fought so hard to build this life, to give her everything she could ever need. But in doing so, had he lost the one thing that truly mattered?

With a heavy sigh, Richard leaned back in his chair, his thoughts drifting to the past. The echoes of old arguments, the harsh words exchanged, the moments of silence that spoke louder than anything ever could—they all haunted him. But no matter how hard he tried, he couldn't shake the feeling that he was losing her.

And that was a loss Richard Jacobs wasn't sure he could bear for many reasons.

****

A few days later, Lacy sat behind her massive oak desk at the State House, dressed in a tailored, cream-colored Chanel suit that hugged her figure perfectly. The soft leather of her red-soled Christian Louboutins added a few extra inches to her already statuesque height. Her long, dark hair was pulled back into a sleek ponytail, and a pair of diamond studs sparkled in her ears—simple yet undeniably expensive. Everything about her appearance exuded power, control, and an impeccable sense of style.

The office itself was a reflection of her status: the tall windows framed with heavy drapes overlooked the bustling state capitol, and the walls were lined with bookshelves filled with legal texts, biographies of great leaders, and a few strategically placed awards. A large portrait of her father, Richard Jacobs, hung on the wall behind her, a constant reminder of the legacy she was expected to uphold.

Today, however, Lacy's mind was preoccupied not with image but with substance. She needed to ensure that the revitalization bill she was championing—a project focused on redeveloping a struggling neighborhood center—was airtight before it went to the subcommittee. It was a cause she genuinely cared about, a step toward enacting the social reforms she believed were necessary to create a more equitable society. But with the legislative session nearing its end, time was running out.

"Lena," Lacy called, her voice echoing slightly in the high-ceilinged office.

Lena Vasquez, appeared in the doorway almost immediately. She was a stunning woman with sharp features, intelligent brown eyes, and a smile that could light up a room. Her beauty was matched only by her brilliance—Lena was whip-smart, quick with a comeback, and had an innate understanding of political strategy that made her invaluable to Lacy's team.

"Lena, I need your help," Lacy said, gesturing to the stack of documents on her desk. "We need to make sure this revitalization bill and the green bill are bulletproof before they go to the subcommittee. I want to anticipate every question they might throw at us."

Lena smiled as she entered, holding a thick binder of documents. "Already on it. Chloe and I have compiled the key talking points, along with a list of potential objections the committee members might raise."

Lacy nodded, feeling a wave of relief. "Good. We have to get this through before the end of the session. If we lose momentum now, it could be another year before we get the chance to speak on it again."

Lena placed the binder on Lacy's desk and opened it to the first section. "I've highlighted some of the more conservative members' concerns about funding and oversight. They'll likely push back on the cost, so we need to be ready with the economic benefits and the long-term savings from investing in these communities."

Lacy scanned the pages, nodding as she absorbed the information. "And what about Whitmore? He's been a thorn in my side since day one."

Lena's expression grew serious. "He's going to be tough, but I think we can appeal to his desire for legacy. If we position this project as something that could define his tenure, we might sway him."

Lacy smiled wryly. "Appeal to his ego—got it. What else?"

"We need to be prepared for questions about the selection process for contractors," Lena continued. "There's always suspicion about cronyism in projects like this, so transparency is key. I've included a section on how we can emphasize the open bidding process and community involvement."

As they worked through the details, Lacy's phone buzzed on the desk, briefly interrupting their focus. She glanced at the screen and saw a message from Brent:

Brent: "Where are you? We need to be at the photo op in 10 minutes. This is important, Lacy."

Lacy sighed, a flicker of annoyance crossing her face. Brent Caldwell, her boyfriend—or rather, the man her campaign team and father wanted her to be with—was a venture capitalist with a perfectly groomed public image. He was tall and handsome, the kind of man who looked good on camera and came from an old-money family that her father approved of. But Brent was also predictable, boring, and, frankly, terrible in bed. Their relationship had grown to one of convenience and optics, not passion or genuine connection.

"Another urgent message from Brent?" Lena asked, noticing Lacy's expression.

Lacy nodded, turning the phone face down on the desk. "He wants me at some photo op. I'll deal with him later—we have more pressing matters."

Lena smirked. "Good call. We can't afford any distractions right now."

They continued refining their strategy, ensuring every angle was covered, every question anticipated. Then, as Lacy prepared herself for the upcoming meetings with her constituents, Lena handed her a list of names.

"First up is Mr. Thompson, a retired schoolteacher who's been advocating for better funding for public schools. He's worried about the latest budget cuts," Lena explained.

Lacy nodded, mentally preparing herself. Education was a topic close to her heart, and she had always admired teachers like Mr. Thompson who continued to fight for their students even in retirement.

"Next on the list is Mrs. Ramirez, a single mother of three who's struggling to make ends meet. She's here to talk about housing issues—specifically, the rising rent prices in her neighborhood and the lack of affordable housing options," Lena continued.

Finally, Lena mentioned a group of young environmental activists who wanted to discuss their concerns about a proposed development project that threatened a local wildlife preserve. "They're passionate and persistent, so we'll need to handle that conversation carefully."

As Lacy prepared for the meetings, she felt a renewed sense of purpose. These were the people she was fighting for—the teachers, the single mothers, the young activists who believed in a better future. They were the reason she had entered politics in the first place, and they were the ones who kept her grounded, even as she navigated the treacherous waters of her father's world.

Just as she was about to step out of her office to meet with Mr. Thompson, her phone buzzed again. Another message from Brent:

Brent: "You can't keep ignoring me, Lacy. We need to talk. Now."

Lacy sighed deeply and slipped her phone into her desk drawer, flipping it to Do Not Disturb. She had more important things to focus on.

"Brent can wait," she said firmly, looking at Lena.

Lena smiled approvingly. "That's the spirit. You've got this."

With a final nod, Lacy gathered her things and prepared to head to her first constituent meeting of the day. As she opened her office door, she greeted Mr. Thompson with a warm smile. It was time to listen, to engage, and to do what she did best—serve her constituents.

Later that day, Lacy returned to her desk after a long day of meetings, her mind still buzzing with the energy of her constituents. As she sat down, she noticed her phone vibrating on the edge of the desk. A new text message from her father flashed across the screen:

"We need to talk about an urgent matter regarding Brent. Come to my office tonight."

Her heart skipped a beat, her fingers tightening around the phone. Whatever this was, it didn't sound good.

****

The grand office of Richard Jacobs was a world unto itself, bathed in the soft glow of lamplight that cast long, flickering shadows across the richly paneled walls. The room was filled with the scent of aged leather and the faint hint of tobacco from the cigar Richard had extinguished earlier. Heavy curtains were drawn across the tall windows, insulating the space from the encroaching night outside. The only sound was the soft ticking of the ornate clock on the mantelpiece and the occasional clink of a chess piece being moved on the board.

Lacy sat across from her father at the massive oak desk, a chessboard set between them. Her designer-clad figure contrasted sharply with the dark, imposing figure of her father, who moved his pieces with the kind of calculated precision that had always unnerved her. He said he needed to speak with her on an urgent matter. Lacy sat there nervously waiting for him to speak. When she was younger, she loved to play chess with her father but now it was an ever-present reminder of the burden he placed on her shoulders from a young age.

The game was more than just a game—it was a ritual, a lesson, a reminder of the power dynamics that governed not just their relationship, but every aspect of their lives.

"Your move," Richard said, his voice low and measured, his eyes never leaving the board.

Lacy studied the pieces, but her mind wasn't entirely on the game. As she absentmindedly reached for her knight, her thoughts drifted to Brent, who had been calling and texting so much she muted him. She pictured the life everyone seemed to expect her to lead: a grand, public wedding with Brent by her side, her father giving her away to a man she didn't love or at times even like—a man who excited her less with each passing day. She imagined the dull routine of their married life—dinners with his business associates, awkwardly timed sex that left her cold, and eventually, children who would grow up in a world of wealth and privilege but devoid of any real passion or connection.

Her hand hesitated above the board as the weight of her thoughts pressed down on her. Her future, the one everyone else had mapped out for her, felt suffocating, like a gilded cage.

"Check," her father's voice cut through her reverie, sharp and unforgiving.

Lacy blinked, realizing she had barely been paying attention to the game. She glanced down at the board, seeing the trap her father had laid out. Her queen was cornered, and her defenses were crumbling.

"Lacy," Richard's tone was cold now, a hint of disappointment seeping in. "You're not paying attention. You're distracted."

She looked up at him, her cheeks flushing slightly. "I'm sorry, Dad. I was just thinking…"

"That's the problem," he interrupted, moving his bishop with a swift, decisive motion. "You're always thinking about the wrong things. In this world, you can't afford to be distracted. Every move counts."

Lacy felt a pang of frustration as she realized she was just two moves away from losing the game. Her father's eyes were on her, sharp and unyielding, and she knew he was not just talking about chess.

"You can't let your emotions cloud your judgment, Lacy," Richard continued, his voice softer now, almost condescending. "If you let sentimentality take over, you'll lose. In this game, there's no room for weakness."

Lacy stared at the board, but the pieces blurred in front of her eyes. She made a move, one she knew was futile and watched as her father easily took her queen, leaving her king exposed and vulnerable.

"Checkmate," he said quietly, his eyes narrowing as he looked at her. "You see what happens when you're not focused?"

Lacy nodded, biting back the words she wanted to say. She felt like a child again, scolded for not living up to his expectations, for not being the perfect queen he had always demanded she be.

Before she could respond, the door to the office opened, and Brent walked in, his expression smug but tinged with annoyance. He was dressed impeccably, as always, in a tailored suit that fit him like a glove. But to Lacy, he looked like nothing more than a well-dressed puppet, a man whose entire life had been shaped by the expectations of others.

"Sorry to interrupt," Brent said, his voice dripping with false politeness. "But we need to talk, Lacy. You missed another photo op today, and it was important."

Lacy sighed, her frustration mounting. "I was busy, Brent. I told you I had to focus on the bill."

Brent's eyes flashed with irritation, his tone hardening. "The bill can wait. This is about us, about the image we're presenting to the public. You can't just ignore that. Your voters want to see a woman with family values, not the single, independent woman image you have now."

Lacy met his gaze, her own eyes narrowing slightly. "Excuse me? First of all, is that all you ever care about—the way things look?"

Brent's jaw tightened, but he kept his voice measured, though the tension was clear. "And why shouldn't I care? We're in the middle of a campaign, Lacy. Every move you make reflects on both of us. We're supposed to be a team."

"We? A team?" Lacy echoed, her frustration bubbling to the surface. "We are not running for anything—I am. And I certainly don't need a teammate who's only interested in how good we look in the press."

Brent's irritation deepened, and he took a step closer, lowering his voice. "You think I'm only in this for appearances? That's rich, coming from you. You're the one who's always so focused on winning, on doing whatever it takes to get ahead."

Lacy's eyes flashed with anger. "I'm focused on making a difference. There's a difference between that and just playing a part, Brent."

"Is that what you think I'm doing?" Brent shot back, his voice rising slightly. "Playing a part? Well, maybe it's time you realize that part of being in the public eye is making sure everything looks perfect, including us."

Richard, who had been silently observing the exchange, finally interjected, his voice calm but firm. "Brent's right, Lacy. The public needs to see that you're not just a strong politician but also a woman who has everything under control, including her personal life."

Lacy bristled at the implication, but before she could respond, her father continued. "We'll make it right. I'm planning a gala next week to raise more funds for the community center. It'll be a big event, and I want you and Brent to attend together."

Lacy's confusion deepened. Her father's sudden enthusiasm for the community center project was out of character. Yet here he was, pushing her to support this project, even planning a lavish gala to raise more money.

She glanced at Brent, who was watching her with a mixture of expectation and impatience. He was waiting for her to comply and agree to the charade they were both participating in. But inside, Lacy felt torn, unsure of what was real and what was just another move in the endless game her father had taught her to play.

"Fine," Lacy said finally, her voice tinged with resignation. "I'll go to the gala.......with Brent. But I have a busy schedule leading up to it, and I need to focus on the campaign."

Brent's expression softened slightly, though his frustration was still evident. "Thank you. That's all I'm asking for—just a little commitment to what we're building here."

Lacy forced a smile, though it didn't reach her eyes. "Of course, I'll see you at the gala."

Richard nodded, satisfied with her answer. "Good. Remember, Lacy, the queen always holds the power. But she uses every piece on the board to her advantage."

Lacy stood, feeling the weight of the conversation settle heavily on her shoulders. She forced another smile at Brent, who still looked less than pleased, and then turned to leave the office. As she walked down the long corridor toward the door, the sense of unease in her chest grew. She couldn't shake the feeling that she was being maneuvered into a life she wasn't sure she wanted, a life that felt more like a carefully constructed facade than anything real.

But for now, she had to play her part, just as she always had.

****

The next morning, sunlight poured through the large windows of Lacy's campaign headquarters, filling the space with a bright, hopeful light. The subcommittee meeting had been a resounding success, and it seemed that the revitalization bill was on track to move forward, gaining the momentum it needed to pass before the session's end. The energy in the room was buzzing with optimism, yet Lacy couldn't shake the lingering unease from her father's odd behavior the previous night—his cryptic message, the tension in his voice. What was he hiding?

Today was debate prep day, and the atmosphere in the office had shifted from excited to tense. Lacy had lost the last debate, and the pressure to perform well in the upcoming one was palpable. Paige, her campaign manager, was already in the conference room with the spin team, preparing for an intense session.

Paige was a woman of sharp intellect and even sharper wit. She stood at the head of the table, her dark skin glowing under the fluorescent lights, her suit impeccably tailored. Her presence commanded attention, her words slicing through the air like a whip, shutting down the bravado of the frat boys-turned-finance bros who made up the spin team.

"Alright, Lacy," Paige began, her voice crisp and commanding as she flipped through her notes. "Let's get down to it. We need to be ready for anything your opponent throws at you. Last time, he hit you hard on lack of executive experience. This time, we counter with your legislative victories and how you've connected with voters on the ground."

Lacy nodded, but as much as she tried to focus on the task at hand, a small knot of anxiety twisted in her stomach. The image of her father's face from last night—his tight, unreadable expression, the strange tension in his voice—kept intruding on her thoughts. What was he hiding? Lacy forced herself to push it aside. This was too important. "I'm ready," she said, her voice steadying as she shoved thoughts of her father and Brent into the back of her mind.

Paige gave a brief nod of approval, but her eyes were sharp, scrutinizing. "Good. Let's start. Derek, you're up."

Derek, one of the more relentless members of the spin team, didn't waste a second. His tone was sharp, eyes narrowing as he spoke, "What do you say to critics who argue that your stance on criminal justice reform is too lenient? You know they're going to paint you as soft on crime."

Lacy took a breath, her mind snapping into gear. "I've always believed that reform and public safety aren't mutually exclusive. We can reduce crime by addressing its root causes—poverty, lack of education, systemic bias—while still holding individuals accountable. It's about true justice, not leniency."

But Derek was already leaning forward, eyes gleaming with the next challenge. "And how do you respond to accusations that you're just a puppet for your father's interests?"

Lacy's jaw tightened. She had been expecting this, but the sting of it still hit like a gut punch. "My record speaks for itself," she replied, keeping her voice even, though her fingers dug into the armrest of her chair. "Every decision I've made has been in the best interest of my constituents. I'm not my father's puppet—I'm my own person, with my own principles."

Paige's gaze flickered, her expression unreadable. Lacy could feel the pressure building, a steady drumbeat against her ribcage. Everyone knew about her father's influence—everyone whispered about it behind closed doors, speculated in headlines. Would it ever stop being a question?

Paige let the silence hang for a moment longer than necessary, then finally called for a break. Lacy leaned back in her chair, exhaling slowly, trying to release the tension coiled in her muscles.

"You did well," Paige said, her tone softening slightly. "But your opponent is going to come at you with everything he's got. Especially when it comes to your father's influence. He'll try to rattle you, make you second-guess yourself."

Lacy nodded, tapping her fingers against the table in a quickening rhythm. "I know. I just have to stay focused. Keep control."

Paige's gaze bore into her, as if testing the strength of her resolve. "And keep your father out of your head," she added, her voice low but firm. "He's not the one running for office. You are."

Lacy met her eyes, a flicker of determination hardening in her chest. "You're right. He's not. This is my fight."

The session resumed, and the spin team leaned in, ready to throw more curveballs her way. Derek, a hint of a challenge in his smile, fired off the next question. "Let's talk about the economy. Your opponent's going to hammer you on taxes and job creation. What's your plan to counter his narrative that you're just another tax-and-spend liberal?"

Lacy straightened in her seat, her posture rigid with readiness. "I'm focused on smart tax reform that benefits working families, not just the wealthy. My plan includes targeted tax incentives for small businesses and tax cuts for working families who are the backbone of our economy. And when we invest in infrastructure and education, we're creating jobs that last—jobs that pay a living wage."

Ryan, another member of the team, jumped in immediately, a skeptical arch to his brow. "But isn't that just more big government overreach? How do you plan to address the concerns of the private sector, who feel stifled by regulations and taxes?"

Lacy didn't miss a beat. "Government should be a partner to the private sector, not a barrier. My plan ensures that businesses have the support they need to grow, without sacrificing the protections that keep our economy stable and fair. It's about balance—protecting our workers and our environment, while still fostering innovation and growth."

Paige began. "It's not just about what you say, Lacy. It's about how you say it. You need to show the voters that you're not just knowledgeable—you're unflappable. They need to see that nothing shakes you, that you're ready for whatever comes your way."

Lacy absorbed the words, her spine straightening with renewed resolve. She had to be ready, not just for the debate, but for the scrutiny, the questions, the inevitable attempts to undermine her. This was about proving something—not just to the voters, but to herself, and maybe, just maybe, to her father, too.

As the session wound down, Derek leaned back, a smirk playing on his lips. "Not bad, Lacy. I didn't think you'd handle that question about your father so smoothly. But you did."

Lacy managed a smile, though her mind was still racing, the lingering unease from last night refusing to fade. "Thanks, I think."

Ryan chimed in with a grin. "What he means is you're ready, confident. And remember, no matter how much your opponent tries to throw you off your game, we're here to make sure you come out on top. We've got your back."

Paige nodded, her tone serious as ever. "They're right. This is a team effort, and we're going to make sure you're ready to walk onto that stage fully prepared. You've got this, Lacy."

"Thanks, everyone," Lacy said, her voice firmer now, steadier. "I'm ready. Let's go win this."

As they began to pack up, Paige fell into step beside her, lowering her voice so only Lacy could hear. "You're showing everyone, including yourself, that you're more than just your father's daughter. You're Lacy Jacobs, and you're going to own that stage. Don't let anything—or anyone—distract you from that."

Lacy met her gaze, feeling a renewed sense of purpose settle over her. "I won't let you down, Paige. And I won't let myself down, either."

The debate was looming, and she knew she had to be ready. Whatever her father was hiding, whatever doubts tried to creep in, they would have to wait. Right now, she had a stage to command, an opponent to defeat, and a future to secure.

With one last look at her team, Lacy walked out of the room, determination hardening her steps. She was ready to take on whatever came her way, even if she had to confront the shadows of her father's influence along the way. This was her moment, and she wasn't going to let anyone take it from her.

CHAPTER 3

The next morning came. Lacy was on her way to meet with Speaker Harold Whitmore, a powerful figure in her party and a man she had publicly clashed with on several occasions. At 68, Whitmore was a relic of a bygone era—a staunchly conservative Democrat, resistant to change, and someone Lacy had once famously referred to as a "dinosaur" during a heated debate. She wasn't looking forward to the meeting, but it was a necessary step in securing his endorsement for her gubernatorial campaign.

As Lacy approached his office, she couldn't help but admire the grandeur of the building, its marble columns and polished woodwork a testament to old-world power. She took a deep breath, straightened her tailored blazer, and pushed open the heavy wooden door to the Speaker's office.

Inside, the room was a study in old money and tradition—dark wood paneling, leather-bound books, and a large desk that seemed to dominate the space. The smell of cigar smoke hung faintly in the air, mingling with the scent of polished leather. But what struck Lacy most was the sight of her father, Richard, sitting comfortably in one of the leather armchairs, a small, satisfied smile playing on his lips. Across from him sat Speaker Whitmore, his expression uneasy, his hands clasped tightly together on the desk.

Lacy froze for just a moment, a rush of confusion flooding her mind. What was her father doing here? This was supposed to be her meeting, her chance to prove herself. A spark of anger flared in her chest. She felt a familiar sense of being undermined by her father yet again came creeping in, the same feeling she'd had so many times before.

"Lacy," her father said, his voice smooth and controlled as he stood to greet her. "I'm glad you could join us."

She forced a smile as she moved further into the room, fighting the urge to turn around and walk out. "Dad," she replied, her voice tight. "I didn't expect to see you here."

Whitmore cleared his throat, his eyes darting nervously between Lacy and Richard. The Speaker was a tall, broad-shouldered man with thinning gray hair and a face etched with the lines of years spent in the political arena. His suit, though impeccable, seemed to hang a little too loosely on his frame, and his eyes, usually sharp and calculating, now seemed to avoid Lacy's gaze.

"Ms. Jacobs," Whitmore began, his voice lacking its usual authority. "I… I've decided to endorse your candidacy for governor. I believe it's the right move for the party, and, well… your father has been very persuasive."

A cold chill ran through her. Persuasive. The word felt like a slap. Richard Jacobs didn't persuade; he commanded, manipulated, maneuvered people like pieces on a chessboard. Her stomach tightened with the realization. This wasn't a win. This was her father, pulling strings behind the curtain.

"Thank you, Mr. Speaker," Lacy said, her voice steady despite the tumult roiling inside her. "But I have to admit, I was hoping for a bit more of a challenge. As a former attorney, I enjoy a good back and forth."

Whitmore forced a laugh, but it sounded hollow, almost painful. "No need for that today, Ms. Ja——— he clears his throat….. Senator Jacobs. Your father and I have come to an understanding."

Lacy glanced at her father. He was watching her closely, his eyes a touch too hard, a touch too knowing. His look said it all: Don't overplay your hand, Lacy. Her heart pounded. He was testing her, reminding her who held the real power here.

"Yes," Richard said, his voice cutting through the tension like a blade. "I'm sure Lacy appreciates your support. It's important for us to present a united front, especially as the campaign heats up."

The words stung. This wasn't about her campaign or her leadership; this was about his game, his control. She felt a wave of frustration, anger, and something else—something colder—fear, perhaps? Fear of just how deep his control over her life ran. Was anything really hers?

"Of course," Lacy said, forcing another smile. The anger simmered beneath the surface, her hands tightening into fists at her sides. "Thank you, Mr. Speaker. I look forward to working with you."

Whitmore nodded, still avoiding her eyes. "Likewise, Senator Jacobs."

As she turned to leave, Richard's voice followed her out the door. "We'll talk more about this later, Lacy. I'm sure you have a busy day ahead."

She nodded tightly and walked out, her heels clicking against the marble floor, each step feeling heavier than the last. She didn't make it far before she heard his footsteps behind her, catching up with her in the stairwell.

"Lacy," Richard called, his tone sharp and unforgiving.

She stopped, her heart pounding in her chest. The anger that had simmered during the meeting now boiled over. She spun around to face him. "What the hell was that? I didn't need your help to get Whitmore's endorsement. This was my job, not yours."

Richard's eyes narrowed, his expression hardening. "Your job? Everything you have, everything you are, is because of me. You think you're here because of your talents alone? Don't be naive, Lacy. You were made by me in every way."

The words hit her like a blow to the gut. She had always known her father was involved in her career, but hearing it laid out like this was different. A reminder that she was still just a piece on his chessboard, a pawn in his strategy.

She shook her head, trying to keep her voice steady. "This—this is why I left the first time. Because of you. Because you can't help but undermine everything I do."

Richard's face flickered with something—pain, perhaps—but he quickly masked it. "Lacy, I'm just trying to help my daughter. I'm a father. What am I supposed to do? Let a man like Whitmore harass you, go after you in public?"

"Not your call! I knew what I was getting into when I chose this job," she snapped. "You're supposed to let your daughter do her job!"

For a moment, they stood there in silence, the air thick with tension. Richard's expression softened slightly, but his voice remained firm. "I did what I thought was best, Lacy. You'll see that, eventually."

She felt a familiar sting behind her eyes, but she wouldn't let herself cry in front of him. "I am a grown woman and I will decide what is best for me. Not you."

Without another word, Lacy turned on her heel and walked away, her pace quickening. She could feel his eyes boring into her back, his presence still looming over her even as she put distance between them.

As she reached her car, her hands trembled as she yanked open the door. She slid inside, slamming it shut, and sat for a moment, her breath coming in short gasps. And then, with a sudden, violent force, she screamed, the sound echoing off the car's interior, releasing all the anger and frustration that had been bubbling inside her.

Her hands gripped the steering wheel, knuckles white, until the wave of emotion passed. She took a few deep breaths, wiping at her eyes with the back of her hand, and started the car. She had to get back to the campaign office. There was no time to dwell on this. No time to feel small.

Back at her office, she walked straight to her desk, ignoring the bustle around her. She flipped the "Do Not Disturb" sign onto her door, closed it firmly behind her, and collapsed into her chair. Her chest was still tight, her breath uneven. She pressed her fingers to her temples, trying to clear her head.

When your heart and mind are clear, her mother used to say, you can see the path ahead.

She stared at the queen chess piece on her desk, like the one her father had given her when she was a child, reminding her to always think two moves ahead. She shook her head at it, feeling a surge of resentment. The piece felt like a taunt now, a reminder of the game she had never asked to play.

Her hands moved to the locked drawer in her desk. She pulled out her journal—the one she kept at work, the one she used when the pressure became too much. Her fingers traced the worn edges of the cover before she flipped it open, grabbing a pen.

The words spilled out before she could stop them, a flood of raw emotion: I'm so tired of feeling weak. So tired of his games, his control. Without my Mom, it's like he has nothing holding him back. How do I fight him and still stay true to myself? Tears streamed down her cheeks as she wrote, her hand moving faster and faster, trying to keep up with the rush of thoughts. She didn't even notice she was crying until the ink began to blur.

She paused, taking a deep breath. She wiped her tears away with the back of her hand, letting out a shaky sigh. After a moment, she put the journal back into the drawer, locking it away again. She glanced in the small mirror on her desk, quickly fixing her makeup, reapplying her lipstick with a steady hand.

Just as she finished, there was a knock on the door. She took another deep breath, forcing herself to steady. "Come in."

Chloe and Paige entered, papers in hand, a small campaign task to go over, another item on the endless to-do list. Paige gave her a quick look, searching her face, but Lacy had already composed herself. She was back to business.

"Alright," she said, voice firm. "What's next?"

They dove into the details, the minutes slipping by as they worked through the afternoon, and by the time the sun began to set, the day was behind them, and the next move was already on her mind.

Later that evening, Lacy found herself at a high-end boutique with Paige, shopping for gowns to wear to the upcoming community center gala hosted by her father. The boutique was a haven of luxury, with racks of designer dresses that shimmered in the soft light, plush velvet chairs in deep jewel tones, and a chandelier that sparkled overhead. The air was scented with expensive perfume, a delicate blend of jasmine and sandalwood, and the soft strains of classical music played in the background, creating an ambiance of refined elegance.

Paige, ever the practical strategist, flipped through the racks with a discerning eye, her fingers dancing over luxurious fabrics—silk, satin, and lace—as she evaluated each gown with the same meticulous attention to detail she applied to campaign strategy. "We need something that makes a statement, Lacy," she said, her tone all business. "You're going to be the center of attention, and we want everyone to remember why you're the best choice for governor."

Lacy nodded, though her mind was still reeling from the confrontation with her father. She forced herself to focus on the task at hand, knowing that appearances mattered more than ever in her world. The right dress could set the tone for the entire evening, and she needed to exude confidence and control, even if she didn't feel it inside.

Paige pulled a deep red gown with a high slit and an elegant, flowing silhouette from the rack. "Try this one," she suggested.

Lacy obliged, slipping into the gown in the fitting room. The fabric felt soft against her skin, and the rich color made her feel bold and powerful, but when she stepped out to show Paige, she felt a pang of uncertainty. Paige, however, was smiling.

"Love this one," Paige said with a grin. "You're going to turn heads in that dress."

Lacy chuckled softly, but she caught sight of another dress on the rack and felt herself drawn to it—a stunning, emerald green gown. The dress had a daring slit, a sleek, fitted silhouette that accentuated every curve, and a one-shoulder neckline that gave it a sophisticated yet modern flair. The rich green fabric gleamed under the boutique's soft lighting, and Lacy couldn't resist.

"This one," she murmured, reaching for it. "It's my favorite color."

Paige's eyes lit up. "Try it on."

Lacy slipped into the gown, feeling the cool, smooth fabric glide over her skin. The dress hugged her body in all the right places, the high slit revealing just enough leg to be elegant yet alluring. She adjusted the one-shoulder strap, feeling a surge of confidence she hadn't felt in weeks. As she stepped out, she saw Paige's reaction and felt a small smile tug at her lips.

Paige's gaze widened with approval. "Wow, Lacy, that's the one. You look stunning—absolutely radiant."

Lacy turned to the mirror, her breath catching. The dress was perfect, the deep green contrasting beautifully with her skin, the fabric shimmering as she moved. "I love it," she said, almost surprised by how much. "It feels... like me."

Paige grinned. "Exactly. That's the power of a good dress—it makes you feel like the best version of yourself."

They shared a satisfied look and, for a moment, Lacy felt a small weight lift from her shoulders. She turned back to admire herself in the mirror, thinking of the gala and the eyes that would be on her, including her father's. She had to show him—and everyone else—that she was her own person, capable and strong.

Paige nodded, pleased. "It's going to make a statement, that's for sure." She paused, then added, "You know, it's been a while since I've seen you this relaxed."

Lacy laughed softly. "Maybe I needed a break from all the politics."

Paige tilted her head. "It's good to see you like this. Sometimes I wonder what you were like before all the campaigning… before all of this."

Lacy hesitated for a moment, feeling a tug at her heart. "Honestly? I don't remember a time when I wasn't in the thick of it. But in college… I guess I was a bit of a nerd, always in the library, but I had my fun, too. A few wild parties, some guys who were… questionable choices." She laughed, a little embarrassed.

Paige's eyes sparkled. "Oh, now you have to tell me more."

Lacy grinned, the champagne she'd been sipping loosening her up. "There was this one guy, Adam. A philosophy major, and he thought he was so deep. We'd stay up all night debating the meaning of life. But let's just say late nights weren't always for talking. I thought he was the most interesting guy in the world and one of the best lovers I'd ever had. That was until I realized he was mostly full of himself."

Paige laughed. "Sounds like my college boyfriend, Derek. He had a huggggggeee….. heart. She winks. He was always protesting something….. until he tried to protest my career choice."

Lacy raised an eyebrow. "And?"

"And I dumped him, of course," Paige said, her grin wide. "No one tells me what to do."

They clinked their glasses, sharing a silent toast to independence.

As the conversation flowed, they continued to try on more dresses, but Lacy kept returning to the emerald green gown. It felt right—like a symbol of her strength and her determination to carve her own path.

By the end of their shopping trip, both women had found their perfect gowns. Paige chose a sleek black dress with delicate lace details that complemented her skin tone. As they admired their choices in the mirror, Lacy felt a sense of satisfaction she hadn't experienced in a long time.

Walking to the register with their dresses in hand, champagne glasses empty, Lacy realized that something had shifted between her and Paige. They were no longer just colleagues—they were friends, allies in a world that demanded so much of them.

And as they left the boutique, laughing about some shared memory from college, Lacy felt a renewed sense of hope—hope that maybe she was finding her way, one step at a time.

****

The night of the gala arrived, and Lacy found herself standing at the precipice of both the event and the upcoming debate. Nerves twisted in her stomach, a tight knot of anxiety that she tried to mask with a confident smile she had perfected over the years. The gala was set to be a grand affair, with all the usual suspects—politicians, donors, and socialites—gathering to support the community center project. But Lacy couldn't shake the feeling that the evening was more about showing herself and Brent off as a power couple than about any real philanthropic effort.

Before arriving, Brent was in full pep talk mode, going over the photo opportunities and the public image they needed to project. He was perfectly groomed, his suit tailored to perfection, but Lacy couldn't help but feel the growing chasm between them.

"You need to smile more," Brent was saying as they pulled up to the venue. "Remember, this is about showing everyone that we're a strong, united front."

Lacy plastered on a smile, though it felt more like a grimace. "I know, Brent. I've done this before."

Brent's hand found hers, giving it a squeeze as they exited the car and stepped into the glare of cameras and flashing lights. Lacy put on her best performance, posing for photos, shaking hands, and mingling with donors. But inside, she felt like she was on autopilot, moving through the motions of a life that didn't feel entirely hers.

As they made their way through the crowd, Lacy spotted her opponent, Senator William Harding, an old-money Republican in his seventies. Harding had been a fixture in the political landscape for decades, a man who had built his career on his connections and deep ties to the establishment. He was the type of politician who believed in preserving the status quo, resisting any change that threatened his and his buddies' carefully constructed world.

Harding was watching her from across the room, his steely blue eyes narrowing as he noticed her approach. He made his way over, his smile all too confident.

"Ms. Jacobs," he said, extending his hand. "I must say, you're looking quite poised tonight."

Lacy took his hand, her grip firm. "Thank you, William. I hope you're ready for the debate."

He chuckled, the sound grating on her nerves. "Of course I'm ready. But don't worry, I'll go easy on you."

Lacy's smile never wavered, though her eyes hardened. "You'd better not. I'm looking forward to a real challenge."

Harding's smile faltered slightly, a flicker of annoyance crossing his face before he masked it with another condescending grin. "We'll see, Ms. Jacobs. We'll see."

The exchange was brief but intense, the underlying tension palpable despite the pleasant tones and polite words. As Harding walked away, Lacy felt a surge of determination. She wasn't just going to win this debate—she was going to dismantle the carefully curated image of a man who had spent his entire career maintaining the status quo at the expense of real progress.

The night continued in much the same way—smiling for photos, faking intimacy with Brent, and delivering a speech that was met with enthusiastic applause. But as the evening drew to a close, Lacy felt the weight of her role pressing down on her.

Just as she was about to leave, her father cornered her, his tall frame blocking her path. He had been watching her all evening, trying to catch her attention, and now that the crowd had thinned, he saw his chance.

"Lacy," Richard began, his tone softer than she expected. "I've been trying to talk to you all night."

Lacy sighed inwardly, feeling the fatigue of the evening catching up with her. "I've been busy. The speech, the photos… you know how these things go."

Richard nodded, his expression more earnest than usual. "I know, sweetheart. But I wanted to apologize for being so pushy with Whitmore. I wasn't trying to undermine you. It's just… when I see someone coming after my family, I can't help but step in."

Lacy felt a pang of guilt as she looked up at her father. He seemed sincere, his usually steely demeanor softened by concern. "I understand, Dad. I do. But I need to shed this 'daddy's girl' image if I'm going to be taken seriously. I need to stand on my own."

Richard looked at her for a long moment, his eyes searching hers. Then he nodded slowly. "You're right. I'll play a more silent role from now on. I'm here to support you, fully. But don't ever forget that you're not just a politician to me—you're my baby girl."

Lacy felt the tension in her shoulders ease slightly. She managed a small smile, rolling her eyes as she did.

Richard chuckled, his laughter warm and genuine. "Can I still hug my baby girl in public?"

Lacy leaned into his embrace, feeling a sense of comfort she hadn't realized she needed. For all his flaws and overbearing tendencies, her father loved her in his own way. And tonight, it seemed he was truly trying to understand what she needed.

After a moment, they pulled apart, and Richard gave her a look of pride. "Go home, get some rest. You've got a big debate ahead, and I know you're going to do amazingly."

Lacy nodded, feeling a renewed sense of determination. "Thanks, Dad. I'll see you later."

She turned to leave, but as she walked toward the exit, she couldn't help but think about how much her father's approval still mattered to her, even after everything.

Brent drove her home, his hand resting on her thigh as he praised her performance. "You were perfect tonight, Lacy. Everyone loved you."

Lacy forced a smile, nodding along as Brent walked her to the door. "Thanks, Brent. I appreciate that."

They arrived at the apartment lobby. The night was quiet, the only sound the faint hum of city traffic below. Lacy fished her keys out of her bag, eager to retreat into the solitude of her apartment. But Brent hesitated beside her, his eyes lingering on her face.

"Mind if I come up for a bit?" he asked, his voice low, almost hopeful.

Lacy's heart sank. She had hoped to be alone, to let the night wash over her in peace, but she could see the anticipation in his eyes. It was a look she'd seen many times before, a mixture of desire and expectation. She knew what he wanted. It was the same routine, the same carefully choreographed dance they'd been performing for months.

"Sure," she replied, the word tasting bitter on her tongue. She tried to smile, but it didn't reach her eyes.

They ascended on the elevator together, the silence between them heavy. Her mind was elsewhere, thinking about the night, the performance, and the emptiness that seemed to follow her everywhere lately.

Once inside the apartment, Brent slipped off his shoes, making himself comfortable as if he belonged there. Lacy busied herself with putting away her bag and coat, trying to ignore the tightness in her chest. Brent was already moving toward her, his hand resting on the small of her back as he pulled her close.

"You really were amazing tonight," he whispered, his breath warm against her neck. "I couldn't take my eyes off you."

Lacy forced another smile, letting him guide her to the bedroom. The door closed behind them with a soft click, sealing her fate for the night.

In the bedroom, Brent's hands were gentle, his touch familiar as he undressed her slowly, savoring every moment. Lacy went through the motions, responding to his kisses, his caresses, with practiced ease. Though it lacked true passion it usually got the job done. But each touch, each sigh of pleasure that escaped his lips, felt like a transaction. A performance within a performance.

When it was over, Brent kissed her forehead, pulling her close as he drifted into a contented sleep. Lacy lay beside him, staring at the ceiling, her mind swirling with thoughts she couldn't quite grasp. The room felt stifling, the sheets too warm, too heavy. She carefully slipped out of Brent's embrace, her movements quiet and deliberate, not wanting to wake him.

The clock on her bedside table read just after midnight. Lacy sighed softly, gathering her clothes from the floor. She felt a pang of something as she glanced at Brent, still sleeping soundly, unaware of the turmoil inside her.

Lacy made her way to the bathroom, closing the door behind her with a soft click. She turned on the shower, the sound of the water a comforting roar that drowned out her thoughts. She undressed slowly, catching a glimpse of herself in the mirror. Her reflection stared back at her, the woman she saw a stranger. There was a hollowness in her eyes, a sadness she couldn't quite shake.

Stepping into the shower, the hot water cascaded over her, washing away the remnants of the night. Lacy leaned against the cool tiles, letting the water flow over her, trying to find some semblance of peace. But the ache inside her wouldn't go away.

Her hand moved almost of its own accord, slipping between her thighs, seeking the release she hadn't found with Brent. Her fingers moved slowly, deliberately, a quiet desperation fueling each stroke. But even as her body responded, the emptiness persisted, a hollow echo that reverberated through her.

She came with a soft gasp, her legs trembling as the tension finally released. But the satisfaction was fleeting, the pleasure a mere whisper compared to the longing that still clung to her. Lacy stood there for a moment longer, letting the water wash away the evidence of her frustration, but it couldn't cleanse the emptiness that gnawed at her.

Afterward, she dried off, her movements slow and deliberate. She dressed in a t-shirt, sweats, and a hat, the comfort of the familiar clothes grounding her somewhat. Brent was still asleep when she crept out of the bedroom, his breathing steady and peaceful. She knew she wouldn't be able to sleep, not with the storm raging inside her.

She left the apartment quietly, the door clicking shut behind her. There was only one place she wanted to go, a place where she could find some semblance of solace, even if it was temporary. Lacy's feet carried her down the familiar path, her thoughts a tangled mess as she walked through the quiet streets.

Sal's Diner was the kind of place that time forgot, and Lacy loved it for that very reason. The vinyl booths were worn and cracked, the jukebox in the corner was filled with songs from decades past, and the smell of sizzling bacon and fresh coffee hung in the air like a comforting embrace. It was the place she ran to when the weight of her world became too much to bear, and tonight was no different.

As Lacy pushed open the door, the familiar chime of the bell above it brought a small, genuine smile to her face. Salvador Jr., or Sal as everyone called him, was behind the counter, flipping burgers with the same ease and rhythm he had when they were kids. His eyes lit up as soon as he saw her, and he tossed the spatula aside, wiping his hands on a towel before walking over.

"Lacy!" he greeted with a grin that seemed to light up the whole diner. His olive skin, thick dark hair, and chiseled jawline made him look like he belonged on a Mediterranean postcard, not in a worn-out diner. But Sal had always been handsome in that easy, unassuming way that had first drawn her to him. "It's been way too long. Thought you'd forgotten about me."

She shook her head, returning his smile. "Never, Sal. Just been… busy."

"Busy being a big shot, I get it," he teased, though his tone was affectionate. "I always knew you'd be someone great. Even back in boarding school, when you were running for class president and I was just goofing off."

Lacy laughed softly, a warmth spreading through her chest. "You weren't just goofing off, Sal. You were the best campaign manager I ever had."

He grinned, a touch of pride in his expression. "Well, you did make it easy. You had all those trust fund kids wrapped around your finger, even though I'm pretty sure they secretly hated your guts."

"Oh, for sure," she said with a smirk. "They were just jealous because I had you on my side."

Sal's smile softened, his eyes twinkling with nostalgia.

"That's why I liked you," Lacy replied, her voice quieter. "You weren't like them. You were… kind. Real. And you took the job seriously. Plus, you were……. a pretty good kisser for a campaign manager."

Sal laughed, a rich sound that seemed to fill the entire diner. "Ah, yes, our first kiss behind the library. Your idea, if I remember correctly. I had no chance."

She chuckled. "And then you went and dumped me. What was up with that?"

Sal's smile faltered for just a second, a flicker of something crossing his face—concern, maybe? He could still see Richard Jacobs in the headmaster's office, his voice low and his gaze steady as he hinted: *Scholarships can disappear, Sal. Businesses can burn down.* Sal had felt a cold sweat on his back, realizing just how far Richard was willing to go. He wanted to argue, to stand his ground, but fear for his future—and his family's—had tied his tongue. Then, just as quickly, the moment passed, replaced by a playful grin. "Biggest mistake of my life," he said, shaking his head as if trying to brush off the memory. "What can I say? I was a dumb kid."

Lacy noticed the brief shift in his expression, a hint of worry in his eyes. She tilted her head slightly. "You okay?"

Sal blinked, quickly shaking off whatever had surfaced. "Yeah, yeah, I'm fine. Just... thinking about how breaking up with you probably ruined my chances of ever running a successful campaign again." He gave a mock sigh of regret, but his eyes twinkled with humor.

"Nice recovery," Lacy quipped, feeling a small pang of curiosity about that flicker of emotion. She decided to let it go. "And for the record, you would have made a great campaign manager. Too bad you chose the diner life."

"Hey, I still get to make speeches," Sal joked, his smile returning full force. "Mostly about the daily specials, but I make them."

Their laughter flowed easily, the years between them melting away. Sal grabbed a plate from the counter and set it in front of her. "Bacon cheeseburger, fries, and an all the ice cream flavored milkshake—just like old times."

Lacy took a bite of the burger, savoring the taste, feeling a little more like herself again. They settled into their old rhythm, talking about everything and nothing—old classmates, current gossip, and a few of their favorite memories.

"God, I just can't believe I know the next Governor of Virginia/Delaware. I just always knew you were going to be someone big," Sal said again, his voice softening as he watched her. "Even back then, you had that fire in you, Lacy."

Lacy felt a lump in her throat. "Sometimes I wonder if it's still there," she admitted. "With everything going on... it's easy to forget….. who I am."

Sal reached across the table, squeezing her hand. "You're Lacy fucking Jacobs," he said with a grin, but his tone held a note of seriousness. "And if all else fails, you can always move here, marry me, and raise those seven kids we talked about in high school."

Lacy burst out laughing, the tension finally breaking. "Oh, right! Our grand plan to populate a small town."

Sal chuckled, his eyes twinkling with mischief. "Hey, I'm still up for it if you are. I'll run the diner, and you can handle the chaos at home."

Lacy grinned, shaking her head. "You forget you've got a wife and a baby on the way, Sal. Maybe……. we'll have to try again in the next lifetime."

Sal's laugh was warm and genuine. "Deal," he said, tapping her hand lightly. "Next lifetime, then."

They talked until the early hours, the conversation ebbing and flowing with ease. Sal's humor was a balm to her soul, and for a while, Lacy forgot about the pressures of her life, lost in the warmth of their connection.

As the sky outside began to lighten with the first hints of dawn, the diner's door jingled open again, and the usual early morning crowd started to filter in—truckers, regulars etc. Lacy finally sighed and pushed herself to her feet. "I should get going," she said reluctantly. "Big day ahead."

Sal stood too, giving her a quick, warm hug. "You've got this, Lacy. Don't let anyone tell you otherwise."

"Thanks, Sal," she whispered, her voice thick with sincerity. "For everything."

As she walked out of the diner, the pale pink of dawn breaking across the sky, Lacy felt a little lighter. She glanced back once more to see Sal already deep in conversation with a regular. And for the first time in a long while, she felt that familiar spark reignite—a reminder of the fire that still burned deep within her, waiting for its moment.

Lacy slipped quietly back into her apartment, her steps light on the hardwood floors. Brent was still sprawled out on the bed, his breathing deep and even. She didn't wake him. Instead, she moved quietly through the apartment, her mind already on the day ahead. There was an interview with Claire Morgan, editor-in-chief of the State Tribune—an opportunity she knew could give her a crucial edge with only a week and a half left until the debate. The early morning with Sal had re-energized her, and she felt ready to face anything.

Lacy arrived at the State Tribune building with a renewed sense of purpose. Claire Morgan was a legend in journalism circles, known for her incisive questions and no-nonsense approach. Lacy had prepared for this interview meticulously, knowing that it could set the tone for the final stretch of her campaign.

The newsroom was buzzing with activity—phones ringing, reporters tapping away furiously at their keyboards, and editors huddling over the latest stories. Lacy was ushered into a sleek conference room, where Claire sat waiting, her presence commanding. A woman in her mid-40s, Claire had sharp eyes and an expression that suggested she missed very little.

"Good morning, Ms. Jacobs," Claire began, her tone polite but firm. "Thank you for taking the time to speak with me today."

Lacy offered a confident smile. "Thank you for having me, Claire. I've been looking forward to this."

Claire nodded, cutting straight to the chase. "Let's dive in, then. Some critics say you lack executive experience—your opponent, Senator Harding, has made that a central point in his campaign against you. How do you respond to those who believe you're not ready to handle the responsibilities of governorship?"

Lacy didn't miss a beat. "I understand the concern, but I think it's important to remember that experience isn't just about years on the job; it's about results. In the Senate, I've authored and passed critical legislation on education reform, healthcare, and criminal justice—all issues that directly affect the lives of our citizens. I've built coalitions, navigated complex negotiations, and delivered tangible outcomes. I believe those accomplishments speak to my readiness."

Claire leaned back, clearly impressed but not giving anything away. "Interesting. But some of your legislative proposals have been criticized as overly ambitious, especially your stance on renewable energy investment. How do you plan to fund these initiatives without raising taxes on the middle class?"

Lacy's eyes gleamed with determination. "I've always believed that the key to growth is innovation. My plan involves reallocating funds from outdated subsidies and investing in green jobs, which will stimulate our economy without coming at the cost of the planet upon which we live. I'm committed to ensuring that our state leads the way in sustainability while protecting middle-class families from having to bail out large corporations who harm this very planet. This isn't about burdening the taxpayer—it's about smart, forward-thinking investment."

Claire's expression softened slightly, though her eyes still held a probing quality. "You talk a lot about change and progress, but what makes you different from every other politician who's made similar promises?"

Lacy smiled, her voice steady. "I'm different because I'm not afraid to fight for what I believe in, even if it means taking on powerful interests, even if it means risking my own standing. I've faced those who've tried to put me in a box, who've underestimated me because of who my father is or where I come from. But I've shown time and again that I'm here to serve the people, not the establishment. My commitment is to them."

Claire seemed to pause, as if reassessing her. "I have to admit, Ms. Jacobs, I didn't expect you to be so… well-rounded. You're certainly making a case for yourself today."

Lacy felt a small surge of annoyance beneath her smile. She was used to people being surprised that she had more to offer than just a pretty face or a wealthy father's name. But she kept her composure. "I appreciate that, Claire. I've worked hard to be prepared for this role and to make a real difference. I'm glad that's coming across."

The rest of the interview continued in a similar vein—Claire firing sharp questions, Lacy responding with poise, determination, and clear vision. By the end, Claire seemed genuinely impressed, nodding thoughtfully as she closed her notebook.

"Well, thank you for your time, Ms. Jacobs," Claire said finally, standing up and extending her hand. "I think our readers will find this enlightening."

"Thank you, Claire," Lacy replied, shaking her hand firmly. "I look forward to reading it."

As Lacy turned to leave, she accidentally bumped into a man entering the conference room, her shoulder brushing his arm. Papers slipped from his hands, and she instinctively bent down to help him gather them up.

"Sorry about that," she said quickly, glancing up only briefly.

"No problem," he replied, not looking at her for more than a second as he straightened up, his focus already shifting back to his work.

They each continued on their way without another word, Lacy moving toward the exit, her mind already shifting to her next task. As she stepped out of the building, she took a deep breath, feeling satisfied. She had handled Claire's questions with confidence and grace, knowing that the interview could help swing the public's perception in her favor.

CHAPTER 4

The day of the debate had finally arrived, and Lacy knew this was her chance for redemption. The last debate had been a setback, but tonight was different. Tonight, she was ready to prove that she could beat Senator William Harding and secure her place as a formidable candidate for governor.

Hours before the debate, the campaign's dressing room buzzed with nervous energy. Paige, ever the meticulous strategist, was running through last-minute preparations with Lacy. Chloe flitted around, ensuring Lacy had everything she needed—water, tea, anything to keep her calm and focused. Lacy sat in the makeup chair, her glam squad expertly applying the finishing touches. The smell of hairspray lingered in the air, mixing with the subtle scent of the chamomile tea Chloe handed her.

As the makeup artist worked, Lacy stared into the mirror, feeling a familiar tightness in her chest. She reminded herself to breathe, to focus. Don't think about the last debate. Don't think about Harding's smug smile or the way he twisted your words. She had to keep her mind clear. But beneath her poised exterior, doubt crept in, whispering to her: What if they see right through you? What if you stumble again?

She pushed the thoughts away, blinking hard. This was no time for self-doubt. She was dressed in a sleek, navy blue dress, elegant yet understated, with a modest neckline and a subtle shimmer that caught the light as she moved. Her pumps were a matching shade, polished and professional, giving her just the right amount of height to command the stage. She glanced at herself in the mirror one last time and felt the wave of determination she needed wash over her. You belong here. You've earned this.

"Remember, Lacy," Paige said, her voice steady and reassuring. "This is your moment. Stay focused, stay calm, and don't let Harding rattle you. You've got this."

Lacy nodded, taking a deep breath as she sipped her tea. "I know, Paige. I'm ready."

Chloe handed her a bottle of water, and Lacy took it, feeling the cool condensation against her fingers. "You've prepared for this, Lacy," Chloe added, her voice soft but encouraging. "Just be yourself up there."

The room was filled with the quiet hum of activity as the team finalized everything. Lacy could hear the faint clatter of keyboards from the spin team in the press room down the hall, already strategizing for the post-debate analysis. The atmosphere was thick with anticipation, the air charged with the weight of what was at stake. She felt it in her bones—the pressure, the expectations.

As she moved from the makeup chair, heading towards the exit, the noises grew louder. The murmur of conversations, the clinking of cups. She felt her heartbeat quicken with every step. The narrow hallway leading backstage seemed to stretch longer, her heels clicking sharply against the polished floor.

What if Harding brings up the family wealth again? What if he twists it into something ugly, something people already suspect—that you're just a privileged girl playing politics?

She felt the familiar twinge of fear. No, focus. Breathe. You're more than that. Much more.

Finally, the moment arrived. Lacy stood backstage, her heart pounding in her chest, but her mind clear and focused. She could hear the muffled sounds of the audience taking their seats, the rustling of papers as the moderators prepared. She adjusted her dress one last time, smoothing out an imaginary wrinkle, and then stepped forward.

As Lacy walked onto the stage, the bright lights momentarily blinded her, but she quickly adjusted. Senator Harding was already there, his presence imposing, his expression smug. They met at center stage for the traditional handshake. Harding's grip was firm—too firm, as if he were trying to intimidate her with a simple gesture. But Lacy remained unshaken, meeting his gaze with unwavering determination.

The debate moderator began with the opening remarks, setting the stage for what was sure to be a tense and closely watched battle. The first few questions were standard fare—economic policy, healthcare, education. Both candidates answered with practiced ease, each trying to one-up the other with statistics and polished rhetoric.

Lacy could feel the audience's eyes on her, their attention wavering between the two candidates. She caught glimpses of nodding heads, a few murmurs from the front rows when she emphasized the need for change in criminal justice. They're listening, she thought, feeling a flicker of hope. She had to keep going, to keep pushing through.

In the press room, the spin team was glued to the screens, watching every move, every word with intense focus. They were ready to jump into action the moment the debate ended, but right now, their job was to analyze, to predict, and to prepare for any angle the media might take.

"She's doing great so far," said Ryan, who had a knack for reading body language. "Harding's trying to goad her, but she's holding her ground."

"Watch his left hand," Karen added. "He's gripping the podium every time she speaks. He's not as confident as he looks."

Paige stood at the back of the room, arms crossed, eyes narrowed in concentration. "We need to be ready if Harding brings up her policy changes. That's her weak spot, and he knows it."

The debate progressed, and it became clear that this was going to be a neck-and-neck showdown. Harding was a seasoned debater, skilled at twisting words and playing to the fears of the electorate. He hit hard, especially on Lacy's recent policy shifts, trying to paint her as inconsistent and out of touch.

"Here it comes," Ryan muttered as Harding pivoted the conversation to Lacy's policy changes. "He's going for the jugular."

Lacy countered with facts and logic, her voice steady, but the tension in the room was palpable. The spin team exchanged glances, ready to react.

"He's framing it like she's pandering," Kate said, her fingers flying across the keyboard as she prepared talking points for the post-debate interviews. "We need to spin this as her being adaptable, responsive to the needs of the people."

"She's got to turn this around," Ryan added, eyes glued to the screen. "If she doesn't, the headlines will be all about her flip-flopping."

"Senator Jacobs," the moderator began, his tone neutral but probing, "your opponent has criticized your recent changes in policy, particularly your shift on criminal justice reform. How do you respond to those who say you're simply pandering to public opinion?"

Lacy took a deep breath, preparing to respond, but Harding cut in before she could speak.

"Ms. Jacobs has indeed changed her policies, but let's be honest about why," Harding said, his voice dripping with condescension. "She wants to be seen as average, as one of the people. But let's not forget, her father is just as rich as I am. She's not fooling anyone."

The words hung in the air, and for a moment, the world seemed to grow quiet around Lacy. She felt a familiar pang of irritation mixed with a deeper sense of dread. There it is. The wealth card. He's trying to make you the out-of-touch rich girl. She glanced around the room, seeing the expectant faces of the audience, the flashing cameras, and then she locked eyes with Paige, who gave her a small, reassuring nod. Lacy looked down at her prepared notes, but something inside her shifted. She knew this was her chance to speak from the heart, to show everyone who she really was.

Back in the press room, the team held their breath. "This is it," Paige whispered. "Come on, Lacy. You got this."

Lacy looked up, her gaze sweeping the room before settling back on Harding. "Senator Harding, fear is a powerful tool, and you've wielded it masterfully tonight. But fear is also a choice. And I choose not to live in fear—of change, of progress, of what the future holds."

The room was silent, all eyes on her as she continued. "Yes, I have changed my policies. And I'm proud of that. When I saw that our criminal justice system was failing our communities, I didn't turn away. I listened to the people. I learned. And I acted. As anyone in a government for the people by the people would do. The changes we made have resulted in fewer community-police interactions, more fully funding programs aimed at reducing gang violence in high-risk areas, and avenues for communities to keep themselves safe. Isn't that what progress looks like?"

In the audience, she noticed a few nods, some murmurs of agreement. A woman in the front row leaned forward, her expression softening. They're with you, Lacy thought, feeling a surge of confidence.

"She's flipping it," Kate said, a note of admiration in her voice. "Keep going, Senator."

"She's turning the narrative on him," Ryan added, grinning. "This is brilliant."

Lacy could see the shift in the audience, their attention fully on her now. "I also changed our gun laws, and you know what happened? We saved lives. Fewer deaths. Fewer tragedies. I changed tax codes to benefit veterans and their families, changed outdated standards for lower-income families to get more kids into programs like Head Start. And yes, I even changed pool hours; the kids threw me a party for that one." The audience chuckled. Lacy continued. "Change isn't something to fear—it's something to embrace. A true leader knows that change is an inevitability, not a possibility, and welcomes it with open arms."

She straightened her spine, her voice steady and strong. "I'm not afraid of change. I'm proof that we can root ourselves in the traditions that matter while progressing toward a future that benefits everyone. Senator Harding, you've spent your career trying to hold us back, trying to preserve a past that benefits only a select few. But the people of this state deserve better. They deserve a leader who isn't afraid to adapt, to grow, to fight for a future where everyone can thrive—not just rich girls like me."

The crowd was hanging on her every word, the tension in the room replaced by a palpable energy. "Our state is rich with resources, and I will ensure those resources are used to make us a world leader in innovation and progress. So no, Senator Harding, I will not apologize for my father's wealth or the opportunities it gave me. I will use those opportunities to root us in the beautiful traditions of the past, like a government for the people by the people, while forging a grand future for us all, only this time it's all people and not just, as Senator Harding says, rich girls like me."

In the press room, the spin team erupted into cheers. "Holy SHIT!!! She did it!" Ryan exclaimed.

Paige allowed herself a small smile of pride. "That's my girl."

As Lacy finished, the room erupted in applause. The crowd's roar was deafening, and it was clear to everyone present that Lacy had won the debate. Harding's face tightened, but he forced a smile as the moderator brought the debate to a close.

In the press room, the spin team was ecstatic. Paige could barely contain her excitement as she watched Lacy's performance. The entire team cheered, hugging and high-fiving each other as they realized the tide had turned in their favor.

Back at headquarters, the celebration continued. Sparkling cider and champagne flowed freely as Lacy's team toasted to their victory. Lacy was glowing, the adrenaline from the debate still coursing through her veins. She raised her glass, a proud smile spreading across her face.

"This was a team victory," she said, her voice carrying over the cheers. "We did this together, and tonight we celebrate together because tomorrow, it's back to work."

The team cheered again, their spirits high as they reveled in the triumph. But as the night wore on and the celebration began to wind down, Lacy slipped away, retreating to her office for a moment of quiet amid the chaos. As she closed the door, the sounds of laughter and clinking glasses became a soft murmur behind her, the buzz of victory dimming slightly.

She leaned back against the door, letting out a slow breath. Her hands, still tingling from the energy of the night, ran over her hair as she tried to process everything. She felt victorious, yes, but something gnawed at her—a realization that had formed in the quiet moments on stage.

The speech I gave wasn't the one on the paper.

She had felt a wave of frustration earlier when she glanced at the prepared notes during the debate—the ones written by her speechwriter. They were polished, carefully constructed, but they hadn't captured what she wanted to say. There had been no fire, no real emotion. They felt like someone else's words, a safety net when what she needed was a springboard. She'd pushed them aside and spoken from the heart, and that was when she felt the audience truly come alive.

Her phone buzzed, breaking her thoughts. She glanced down to see a text from her father. The message was uncharacteristically sweet, offering words of support and pride. It was a small gesture, but it made her heart swell. She hadn't expected such kindness from him, and it only added to the layered emotions of the evening.

Just as she was about to respond, Paige walked in, a wide smile on her face. "Lacy, you were amazing tonight. This really is your moment."

Lacy nodded, her thoughts sharpening as Paige spoke. She felt the tension in her shoulders release, a knot of anxiety she hadn't even realized she was carrying suddenly unraveling. "Paige, I'm breaking up with Brent."

Paige's smile faltered, replaced by a look of surprise. "Are you sure?"

"Positive," Lacy replied, the firmness in her voice surprising even herself. "I realized tonight that I'm tired of playing it safe. Brent... he keeps me in this box, and I've stayed there because it was easy, because it was expected. But I need to be free of that. I need to be true to myself, no matter the cost."

Paige nodded slowly, understanding dawning on her face. "I get it."

"And that means I also want you to fire the speechwriter," Lacy continued. "The words on that page tonight lacked depth, lacked authenticity. They weren't mine. I want someone who can capture my real voice."

Paige's eyebrows lifted in surprise, but she nodded, already thinking ahead. "We'll handle the breakup story but you have to handle the actual breakup!

Lacy considered for a moment, her jaw tightening slightly. " Deal. Get ahead of it. Craft a joint statement, if possible; I'll see if Brent will agree to an amicable split. If not, we'll make sure it doesn't overshadow our message."

Paige smiled, a glimmer of pride in her eyes. "We'll make it happen. I'm on it."

As Paige left, Lacy felt her body relax further, her shoulders loosening, the tension in her neck easing as if a weight had been lifted. She stood up, rolling her shoulders back, and felt a lightness she hadn't felt in months, maybe even years. She hadn't realized how much she'd been holding back—how much she'd been compromising who she really was to fit into everyone else's expectations.

She glanced back at her phone, reading her father's text again. His words of support were a welcome surprise, but she couldn't help but wonder what his real thoughts were. Would he truly back her, or was this just another maneuver in his own playbook? The thought flickered across her mind, but she pushed it aside for now.

With a contented sigh, she slipped her phone into her bag and headed out of her office, feeling a sense of renewal. The campaign would continue, and there were battles yet to be fought, but tonight had been hers to savor. She had spoken from the heart and felt the power of her own voice resonate. She was done hiding behind prepared words or an image that wasn't her own.

But as she walked down the hallway, a thought pricked at her— what would Brent do? How would he react to the breakup? She pushed the thoughts away, knowing she'd face whatever came next. Still, a whisper of doubt lingered at the edges of her mind. I can handle this. I have to.

She had proven herself, and she would continue to prove herself. No opponent, no challenge, could take that away from her.

****

A few days after the debate, Lacy found herself in her kitchen, preparing a homemade dinner. The smell of rosemary and garlic filled the air as she carefully basted a roast chicken, the skin turning a perfect golden brown in the oven. She had set the table with her best china, the soft glow of candlelight reflecting off the polished silverware. A bottle of white wine stood on the counter, as she arranged a salad of mixed greens, cherry tomatoes, and shaved Parmesan. Everything was perfect, but there was a knot in her stomach that had nothing to do with the meal.

Tonight, she was going to break up with Brent.

Lacy took a deep breath and glanced at the clock. Brent would be arriving any minute. She straightened her dress—a simple but elegant navy sheath she had chosen carefully, something that made her feel confident and composed. The doorbell rang, and Lacy felt her heart skip a beat. She wiped her hands on a towel, feeling a slight tremor in her fingers, and went to answer the door.

Brent stood there, looking as polished as ever in a crisp white shirt and slacks. He smiled as he stepped inside, leaning in to kiss her on the cheek. "Something smells amazing," he said, his voice warm.

Lacy forced a smile, feeling her lips twitch slightly. "Thanks, I hope you're hungry."

They sat down to dinner, and Lacy kept the conversation light—small talk about the campaign, the debate, anything to avoid the growing tension that sat like a stone in her chest. As they finished the meal and moved to the living room for dessert, she felt a flush of heat rise up her neck. She knew she couldn't delay any longer.

"Brent, there's something I need to talk to you about," she began, her voice wavering slightly despite her efforts to keep it steady.

Brent looked up from his slice of chocolate cake, his expression suddenly wary. "What is it?"

Lacy took a deep breath, her hands clenching and unclenching in her lap. "I've been doing a lot of thinking, and I've realized that we're not… compatible. We want different things, and it's not fair to either of us to keep pretending that this is working."

Brent's face hardened, his eyes narrowing. "What are you saying, Lacy? That you want to break up?"

She nodded, feeling her throat tighten painfully. "Yes, Brent. I think it's best if we go our separate ways."

Brent sat there in stunned silence for a moment, his eyes searching her face as if trying to find some hint that this was a joke. When he spoke, his voice was quiet, almost pleading. "I don't understand… We've been through so much together. Why now?"

Lacy's heart ached at the look on his face, and she wished, just for a moment, that she could take it all back. But she pushed that thought away. "Because I need to focus on the campaign. On myself. I've felt… stuck, Brent. Like I've been holding back. And it's not fair to you either. You deserve someone who's all in."

Brent's eyes glistened, and for a second, Lacy thought he might cry. "All this time, I thought we were building something. But I guess I was wrong."

"Brent, it's not that…," Lacy said gently. "It's just… not what I want anymore.".

His face crumpled for a moment, but then he seemed to regain his composure, his expression hardening into something colder. "So, what happens now?" he asked, his tone clipped. "You're just going to walk away like none of this ever mattered?"

Lacy inhaled slowly, steadying herself. "No, of course not. I think we should handle this with dignity. I've already thought about the best way to manage this, both for us personally and for the campaign. We can release a joint statement saying we've decided to remain friends and that you'll be supporting me, cheering me on… and that you can't wait to vote for me on November 3rd – all that blah blah, and I'll wish you the best and thank you for your support."

Brent's mouth dropped open, and for a moment, he just stared at her. Then, his face twisted into a sneer. "You're a piece of work, Lacy. You really think I'm just going to play along with your little narrative?"

Lacy flinched at his words, but kept her composure. "I'm just trying to do this the right way, Brent. We both have reputations to protect, and this way, we both come out of it with our dignity intact."

"Dignity?" Brent's voice rose, his calm facade beginning to crack. "Is that what you think this is about? A PR strategy? God, you're just like your father—cold, calculating. You use people, then discard them when they're no longer useful to your littles schemes."

The words hit her like a slap. Her heart pounded, a mix of anger and hurt surging up through her. "That's not fair, Brent. I care about you. I never wanted to hurt you, but I have to be true to myself."

Brent stood up abruptly, his chair scraping loudly against the floor. "True to yourself?" he shouted. "Don't kid yourself, Lacy you don't even know who that is. You're nothing without your father. No one would even know your name if it weren't for him. You're just another spoiled rich bitch pretending to care about things she knows nothing about!"

Lacy's hands trembled, her face flushing hot with anger. She stood up, her voice rising to meet his. "And you think you're any better? You let him use you. You played along with his games because it suited you. If anyone's a puppet here, it's you, Brent. So don't stand there and call me nothing when you've spent the last year doing his bidding. And by the way, I'm dumping you because when it wasn't my father's hand up your ass—it was a fucking stick!"

Brent's face reddened, his fists clenching at his sides. "That's not—" he started, but then his words faltered. "I never—"

"No, Brent. You did. And that's what this has always been about," Lacy interrupted, her voice firm. "You thought you could climb your way up by being with me, but you were only ever interested in what you could gain. At least I'm honest about what I want."

For a moment, they stood there, locked in a battle of wills, neither willing to back down. Then Brent let out a bitter laugh. "You're going to regret this, Lacy," he spat, grabbing his jacket. "You think you're so much better than everyone, but you're just like him. And people will see it. They always do."

He turned and walked to the door, yanking it open. Lacy followed, her chest heaving with emotion. "I never wanted it to be like this," she whispered, but he didn't look back.

He paused at the doorway, his back to her. "You did it anyway," he muttered, and then he was gone, the door slamming shut behind him with a final, echoing thud.

Lacy stood there, her breath coming in sharp, uneven gasps. The silence of the apartment pressed in around her, the only sound her own heartbeat pounding in her ears. She had known this wouldn't be easy, but she hadn't expected it to feel like this—so raw, so exposed.

For a moment, she felt a stab of doubt. Had she done the right thing? Was she really like her father, ruthless and calculating? She shook her head, trying to push the thought away, but it lingered, gnawing at her resolve. She had made her decision. She had to own it.

She sank down onto the couch, her head in her hands. The room felt colder now, the candlelight flickering uncertainly in the dimness. Her phone buzzed in her pocket, pulling her back to reality. She glanced at the screen. It was her father.

She hesitated, her fingers hovering over the answer button. Why was he calling now? Was this just another attempt to manipulate her, or did he genuinely care?

She wiped her eyes and answered. "Hi, Dad."

"Lacy," Richard's voice was uncharacteristically gentle. "How are you doing?"

Lacy swallowed hard, her voice strained. "I just broke up with Brent."

There was a pause on the other end of the line before Richard spoke again. "Lacy, these things are never easy, but sometimes they're necessary."

Lacy frowned, caught off guard by his unexpected sympathy. "Why are you being so… supportive? It's not like you."

Richard chuckled softly, his tone almost affectionate. "Can't a father care about his daughter's well-being?"

Lacy forced a small smile, but suspicion gnawed at her. "I guess so. It's just… unusual."

"Well, don't question it," Richard said, his tone light. "Take care of yourself, okay?"

"I will," Lacy promised. "Thanks, Dad."

As she hung up, she stared at her phone, a mixture of doubt and comfort swirling within her. She wanted to believe her father's tenderness was genuine, but she knew better than to take it at face value. There were always strings attached with him. Always.

With a deep breath, Lacy stood up, feeling a tremor in her legs. Tonight had been hard, but she felt something shift inside her—like a weight had lifted. She knew she'd face fallout from this, both in her personal life and on the campaign trail. But for the first time in a long time, she felt like she was making choices for herself, and no one else.

She glanced around the apartment, feeling the quiet settle in. She had won a battle tonight, but the war was far from over.

Brent arrived at the Jacobs' home with a mix of rage and desperation simmering just beneath his polished surface. The grand estate loomed large and imposing in the evening light, its manicured lawns and tall wrought-iron gates a stark reminder of the power and wealth he was up against. His hands felt clammy as he wiped them against his trousers, forcing himself to walk up the steps to the heavy front door.

A maid ushered him into Richard's office, a room that felt more like a fortress than a place of work. Dark wood paneling lined the walls, and the smell of cigar smoke lingered in the air. Richard sat behind a massive mahogany desk, his chair turned slightly away from Brent, looking out over the sprawling garden. The silence was suffocating.

Richard slowly turned to face him, a cool, assessing look in his eyes. "Brent," he said, his voice deceptively calm. "What brings you here tonight?"

Brent's jaw tightened, his anger bubbling to the surface. "Lacy broke up with me," he began, his voice strained with a mix of frustration and sadness. "And I want you to fix it. Tell her to take me back."

Richard's expression barely shifted, but his eyes grew colder. "And why, exactly, should I involve myself in your... romantic troubles?"

Brent stepped forward, his fists clenching at his sides. "Because she's acting like a frigid, stuck-up bitch!" he spat out, his voice cracking with emotion.

Richard's eyes narrowed, and his face remained perfectly still. "You would be wise to remember," he said slowly, enunciating every word, "that you are speaking to her father."

Brent flinched but pressed on, his desperation overtaking his sense. "I don't care, Richard! I need her back, damn it. You know how much I've put into this relationship. She's trying to make me look like a fool with this whole 'amicable breakup' nonsense. You need to tell her to reconsider."

Richard leaned back in his chair, a faint smile playing on his lips. "Tell me," he asked, his voice dangerously calm, "what exactly did Lacy say to you?"

Brent shifted nervously. "She wants to put out some joint statement, pretend we're still friends, have me say I'm cheering her on. She even wants me to say I'll vote for her. It's a joke. She's trying to humiliate me."

Richard's smile widened slightly. "And what do you expect me to do about it?"

Brent's frustration peaked, his voice rising. "I want you to tell her to take me back! Make her see reason. She listens to you—she always has. You can convince her."

Richard studied him for a moment, tapping his fingers against the armrest of his chair. "Brent," he began slowly, "it would be in your best interest to accept Lacy's offer. Save face. Walk away with some dignity."

Brent's face twisted with anger. "Fuck you," he snarled. "Just like I used to fuck your daughter. You think I'm going to take her scraps and your shit? I'm going to tell everyone that your daughter is a stuck-up bitch and a lousy lay."

Richard's eyes flickered with something dark and dangerous. He stood up slowly, moving around the desk with deliberate calm. Brent's bravado wavered as Richard closed the distance between them, each step slow and measured.

When Richard reached him, he didn't stop. He cupped the back of Brent's neck with a firm, almost fatherly grip, and leaned in close, his breath warm against Brent's ear. "Son," he said softly, pausing just long enough to make Brent's heart hammer in his chest. "Now, if you do that, I'm going to have to kill you. Cut your head off and mail it to your mother for Christmas."

Brent's bravado shattered. He tried to look away, his eyes darting nervously, but Richard's grip tightened slightly, holding him in place. "But don't worry," Richard continued, his tone almost playful, his smile sickeningly sweet. "I'll slit her throat too, so she can join you in hell. Because if you mess with my family, I kill yours. Okay?"

Brent's face drained of color. He felt a cold sweat break out on his forehead. "Richard, I didn't mean—"

Richard's smile didn't falter. He smacked the back of Brent's neck lightly, like a warning. "Be wise, son. Take what she offers. And get the fuck out of my house."

Brent stumbled back, his eyes wide with fear and shock. He opened his mouth to say something, anything, but no words came out. He turned and fled, nearly tripping over his own feet as he rushed to the door, his breath coming in short, panicked gasps.

Richard watched him go, his expression calm, almost amused. He returned to his desk, picked up his cigar, and took a slow, deliberate puff, the smoke curling around him like a veil.

"Goodbye, Brent," he murmured softly, as if dismissing a child who had overstayed his welcome. He tapped the ash from his cigar into a crystal tray and leaned back, a small, satisfied smile playing at the corners of his mouth.

Brent slammed the door behind him, his heart racing, his mind spinning. He knew he had pushed too far, and now he understood— Richard Jacobs was not a man to be crossed.

Days went by with no word from Brent. Lacy tried to focus on her campaign, pushing the breakup to the back of her mind. But it lingered, a dull ache she couldn't quite shake. Every so often, a flicker of doubt would surface—Did I make the right choice? Will he try to sabotage me? But she buried those thoughts, knowing there was too much at stake to dwell on them now.

One afternoon, Chloe came rushing into her office, a broad grin spread across her face.

"Lacy, you're not going to believe this," she said, waving a piece of paper in the air.

"What is it?" Lacy asked, looking up from her desk, trying to read Chloe's excitement.

"It's an email from Brent," Chloe said, her voice bubbling over with excitement. "He signed the joint statement and endorsed you fully!"

Lacy's eyes widened in surprise. "He did?"

"Yes!" Chloe practically bounced on her feet. "Paige, get in here!"

Paige appeared in the doorway, curiosity etched on her face. "What's going on?"

"Brent signed the statement and endorsed Lacy," Chloe explained, still beaming.

Paige's face broke into a smile, and she turned to Lacy. "That's amazing! I guess he finally came around."

Lacy felt a mixture of relief and suspicion tugging at her. "Yeah, I guess he did..." She couldn't help but wonder what had changed. Was this a genuine decision, or was something else at play? Her mind flashed to her father, but she quickly pushed the thought away. Maybe Brent realized it was better to be gracious than bitter.

Just then, Richard walked into the office, his expression curious. "What's all this excitement about?"

Lacy turned to him, feeling a warmth spread through her chest. "Dad, Brent agreed to the joint statement. He says he fully supports my campaign."

Richard's eyes softened, a pleased smile curling on his lips. "That's wonderful news, Lacy. I'm proud of you."

Unable to contain herself, Lacy impulsively hugged her father. It felt good, almost natural, and for a moment, she allowed herself to bask in the rare tenderness between them. "Thank you for not butting in, Dad," she murmured, pulling back to look at him.

Richard chuckled, hugging her back. "I'm learning to let you handle things on your own."

Lacy laughed softly, feeling lighter than she had in days. "I appreciate that," she replied, smiling up at him. "I really do."

As they pulled apart, Richard's phone buzzed in his pocket. His smile faded just a touch, and he glanced at the screen. "Excuse me for a moment," he said smoothly, stepping out of the office to take the call.

Outside, Richard's voice was low, his tone calm and controlled. "Thank you for being so cooperative, Brent," he said, a slight smile playing at the edges of his lips.

On the other end of the line, Brent's voice was curt and laced with bitterness. "Whatever, Richard. I did what you asked. Now leave me and my family alone."

Richard's smile didn't waver. "Of course," he replied smoothly, his tone dripping with a polite menace. "But remember, Brent, it's always in your best interest to stay on my good side."

Brent's breath hitched, a slight tremor in his voice now. "Yeah... I get it."

Richard paused for a moment, his smile growing sharper, almost predatory. "Good," he said softly. "Because it would be a shame if things... escalated, wouldn't it?"

There was a brief silence on the line before Brent muttered, "Just keep your word, Richard."

"Oh, I always do," Richard replied, his tone light, almost playful. "You have my word. As long as you keep yours."

He ended the call without waiting for a response, slipping his phone back into his pocket. His smile broadened as he returned to the office, a look of satisfaction in his eyes.

Lacy glanced up as he walked back in, trying to read his expression. "Everything okay?" she asked, her tone casual, though her heart quickened slightly.

"Everything's fine," Richard said with a reassuring smile, but there was a glint in his eyes that she couldn't quite decipher. "Just some business to attend to."

Lacy nodded, her suspicions momentarily quelled,. What exactly is his business? she wondered, feeling a slight chill despite the warmth of the room.

Richard clapped his hands together, his demeanor shifting back to jovial. "Let's celebrate this victory, shall we?"

Lacy smiled, trying to push the unease aside. "Absolutely," she agreed, but as she turned back to her desk, a nagging doubt crept back in, whispering that with her father, nothing was ever truly as simple as it seemed.

Later that afternoon, the office buzzed with activity as Lacy and her team continued interviewing candidates for the vacant speechwriter position. Chloe had scheduled five interviews back-to-back, and each candidate seemed less impressive than the last.

After the third candidate, Lacy glanced at her watch, feeling a dull throb forming behind her eyes. Her patience was wearing thin, her frustration growing with every passing minute. She drummed her fingers lightly on her desk, wishing for a miracle—or at least someone who actually understood what she needed.

"Let's hope the next one can string a coherent sentence together," Paige muttered under her breath as the door opened for the fourth candidate.

By the time the last candidate, exited with a hollow promise of "selling the brand," Lacy could feel the tension in her shoulders creeping up her neck. She let out a sigh, leaning back in her chair. "Is this really the best we can find?" she murmured, half to herself.

And then Benjamin Carter walked in.

The atmosphere in the room seemed to shift almost instantly. Benjamin was tall and broad-shouldered, his skin sun-kissed and bronzed. His long, curly black hair was pulled back into a neat bun, and his brown eyes were warm and kind, yet quietly confident. Tattoos peeked out from beneath the sleeves of his shirt—intricate lines and symbols that hinted at stories she wanted to know. He carried himself with an ease that commanded attention, but without arrogance.

Lacy sat up straighter, her curiosity piqued. Finally, someone who looks like he actually wants to be here.

"Mr. Carter, it's a pleasure to meet you," she said, extending her hand.

Benjamin smiled, a slow, genuine smile that immediately softened the tension in the room. "Please, call me Ben. The pleasure is mine, Senator Jacobs."

"Call me Lacy, please," she replied.

As they sat down, Lacy found herself studying him, not just his appearance, but his demeanor. There was something about the way he held himself, something genuine, almost magnetic. She noticed how he waited for her to speak, unlike the others who had been all too eager to fill the silence with their own voices.

Paige leaned forward, her eyes scanning his resume. "So, Ben, you were an elementary school teacher before moving into activism. That's quite a shift. What motivated you to make that change?"

Ben nodded, his gaze steady. "I loved teaching, but I realized that the issues my students faced went far beyond the classroom. They were dealing with poverty, community violence, systemic inequality. I couldn't just sit back and teach them to read and write when I knew they needed so much more. That's what led me to get involved in activism and policy change."

Lacy found herself leaning forward, her chin resting on her hand. She liked the way he spoke—direct, with a quiet conviction that made her want to listen more. *He cares about the same things I do,* she thought. *And he understands that change isn't just about big speeches; it's about the impact on real people's lives.*

"And what made you want to apply for this position?" Lacy asked, genuinely curious.

Ben's eyes softened as he spoke. "I watched your debate, Senator Jacobs......Sorry. Lacy. The way you spoke about change, about progress—that's the kind of leadership I want to support. Plus, I've always loved proving people wrong when they say you can't get a job with a BA in English," he added with a playful grin.

Lacy laughed, a bright, genuine sound that filled the room. She quickly hid her smile, feeling a small flush of embarrassment. Their eyes met for a brief moment, a flicker of connection that neither of them acknowledged.

Paige's voice cut in, more serious now. "You mentioned policy change. How do you plan to incorporate that experience into writing for a political campaign?"

Ben didn't hesitate. "My experience has taught me that words matter. The way we communicate our message can be the difference between passing a bill and watching it fail. I want to bring that level of precision and impact to your speeches, Senat—— Lacy. It's not just about sounding good—it's about making a real difference."

Lacy nodded slightly, her gaze never leaving his. She could feel something stirring within her, a sense of possibility. *Maybe this is what we've been missing.*

Chloe, who had been taking notes, looked up with a smile. "What about working under pressure? This campaign moves fast, and we need someone who can keep up."

Ben's smile widened slightly. "I'm used to working under pressure. Whether it was managing a classroom full of kids or organizing a protest, I've learned to stay calm and focused. I know how to prioritize and deliver, no matter how tight the deadline."

Lacy found herself nodding again, feeling an unexpected spark of excitement. He gets it, she thought. He really gets it.

"Your background is impressive," she said, trying to keep her tone professional. "But what makes you think you're the right fit for this role?"

Ben's smile faded slightly, replaced by a look of earnest determination. "Because I believe in what you're doing. I believe in your vision, and I want to be part of making it a reality. I'm not here to write pretty words—I'm here to help you create meaningful change."

Before Lacy could respond, Paige cut in with a grin. "You're hired. Start tomorrow morning."

Lacy blinked, momentarily surprised, but Ben's face lit up with excitement.

"Thank you!" Ben said, beaming. "I won't let you down."

He shook their hands, his grip firm, and left the room with a confident stride. As the door closed behind him, Lacy turned to Paige, a mix of amusement and frustration on her face.

"DIBS!" Paige professed loudly.

"No fair! I was totally gonna call dibs!!" Chloe whined.

Lacy shook her head, rolling her eyes with a hint of a smile. "Nobody calls dibs on the new guy……… or any human, for that matter," she said, trying to sound stern, but there was a playful edge to her voice. "And, for the record, I need everyone to promise not to try and sleep with Ben or sexually harass him—or anybody else for that matter."

Chloe and Paige exchanged amused glances and then, with mock seriousness, raised their hands in the Girl Scout salute. In unison, they repeated in a half-teasing tone, "We promise not to try and sleep with Ben or sexually harass him or anybody else for that matter."

Lacy couldn't help but laugh, and soon the whole room was filled with their laughter. "Alright, let's go grab dinner at The Carlton," Lacy said, grinning. "We've earned it after today."

Paige grinned back. "That sounds perfect."

Chloe chuckled, her eyes still lingering on the door where Ben had just left. "I've got some prep work for tomorrow. You two go ahead and enjoy."

A few minutes after Lacy and Paige left for dinner, Richard returned to the office, his presence immediately commanding attention. He glanced around, pretending to look surprised. "Ah, Chloe," he said smoothly, "I was hoping to catch Lacy. But since you're here, maybe you can help me with a few things?"

Chloe stood up quickly, feeling a bit flustered. "Of course, Mr. Jacobs," she replied, her voice a little too eager.

Richard moved closer, taking her hand and pressing a light kiss to it. "Call me Richard," he said with a charming smile.

Chloe blushed and smiled back, trying to keep her composure. Richard slowly began to walk around the office, his fingers brushing lightly over the back of a chair, then the edge of Lacy's desk. His eyes seemed to take in every detail, his expression thoughtful.

"So, tell me," Richard began casually, "How is the campaign shaping up? What's the team's morale like these days?"

Chloe watched him as he moved, slightly mesmerized. "Everyone's working really hard," she said. "The debate win has given us a boost. The team feels more energized."

Richard nodded, his hand trailing over a stack of papers on a side table, his gaze flicking back to Chloe. "Good, good… And what about Lacy? Is she feeling the pressure?"

"She's determined," Chloe replied, eager to be helpful. "I think she's in a really good place, especially after the last debate."

Richard smiled approvingly. "That's what I like to hear. A focused leader makes all the difference." He moved toward a framed photograph of Lacy with a group of young supporters, studying it for a moment before continuing. "And no concerns or… internal conflicts I should know about?"

Chloe hesitated slightly. "Nothing major, just the usual stress of a campaign."

Richard turned back to her, still smiling, but with a hint of something sharper in his eyes. "Excellent. Thank you, Chloe, for the insight. I appreciate your dedication to Lacy and the campaign."

He took her hand again, his grip firm but gentle, and kissed it lightly once more. "It's been a pleasure speaking with you," he added, his tone warm but deliberately vague.

Chloe nodded, smiling as Richard released her hand and made his way toward the door. He paused just before leaving, his eyes sweeping over the room one last time. "Take care, Chloe," he said softly before stepping out, his footsteps echoing in the hallway as he disappeared from sight.

The office was quiet again, save the faint buzz of a distant conversation. Chloe stood there for a moment, unsure of what to make of their exchange, but feeling the warmth in her cheeks from Richard's attention.

Later that night, Lacy found herself in her apartment, craving some much-needed relaxation. She kicked off her heels, slipped into a pair of comfy socks, and cranked up her favorite playlist. The sound of soulful R&B filled the room as she moved to the kitchen, grabbing ingredients to make cookies. The familiar rhythm of the music was a balm, the smooth notes wrapping around her like a warm blanket.

As she mixed the dough, her mind drifted back to the interview with Ben. There was something about him—his quiet confidence, his sincerity—that lingered in her thoughts. Why was she thinking so much about a man she'd only just met? She shook her head slightly, trying to dismiss the thought, but it clung to her, unwilling to be brushed aside.

The cookies went into the oven, and Lacy poured herself a glass of wine. She let the rich, buttery aroma fill the apartment, savoring the comfort it brought. The glow of the lamplight cast soft, warm shadows across the room, while the deep red of her favorite blanket draped over the arm of the couch seemed to beckon her to sit and relax. She swayed gently to the music, letting the tension of the day slowly ebb away.

She couldn't help but smile as she moved around the kitchen, the rhythm of the R&B blending with the faint hum of the oven. For a moment, she allowed herself to forget the pressures of the campaign, to enjoy the simple pleasure of a quiet evening at home.

Once the cookies were done, she settled onto the couch with a plate full of them, still warm and gooey from the oven. She wrapped herself in the blanket, feeling its soft texture against her skin, and opened her journal. She started to write, capturing her thoughts from the day—the highs and lows, the excitement of the debate victory, the bittersweet breakup, and the unexpected connection with Ben.

As she wrote, she felt a sense of peace settle over her. Yet, even as the words flowed easily, her mind wandered back to Ben. Why did he keep popping up in her thoughts? She shook her head, feeling a mix of curiosity and irritation. She knew she couldn't afford distractions— not now, not when the debate win was still fresh. But somehow, he had slipped past her guard, and she found herself wondering.

What would it be like to work with him every day? She pictured him in the office—his calm presence steadying the chaos around him. Could he handle the intensity of her world, the relentless pace of the campaign? She wondered how Ben would handle the pressure, the scrutiny. There was something about him that seemed adaptable, but also… different.

Lacy flipped on the TV, finding an old episode of Law & Order: SVU to unwind to. Curling up on the couch, she nibbled on her cookies, trying to lose herself in the familiar storyline. Yet, her mind kept circling back to Ben.

She wasn't looking for a distraction, especially not now, but she couldn't deny the pull of her curiosity. Maybe it was just the adrenaline of the debate, or the long day catching up to her. Or maybe it was something more.

Eventually, she drifted off to sleep, the TV still playing softly in the background, her journal and cookie plate resting on the coffee table. The glow from the lamplight cast a soft, warm hue over the room, and the faint rhythm of the music played on, a lullaby for a mind that refused to completely rest.

It had been a long day, but as Lacy lay there, surrounded by the warmth of her home and the comfort of her own company, she felt a strange mixture of calm and anticipation. Maybe tomorrow would bring more answers.

For now, though, she knew she was exactly where she needed to be.

CHAPTER 5

The State Tribune newsroom was almost deserted, the hum of computers and the distant sound of a late-night radio show the only noises breaking the silence. The faint smell of burnt coffee lingered in the air, a testament to the hours already logged by the few remaining journalists scattered throughout the office. The harsh fluorescent lights cast long shadows over the rows of desks, their beams glinting off the cluttered piles of papers and half-empty cups that littered the room.

In the corner, slumped over his desk, was Jake Marlowe, a young reporter with a keen eye for a story and an insatiable curiosity that often got him into trouble. Tonight, he was supposed to be working on a piece about the upcoming local elections, focusing on Mayor Harold Blake of Lacy's district—a man known for his integrity, a rarity in the murky waters of state politics.

Mayor Blake was in his late fifties, a tall, imposing figure with a shock of silver hair and a deep, resonant voice that commanded attention. He had earned a reputation as a no-nonsense leader, a man who had taken on corruption within the city with a fierce determination that had won him both admirers and enemies. Blake had served as mayor for three terms and was now running for a fourth, his platform centered on maintaining transparency and accountability in government—values that had made him a thorn in the side of the state's most powerful businessmen.

Jake had been researching Blake's career, piecing together a profile of the mayor that would highlight his accomplishments and the challenges he had faced. But as he dug deeper, he stumbled upon something unexpected—a buried story from a few years back, barely mentioned in the archives. It was a brief report about an assassination attempt on Mayor Blake, an incident that had been quietly swept under the rug. The article mentioned a heroic cop, Michael Hayes, who had intervened and saved the mayor's life. Intrigued, Jake tried to find more information about Hayes, but the trail was cold.

Jake leaned back in his chair, frowning. Why had the story of a thwarted assassination been buried so quickly? The headline was sensational enough to have been front-page news for days. Instead, there was just a single, sparse article—no follow-ups, no interviews with the officer who had saved the mayor. And the more Jake thought about it, the more it bothered him. It was like a puzzle with a missing piece that refused to fit.

The assassination attempt had happened in broad daylight, just outside Blake's office. According to the scant details in the report, a man had approached the mayor with a gun, but before he could fire, Officer Michael Hayes had tackled him, disarming the would-be assassin and preventing what could have been a tragedy. The assailant had been arrested, but the story had quickly disappeared from the headlines.

Why? Jake wondered, his fingers tapping absently on the desk. And why had Hayes, a hero by any measure, suddenly quit the force just a few weeks later and disappeared from town?

He had tried to contact Hayes, searching through old police records, social media, and even reaching out to former colleagues, but it was as if the man had vanished into thin air. The only thing Jake had managed to find was a vague connection between Hayes and the Jacobs family—the wealthiest and most powerful family in the state, headed by the enigmatic Richard Jacobs.

Jake's pulse quickened. The Jacobs family. They were known for their influence, their sprawling business empire reaching into every corner of the state, but their name also came with whispers of darker dealings—rumors that never quite made it to the front page. And then there was Amanda Jacobs, Richard Jacobs' wife. She had died under mysterious circumstances not long after Hayes had left town. The official story was that it had been an accident, but the timing was suspicious—too close to Hayes' departure to be a coincidence.

Jake rubbed his temples, feeling the pressure building behind his eyes. Was it just a hunch, or was there something more? Every instinct told him that the story hadn't ended with the assassination attempt— that there were threads connecting Hayes, the Jacobs family, and perhaps even Amanda's death. He felt a bead of sweat form on his brow and wiped it away, trying to focus.

He clicked through the sparse records again, looking for anything he might have missed. A detail, a name, something. Why would Hayes have any connection with the Jacobs family? And why leave town so suddenly?

He pulled up a fresh document, his fingers hovering over the keys. Jake knew he should be writing about Mayor Blake's integrity and his campaign for re-election, but this story felt bigger, more urgent. If Richard Jacobs had ordered a hit on Mayor Blake, he thought, was it because Blake was too incorruptible? Was he standing in the way of some larger plan? And how did Hayes fit into it all?

The questions swirled in Jake's mind, and he felt a jolt of adrenaline. His hands trembled slightly as he began to type, the rapid clicks of the keys breaking the silence of the empty newsroom.

He reached for his phone, scrolling through his contacts, searching for someone who might have known Hayes, someone who could shed light on his sudden departure. He knew he was straying from his original assignment, but he couldn't let this go. He dialed a number, pressing the phone to his ear. The phone rang, piercing the silence of the newsroom. His heart pounded in his chest.

The line clicked, and a voice on the other end answered, groggy but curious. "Hello?"

"Hi, this is Jake Marlowe from the State Tribune," Jake said quickly, his voice steady despite the late hour. "I'm working on a story about Michael Hayes, and I was hoping you could help me. It's about something that happened a few years back—an assassination attempt on Mayor Blake."

There was a pause on the other end, and for a moment, Jake feared the line would go dead. But then the voice spoke again, more awake, more cautious. "It's after fucking midnight! Why are you asking about Officer Hayes? He left the force over a decade ago."

"I know, and I'm sorry to bother you this late," Jake replied, leaning forward in his chair, his grip tightening on the phone. "But something doesn't add up. And I think it's connected to Richard Jacobs. I need to know what happened to Hayes, why he left town, and what role the Jacobs family played in all of this."

The silence that followed was heavy, thick with tension. Jake felt his pulse quicken, his breath shallow. He wiped his damp palms on his jeans, waiting.

Finally, the voice spoke again, low and serious. "If you're digging into this, be careful. Richard... he doesn't like people poking around in his or his family's business. And if Hayes was involved with them, there's a reason he left town. A reason you might not want to know."

Jake swallowed, feeling his mouth go dry. But he couldn't back down. "I'm not afraid of the truth," he said, his voice firm.

"But you should be afraid of Richard Jacobs," the voice replied, before the line went dead with a sharp click.

Jake lowered the phone slowly, the warning ringing in his ears. His hands were trembling now, but he felt a surge of determination. I'm onto something big, he thought, something that could change everything.

He turned back to his computer, his fingers flying across the keyboard, piecing together the threads of the story. He knew he was stepping into dangerous territory, but the truth was out there, and he was going to find it—no matter what it cost.

The first light of dawn began to creep through the windows, casting a pale glow over the newsroom. Jake didn't notice. He was too focused, too caught up in the thrill of the chase. This was only the beginning.

CHAPTER 6

Ben's first day at the campaign office began with Chloe and Paige leading him through the bustling maze of desks and computers. The office buzzed with energy, staffers moving quickly, their conversations a low hum of urgency and excitement.

Chloe, always the warm one, gestured enthusiastically as they moved through the open space. "This is the bullpen," she explained. "Where the magic happens. And over there," she pointed to a corner desk cluttered with coffee cups and sticky notes, "is Jason, our head of Communications."

Jason looked up from his computer, gave a brief nod, and adjusted his glasses. "Nice to meet you, Ben," he said with a slight smile. "Hope you're ready for the chaos."

Ben grinned. "I thrive in chaos."

"Good answer," Jason replied before turning back to his screen.

Chloe and Paige led Ben down a narrow hallway to Lacy's office. Chloe knocked, and they heard a muffled, "Come in!" They opened the door to find Lacy typing furiously, her fingers a blur over the keyboard. She didn't even look up, her eyes focused intently on the screen.

Ben cleared his throat. "Is this a good time?"

Lacy glanced up, her professional smile in place, but she didn't stop typing. "Of course, come on in," she replied smoothly, her hands still dancing over the keys.

Ben stepped inside, feeling a little awed by her multitasking prowess. "I believe I'm scheduled to have lunch with you today. Your treat, apparently."

Lacy laughed, finally pausing in her typing to give him her full attention. "I make it a point to take all my senior staffers out to lunch. I threw a bowling party for everyone to get to know me and each other better. It's important to me that we're all connected."

Ben liked that she seemed so genuine, a contrast to the polished figure people saw on TV and in magazines. He smiled. "So, where do we go?"

Lacy leaned back in her chair, still smiling. "Your choice. Where would you like to go?"

Ben didn't hesitate. "There's this great old burger joint just outside of town. They make these amazing greasy burgers and milkshakes. It's called—"

"Sal's!" they both said at the same time, their smiles widening.

For a moment, they just stood there, smiling at each other before realizing they were locked in a gaze. Lacy's cheeks flushed slightly as she cleared her throat. "I love that place."

Ben chuckled. "So do I. Funny I've never seen you there."

Lacy shrugged, her eyes twinkling with amusement. "I prefer to eat a greasy burger when no one is watching."

They both laughed, the moment light and easy. "That place and I go way back," Lacy added, leaning forward on her desk. "I even dated the owner's son once."

Ben's eyebrow arched playfully. "No jilted ex-lovers I'll have to fight off, right?"

Lacy laughed. "No worries there. We're good."

They decided to head out to Sal's, and soon enough, they were on the road, the small diner coming into view. As they entered, the smell of fried onions and sizzling beef filled the air, a comforting aroma that instantly made them both smile.

Sal and Sal Jr. were behind the counter, and Sal Jr.'s very pregnant wife, Anne, sat at a nearby table, her feet propped up on another chair, reading a magazine. The diner was nearly empty, save for a few older regulars sipping coffee in the corner.

Lacy slipped Sal a few extra bills discreetly. "To keep the riff-raff away while we have lunch," she whispered.

Sal grinned, handing her back the money. "I'd do that for free, Lacy."

Sal Jr. spotted them and came over, his face lighting up. "Lacy! Great to see you!" He turned to Ben, who nodded in greeting.

Lacy smiled warmly. "Sal Jr., this is Ben. New on the team. Ben, this is Sal Jr., an old friend and that's his lovely wife, Anne."

Mary-Anne let out a loud, almost comically exaggerated laugh. "Should I be worried about you being around my man, Ms. Jacobs?" she joked in her thick Greek accent.

Lacy grinned. "No need, Mary- Anne. I promise."

Sal Jr. rolled his eyes, still smiling. "Back to the kitchen with you, woman," he teased. "And get them some waters."

Mary-Anne laughed, patting her belly. "I'm coming, I'm coming," she replied, waddling off to grab glasses.

Ben and Lacy found a booth by the window, the red vinyl seats cracked but comfortable. "The usual?" Sal Jr. called from the kitchen.

Lacy nodded, looking at Ben. "Trust me, you'll want the classic bacon cheeseburger and fries. And don't forget my milkshake made with Neapolitan ice cream."

"Deal," Ben agreed, relaxing back into his seat.

They started with small talk about the campaign, the recent victories, and their mutual admiration for Sal's greasy menu. Ben was clearly thrilled to be on board. "I'm grateful for this opportunity,

Lacy," he admitted, his tone sincere. "I've always wanted to work somewhere I could make a real impact."

"I'm glad to have you," Lacy replied genuinely. "You have a unique perspective, and I think it'll help us connect with more voters."

When the food arrived, it was everything they hoped for. The burgers were juicy and perfectly seasoned, the fries crisp and golden, and the milkshakes thick and creamy.

They ate, chatting about lighter topics. Ben shared his hobbies—fishing, writing, hanging out with his childhood friends, reading, and spending time with his family. Lacy listened, intrigued, enjoying the ease of their conversation.

Their talk turned more serious, touching on the shared experience of losing a parent young. "It changes you," Ben said softly, his voice thoughtful. "Makes you grow up faster, I guess."

Lacy nodded, her gaze meeting his. "Yeah… it makes you tough, but it also makes you appreciate every moment. It's like, what I wouldn't give for another hour with my mom."

Their eyes locked, and for a moment, there was a shared understanding, a silent connection. But then, something else flickered between them, a spark that caught them both by surprise. They quickly looked away, both smiling nervously.

Before either could speak again, Lacy's phone rang, breaking the moment. She glanced at the screen. "It's Paige."

She answered, and Paige's voice came through, tense. "Lacy, we've got a small emergency. The speechwriter you fired—he's upset and tweeting about you. And it's gaining traction."

Lacy blinked, stunned. "What? I thought we parted on good terms… I even offered to help him find a new job!" She could feel her pulse quickening, the initial surprise shifting into a mix of confusion and frustration. She had been careful, thoughtful, even overly kind in letting him go.

Lacy stood up, preparing to leave the booth. "Okay, I'll—"

But before she could finish, Paige pushed through the door of the diner, her phone still to her ear. "Never mind that, I'm here already."

Ben raised his eyebrows, sensing the urgency. Paige marched over, her face set with determination. "Ben, I'm going to need you in on this, too."

Lacy quickly unlocked her phone and pulled up Twitter. Her heart sank as she scrolled through the tweets. At the top was one from her former speechwriter, David King, a middle-aged man with a well-groomed beard and a penchant for dramatic flair. His tweet read:

"Unbelievable how @LacyJacobs pretends to care. Fired me without warning! Claimed it was 'for the best' but just couldn't handle my integrity. #LacyLies #TruthHurts #PoliticsAsUsual #DontTrustLacy."

Beneath the tweet, a thread of replies piled up—some expressing sympathy, others seizing the chance to criticize Lacy's character. The hashtags he'd created were beginning to trend in the local political circles, and she could already see several smaller accounts latching on, amplifying the negativity.

Paige pulled out a chair and sat down, speaking quickly. "David's got over 10,000 followers, and his thread is catching fire. We need to act fast before this snowballs. I thought he was happy with how we handled everything."

Ben leaned over Lacy's shoulder, reading the tweet again. "What exactly did you say to him when you let him go?"

Lacy ran a hand through her hair, trying to recall every detail. "I was polite, told him we needed a different voice to better match the campaign's new direction. I even offered to help him network and find another position... I thought he understood. He seemed fine with it at the time. I didn't expect this." She shook her head, a wave of frustration washing over her. "This is the last thing we need right now."

Paige nodded, her face serious. "It doesn't help that he's spinning the narrative to make it seem like you fired him for speaking the truth."

Ben studied the tweets, then leaned back in his chair, thinking. "We need to counter this with authenticity—your strongest asset. You have a lot of people who trust you, Lacy. We just need to mobilize them."

Before they could strategize further, Lacy's phone buzzed again. It was Chloe, and her voice was urgent. "Lacy, get on Twitter. Now."

A chill ran through Lacy's spine as she exchanged a quick look with Paige and Ben. "What is it?" she asked, her voice tense. She pulled up the app again, fearing the worst.

Paige leaned closer, peering over Lacy's shoulder. "Okay, everyone breathe… Let's see what's happening."

As they refreshed their screens, a new hashtag caught their attention: #LacyLifts. And below it, a stream of tweets flooded in, like a wave turning the tide.

The first one was from a woman named Angela Mendez, who ran a local community center. Her tweet read: "@LacyJacobs was the only politician who fought for us when our funding got cut. She showed up when no one else did. I stand with her. #LacyLifts"

Another tweet from Tom Reilly, a small business owner: "Had the privilege of meeting @LacyJacobs at a town hall. She listened, really listened. That's rare in politics. #LacyLifts"

Ben's eyes widened as more and more tweets flooded in, recounting personal stories of Lacy's kindness and integrity. A teacher wrote:
"@LacyJacobs helped save our after-school program. Without her, hundreds of kids would have been left without a safe place to go. #LacyLifts"

And then, even more came—flooding in by the dozens, then hundreds. A firefighter's widow wrote: "Lacy Jacobs was the only one who reached out to our family when we lost my husband. I'll never forget that. #LacyLifts"

A small chuckle escaped Paige's lips as she scrolled through, her shoulders relaxing. "Looks like David's attack is backfiring spectacularly."

Lacy stared at her phone, blinking back tears. "I… I can't believe this," she whispered, her voice catching in her throat. "I never expected this."

Paige grinned, patting Lacy's shoulder. "See? People know the real you. They're not buying into his bullshit."

Ben nodded, his expression warm. "Looks like you've got an army behind you, Lacy."

As more tweets continued to pour in, Lacy read a few more aloud, her voice trembling with emotion:

A tweet from a young woman read: "@LacyJacobs helped me get a scholarship I never thought I'd qualify for. She didn't have to, but she did. She cares about people. #LacyLifts"

Another from a retired veteran: "Lacy Jacobs always stood up for vets. I'm with her. #LacyLifts"

Lacy felt a wave of gratitude so intense it almost knocked her breath out. She blinked hard, trying to keep her composure, but her eyes welled up despite her best efforts.

Ben smiled softly at her, his voice gentle. "You've made a real impact on people's lives, Lacy."

Lacy nodded, swallowing hard. "I guess I underestimated… how much they cared."

Paige, still scanning her phone, added with a sly grin, "And don't forget, social media's fickle. This wave of support is something real. It's personal."

Ben leaned forward, his expression more serious now. "So, what's our next move? We should acknowledge the support somehow, make sure people know we see them and appreciate them."

Lacy nodded, determination setting back in. "We will. But first, let's get back to the office. We need to regroup and figure out a more strategic response."

Paige agreed. "Good idea. We can capitalize on this momentum, but we need to do it right."

They quickly settled their bill, thanking Sal and his family for their hospitality. As they stepped outside, the air felt fresh and invigorating, a light breeze cutting through the afternoon heat.

On the drive back to the office, Lacy stared out the window, feeling a mixture of relief and renewed purpose. For the first time in a long while, she felt the weight of public scrutiny lift just a little. The support had been overwhelming, but it was also a reminder of why she was doing this—who she was fighting for.

Back at the office, they moved quickly into action. Paige got on a call with the social media team, strategizing the next steps. Ben was already drafting a statement of gratitude for Lacy to post, something genuine and heartfelt.

Lacy stood in the middle of the office, taking a deep breath as the team buzzed around her. The adrenaline from the unexpected turn of events was still rushing through her veins, but she felt more grounded now, her resolve stronger than ever.

"We've got this," she whispered to herself, feeling a small smile tug at her lips. She looked around at her team—Paige, Ben, Chloe, all of them working tirelessly, ready to fight back with her. She knew she wasn't alone. She had her people, her purpose, and, most importantly, her integrity.

They were going to turn this around.

And as the office buzzed with energy and excitement, Lacy felt a spark of something new—hope. A belief that maybe, just maybe, they could win this battle and every one that lay ahead.

****

It had been an action packed first few weeks for Ben, when he walked into the campaign office, the atmosphere buzzing with activity. Posters of smiling veterans with service dogs adorned the walls, surrounded by papers detailing every aspect of the upcoming event, "Paws for a Cause." The scent of fresh coffee hung in the air, mingling with the faint vanilla from Lacy's candle. He noticed how everything seemed to have been arranged with a purpose: stacks of pamphlets on tables, press releases in neat piles, and a large, colorful banner draped across the back wall, proclaiming the event's slogan, "Healing Together."

He felt a mixture of excitement and anticipation as he navigated the busy room, nodding politely at staffers who were engrossed in their tasks. Finally, he spotted Lacy in the conference room, deeply focused on a document. She looked up as he approached and smiled, a professional but warm expression that made his chest tighten, just a little.

"Ben!" she greeted him with enthusiasm. "I really want to say you've done an amazing job these past few weeks. Jason is so pleased." She leaned in slightly, lowering her voice to a playful whisper. "He likes you way more than he ever liked David."

Ben chuckled, relieved to hear it. "That's good to know."

Lacy laughed softly, nodding towards the stack of papers in front of her. "Alright, let's get started. This event—Paws for a Cause—it's the first of many, and it's crucial for us. We want to use it to show our commitment, not just to veterans but to everyone in the community. 'Paws for a Cause' is about giving purpose to puppies that were too gentle for police work by matching them with veterans struggling with PTSD. This is just one piece of my larger initiative to better care for our vets here at home—expanding VA services, improving mental and physical healthcare, increasing transparency in the transition process, and creating a wellness task force that puts veterans first, without unnecessary law enforcement involvement."

Ben glanced around at all the material, impressed but still curious. "I'd love to know more about why you chose this particular policy platform. It would help with crafting the speech."

Lacy's expression softened, her posture relaxing a little. "Did you know 22 veterans die every day waiting for services from our nation's VA and that's just the ones we know about?" she asked, her voice quieter now, more reflective.

Ben blinked, his attention sharpening. "I've heard that, yeah."

Lacy nodded slowly, her eyes taking on a distant look. "I went to a conference on veterans' affairs a couple of years ago, and when I heard that statistic, I almost cried. I knew we had to do something… more." She took a deep breath, her gaze steady but filled with emotion. "This event… yes, I want the press, I want people to see how good this program is, and yes, it will help my political career. But," she paused, moving to sit directly in front of Ben, "the non-politician side of me just doesn't want to lose another mother, friend, sister, dancer, teacher, or father."

Ben could see the emotion welling in her eyes, her usual composure faltering for just a moment. "People are hurting….badly," she continued, her voice trembling slightly, "and I really want to fix that. This policy is part of a larger plan of change aimed at taking care of people, especially veterans, and seeing no more lives lost here at home."

Lacy seemed to catch herself, quickly recomposing, and she laughed lightly, wiping her eyes with the back of her hand. "Does that help?" she asked, her smile returning, though still touched with the sincerity of her words.

Ben smiled back at her softly, touched by her openness. "It does. It helps to know you actually care," he said quietly, pausing for a moment before continuing. "I had a friend, Michael 'Mickey' Ortega… We were a group of six, tight as brothers. Mickey was the combat vet, two tours in Iraq and Afghanistan. When he got back from the second one," Ben sighs, "he was different and it was so hard for him… he struggled so much….we tried so hard to be there for him. All of us, including his mom, felt….we all felt…. so helpless. Then one day, he… he wrote he was tired of struggling… and being a burden to us………." Ben's voice tightened as he spoke, the pain evident in his eyes.

Lacy reached out and touched Ben's elbow gently, her voice filled with empathy. "I'm so sorry for your loss, Ben. I can't imagine what that must have been like for you… or for him."

He nodded, taking a breath to steady himself. "He wasn't a burden but that's why this is so important to me, too. I've seen what happens when we don't do enough." Ben said softly, his voice filled with genuine appreciation.

Lacy nodded in understanding, clearing her throat, clearly moved. She shifted back to business mode, tapping her notepad. "Alright, so… let's make sure this speech moves people in this way, too! We need to start with a story—something that captures attention immediately."

Ben agreed, "How about we start with a real story? A veteran, someone whose life was changed by a service dog… We show their journey, the struggles before and the healing after."

Lacy's eyes lit up, and she nodded eagerly. "Yes, perfect. Then we transition into how our program is expanding that kind of impact. And we'll bring in the science—how these dogs are more than pets, they're lifelines."

"The science is key," Ben agreed, his voice full of conviction. "It's one thing to make people feel, but we also need to make them understand that this is a practical, effective solution."

Lacy smiled, feeling the rush of inspiration flowing between them. "And we end with a call to action," she continued, leaning in with enthusiasm. "A reminder that it's our duty to care for veterans for the rest of their lives."

Ben nodded, their gazes locking again, that familiar spark of connection flaring up. The room seemed to buzz with the energy of their collaboration, a shared passion that was both exciting and a little daunting.

"Absolutely," he murmured, feeling the intensity of the moment. "You're speaking from the heart, and that's what people will respond to."

She gave his arm a gentle squeeze, a moment of quiet gratitude passing between them. "Thank you, Ben. I couldn't do this without you."

Ben's smile deepened, his admiration for her growing stronger. "It's my pleasure, really. You're going to make a real difference with this."

She pulled away, the moment lingering just a touch longer than necessary. "I have to head out now," she said, gathering her things. "One last push for community center funding on the Senate floor tonight."

Ben chuckled, his eyes following her. "You're making speeches left and right. Go give 'em hell, Lacy."

She grinned, grabbing her bag. "I always do. And I'll leave this speech in your capable hands. Ready for me by morning?"

"Consider it done," he replied confidently. "Good luck tonight."

Lacy nodded, pausing at the door. "See you tomorrow, Ben."

He watched as she left, the door clicking shut behind her, feeling the warmth of her touch still lingering on his arm. For a brief moment, he allowed himself to remember Mickey—their laughter, the dreams they'd shared, and the pain of losing him. It made him more determined than ever to help Lacy succeed.

Turning back to the scattered notes, he settled at his desk. He felt the weight of their shared mission, but also a deep sense of purpose. He wasn't just writing a speech—he was helping shape a movement that could save lives. And that, he realized, was worth every ounce of effort.

The office grew quieter, the flickering candle on Lacy's desk cast soft shadows on the wall, and Ben got to work, determined to make this speech as perfect as the cause it championed.

Lacy had spent this entire session pushing SB1222 through every stage of the legislative process. She'd fought tooth and nail in subcommittee meetings, weathering skepticism and criticism from colleagues who dismissed the community center as an unnecessary expense. She'd navigated the sharp elbows and power plays in committee hearings, building unlikely coalitions and painstakingly winning over those who had the power to kill the bill. Now, after two previous attempts on the Senate floor, SB1222 was finally back for a third and final vote.

The grand chamber of the State House was bathed in the warm, golden light of the early evening sun filtering through the tall, ornate windows. The air was thick with anticipation as Lacy stood at the podium, her heart pounding in her chest. This was it—the final push to secure funding for the community center she had fought so hard for. The walls of the chamber, lined with rich wood paneling and historic portraits, seemed to close in around her, the weight of history and expectation pressing down on her shoulders.

In the balcony above, her father sat among the spectators—lobbyists, political aides, and a smattering of visitors who had come to witness the proceedings. His presence was a steadying force, but also a reminder of the high expectations she carried on her shoulders. Lacy felt the familiar twist of anxiety in her stomach as she caught his eye. He nodded to her with a small, approving smile—a look she knew all too well. It was a look that said, "Show them what you're made of." She wanted so desperately to meet that expectation, but a small voice in the back of her mind whispered, "What if I can't?"

The Speaker of the House, Harold Whitmore, called the session to order, his gravelly voice echoing through the chamber. "The floor recognizes Senator Lacy Jacobs, presenting SB1222 for the final vote."

Lacy took a deep breath, her hands gripping the edges of the podium. She looked out over the sea of faces—colleagues, allies, and opponents alike. She could feel the tension in the room, a tight coil waiting to spring. She couldn't afford to let her nerves show. "Mr. Speaker, esteemed colleagues," she began, her voice steady but filled with emotion. "Today, I stand before you not just as a senator, but as a member of this community, to urge you to consider the importance of SB1222. This bill is not just a line item in a budget—it is a lifeline for the people it will serve."

As she spoke, Lacy felt her voice growing stronger, carried by the passion she felt for the cause. She painted a vivid picture of what the community center would mean—the programs for at-risk youth, the health services for the elderly, the support groups for veterans. She knew that every word mattered, every moment was a chance to sway a wavering vote. "This isn't just a building," she thought, "it's a chance for me to prove what I'm capable of beyond my father's influence." Her gaze flicked briefly to her father, still watching from the balcony, his expression unreadable.

"In times of division and uncertainty, it is our duty to come together and invest in the future of our communities," Lacy continued, her voice resonating with conviction. "This center is a testament to that commitment. It is an opportunity to give back, to lift up those who need it most, and to create a legacy that we can all be proud of." She felt the intensity of the moment—a crucial step in her career. Her thoughts were interrupted by a sudden image of her father, his smile slipping if this vote didn't pass. But she pushed it away, determined to stay focused.

The chamber was silent after she finished, and Lacy could feel her heart pounding so hard she wondered if others could hear it, too. She took a deep breath, her knuckles white against the podium as she waited for the outcome. But she forced herself to stay calm, her face betraying none of the inner turmoil.

"The clerk will open the roll for voting on SB1222," Speaker Whitmore announced, and Lacy watched the board intently. Green lights began to blink on, one after another, interspersed with red. Her breath hitched. She exhaled slowly, feeling the tightness in her shoulders begin to ease, even as the tension in the room reached its peak.

Finally, Speaker Whitmore's voice cut through the thick air. "Will the clerk close the roll?"

Lacy held her breath again, the seconds stretching out into eternity. The final tally appeared: 26 Yays, 24 Nays.

"SB1222 passes with a vote of 26-24," Speaker Whitmore announced.

A wave of relief washed over her, and she let out a breath she hadn't realized she was holding. Her shoulders sagged slightly, and she caught herself, quickly straightening her posture. She had to look composed, even in victory. But inside, her heart was soaring. She glanced up at her father and saw his rare, genuine smile. For a moment, it felt like she'd won his approval, not just the vote.

As the chamber gradually emptied, Lacy exchanged a few quiet congratulations with her colleagues, but already her mind was turning to the next challenge.

Later that night, Lacy drove home through the dimly lit streets, her thoughts still spinning. As the city lights blurred past her car window, she felt a strange mix of triumph and apprehension. The victory in the Senate was just the beginning. The community center's funding was secured but now came the hard part—delivering on her promises. She had made so many commitments to so many people. Could she keep them all?

Finally home, she sank into the plush cushions of her couch, her body sinking into the soft fabric with a sigh. The exhaustion hit her like a wave, the adrenaline of the day finally giving way. Her apartment was quiet, save for the distant hum of traffic and the comforting glow of the city lights filtering through the curtains. She kicked off her heels, her feet sinking into the soft, cool rug beneath her.

Her phone buzzed on the coffee table. She reached for it, scanning the screen. It was an email from Ben. The subject line simply read, "Draft of Paws for a Cause Speech."

A small smile tugged at her lips. Even in her exhaustion, she felt a flicker of warmth. She opened the email:

Lacy,

Attached is the draft for the Paws for a Cause speech. I think it's coming together really well. Take a look when you get a chance. I'm confident this will resonate with everyone. Enjoy your evening and try to get some rest—you've earned it.

Ben

Lacy smiled wider, her fingers hovering over the keyboard. She wanted to dive into the draft right away, but she felt the weight of her fatigue pulling her eyelids down. She quickly typed a reply:

Ben,

Thank you for getting this done so quickly. I can't wait to read it, but I think I'll save it for tomorrow. I promise I won't interrupt your day off. You deserve it after all your hard work.

Tonight was a success—SB1222 passed! I couldn't have done it without your support.

Goodnight, Lacy

She hit send, then leaned back into the cushions, the soft fabric enveloping her. For a moment, she felt truly at peace. But then, a thought crept in—what if this was just the beginning? What if the passage of SB1222 brought more scrutiny, more challenges, more battles to fight? She could almost hear her father's voice: "This is the easy part, Lacy. Winning is one thing; keeping it is another."

She shook off the thought, deciding to let tomorrow worry about itself. For tonight, at least, she had won. Her muscles relaxed, her fingers tracing the texture of the couch fabric. The soft glow of the lamp beside her bathed the room in a warm, comforting light. She closed her eyes, allowing herself to drift into a well-earned sleep, feeling, for once, that she was exactly where she was meant to be.

The next day was one of those ordinary campaign days that Lacy had grown all too familiar with—packed with back-to-back meetings, phone calls, and endless staff briefings. The sun poured through the windows of the campaign office, casting warm, golden light across the room, but Lacy barely noticed. She was at her desk, flipping through notes for her upcoming appearances, her mind churning through the countless details that needed to be managed. The office buzzed with the usual chaos—phones ringing, keyboards clacking, staffers darting around like bees. The smell of strong coffee mixed with the faint scent of lavender from the air freshener someone had sprayed earlier.

Across from her, Paige was flipping through a printed copy of Ben's speech for the upcoming Paws for a Cause event. Lacy tried to focus on her notes, but she couldn't help but feel a flutter of anticipation every time Paige turned a page. She hated to admit it—even to herself—but there was something about knowing that Ben had stayed up late to perfect this speech that made her stomach twist in a way that was both thrilling and unnerving.

Paige let out an appreciative whistle, pulling Lacy from her thoughts. "Lacy," she said, looking up with a gleam in her eye, "I gotta say as your campaign manager, I love this speech. It's amazing—probably one of the best we've had. But as your friend…" She grinned mischievously. "I kind of want to fuck that man."

Lacy burst out laughing, a little too loudly, trying to mask the sudden rush of heat to her cheeks. "Paige, you're terrible!" she teased, but she felt her face flush.

"Seriously, though," Paige continued, leaning back with a satisfied smile. "The way he captured your vision, your passion for this cause… It's not just good—it's inspiring. And if you weren't already convinced that he had a crush on you, this speech would be all the proof you need."

Lacy's smile faltered for just a second. She pushed a loose strand of hair behind her ear, trying to sound casual. "It's not like that," she said, more to herself than to Paige. "Ben's just… he's incredibly dedicated. He believes in what we're doing."

Paige raised an eyebrow, clearly unconvinced. "Uh-huh. Well, whether or not there's more to it, this speech is going to be an incredible one. You two make a hell of a team."

Lacy felt a twinge of uncertainty. Did they? She quickly shifted in her chair, trying to hide her unease. "Yeah, well, we'll see how it goes," she said, her voice a bit too breezy. "Anyway, let's go grab some lunch before the staff meetings. I could use a break from all this."

Paige caught the deflection and smirked. "Changing the subject, are we? Fine, fine. Lunch it is."

Lacy stood, smoothing her skirt with a deliberate motion. "Yes, lunch," she said, a little too brightly. "I need to clear my head. If I don't, I might just lose it in one of these meetings." Her voice was half-joking, half-serious. Today was critical—the upcoming events needed to be perfect, and every moment of preparation counted. If they didn't pull everything together flawlessly, they risked losing momentum—and maybe even funding.

They headed toward the door, and Lacy could hear the faint buzz of a news segment playing in the background, the sound of political commentary mingling with the busy hum of the office. As they walked out, she glanced at the rows of posters lined up for their next event and couldn't help but feel the weight of the campaign press down on her shoulders.

Paige's voice broke through her thoughts. "Don't forget, we've got that dinner next week with the donors from the Northeast. We need to strategize."

Lacy nodded, grateful for the change in conversation. "Yeah, there's a lot riding on that night… and on the next few weeks." She tried to push thoughts of Ben from her mind, focusing instead on the stakes ahead.

They stepped outside, the crisp air hitting her face and reminding her just how much was at stake. As she took a deep breath, the fluttering in her chest settled, replaced by a familiar determination. Today, tomorrow, and every day until the election—all of it mattered.

Lacy glanced at Paige and smiled. "Alright, let's do this."

But as they walked down the street toward the café, Paige couldn't resist one last dig. "And maybe over lunch, you can tell me more about how 'not like that' things are with Ben."

Lacy laughed, shaking her head.

****

Fifteen minutes from where he grew up, in a modest but well-kept apartment complex, Ben was waking up to the soft light of the morning sun filtering through his blinds. His apartment was simple, yet comfortable—a reflection of his no-nonsense personality. The walls were a muted gray, with framed photos of his family and friends hanging in neat rows. A small bookshelf in the corner was filled with well-worn paperbacks, and the living room boasted a worn but comfortable couch, a flat-screen TV, and a coffee table littered with the remnants of last night's reading.

Ben yawned and stretched, his muscles sore from yesterday's workout. He rolled out of bed and headed to the bathroom, where he brushed his teeth and splashed cold water on his face, the bracing chill waking him up completely. Afterward, he changed into his workout clothes—a simple pair of shorts and a faded T-shirt—before heading to the small area in his living room that he had designated as his workout space.

The morning air was cool, but Ben quickly warmed up as he began his routine. He started with push-ups, his muscles flexing with each controlled movement, the familiar rhythm calming his mind. He followed up with a series of squats, lunges, and sit-ups, pushing his body to its limits as the sweat began to bead on his forehead. He relished the burn in his muscles, the way his body responded to the challenge. It was a ritual for him, a way to clear his mind and prepare for the day ahead.

After an hour of lifting weights and completing his usual circuit, Ben was thoroughly exhausted, but in the best way. He took a moment to catch his breath, then headed to the bathroom for a quick, refreshing shower. The hot water soothed his aching muscles, washing away the sweat and leaving him feeling invigorated.

Dressed in jeans and a casual button-down shirt, Ben moved to the kitchen, where he began preparing breakfast. He loved to cook, and his kitchen, though small, was well-equipped for his culinary experiments. The smell of sizzling bacon filled the apartment as he cracked a few eggs into a pan, the soft sound of them frying adding to the comforting atmosphere. He added a sprinkle of cheese and some freshly chopped herbs, his movements practiced and precise.

The breakfast was simple but hearty—scrambled eggs, crispy bacon, and whole-grain toast. Ben poured himself a cup of freshly brewed coffee, the rich aroma filling the air as he sat down to eat. He savored each bite, enjoying the quiet of the morning.

After breakfast, Ben grabbed his keys and headed out to visit his grandmother, Dianna—whom he affectionately called Nonie. She had raised him after both his parents were killed in a hit-and-run accident when he was just seven years old. Her home was in the same neighborhood where he'd grown up, a close-knit community where everyone knew each other.

Nonie's house was a charming old-world bungalow, with ivy creeping up the stone walls and flower boxes overflowing with colorful blooms. The front porch had a wooden swing, where Nonie loved to sit on warm afternoons, a glass of sweet tea in hand. The inside of the house was filled with vintage furniture, lace doilies, and shelves lined with books and knickknacks collected over a lifetime. The scent of jasmine, her favorite, always lingered in the air, and the warmth of the home felt like a comforting embrace.

Ben parked his car in the driveway and let himself in, the familiar creak of the front door bringing a smile to his face. "Nonie?" he called out as he walked into the living room, where he found her curled up in her favorite armchair, a patchwork afghan draped over her legs.

"Benji, my sweet boy," Nonie greeted him with a warm smile, her voice tinged with affection. Her silver hair was pulled back into a loose bun, and though she was in her late sixties, her eyes still sparkled with the wisdom and humor that had seen her through so much in life. Today, however, she looked a bit more tired than usual, and Ben could see the stiffness in her movements as she shifted in her chair.

"My feet are giving me trouble today," she admitted, a touch of frustration in her voice as she tried to get comfortable.

Ben's heart softened as he looked at her, his protective instincts kicking in. "Let me see what I can do for ya, Nonie," he said, heading to the bathroom to fill a small tub with warm water. He added some Epsom salts and carried it back to the living room, setting it down in front of her chair.

Nonie gave him a grateful smile as he gently lifted her feet into the warm water. "You always know just what I need. Ben smiled, taking a seat next to her as she relaxed into the soothing warmth.

As they sat together, they talked about everything and nothing— Ben's work, the latest neighborhood gossip, and the little things that made life sweet. Eventually, the conversation turned to Lacy, and Nonie's eyes lit up with curiosity.

"So, this Lacy," Nonie began, her tone playful. "You seem to talk about her a lot. Do you like her?"

Ben chuckled, shaking his head. "Nonie, it's not like that. I just… I believe in what she's trying to do. She's different, you know? She actually cares."

Nonie raised an eyebrow, her smile teasing. "Different, hmm? You sure there's nothing more to it than that?"

Ben rolled his eyes, but he couldn't help the smile that tugged at his lips. "You're impossible, Nonie."

"Mmmmhmmmmmm," she quipped, giving his hand a gentle squeeze.

They chatted for a while longer, Ben sharing stories from his week and Nonie offering her usual mix of wisdom and humor. When lunchtime rolled around, Ben insisted on making her something to eat, preparing a simple but delicious meal of tomato soup and grilled cheese sandwiches—her favorite. They ate together in the cozy kitchen, the sunlight streaming through the lace curtains, casting a warm glow over the room.

After lunch, Ben helped Nonie to her bedroom. "I'll be back soon," he promised, leaning down to press a kiss to her forehead.

"You'd better," Nonie replied, her voice soft but firm. "Don't be a stranger, Ben. I like hearing about your life."

"I won't," Ben assured her, giving her hand one last squeeze before heading out. He glanced back at her as he reached the door, smiling at the sight of her already drifting off to sleep. Nonie was the most important person in his life, and he would do anything to make sure she was taken care of.

That evening, Ben headed over to his friend Sam's house for poker night—a rare treat for him, considering how busy his schedule usually was. Sam's place was a cozy, well-lived-in home on a quiet street, where he lived with his wife and two young kids. The house was always filled with laughter and the smell of something delicious cooking in the kitchen.

Ben was excited to see everyone; it had been too long since he'd been in town, and his boys weren't the only ones who wanted to catch up. But tonight wasn't about anyone or anything that didn't involve good cards, cold beer, and a little friendly shit talking.

When Ben arrived, he was greeted by the familiar sight of his four closest friends—Sam, Josh, Daniel, and Tony—gathered around the large dining table that had been cleared off for the game. Each of them was at a different stage in life: Sam, married with kids and playing the unofficial 'dad' of the group; Josh, engaged and already stressing over wedding plans; Daniel, the practical one who'd just bought his first home and seemed to have an answer for everything; and Tony, the perennial bachelor who could always be counted on for a good time and a bad idea.

"Look who finally decided to show up," Sam called out as Ben walked in, leaning back in his chair with a grin.

"Yeah, we were beginning to think you'd forgotten about us," Josh added with a laugh.

Ben chuckled, raising his beer in a mock salute as he took a seat at the table. "You know I wouldn't miss this. Just been busy."

"Busy with what, exactly?" Tony teased, waggling his eyebrows. "Or should I say, with who?"

The guys erupted into laughter, their camaraderie and ribbing a staple of their friendship. Ben shook his head and laughed along, a smile spreading across his face. "You guys are ridiculous."

As the night wore on, the poker game got into full swing. The table was covered in beer bottles and plates of bar food—nachos, wings, and fries—each bite filling the room with the smell of greasy indulgence. The sound of cards being shuffled and chips clinking together mingled with the constant banter, creating an atmosphere of easygoing fun and nostalgia.

At one point, Tony, who had been sipping on his beer, leaned back in his chair and grinned at Ben. "So, I saw a picture of that Lacy Jacobs on TV the other day," he began, his tone playful. "If I was single and working on that campaign, I'd be all over that."

The table burst into laughter and high-fives, the guys relishing the chance to poke fun at Ben. He laughed along, though he scoffed at their antics. "It's not like that, Tony. Lacy's… she's smart, funny, and she's got a vision for making things better. She's different from what you see on TV."

"Yeah, yeah," Sam chimed in, smirking. "But what else have you seen that….. ain't on TV?"

More laughter ensued, and Ben rolled his eyes, though he couldn't help but smile at their ridiculousness. "Ben, you better watch out," Tony teased, throwing a sideways glance at Ben. "You're way too good at this game. How do we know you're not secretly counting cards?"

Ben smirked, taking a swig of his beer. "Wouldn't be fair if I told you, now would it?"

The table erupted in laughter again, the camaraderie between the friends as natural as breathing. They had been doing this for years—ever since their teenage days. Some things never changed, and poker night was one of those traditions that kept them connected, no matter how busy life got.

As the game continued, the room buzzed with energy, the clink of poker chips and the rustle of cards creating a familiar rhythm. But amid the jokes and laughter, Ben's phone vibrated in his pocket. He glanced down at the screen and saw Abby's name flashing.

Without hesitation, Ben excused himself from the table, getting up and heading toward the hallway for some privacy. His friends shot him knowing looks, but he ignored them, his focus already shifting.

He pressed the phone to his ear as he walked into a quieter part of the house. "Abby," he said, his voice softening as he spoke her name.

"Hey," Abby's voice came through the line, soft and sultry, with that familiar mix of sweetness and longing. "Are you busy?"

Ben leaned against the wall, closing his eyes for a moment as he let the sound of her voice wash over him. "Not too busy for you," he replied, his tone taking on a more serious, almost commanding edge. "What do you need?"

There was a brief pause on the other end, and Ben could almost picture Abby biting her lip, hesitating just a moment before she answered. "I want Sir to come over and fuck me," she said, her voice dropping to a whisper, laced with anticipation.

Ben's breath caught in his throat, a surge of desire flooding through him at her words. He loved the way she surrendered to him, the way she trusted him to take control. His voice, when he spoke, was low and firm, a stark contrast to the playful tone he had used with his friends moments ago. "Good girl. I'll be over in twenty minutes. You know how I like you to wait for me."

"Yes, Sir," Abby replied, her voice barely audible but filled with the need that Ben knew all too well.

"Good," Ben said, his tone leaving no room for argument. "Be ready."

With that, he ended the call, his mind already shifting gears. He took a deep breath, composing himself before heading back to the poker table. His friends were still engrossed in the game, but as soon as they saw him returning, the teasing began.

"Leaving us so soon?" Josh called out, smirking as he shuffled the deck of cards.

"Whipped!" Sam chimed in, making exaggerated cracking noises with an imaginary whip, sending the rest of the guys into fits of laughter.

Ben just shook his head, laughing along with them. "You guys wish you had someone waiting for you like I do," he shot back, grabbing his jacket from the back of his chair and sliding it on.

"Yeah, yeah," Daniel said, grinning. "Just make sure you don't lose all your money before next poker night."

Ben smirked, his mind already on the night ahead. "Don't worry, I'll be back to take all your money next time. But for now, keep your two dollars, Danny Boy."

As he left, his friends' laughter echoed behind him, but his thoughts were already on Abby and the way her voice had sent a thrill through him. He knew what she wanted—what she needed—and he was more than ready to give it to her.

The night was cool as Ben stepped outside, the air crisp against his skin. He felt a mix of anticipation and excitement as he climbed into his car and started the engine, the familiar rumble grounding him. As he drove through the quiet streets, the memories of poker night faded into the background, replaced by thoughts of Abby and what was about to happen.

Twenty minutes later, Ben pulled up to Abby's place. The lights were dim inside, just as he had instructed her to keep them. He could already feel the tension building in his chest, a potent mix of desire and control that he would soon release.

Abby knelt in the center of her bedroom, the dim light casting shadows over the room that was her private sanctuary. Dressed in nothing but black lace panties, she was a vision of submission, waiting for the man who had come to dominate her thoughts and desires. Around her, the space reflected her secret life—leather restraints hung neatly on the wall, a chest in the corner filled with toys, and a full-length mirror reflecting her anticipation. The air was thick with the scent of jasmine, the only light coming from a single candle flickering on the nightstand.

The front door clicked open, and she heard the familiar sound of Ben's footsteps. Her heart raced, her breath quickening in time with the rhythm of her pulse. She could sense the shift in him the moment he entered the house, the quiet, laid-back man she knew by day transforming into the dominant force she craved at night.

Ben stepped into the room, his presence filling the space, the energy crackling between them. He stood in the doorway for a moment, his eyes taking in the sight of her—kneeling, vulnerable, waiting. A small smile tugged at his lips as he closed the door behind him.

"Good girl," Ben murmured, his voice deep and commanding as he approached her. "You've been waiting for me, haven't you?"

"Yes, Sir," Abby whispered, her voice trembling with a mix of nerves and excitement. She kept her eyes down, focusing on the floor, knowing better than to look up without permission.

Ben reached down, his hand brushing over her cheek before sliding into her hair, gripping it firmly as he tilted her head back, forcing her to meet his gaze. His eyes were dark with desire, the control he exerted over her making her shiver.

"You're so beautiful when you're like this," he said, his voice low and rough. "So ready to be used."

"Yes, Sir," Abby repeated, her body quivering in anticipation. She wanted him—needed him—to take control, to remind her of the power he had over her.

Ben's hand slid from her hair to her chin, his thumb brushing over her lips. "Open," he commanded, his tone leaving no room for hesitation.

Abby parted her lips, her breath hitching as he unbuckled his belt, the leather strap sliding through the loops with a soft, tantalizing sound. He unzipped his pants, pulling them down just enough to free his already hard length. His grip on her chin tightened as he guided her mouth to him, his tip brushing against her lips.

"Show me how much you've missed me," he ordered, his voice dark with expectation.

Without another word, Abby wrapped her lips around him, her tongue swirling as she took him deeper, her submission complete. The feel of him in her mouth, the taste of his skin, sent a rush of heat through her body. She reveled in the control he held over her, the way he guided her movements with a firm hand in her hair.

Ben groaned, the sound vibrating through the room as he thrust into her mouth, his control absolute. "That's it," he growled, his voice a mix of pleasure and authority. "Take it all."

Abby's throat tightened around him, her gag reflex barely held in check as she worked to please him, every inch of her body attuned to his commands. He held her there for a moment, his hips rocking gently, savoring the control he had over her.

Finally, he pulled back, his grip on her hair loosening just enough for her to catch her breath. "On the bed," he ordered, his voice a dark promise of what was to come.

Abby scrambled to obey, crawling onto the bed and positioning herself on all fours, her body trembling with anticipation. She didn't have to wait long. Ben was behind her in an instant, his hands rough as they gripped her hips, pulling her back against him. The fabric of her panties was no barrier as he yanked them aside, his fingers slipping between her legs, finding her wet and ready.

And then he was inside her, filling her in one rough thrust that made her cry out, her body arching as he took her hard and fast. The sound of skin against skin filled the room, each thrust sending shockwaves of pleasure through her, her mind spinning as he pushed her to the edge. Ben's grip on her hips was bruising, his dominance overwhelming, and Abby surrendered to it completely, her body moving in time with his, matching his intensity.

He didn't let up, driving into her with a force that made her scream his name, her nails digging into the sheets as she clung to the bed. The pleasure built inside her, each thrust bringing her closer to the brink until she couldn't hold back any longer.

"Come for me, Abby," Ben commanded, his voice a dark, seductive growl.

And she did, her body shattering around him as she came, her climax ripping through her with a force that left her trembling and gasping for breath. Ben wasn't far behind, his rhythm growing erratic as he chased his own release, finally spilling on the bed near her with a guttural groan.

They collapsed onto the bed, their bodies entwined, both of them breathing heavily in the aftermath. Ben wrapped his arms around her, pulling her close as they lay there, the room filled with the scent of sex and sweat.

For a long moment, they were silent, the only sound the soft rustle of the sheets as they shifted, finding comfort in each other's warmth. Eventually, Ben spoke, his voice soft and more like his everyday self.

"Tonight was great," he murmured, pressing a kiss to her forehead.

Abby smiled, her body still humming with the aftershocks of their lovemaking. "Always is," she whispered, her voice filled with contentment.

They lay together in the stillness, the heat of their bodies slowly fading as they talked in hushed tones. They shared stories and laughter, their connection deepening in the comfort of the moment. After a while, Ben sat up, stretching lazily before swinging his legs over the side of the bed.

"Be right back," he murmured.

Abby watched as he padded softly across the room, disappearing into the hallway. A few moments later, she heard him rummaging in the kitchen, the familiar sound of cupboards opening and closing. He returned with a glass of water in one hand and a banana in the other, a small smile on his lips.

"Thought you might need this," he said, handing them over. "Replenish the reserves."

Abby took the glass and fruit, a surprised laugh escaping her. "Always taking care of me," she teased, but her voice was warm, touched by his thoughtfulness. Ben just grinned and settled back beside her, his eyes never leaving her face.

After a while, Ben's tone shifted, becoming tender. "So, what do you say to dinner sometime?"

Abby stiffened, pulling back just enough to look at him. "Ben, I thought we agreed to keep this just a casual thing," she reminded him, her voice edged with surprise and a hint of panic.

Ben's laid-back demeanor kicked back in instantly. "I know, I know. It was just as friends, nothing more," he said, his hands going up in a playful gesture of surrender. "Thought it might be nice."

Abby's heart softened, but she kept her resolve. "We broke up for a reason, Ben," she said, trying to sound firm, though a trace of regret slipped into her voice.

"I know," he replied gently. "I'm not trying to change anything. Just…offering."

Before Abby could say more, Ben's phone buzzed on the nightstand. He picked it up, his eyes lighting up as he read the screen.

It was Lacy, emailing him about the speech. Her words were full of praise, calling him an incredible talent and assuring him that he had a job with her for as long as she was in office.

Ben's smile grew, his heart swelling with pride. He wasn't sure if it was the compliment or the promise of stability that made him feel this way. He hadn't realized he was still smiling when Abby asked, "What's up?"

He didn't look up from his phone. "It's Lacy….. Senator Jacobs. She's just thanking me for the speech."

Abby tried to keep her face neutral, but a flicker of jealousy crossed her features. "How's the job going?" she asked, aiming for casual.

Ben launched into an explanation, his words flowing easily as he talked about the campaign and the impact they were making. But as he spoke, it became clear that his thoughts were focused on Lacy. He spoke about her with a quiet admiration, almost poetic, his voice filled with a respect that stirred something in Abby—something she didn't want to acknowledge.

Pushing down the unease, she made a comment, her tone more clipped than intended. "Be careful with her, Ben. You know all politicians are snakes."

Ben chuckled softly, leaning over to press a kiss to her forehead. "Thanks for looking out for me," he said warmly. "But don't worry. Lacy and I aren't even friends. We just work together."

Abby forced a smile, trying to brush off her lingering annoyance. But as she watched Ben get dressed, his movements casual and unhurried, she couldn't help but ask, "You're not staying tonight?"

Ben shook his head, offering her a small, apologetic smile. "Not tonight. I've got to be up early for work. We leave on the campaign bus for her next event in two days," he explained, a flicker of excitement in his tone that Abby couldn't miss.

She nodded, trying to keep her disappointment from showing. "See you soon, then," she said, forcing a lightness into her voice that she didn't feel.

Ben leaned down, pressing a soft kiss to her lips. "Yeah, see you soon," he replied, his voice warm. With one last look, he turned and walked out, leaving Abby alone in the dim light.

As the door closed behind him, Abby sat up, pulling the blanket around her shoulders. The room felt emptier now, their earlier intimacy replaced by a cold void. She couldn't shake the unease gnawing at her, a mix of jealousy and fear that settled in her chest.

After a few minutes, she reached for her laptop, hesitating before typing "Lacy Jacobs" into the search bar. She knew it was irrational, but she needed to understand what made this woman so special—what had captured Ben's attention so completely.

The search results filled the screen, and Abby's eyes narrowed as a mix of curiosity and dread tightened her stomach. She clicked on a news article detailing Lacy's rise in politics, her commitment to veterans, her impressive track record. The article was glowing, full of praise for Lacy's leadership and her ability to connect with people deeply.

Abby's gaze lingered on a photo of Lacy—tall, confident, with a smile that radiated warmth and intelligence. She was undeniably beautiful, but it was more than that. It was the way she carried herself, spoke with conviction—Ben's admiration for her made perfect sense.

Her chest tightened as she continued to read. Lacy Jacobs was impressive, someone who seemed to have it all. And Abby couldn't help but wonder: Was Ben falling for her? Had she made a mistake keeping their relationship strictly physical, pushing him away?

The thought of losing him to someone like Lacy—a woman who seemed to embody everything Abby wasn't—filled her with a cold, gnawing fear. But what could she do? She had chosen this, chosen to keep things casual, to avoid getting her heart broken again.

Abby had always been the woman who turned heads without trying. Her long, chestnut hair fell in soft waves past her shoulders, and her green eyes were striking against her fair skin, giving her an air of quiet intensity. Her lithe, athletic build, honed from years of hiking and running, was a testament to her restless spirit. A delicate tattoo of a compass rose adorned her left wrist, a symbol of her desire to explore the world beyond the small town where she and Ben had grown up.

Their relationship had always been intense, a fiery connection born from their high school years. They were each other's first love, their chemistry undeniable. But as high school ended, their dreams diverged. Ben loved their small community, the tight-knit fabric of familiar faces, the sense of belonging that came from being rooted in one place. Abby, on the other hand, felt confined by the town's limits. She craved the thrill of the unknown, the excitement of new experiences, and the idea of spending her life in the same place felt suffocating.

The tension between them reached a breaking point when Abby received an opportunity to study abroad in Europe. Ben, who had been accepted to a nearby state school, felt betrayed by her decision to leave. They argued for weeks until they finally had the conversation that changed everything.

And so, with tears in her eyes, Abby left for Europe, and Ben stayed behind. They broke up officially before she boarded the plane.

Now, as Abby stared at Lacy's image on her screen, the old fears resurfaced. Ben had always been her anchor, but Lacy represented everything Abby wasn't—stability, purpose, and a deep connection to the very community Abby had always wanted to escape.

The thought gnawed at her. What if Ben had finally found someone who shared his love for the community? Someone who wouldn't leave him behind?

As the night wore on, Abby's doubts grew. She had always been the one to leave, the one who couldn't be tied down. But now, for the first time, she wondered if she was making a mistake—one that might cost her the only man she had ever truly loved.

CHAPTER 7

The city of Norfolk, Virginia pulsed with coastal energy, where history met hustle and the waterfront shimmered. Nestled against the edge of the Elizabeth River, the skyline sparkled in the fading light, its modern architecture blending seamlessly with old naval brickwork and historic warehouses converted into vibrant art spaces.

The Norfolk Marriott Waterside stood proudly near the river's edge, its sleek glass facade catching the sunset and reflecting back streaks of orange, coral, and gold. Boats rocked gently at the nearby marina, their masts swaying to the rhythm of the breeze, while the distant honk of a ferry echoed across the water. Palms and planters lined the broad walkways that curved along the waterfront promenade, where joggers, tourists, and street musicians mingled beneath a sky streaked with cotton candy clouds.

As the campaign bus pulled up to the hotel's elegant entrance, Lacy glanced out the window and took in the scene—locals gathered around fire pits on the outdoor patio, the scent of sea air mingling with grilled seafood and roasted garlic drifting from nearby restaurants. A jazz trio played on the corner, their music weaving into the ambiance like another layer of charm.

Despite the day's campaign chaos, something about Norfolk—its calm tides, deep harbor air, and anchored strength—made Lacy feel like she could breathe again. But only for a moment.

Lacy stepped off the bus first, her heels clicking softly against the pavement. She wore a tailored navy blue blazer and skirt, a crisp white blouse peeking out from underneath. Her hair was pulled back in a sleek ponytail, her makeup just enough to highlight her sharp features. She moved with purpose, making eye contact with everyone they passed, her smile friendly but her stride firm and steady.

Ben descended the steps behind her, his casual style on full display—dark jeans, a gray button-down with the sleeves rolled to his elbows, his dark hair tousled from the bus ride. He looked more ready for a casual night out than a campaign stop, but his easygoing smile drew a few curious glances from passersby.

Paige followed, her black pantsuit contrasting with a bright red blouse, moving with the efficiency of someone always a step ahead. Chloe brought up the rear in black slacks and a lavender blouse, her focus already on her tablet as she confirmed details for tomorrow's event.

As they made their way into the hotel, the group's energy was lively. Chloe, juggling two phones, murmured, "Venue's confirmed, but still waiting on catering." She barely paused to breathe. "And Lacy, don't forget you've got a donor meet-and-greet tonight at 8."

Lacy nodded, though her focus had already shifted. Paige caught up to her, flipping through a stack of papers. "And we still need that campaign memo for tomorrow," she reminded, though there was a playful glint in her eye.

Lacy groaned in mock annoyance and shot a glance at Ben. "Then what are we paying Ben for?" she joked, though there was a flash of curiosity as she gauged his reaction.

Ben grinned, his eyes lingering a little too long on the hotel bar they passed. "Nope! I'm hitting up that bar tonight. You're on your own," he teased back, his smile easy and carefree. But he felt a twinge of something else when he caught the amused sparkle in her eyes.

Lacy dropped her bags and turned to face him, grinning. "Rock, paper, scissors for it," she challenged, her tone light but her eyes dancing with mischief.

Ben laughed, setting his own bag down. "You're on," he agreed.

They squared off, hands poised in the air. "Rock, paper, scissors, shoot!" they chanted together.

Ben's scissors cut through Lacy's paper. She groaned in defeat but refused to back down. "Best two out of three."

He chuckled. "You got it."

They played again. Lacy threw rock; Ben threw paper. She dragged out a playful groan of "Fiiiiine," tossing her hands up. "You win, Ben. Enjoy your night at the bar. I'll write the memo."

Ben laughed, slinging his bag over his shoulder. "I'll hold you to that. But if you need help, you know where to find me," he said, catching her eye as they reached the elevator.

Their rooms were side by side, and Ben grinned. "Just don't throw any loud parties in your room tonight. I need my beauty sleep," he teased.

Lacy smirked, a playful glint in her eyes. "Mad you're not invited?"

Ben shot back with a mock-pout. "Well, I don't want to go to your stinky party anyway."

She laughed, giving him a gentle push on the arm. Her hand brushed against the firm definition of his biceps, and for a moment, she wondered how good it might feel to be held in those arms. The thought alarmed her so much that she stepped back abruptly—and tripped, stumbling backward.

Ben reached out instinctively to steady her, but her momentum pulled him down with her. They landed in a heap, Ben on top of Lacy.

He grinned down at her, eyes twinkling with amusement. "Is this a good time to ask for a raise?"

Lacy burst out laughing, pushing him off as he rolled to the side. "Get off me, you idiot!" she teased, but there was a softness in her tone as she accepted his hand and let him help her up.

Ben's grip was firm, steady. Once they were standing, he asked, "You okay?" But Lacy, for a few seconds, was only aware of the fact that he was still holding her hand, and how good it felt when he was on top of her. The realization made her cheeks flush, and she quickly dropped his hand, stepping back.

"Yeah, I'm fine," she stammered, embarrassed for so many reasons she couldn't count. "Sorry about that." She turned quickly, fumbling with her room key, desperate to escape the moment. "See you in the morning."

Ben watched, confused, as she disappeared into her room, then shrugged and went into his own.

Inside, Lacy closed the door and leaned against it, her heart racing. "Get it together," she whispered to herself, shaking her head, trying to banish the warmth spreading through her chest.

Ben, in the hallway, was still trying to figure out what had just happened. He hesitated a moment, then shook his head with a half-smile and went into his room.

A few minutes later, there was a knock at Lacy's door. She opened it to find Paige standing there, a stack of papers in one hand and a takeout coffee cup in the other.

"Hey there, future governor," Paige greeted with a wry smile.

Lacy laughed softly, trying to regain her composure. "Is this a social visit or campaign-related?" she asked, though her heart still raced.

Paige's expression turned mock-serious. "The only action I'm getting lately is from my rose toy, so... I'm sorry to say it's campaign-related," she quipped, grinning as Lacy burst into laughter.

"Alright, then," Lacy said, shaking off her embarrassment as she moved to the small table by the window. Paige joined her, and they spread out the papers, diving into the details of tomorrow's big event.

For the next few hours, they worked together in comfortable collaboration, refining talking points, reviewing the event schedule, and making sure every detail was perfect. As the night wore on, their usual rhythm returned, filled with the sound of their voices and occasional bursts of laughter. Despite the hard work, the camaraderie they shared made it all feel less like a chore and more like a partnership.

Outside,Norfolk Marriott settled into the quiet of the night, the lights in the windows slowly dimming. Inside, the warmth and energy of Lacy's campaign team buzzed with anticipation for the challenges and triumphs that tomorrow would bring.

The State Tribune newsroom was mostly empty, save for the soft glow of a few desk lamps and the hum of computers that whirred into the late hours. Jake was on the verge of something big—a story that had gnawed at him for weeks. What began as a simple profile on Mayor Harold Blake, a man with a reputation for unshakable honesty, had spiraled into something darker. As Jake dug deeper, the facts started to twist, leading him down a path far more dangerous than he had expected. The key seemed to be Officer Michael Hayes, the hero cop who had foiled an assassination attempt on Blake several years ago.

It was a day seared into the city's memory. The mayor had been leaving a charity event when shots rang out, sending the crowd scattering. Hayes had tackled Blake to the ground, shielding him with his own body, before chasing down the gunman and taking him down. But soon after, Hayes vanished—quitting his job, leaving the state, and disappearing completely. The incident was buried in the archives, barely mentioned again, and every lead Jake followed hit a dead end.

Jake had spent countless nights in the office, sifting through old police reports, court records, and any scrap of information he could find. He was close—he could feel it. But he needed more than just a hunch or a few circumstantial connections; he needed something concrete to convince his boss, Claire Morgan, that the story was worth pursuing.

Claire was a legend in the newsroom. In her early 40s, she had a reputation for exposing corruption and taking down criminals without batting an eye. She was sharp, relentless, and fiercely protective of her team. But she had no patience for wild goose chases. If Jake wanted her to back him, he needed something definitive—something she couldn't ignore.

Jake's thoughts were interrupted by the familiar click of Claire's heels approaching. Quickly, he shuffled his papers, sliding the ones related to Hayes into a drawer, and pulling up his notes on Mayor Blake. The mayoral profile was due soon, and he needed to keep up appearances.

"Jake." Claire's voice was sharp as she stopped by his desk, her piercing blue eyes taking in the chaos of his workspace. Despite the late hour, she looked as put-together as ever—dark hair neatly pinned back, crisp blouse, tailored slacks. She was a picture of authority.

"Hey, Claire," Jake greeted, glancing up with a casual.

"Just wrapping up the piece on Mayor Blake. I think it's coming together nicely."

Claire raised an eyebrow. "Is that so?" Her tone was skeptical. She leaned over his desk, scanning the hastily arranged notes. "You've been burning the midnight oil a lot lately. Care to share what's really going on?"

Jake shifted in his seat, his shirt sticking to his skin as he felt the sweat trickle down his back. He kept his expression neutral. "Just making sure I get all the details right," he replied, tapping the papers in front of him. "Blake's got a lot of layers. Want to make sure I'm capturing the whole picture."

Claire studied him for a long moment, her gaze piercing. Then, she straightened, crossing her arms. "Jake, I didn't get to where I am by ignoring my gut," she said, her voice firm but not unkind. "And my gut's telling me you're onto something bigger than a mayoral profile. If you've got a lead, you need to let me in on it."

Jake hesitated. This story was more than just another assignment for him—it was personal. Years ago, he'd gone after a government corruption case that had blown up in his face. His source had been unreliable, and the story collapsed, costing him his reputation and nearly his job. Some in the newsroom still whispered about it, doubting if he'd ever make a real comeback. This was his chance to prove them wrong, to show he was still the relentless journalist who wouldn't back down from the truth.

But it wasn't just about professional redemption. Deep down, Jake had a fierce belief in what journalism could accomplish. He'd seen too much of the damage that corruption could do—families torn apart, communities left to crumble. To him, getting this story right wasn't just career salvation; it was a moral duty. Someone had to hold people like Richard Jacobs accountable, and if no one else would, it had to be him. He needed to know he could still make a difference, that he could still look in the mirror and see a journalist willing to dig deep, no matter how dangerous the story became.

"I'm just chasing a few leads," he admitted, giving her a half-truth. "Nothing concrete yet. But if something pans out, you'll be the first to know."

Claire didn't look entirely satisfied, but she nodded, her expression softening just a fraction. "Alright, Marlowe," she said, "but don't go running yourself into the ground chasing shadows. And remember, we're on deadline for that Blake piece."

"I know, I know," Jake replied, forcing a light-hearted tone. "I'll have it ready."

With one last searching look, Claire turned and headed back toward her office. Jake breathed a sigh of relief, but as soon as she was out of sight, he pulled the hidden documents back onto his desk. His mind raced with the new connections he was piecing together.

Earlier that day, Jake thought he'd finally caught a break—a tip from a retired detective who swore he knew where Hayes was hiding. Jake had called the number immediately, the gravelly voice on the other end sounding cautious, almost paranoid. They arranged to meet at a rundown diner on the edge of town, the kind of place where no one asked questions and the coffee tasted like motor oil.

Later that evening, Jake had arrived early, his pulse quickening as he scanned the nearly deserted diner. He ordered a cup of that god-awful coffee, his eyes flicking to the door every few seconds. Minutes ticked by, stretching into what felt like hours. No detective showed up. The diner's lone waitress cleared her throat and nodded toward his table. Confused, Jake looked down and noticed a folded napkin he hadn't seen before.

His stomach tightened as he picked it up. Two words, scrawled in red ink, stared back at him: "Nice try."

His heart thudded in his chest. Someone was onto him, watching him—maybe closer than he realized. Jake crushed the napkin in his hand, a fresh wave of frustration and dread washing over him. Another dead end. Another reminder that he was getting closer to something someone didn't want him to find.

He looked back at the notes on his phone, scrolling through a maze of scribbles and hastily saved clippings. And there it was—the address he'd nearly overlooked before. A small, remote town hidden in the mountains of the western part of the state, barely a blip on the map. His heart quickened. This was it—the lead he'd been chasing.

A place mentioned in passing in a decades-old news article, a grainy photo showing Officer Michael Hayes in the background, looking over his shoulder like he was waiting for a shadow to move. The wary expression on Hayes's face stuck with him, a flash of fear or guilt—or both. Jake's gut twisted; he knew this was the thread he needed to pull.

He needed to crack this wide open, and he needed to do it fast, before anyone else caught wind of what he was digging into. His fingers flew over the keyboard, diving deeper into the rabbit hole. He couldn't afford another dead end, not when he was this close.

Because this wasn't just about a corrupt businessman or a missing cop. This was personal. It was about redemption, about proving that he still had what it took to bring the truth into the light, no matter how deep it was buried. Jake Marlowe had a lot to make up for—and he wasn't about to stop until he had every piece of this story laid out in front of him.

The night stretched on, his determination sharpened by every flicker of new information. He leaned closer, eyes scanning each line with laser focus, the coffee in his cup long gone cold. The pieces were all there, scattered and fragmented; he just needed to find the one that would make them all click together.

And when he finally did, when the whole picture snapped into place, all those sleepless nights, all the exhaustion and doubt, would be worth it. He was close—so close he could almost see the headline.

But for now, all he had was an address and the promise of another sleepless night.

****

The donor meet-and-greet was held in a beautifully restored atrium of the nearby Chrysler Museum. Artful chandeliers hung from the high ceilings, casting a warm, golden glow over the space. The walls were painted a rich cream color, with intricate gold molding that added a touch of grandeur. Round tables draped in crisp white linens were scattered throughout, each adorned with simple floral centerpieces that gave off a subtle, sweet fragrance. A string quartet played softly in the corner, their music weaving through the low hum of conversation and laughter.

The room was filled with donors who wore business casual attire—men in well-fitted blazers with open-collared shirts, women in elegant but understated dresses or chic pantsuits. There was an easy, relaxed energy in the room as people mingled, their conversations punctuated by the soft clinking of wine glasses. Lacy moved through the crowd with ease, her smile warm and genuine as she greeted each guest, making them feel seen and heard.

As she engaged in a lively conversation with a group of donors, Lacy felt a familiar presence enter the room. She glanced up and saw Ben standing near the entrance, looking effortlessly handsome in a dark suit jacket over a crisp white shirt, the top button undone for a hint of casual ease. His eyes found hers across the room, and for a moment, he simply stared, his expression softening as he took in her appearance. He gave her a small, almost shy smile, not wanting to interrupt but unable to resist acknowledging her.

Lacy smiled back, warmth spreading through her chest at the sight of him. She waved him over, eager to introduce him to the group.

"Everyone, I'd like you to meet Ben, my amazing speechwriter," she said, her voice filled with genuine pride as Ben approached.

Ben, ever modest, gave a polite nod and a friendly smile. "I'm just the guy who writes down the smart things Lacy says," he joked, trying to deflect the attention.

One of the donors, an older gentleman with a silver beard and a sharp suit, chuckled. "So you're the reason her speeches are so good?"

Ben shook his head, his smile widening. "Absolutely not," he replied sincerely. "I'm just a wordsmith who gets to capture all of her hard work, intelligence, and grace in a speech. But that's not a hard job because Senator Jacobs is truly phenomenal."

A few of the donors exchanged impressed glances, their smiles widening as Ben spoke with quiet admiration. Lacy felt a warmth in her cheeks, a rare moment of flattery that genuinely touched her.

As the group began to disperse, Lacy turned to Ben, her eyes sparkling with gratitude. "Thank you, Ben," she said softly. "Your extra check is in the mail," she added with a playful smile.

Ben chuckled, shaking his head. "I would have done it for free," he joked back, but the sincerity in his eyes didn't go unnoticed.

Before Lacy could say anything more, Paige appeared at her side, gently pulling her away. "Come on, Lacy, there are more donors to meet," she said with a grin, though there was a hint of urgency in her voice.

Lacy gave Ben a quick smile before letting Paige guide her across the room. The rest of the evening passed in a blur of handshakes, introductions, and engaging conversations. The event was a success, with donors promising their continued support, leaving Lacy feeling both relieved and energized.

As the night drew to a close and the guests began to leave, the once-bustling ballroom grew quiet. Lacy slipped off her heels and wandered to the center of the room, her bare feet sinking into the plush carpet. The string quartet had long since packed up, but someone had left a playlist running through the speakers. The soft, soulful notes of K-Ci & JoJo's All My Life filled the empty space, wrapping around Lacy like a warm embrace.

She began to sway gently to the music, her eyes closing as she let herself get lost in the melody. For a moment, she was just a woman—not a senator or a campaigner—simply herself, relishing the rare opportunity to let go.

Unseen, Ben slipped quietly back into the room. He paused in the doorway, his breath catching in his throat as he watched Lacy move, her body swaying gracefully, bathed in the soft light of the chandeliers. She looked ethereal, completely absorbed in the music. He felt an unexpected tug at his chest, a mix of admiration and something deeper. He didn't want to break the spell, but he couldn't help the way his eyes traced her movements, mesmerized.

He stood there, silent and still, letting the moment linger. He watched the way the dress clung to her curves, the way her hair fell in soft waves around her face. She looked different—softer, almost vulnerable. He swallowed, suddenly aware of how close he felt to her, even from across the room.

Finally, Ben cleared his throat softly. Lacy jumped, her eyes snapping open, a sheepish smile spreading across her lips. "Don't tell anyone you saw that," she laughed, her embarrassment clear.

Ben smiled, his eyes warm as he stepped forward. "Your secret is safe with me," he promised, his tone teasing.

"But feel free to tell everyone I have killer dance moves." Lacy giggled, doing a small, playful dance move, making Ben chuckle. Yet, there was something about his gaze that made her feel more self-conscious than usual, a feeling that was oddly pleasant.

"Mind if I join you?" Ben asked, his voice a little more serious now as he stepped closer.

Lacy hesitated, her mind flashing with warnings about boundaries. "I shouldn't... but I want to?" She took a breath and nodded, allowing Ben to take her hand. As he pulled her gently into his arms, she felt a shiver of anticipation.

They began to sway slowly to the music, their movements careful, almost as if they were afraid to break the spell. At first, they kept a respectful distance, their bodies moving in sync but not fully touching. But as the song built, the distance between them closed. The pull between them, always present but unspoken, drew them closer. She could feel the warmth of his chest against hers, his strong arms around her. It made her feel safe and exposed all at once.

The music swelled, and they moved as if they had danced like this a thousand times before. Lacy found herself relaxing into Ben, her head resting lightly on his shoulder. It felt... right. She closed her eyes, letting herself sink into the moment, forgetting everything else.

As the final notes of the song played, Lacy slowly pulled back, just enough to look up at Ben. "Thank you for the dance," she whispered, her voice barely audible over the fading music.

Ben stared down at her, his eyes dark with something she couldn't quite place. Their gazes locked, and for a moment, it felt like the whole world had fallen away, leaving just the two of them suspended in this quiet, intimate space. It was the prelude to a kiss, the kind of moment that teetered on the edge of something more.

But before either of them could act on it, Paige's voice cut through the air, shattering the delicate tension. "There you two are! The cars are here to take us back to the hotel."

They jumped apart, both feeling the flush of guilt at being caught in such a vulnerable moment. Lacy quickly composed herself, giving Paige a tight smile as she turned to gather her things.

The ride back to the hotel was quiet. Paige chattered on about the donors and their commitments, but Lacy and Ben sat side by side in silence, their shoulders occasionally brushing. Each touch sent a jolt of awareness through them. The tension from their dance lingered, unspoken but impossible to ignore.

When they arrived at the hotel, they walked side by side to their rooms. The hallway was dimly lit, the only sound the soft rustle of their clothing as they moved. They stopped in front of their doors, standing there for a moment, the air thick with what was left unsaid.

"Goodnight," Lacy said softly, her voice tinged with a hesitance that hadn't been there before.

"Goodnight," Ben replied, his tone equally tentative.

Lacy quickly slipped into her room, closing the door behind her before leaning against it, her heart racing. She wasn't sure what had just happened between them, but she knew it was something she couldn't easily dismiss.

In their separate rooms, both Lacy and Ben went through the motions of getting ready for bed, their minds racing with thoughts of the other. Lacy slipped off her dress and hung it neatly in the closet, her fingers lingering on the fabric as if it still held the warmth of Ben's touch. She caught her reflection in the mirror, noticing the flush on her cheeks, the brightness in her eyes. She sighed, shaking her head as if to dismiss the thoughts that crowded her mind.

What am I doing? she wondered, running a brush through her hair. This isn't part of the plan.

She knew better than to mix business with anything personal, especially in the midst of a campaign. Yet, the way Ben had held her, the softness in his voice, had felt like a promise of something more—something she wasn't sure she was ready for but couldn't help being drawn toward. She slipped into her pajamas, trying to convince herself that it had just been a dance, nothing more. But even as she brushed her teeth and washed her face, she could still feel the ghost of his hands on her waist, the warmth of his breath near her ear.

Meanwhile, in the room next door, Ben unbuttoned his shirt and tossed it over a chair, his mind replaying the dance in slow motion. He could still feel the weight of her in his arms, the way she had relaxed against him, her head resting lightly on his shoulder. He kicked off his shoes, letting them fall to the floor with a soft thud, and stared at his reflection in the mirror, running a hand through his tousled hair.

What the hell am I doing? he thought, rubbing the back of his neck, feeling the tension still there. He had always been good at keeping things professional—at knowing where the line was and staying on the right side of it. But tonight had blurred that line in ways he hadn't anticipated. He tried to focus on the campaign, on the deadlines and the speech drafts waiting for him, but his thoughts kept drifting back to the way Lacy's body had felt pressed against his.

Ben paced the room for a moment, then stopped, staring at the thin wall that separated his room from Lacy's. He felt an urge to knock on her door, to say something—anything—that would bring them back to the easy camaraderie they had shared before tonight. But he hesitated, sensing that things were different now, and he wasn't sure how to navigate this new territory. He took a deep breath and decided against it, instead walking over to the window and staring out at the dimly lit parking lot below, his mind churning with possibilities.

In her room, Lacy slipped under the covers, pulling the comforter up to her chin. She lay there for a moment, staring at the ceiling, listening to the quiet hum of the hotel. She could almost feel the tension between her and Ben as a tangible thing, lingering in the air, refusing to dissipate.

Get it together, Lacy, she told herself firmly. You're here to win an election, not to get caught up in... whatever this is.

Yet, as she closed her eyes, trying to will herself to sleep, her thoughts kept circling back to the way he had looked at her, like she was the only person in the room. She wondered if he was thinking about her too, and the thought sent a shiver down her spine. She turned over, punching her pillow lightly, trying to find a comfortable position, but sleep felt a million miles away.

Ben finally decided to distract himself by reviewing the latest campaign notes, but the words on the page seemed to blur together. He couldn't concentrate, not with the scent of her perfume still lingering in his senses, not with the memory of her laughter echoing in his mind. He tossed the papers aside and flopped down on the bed, staring up at the ceiling, feeling a mix of frustration and longing that he couldn't quite shake.

Minutes passed. Then more. Neither of them could sleep. The silence of the night grew heavier.

Lacy lay in bed, staring at the ceiling, her thoughts still circling back to Ben. She could feel the steady rhythm of her heartbeat, the faint hum of the hotel air conditioning, and the distant murmur of footsteps in the hallway. But her mind kept replaying the moments from earlier—the way his eyes softened when he looked at her, the warmth of his hand on her back as they danced.

I shouldn't be thinking about him like this, she scolded herself, trying to banish the image of his smile, the sound of his laughter. She was running a campaign, juggling deadlines, navigating the complexities of politics. There wasn't room for... whatever this was. Yet, every time she closed her eyes, she saw him—standing in the ballroom doorway, watching her with that look she couldn't quite decipher.

She sighed, turning onto her side, pulling the covers tighter around herself. Why does it feel so complicated? she wondered. She knew she should shut it all out, refocus on what was important, but her thoughts kept wandering back to Ben and the way he had made her feel tonight—seen, understood, maybe even desired.

In the room next door, Ben lay flat on his back, staring at the ceiling. His mind raced with images of Lacy—the emerald dress that had hugged her curves, the way her hair had framed her face, softening her features. He replayed their dance over and over, the subtle weight of her against him, the moment he had almost leaned in closer.

What are you doing, man? he thought, running a hand over his face. He knew he was crossing a line in his mind, wandering into territory that was best left unexplored. But he couldn't help it; the pull was too strong. He'd seen a side of her tonight that he hadn't expected—vulnerable, playful, almost... free.

He shifted in bed, trying to find a comfortable position, but every turn only seemed to remind him of how close he'd been to her, how easily he could still feel the rhythm of her body moving with his. Focus on the job, Ben, he told himself. This is a campaign, not some romantic movie.

But the thought of her—her laughter, her warmth, the spark in her eyes when she looked at him—was impossible to ignore. He felt the faint ache of something he didn't quite want to name, a longing he hadn't felt in a long time.

Lacy turned onto her other side, her mind drifting to the unspoken connection that had simmered between them tonight. She felt a flutter in her chest, a mixture of excitement and fear. What does he think of me? she wondered. Did he feel it too? She tried to push those thoughts away, but they kept coming back, persistent and unwelcome.

Ben's mind, meanwhile, replayed her words from earlier—"Your extra check is in the mail." The playful tone, the hint of something more beneath the surface. He wondered if she'd felt that same spark, if her thoughts were just as tangled as his. He wanted to know, needed to know, but didn't dare to cross that line. Not yet.

Minutes ticked by, the night stretching on. Neither of them moved, lying there in the dark, their breaths steady, but their minds anything but calm.

Gradually, the weight of exhaustion began to settle in. Lacy's eyelids grew heavy, her thoughts slowly blurring around the edges. She could still feel the imprint of his touch, the way his hand had rested lightly on her back. She whispered a soft sigh into the quiet of her room, and finally, sleep began to claim her, pulling her under with dreams that carried the echoes of their dance.

In the next room, Ben's body relaxed into the mattress, the tension easing from his shoulders as his breathing slowed. He closed his eyes, surrendering to the pull of sleep. But even as he drifted off, his last conscious thought was of Lacy—her smile, her scent, the way she'd felt so right in his arms.

And so, in separate rooms, they both finally succumbed to sleep, still connected by the threads of what had passed between them that night, unaware that their dreams were filled with the same thoughts, the same questions, and the same impossible "what ifs."

The alarm blared at 5 a.m., pulling Lacy from a restless sleep filled with fragments of dreams she couldn't quite remember. She groaned, slapping at the snooze button before reluctantly dragging herself out of bed. Today was the big day—the Paws for a Cause event she'd been planning for months. It was a cornerstone of her campaign, and she needed it to go perfectly. Despite the nerves fluttering in her stomach, she was determined to make this day a success.

After a quick shower, Lacy stood in front of the mirror, trying to decide on her outfit. Today's look needed to be casual but polished. She chose a pair of dark-wash jeans that hugged her figure, paired with a white blouse that had delicate lace detailing along the collar and sleeves. Over it, she wore a soft, tailored blazer in a light beige color. She slipped on a pair of tan ankle boots that were comfortable yet stylish, perfect for a day spent walking around and interacting with people. Her hair was pulled back into a loose, low ponytail, and she kept her makeup natural, with just a hint of color on her lips.

As she applied a final swipe of lip gloss, Lacy caught her own reflection in the mirror, her mind flashing back to the previous night. The dance with Ben, the way his arms had felt around her, the intensity in his eyes—it all felt too real, too close. She was a grown woman, she reminded herself. Ben was an attractive guy, and it had been a while since she'd let herself feel anything like that. She rationalized the vivid daydreams about him as nothing more than pent-up emotions needing an outlet. It doesn't mean anything, she told herself firmly. She had a job to do today, and there was no need to act weird around him.

Breakfast was at 5:30 a.m. sharp, and by the time Lacy made it downstairs, the dining room was already buzzing with activity. The team had gathered at a long table near the window, sunlight just beginning to filter through the curtains. Paige was already halfway through a cup of coffee, her dark hair pulled into a sleek ponytail. She was dressed in a simple black blouse and slacks, looking effortlessly professional despite the early hour. Ben was seated beside her, stirring sugar into his coffee. He wore dark jeans and a light blue button-down shirt with the sleeves rolled up, his hair still slightly tousled from sleep.

Lacy approached the table, her heart skipping a beat when she saw Ben glance up at her with a smile. She forced herself to act normal, reminding herself there was nothing to be nervous about. But when Ben reached out to touch her back lightly, just to get her attention, she nearly jumped out of her skin.

"You okay?" Ben asked, his brow furrowing slightly as he took in her reaction.

Lacy quickly composed herself, offering a tight smile. "Yeah, just nervous about today, I guess," she replied, hoping he hadn't noticed the way her pulse had spiked at his touch.

Ben's expression softened, and he gave her a reassuring smile. "You're going to do great, Lacy. You always do."

Something about the way he said it made that familiar warmth spread through her chest again, but she quickly pushed the feeling aside. She had a full day ahead of her, and there was no time to get distracted.

The event kicked off without a hitch. The venue—a spacious park in the heart of Norfolk—was filled with the sounds of excited chatter, barking dogs, and the laughter of children. Booths were set up around the perimeter, offering information on pet adoption, veteran services, and local community programs. The sun was shining brightly, casting a warm glow over the scene, and the air was filled with the scents of fresh grass and grilled food from nearby vendors.

Lacy moved through the crowd with practiced ease, shaking hands, posing for pictures, and chatting with attendees. Ben and Paige stayed close by, each of them busy in their own rights. Ben seemed focused on ensuring everything ran smoothly, his usual laid-back demeanor replaced with a quiet determination. Lacy couldn't help but notice how good he looked in the casual setting, even as she tried to focus on the task at hand.

As the day wore on, Lacy found herself caught up in the energy of the event. She fawned over puppies with the same enthusiasm as the children who begged their parents to let them take one home. She thanked veterans for their service with genuine emotion, shaking their hands and listening to their stories. And when it was time for her speech, she delivered it with a passionate determination that left the crowd applauding and cheering for more.

The speech had gone exactly as they had intended—powerful, heartfelt, and deeply resonant with everyone in attendance. Ben watched her from the side of the stage, pride mixing with a deeper, more confusing emotion that tightened in his chest. She was incredible, and he couldn't deny the admiration he felt for her, both as a leader and as a woman. But seeing her like this—so alive and in her element—made him realize just how complicated his feelings were becoming.

By 3 p.m., the event was winding down. The once-crowded park had started to thin out, with many of the attendees heading home with newly adopted pets in tow. Lacy was just finishing up a photo op with a wiggly golden retriever puppy that couldn't stop licking her face. She laughed, trying to hold onto the squirming bundle of energy, her face alight with joy.

Ben approached her just as the photographer snapped the last few pictures. "You did an amazing job today," he said, his voice filled with genuine admiration.

Lacy managed to wrangle the puppy into a more manageable position, turning to Ben with a smile. "Thank you, Ben. But this was a team effort. I'm nowhere without you guys."

Her words touched him more than he expected, and he was about to say something more when a voice he hadn't expected to hear called out, "Hey, baby!"

Before Ben could fully process what was happening, Abby appeared beside him, pulling him into a kiss. Shocked, his chest tightened as he felt Lacy's gaze on him—her expression a mix of surprise and something else, something that looked like hurt. He froze for a moment before gently pulling away from Abby, turning to Lacy, who still held the puppy, her face carefully composed but her eyes flashing.

A wave of something—anger, jealousy, frustration?—hit her before she could shove it down. She was supposed to be focused, not feeling like this.

Lacy forced a polite smile. "Hi, I'm Senator Jacobs," she introduced herself, her tone professional but with a slight edge.

Abby gave Lacy a quick once-over, her smile almost too sweet. "Hi, I'm Abby, Ben's high school sweetheart," she said, her voice dripping with familiarity, her gaze holding a touch of challenge.

Ben felt a knot tighten in his stomach. Seeing Lacy's expression— her eyes, so bright a moment ago, now guarded—made his heart sink. He wanted to explain, to say something that would make it right, but the words wouldn't come. He stood there, helpless, as the moment stretched on.

Lacy's smile tightened, and she responded with a smoothness that belied the tension beneath. "I have to go find this little guy a home," she said, gesturing to the puppy. "It was nice meeting you, Gabby," she added.

Abby's smile faltered, irritation flickering in her eyes. "It's Abby," she corrected, her voice a bit sharper.

"Right, sorry," Lacy replied, her tone saccharine as she turned and walked away, heading toward Paige and Chloe.

Paige, who had been watching from a distance, raised an eyebrow as Lacy approached. "So much for me hittin' that," she quipped, her eyes flicking over to where Abby was still talking to Ben, touching him softly as she spoke.

Lacy forced a laugh. "Yeah, well, looks like it was just a fleeting moment," she said, trying to sound nonchalant as she focused on finding the puppy a home. She resolved not to care, telling herself that last night had been exactly what she thought—a moment of weakness she'd needed to release some pent-up tension.

Meanwhile, Ben and Abby stepped aside, away from the remaining crowd. He kept glancing around, his jaw tight, feeling embarrassed about how this must look to everyone—including Lacy. Especially Lacy.

"What are you doing here, Abby?" Ben's voice was low, but the frustration simmered beneath the surface.

Abby crossed her arms, her tone defensive. "I wanted to see you. What's the problem if I'm here? Unless you're with someone, or trying to be?"

Ben let out a sharp breath, running a hand through his hair. "Are you serious, Abby? What is this….petty jealousy? You show up out of nowhere, say you want something casual, then pop up at my job kissing me talking about high school sweethearts like you didn't leave me all those years ago. I'm tired of this."

Her eyes softened, her voice taking on that familiar pleading note. "I'm sorry, Ben. I really am. I know I've messed up. But I want you back. I wanna work it out. I miss you so much."

Ben felt a stab of irritation. He'd heard these words before, the same promises, the same half-hearted attempts. He couldn't help but think of Lacy and what she must be thinking right now. He'd felt something last night—something real, something that wasn't tangled up in years of drama and confusion. But now, with Abby here, he just felt exposed.

"Abby, we've been doing this for years," he said, his voice strained. "You come back, you leave. I need something... more stable, something real. Not whatever this is."

Abby stepped closer, her hand reaching for his arm, her touch soft, almost desperate. "I mean it this time, Ben. I want to try. I miss us. I need us,"

Ben clenched his jaw, feeling a rush of conflicting emotions. He wanted to push her away, tell her he was done for good, but he hesitated. He was tired of being caught in this endless loop with Abby, tired of feeling like he was always waiting for the other shoe to drop. He glanced over his shoulder, his gaze drifting back to where he'd last seen Lacy, wondering what she must think of him now, tangled up with his past like this.

"Abby, I'm at work," he said more firmly, his tone edged with frustration. "This isn't the time or the place."

She ignored his protest and leaned in, trying to kiss him again, but Ben stepped back, holding her gently at arm's length, his patience wearing thin. "No, Abby. Not here, not now."

A flash of hurt crossed her face, quickly replaced by irritation. "Why not? Because of her?" Abby's eyes darted in Lacy's direction. "Is that it? You think she's any different?"

Ben felt heat rise in his cheeks, his embarrassment giving way to annoyance. "Lacy has nothing to do with this," he snapped, a bit too quickly. "This is about you and me, and the fact that you don't know what you want until it's convenient for you."

Abby's expression hardened, her lips pressing into a thin line. "I see," she said, her voice cold now. "So, you're just going to pretend like we never mattered?"

Ben shook his head, feeling a mix of frustration and something close to regret. "We did matter, Abby, but it's been years of this. Years of trying, of you leaving, of me picking up the pieces. I'm sick of it."

She hesitated, looking like she might argue more, then let out a slow breath. "Fine. I'll go," she said softly, but there was a challenge in her eyes.

Ben sighed, feeling his anger softening into weariness. "Abby, look… when I get back into town, we can talk, okay? But not like this, not here."

She seemed to consider his words for a moment, then nodded slowly. "Alright," she agreed, but there was a slight edge to her smile. "I'll be waiting."

She gave him a quick peck on the cheek, her lips barely brushing his skin. Then, without another word, she turned and walked away.

Ben watched her go, feeling frustration, as the knot in his stomach tightening. He glanced back toward Lacy, but she was already turning away, pretending to be engrossed in a conversation at a nearby booth. He wanted to call out to her, to explain, but he felt stuck—trapped between his past and whatever possibilities he'd felt spark to life last night.

Dammit, he thought, his chest tightening again. Last night meant something. He wanted to reach out, to explain, but the moment had slipped through his fingers, and now he felt more uncertain than ever.

The rest of the day passed in a blur of activity. The event had been a resounding success, with dozens of dogs finding new homes and plenty of positive feedback from attendees. But as the day wound down, Ben couldn't shake the image of Lacy's face when she saw Abby kiss him.

Later that evening, back at the hotel, Ben and Lacy found themselves alone in the elevator, the tension between them palpable. The elevator was silent except for the soft hum of the machinery as it ascended to their floor. Ben cleared his throat, deciding to try and explain. "I'm sorry about earlier," he began, his voice quiet. "About Abby—"

Lacy's smile felt stiff, like a mask. She wanted to say something cutting, something that would make her feel in control again, but the words wouldn't come. Instead, she forced a light, dismissive tone. "Don't worry, Ben. I get it," she said, offering a small, friendly smile. "Just try and keep your personal life away from the campaign," she continued, her tone very firm but never unfriendly.

The elevator dinged, signaling their arrival on their floor. They stepped out, walking down the hallway side by side, but the distance between them felt wider than ever. As they reached their doors, Lacy turned to him with a playful grin, trying to lighten the mood. "Don't forget—the bus leaves early," she teased, her tone friendly and casual.

Ben managed a small smile, but inside, he felt a mix of frustration and regret. Whatever had happened between them last night, whatever connection they had felt, was slipping away. Lacy was shutting down any possibility of anything more, and he knew he had no choice but to respect that.

"Got it," he replied, his tone matching hers as he gave her a nod.

Lacy smiled one last time before quickly disappearing into her room, leaving Ben standing in the hallway. He lingered for a moment, staring at her closed door, before turning and entering his own room.

They both showered in their separate rooms, trying to wash away the events of the day. But as they sat on the edge of their beds, their minds couldn't help but wander back to that moment in the elevator, the unspoken tension between them. They both knew they had crossed a line, and as they lay down to sleep, they couldn't shake the feeling that something important had just slipped through their fingers.

For now, they were back to being professional, friendly colleagues. But the memory of last night, and the undeniable chemistry that had sparked between them, lingered in the back of their minds as they drifted off to sleep, each wondering what might have been if things had played out differently.

CHAPTER 8

Richard Jacobs, the man who ruled this empire, sat behind his massive mahogany desk, his fingers drumming lightly against the polished surface. He was a tall, imposing figure, his silver hair slicked back to accentuate his sharp features. His tailored suit fit him perfectly, a subtle testament to his wealth and influence. But it was his eyes that truly commanded attention—cold, calculating, devoid of any emotion.

He took a slow sip from his glass, savoring the burn of the whiskey as it went down. His phone buzzed on the desk. Richard glanced at the screen, a slight frown creasing his forehead. The number was one he recognized—one that only contacted him when there was a problem demanding his attention. Setting the glass down with deliberate precision, he picked up the phone, his voice a low growl.

"Speak," Richard commanded, his tone leaving no room for hesitation.

"Mr. Jacobs," came the voice on the other end, clipped and professional, yet tinged with the slightest hint of nervousness. "We've got a situation. Someone's been asking questions about Michael Hayes and… well, about you."

Richard's fingers tightened around the phone, his expression darkening. "Who?" he demanded, his voice cold as ice.

"A reporter," the man on the line replied. "Name's Jake Marlowe. Works for the State Tribune. He's been digging into Hayes' disappearance and the… incident with Mayor Blake."

There was a pause on the line, the weight of the words hanging in the air. Richard's mind raced, though his face remained impassive—a mask of controlled fury. He had taken great care to bury the past, to ensure that the truth about Michael Hayes and the failed assassination attempt on Mayor Blake never saw the light of day. And now, it seemed, someone was trying to unearth it.

"Should I take care of it?" the informant asked cautiously, the implication clear.

Richard's lips curled into a cold smile. "No," he replied softly, his voice almost a whisper. "Send me his information."

There was a brief pause before the man on the other end answered, "Yes, sir. I'll have it to you in a moment."

The call ended with a click, and Richard set the phone down, his mind already working through the possibilities. A few seconds later, his phone buzzed again with a notification. He picked it up, his eyes narrowing as he opened the file.

A picture of Jake Marlowe filled the screen—a young, determined-looking reporter with a hint of stubbornness in his eyes. Below the photo, a dossier laid out basic details: age, background, recent articles, even his home address.

Richard's gaze lingered on the image, his eyes narrowing as if trying to see deeper into the man's intentions. What do you want, Jake? he thought, his voice low and menacing, almost as if he could speak to the photograph itself.

Memories flickered at the edge of his mind, unbidden. The weight of Amanda's body in his arms, her skin cold and lifeless. Blood spreading across the floor of his study, her eyes half-closed, unseeing. Richard had stood there, tears hot and unexpected on his cheeks, then flowing freely as he blinked them away. He had made a call with steady hands and a steady voice: "Get over here. Now. And clean this mess up." No tremor, no hesitation. Just cold command. He'd left the room, Amanda's body still sprawled on the floor, the study door closing behind him like the lid of a coffin.

He had learned that day what it took to survive, to bury things so deep no one could find them. And now, this reporter—Jake Marlowe—was poking around in things that should have stayed dead.

Richard exhaled slowly, forcing himself to remain calm. Marlowe didn't know who he was dealing with. Not yet. But he would soon enough.

Richard leaned back in his chair, fingers steepled, his eyes narrowing further as he considered his options. He had dealt with threats before. Rivals. Enemies. They all thought they could take him down. They had all been proven wrong.

Let's see how much you really know, he thought, a dangerous glint in his eyes. He would watch Marlowe, find his weaknesses, and then decide when and how to strike. Richard Jacobs hadn't risen to power by being careless. He would handle this the way he handled everything else: with patience, precision, and an iron will.

Outside, the city lights glittered in the night, unaware of the storm brewing within Richard's mind. This was a game. And Richard had no intention of losing. Not again.

****

The State Tribune office was bustling with the usual midday energy—phones ringing, reporters typing furiously at their desks, and the hum of conversations filling the air. But amidst the organized chaos, one man stood out like a sore thumb.

Jake Marlowe looked like he had been dragged through the wringer. His clothes were rumpled, the once crisp button-down shirt now wrinkled and untucked, his tie loosened and askew. Dark circles clung under his bloodshot eyes, evidence of too many sleepless nights spent chasing a story that was quickly consuming him. His hair was a mess, as if he hadn't bothered to run a comb through it in days, and the five o'clock shadow on his jaw suggested he had forgotten to shave more than once.

Clutching a disheveled folder of notes and printouts, Jake made his way through the newsroom, barely acknowledging the greetings from his colleagues. His mind was laser-focused on one thing: convincing his boss that what he had uncovered was more than just a hunch.

Claire Morgan's office door was slightly ajar, the frosted glass etched with her name and title. Jake could see her inside, sitting behind her desk, glasses perched on her nose as she reviewed a stack of papers. She looked as composed and sharp as ever, her dark hair pulled back into a sleek ponytail, and her tailored suit giving her an air of authority that was impossible to ignore. The scent of her signature lavender perfume wafted faintly into the hallway as Jake approached.

He took a deep breath, steeling himself, and knocked on the doorframe before stepping inside. "Claire, we need to talk," he said, his voice rough from lack of sleep and too much coffee.

Claire looked up from her work, her eyes narrowing slightly as she took in his appearance. "Jake," she said, her tone neutral but laced with concern. "You look like hell. What's going on?"

Jake didn't bother with pleasantries. He walked straight to her desk and dropped the folder in front of her, the papers spilling out slightly as it landed with a thud. "I've been working on something bigger than that mayoral profile," he said, his voice urgent. "This is about Richard Jacobs. I think he's running a front for money laundering, drug cartels—God knows what else—and I think he's using Lacy Jacob's community center as a headquarters for his operations."

Claire's eyes flickered with interest, but her expression remained guarded as she leaned back in her chair, crossing her arms. "That's a hell of an accusation, Jake," she said slowly, her tone measured. "What makes you think this?"

Jake's hands shook slightly as he flipped through the papers, pulling out a few key documents and laying them in front of her. "I've been digging into Michael Hayes, the cop who disappeared after the assassination attempt on Mayor Blake. All the evidence points to him being involved with the Jacobs family before he vanished. I tracked down some of his last known movements—there's a connection, Claire, I'm sure of it."

He ran a hand through his messy hair, frustration evident in his voice. "Look, I know it sounds crazy, but think about it: What better place to run dirty dealings than in that shitty neighborhood? It's the perfect cover—no one would suspect a thing."

Claire's expression darkened, her eyes flashing with anger. "Watch your mouth, Jake," she snapped, her voice cutting through the air like a knife. "I grew up in that 'shitty neighborhood.' Don't talk about it like it's some cesspool just because people like Richard Jacobs try to take advantage of it."

Jake's face flushed, realizing his mistake. "I'm sorry, Claire," he mumbled, genuinely contrite. "I didn't mean it like that. I just—"

"Enough," Claire interrupted, holding up a hand. She took a deep breath, her expression softening just a fraction. "Let's get back to your theory. You're saying Richard Jacobs is using his daughter's community center as a front for criminal activity. But you don't have any proof, just a bunch of half-baked ideas and rumors. And where's your story on Mayor Blake? That was due this morning."

Jake's shoulders slumped slightly, the weight of her words hitting him hard. "Forget the mayoral profile, Claire. This is huge. If I'm right, this could take down one of the most powerful men in the state."

Claire sighed, leaning back in her chair as she considered his words. "Jake, do you have any idea what you're up against here? Richard Jacobs isn't just some small-time crook. He's connected. And the owner of the State Tribune happens to be a personal friend of his. If you bring me gossip and hearsay, it's going to backfire, and you'll be out on your ass."

Jake's jaw clenched, frustration boiling over as he stared at her. "What happened to you, Claire? You used to chase stories like this without hesitation. Now you're just selling out, protecting the status quo."

The room fell into a tense silence. Claire's expression darkened, her eyes narrowing into a dangerous glare. When she spoke, her voice was low and menacing. "Call me a sellout again, and I'll have you writing obituaries for the rest of your career. Now, get out of my office."

Jake swallowed hard, realizing he had crossed a line. He grabbed his folder and stormed out of the office, slamming the door behind him. His heart pounded in his chest as he made his way back to his desk, his mind a whirlwind of anger and determination.

Once at his desk, he slammed the folder down, the papers scattering across the surface. He took a few deep breaths, trying to calm the storm of emotions swirling inside him. But the fire in his gut wouldn't be extinguished. He knew he was onto something— something big. And he wasn't going to let Claire or anyone else stop him from getting to the truth.

With renewed resolve, Jake pulled up his computer and entered the address he had found for Michael Hayes. It was in a small town in the mountains to the west of the state—far enough away to have slipped under the radar, but not so far that it couldn't be reached within a day's drive.

He glanced at the clock. He needed to submit the mayoral profile—he couldn't afford to lose his job, not when he was this close. With a sigh, Jake opened the draft and quickly polished it up, making sure it was ready for submission. It was good, but it lacked the fire and passion he felt for the story he really wanted to write.

As soon as the article was sent off, Jake grabbed his jacket and headed for the door. He needed to clear his head, to figure out his next move. But one thing was certain—he wasn't going to let this go. Michael Hayes was the key, and Jake was determined to track him down, no matter what it took.

As he left the State Tribune office and stepped out into the brisk afternoon air, Jake knew he was on a collision course with something much bigger than himself. And this time, he wasn't backing down.

The atmosphere at the Jacobs campaign headquarters was electric. With just under five months until the election, the team had been working around the clock to build momentum and close the gap between Lacy and her opponent. The scent of freshly brewed coffee mingled with the sugary aroma of doughnuts, a staple for these long strategy sessions. Papers rustled, voices murmured, and the soft buzz of phones created a steady background hum.

Lacy sat at the head of the table, casually nibbling on a glazed doughnut as the meeting wound down. Her navy blazer draped over the back of her chair, leaving her in a simple white blouse with sleeves rolled up to her elbows. Despite the intensity of the campaign, there was a faint smile on her lips. They were making progress.

Paige paced around the room, her eyes sparkling, unable to stop herself from bouncing slightly on the balls of her feet. Her energy crackled like electricity. As the last of the team members filtered out, Paige edged closer to Lacy, her voice dropping to a conspiratorial whisper.

"Lacy, guess what?"

Lacy looked up, her brow furrowing slightly, doughnut halfway to her mouth. "What is it?"

Paige glanced around, making sure no one was within earshot. Her grin widened, her voice barely contained. "We started the campaign polling at 20 points behind. Well, I didn't want to say this in front of everyone, but we are now polling at 3%!"

Lacy blinked, the words taking a second to register. Then it hit her. She set the doughnut down, her breath catching. "Are you serious?"

Paige nodded, her excitement bubbling over. "Yes! Can you believe it? We're closing the gap, and we still have time to make up the rest. This is huge, Lacy!"

Joy surged through Lacy, pushing her to her feet. Before she knew it, she and Paige were jumping up and down, hugging and laughing, caught in a moment of pure celebration. "We've got this!" Lacy exclaimed, her voice ringing out in the room, her heart racing.

Paige grinned wider, still bouncing with joy. "We've just got to keep pushing. We're going to make it!"

The room seemed to hum with their shared energy as they caught their breath, their laughter subsiding into wide, exhilarated smiles. Lacy's mind flickered briefly to what needed to come next—the door-to-door efforts, the town hall meetings, the ads they needed to fund. But she shoved those thoughts aside, letting herself savor this win for just a moment longer.

"How about we celebrate with a proper lunch?" Lacy suggested, still beaming.

Paige nodded eagerly. "Absolutely! Let's do it. We've earned it."

They grabbed their jackets, the buzz of victory still tingling in their veins. They knew there was more to do, more work ahead. But today, they had a reason to celebrate.

Meanwhile, in a small, cozy diner in Ben's hometown, the smell of frying bacon and freshly brewed coffee filled the air. The diner was a local institution, owned by the same family for generations. Framed photographs of the town's history lined the walls, and the checkered cloths covering the tables whispered of countless memories. The waitresses, all grandmothers of the town, moved with a practiced familiarity born of decades. The food was hearty, the portions generous, and the service felt like being at your grandmother's house.

Ben walked in, immediately spotting Abby seated at a booth near the window. She waved him over, a hopeful smile on her face. Her chestnut brown hair fell in loose waves around her shoulders, and her soft pink sweater complemented her dark jeans. Her eyes sparkled, but Ben couldn't tell if it was from excitement or nerves. He offered a smile in return, though it faltered slightly. His sandy hair was tousled, and his casual navy shirt seemed to hang a little heavier on his shoulders than usual.

As he slid into the booth, Abby reached across the table and touched his hands, her fingers warm, a little too eager. "I'm so glad you came," she said softly.

Before Ben could reply, their favorite server, Gladys, approached with a broad smile. In her late 70s, with a shock of white hair pinned up and a floral apron over her uniform, she had a face that radiated kindness and a touch of mischief.

"Well, well, look who's here," Gladys said, her voice rich with warmth. "Ben and Abby, back together again? You two always were my favorite couple."

Ben returned the smile but didn't confirm anything. "Good to see you, Gladys. What's the special today?"

Gladys winked, clearly not fooled. "Oh, the usual—meatloaf with mashed potatoes. But I'll let you two lovebirds decide."

Ben glanced at Abby, who nodded with a small, shy smile. "We'll take the special," he said, handing the menus back.

As Gladys moved away, Abby's smile faded. She leaned in closer, her voice more serious. "Ben, I'm glad we're here. I'm glad we're trying again."

Ben frowned slightly. "Trying again?" he echoed, keeping his tone calm. "Abby, when did we decide that? You told me you were just visiting family for a while."

Abby took a breath, reaching into her purse and pulling out her phone. She slid it across the table, showing him pictures of houses. "I've already started looking at homes, Ben. Here. For us. To start the family you've always wanted. I'm ready now."

Ben stared at the screen, emotions swirling in his eyes. Abby leaned in further, her voice dropping to a softer, almost coaxing tone. "I'm ready to live the simple life with you. A home, kids, a two-car garage… everything. We can even start…… practicing making that family."

Ben chuckled, but it came out forced, quickly turning into a sigh. He set her phone back on the table, shaking his head slightly. "Abby… my life isn't just 'simple' or 'ordinary.' It's not some plan B you settle for when everything else doesn't work out."

Abby blinked, taken aback. "That's not what I meant—"

He cut her off gently. "But that's how it feels, Abby. You're talking about kids, houses, garages… like it's some script you think I want. But I want someone who wants those things for real, not someone who thinks they're settling for it."

She leaned back, her smile completely gone, replaced by confusion and a hint of hurt. "Ben, I thought this was what you wanted—"

"We decided not to be together," Ben said, his voice steady but sad. He took out his wallet and placed some cash on the table. "I think we also should stop sleeping together."

As he started to rise, Abby's voice, small and crestfallen, stopped him. "Is it because of her?"

Ben paused, then shook his head slowly, his expression resolute. "No, Abby. It's because of me. I need to stop waiting for someone to fit into a life I already love."

With that, he turned and walked out, leaving Abby staring after him, the echo of his words hanging in the air between them.

Ben pushed open the diner's door, the bell above it tinkling softly. He stepped outside into the crisp evening air, exhaling deeply as if trying to release the tightness in his chest. He took a few steps, but then heard the door creak open behind him.

"Ben," Gladys called after him, her voice gentle. He turned to see her stepping out, wrapping her thin cardigan a little tighter around her shoulders against the chill. Her kind eyes studied him for a moment. "You okay, hon?"

Ben offered a faint smile. "I'll be fine, Gladys. But it's… really over this time."

Gladys nodded slowly, her expression understanding. "Maybe that's for the best, Ben. Abby's got her path, and it looks like you've got yours."

He sighed, nodding. "Yeah. I guess so."

Gladys hesitated, then added, "Just as well, you know. The diner's closing at the end of next month."

Ben's brow furrowed in surprise. "Closing? Why?"

She shrugged, trying to keep her tone light, but there was a shadow of weariness beneath it. "Not much cash flow these days. People aren't eating out like they used to, and my knees don't take to running around anymore." She paused, glancing back at the cozy glow of the diner. "It's been a good run, though. This place… it's seen a lot of lives come and go."

Ben's expression softened. "I'm sorry, Gladys. I know how much this place means to you."

She waved a hand dismissively but smiled warmly. "Oh, don't you worry about me, darling. It's just another chapter, right?" She looked at him with a knowing glint in her eye. "Besides, I think you could use a new chapter yourself."

He chuckled, a small, genuine sound that felt strange in his chest after everything. "Yeah, maybe I could."

Gladys stepped closer and put a hand on his arm, her grip surprisingly firm for her age. "You're a good one, Ben. Don't you ever doubt that. Whatever happens next, just make sure it's something that makes you happy. And hey, you'll always have a friend in me, even if the diner's gone."

Ben nodded, a lump forming in his throat that he didn't quite expect. "Thanks, Gladys. I'll miss this place… and you."

Her eyes crinkled as she smiled. "Oh, you'll see me around. I'll be that old lady feeding the ducks by the pond or causing trouble at bingo night." She winked, and for a moment, Ben felt a lightness in his chest, a hint of warmth pushing back against the ache.

He laughed softly. "I'll hold you to that."

Gladys patted his arm one more time. "Take care, Ben. Remember, sometimes endings aren't so bad. They make room for new beginnings."

He nodded again, feeling a strange mixture of sadness and hope. "Yeah… I guess they do."

He watched her turn and walk back into the diner, the door closing with a soft jingle. Ben stood there for a moment, the night air cool against his skin. He still felt the weight of his conversation with Abby, the unresolved emotions swirling within him. But somehow, he felt just a bit lighter, a bit more open to whatever might come next.

He took a deep breath, then slowly turned and walked away, his steps steady, though his heart was still finding its rhythm.

The day had been long, and Lacy was just wrapping up the last of her tasks when her phone buzzed. She glanced at the screen and saw her father's name. Smiling, she answered quickly, glad to have a moment to connect with him.

"Hey, Dad," she said warmly, leaning back in her chair.

"Lacy," Richard's voice came through the line, smooth as always but with a hint of something that made her pause. "I'm going to have to cancel our Thursday dinner. Something's come up with business, and I'll be out of town."

Lacy's smile faded slightly, a touch of worry creeping into her voice. "Is everything okay?"

"Of course," Richard replied, his tone reassuring. "Just some last-minute preparations for my 65th birthday party, and a few business matters that can't wait. But don't worry, I'll be back in time for the party, and I can't wait to see you there. You can invite anyone you'd like, by the way."

Lacy relaxed a bit, the mention of the party reminding her that her father always had things under control. "Okay, Dad. I'll see you then. And don't work too hard."

Richard chuckled. "You know me, Lacy. I'll be fine. Take care of yourself, sweetheart."

"Will do. Love you, Dad."

"Love you, too," he said before the call ended.

Lacy sat for a moment, her mind lingering on the conversation. She trusted her father, but there was always that small part of her that worried when he mentioned business. Shaking off the thought, she turned back to her desk just as Chloe entered the room with her usual clipboard in hand.

"Hey, Lacy," Chloe greeted, her energy as vibrant as always. "Just wanted to give you a quick rundown of tomorrow's schedule. We've got a few meetings in the morning, followed by a community outreach event. And don't forget, there's a campaign event with your opponent coming up next week. Paige is going to want to start prepping for that soon."

Lacy nodded, her mind shifting back to campaign mode. "Got it. Thanks, Chloe. Anything else?"

Chloe smiled and shook her head. "That's it for now. But Lacy, seriously, you've been working nonstop. Maybe take a break tonight?"

Lacy laughed softly. "I was planning on a late night, actually. But you should take your own advice—go out, enjoy being young and single."

Chloe grinned, clearly not needing to be told twice. "If you insist, boss! I'll head out then. Have a good night!"

"Goodnight, Chloe! And no emails or phone calls, okay? Just go have fun."

Chloe nodded enthusiastically, her excitement palpable. "You got it!" she called out as she hurried out the door.

Lacy watched her leave, a fond smile on her face. She turned back around in her chair, ready to settle in for the evening, when she heard footsteps behind her. Thinking Chloe had forgotten something, she didn't turn around.

"Didn't I tell you to get out of here—" she began playfully, only to stop mid-sentence when she realized it wasn't Chloe standing in the doorway.

It was Ben.

Ben stood in the doorway, his usual calm, confident self, though he feigned a look of hurt as he walked in. "Ouch. You really want me gone that badly?" he teased, his eyes twinkling with amusement.

Lacy laughed, rolling her eyes. "You know I didn't mean you. What are you doing here?"

He shrugged, casually stepping further into the room. "I've got a few things to type up for the campaign, and I thought I might focus better here. I didn't expect the place to be so empty."

Lacy nodded, understanding. "Well, I was planning on working late anyway. How about some company while you work?"

Ben smiled, the easygoing warmth that made him so likable evident in his expression. "Of course. I'd like that."

The hours passed in a blur of work, laughter, and takeout. The once pristine office was now scattered with notebooks, papers, laptops, and Chinese food containers. Lacy had swapped her business attire for a giant T-shirt and sweatpants, her hair piled into a messy bun, glasses replacing her usual contacts. She was in full comfort mode, her guard down in a way she rarely allowed during campaign hours.

Ben was similarly dressed down in a simple gray T-shirt and jeans, a red pen behind his ear as he worked through the notes in front of him. They had been eating and talking for hours, the conversation flowing naturally between work and personal topics. The late-night quiet of the office was punctuated only by the occasional clatter of chopsticks against takeout boxes and the soft hum of the air conditioning.

At one point, Ben reached for one of the cookies that had been sitting in a container on the desk. He bit into it and paused, his eyes widening in pleasant surprise. "Damn, this is amazing. What bakery did you get these from?"

Lacy looked up from her notes, hesitating for a moment before she replied, a small, proud smile on her face. "I made them."

Ben raised an eyebrow, clearly impressed. "No way. You baked these?"

She nodded, her smile widening. "My mom used to bake all the time when I was a kid. She'd sing while she worked, and the house would always smell like cookies or pies. It's one of the things I really miss about her." Her voice softened slightly, a wistful note creeping in.

Ben could see the genuine emotion in her eyes, the way she seemed to momentarily drift back to a different time. Surprised by this rare glimpse into her past, he felt an unexpected tug in his chest. Without thinking, he reached out and touched her hand, a simple gesture of comfort. "She sounds like a wonderful person," he said quietly.

Lacy looked down at their hands, then back up at Ben, their eyes meeting and holding for a beat longer than usual. "She was," she said softly, a hint of vulnerability in her expression.

Ben felt a flicker of something—an awareness, perhaps, of how rarely he saw this side of her. He cleared his throat, sensing the moment shift between them. "What about you?" Lacy asked, her voice gentle. "What were your parents like?"

Ben's expression grew a bit more serious as he leaned back in his chair. "My mom... she was a nurse. The kind who'd stay late to comfort a patient, who'd go out of her way to make people feel cared for. She was strong but so kind. And my dad, he was an artist—a painter and photographer. He had this way of seeing the world that was almost magical. He used to say that there was beauty in everything, even in the most ordinary places."

He paused, his voice growing softer. "They were different from each other in so many ways, but they were both passionate and full of life. They loved deeply... and they made our house feel alive, like anything was possible."

Lacy listened, her heart aching a bit at the tenderness in his voice. "They sound incredible, Ben," she said softly.

He smiled, though there was a sadness in his eyes. "They were. But they died in a hit-and-run accident when I was seven. After that, my grandmother raised me. She'd just lost her husband, so it was just the two of us for a long time."

Lacy felt the weight of his words, the years of loss and resilience that shaped him. "I'm sorry, Ben," she said sincerely.

He shrugged lightly, the sadness fading as he continued, "My grandmother… she's something else. She stepped up without a second thought. Sweet but tough, but with a sense of humor that could make anyone laugh. I owe a lot to her."

Lacy chuckled softly. "She sounds amazing."

"She is," Ben agreed, the fondness in his voice evident.

The tension that had lingered between them since Norfolk seemed to dissipate completely. What remained was a friendly, comfortable camaraderie that felt natural and right. They continued working until about 1:30 in the morning, finally calling it a night when both of them were too tired to think straight.

As they packed up their things and prepared to leave, Lacy smiled at Ben, feeling genuinely grateful. "I'm glad we did this," she said, her voice softer than before.

Ben returned her smile, nodding in agreement. "Yeah, me too." Their eyes met again, and for a moment, the air felt different—charged with something unspoken yet understood.

They walked out of the office together, heading to their separate cars. As Ben glanced at Lacy, even in her T-shirt and sweatpants, he found himself struck by how beautiful she looked—how much she radiated warmth and strength. It wasn't just her appearance; it was the way she carried herself, the way she made others feel seen.

He realized there was no harm in admiring a friend—especially one as remarkable as Lacy. With that thought, he got into his car and drove home, feeling content with the way the night had gone. The lingering tension had been replaced with something much better—mutual respect, understanding, and a sense of something new unfolding, even if he couldn't quite name it yet.

CHAPTER 9

The drive to the small, rural town of Reston where Michael Hayes had last been seen was long and quiet. The landscape shifted from the bustle of the city to the stillness of the countryside. Jake Marlowe had spent the hours on the road replaying the details in his mind, mentally preparing himself for what he might find. The further he drove, the more isolated the world became—fields stretching out for miles, punctuated by the occasional farmhouse or rusted barn. It was the kind of place where secrets could easily be buried and forgotten.

He needed this story so badly that he craved it. After the humiliation of his last big piece falling apart due to an unreliable lead in the government corruption scandal, Jake's reputation had taken a hit. This time, he was determined not to let anything slip through the cracks. Finding the truth about Michael Hayes might be his shot at career redemption and, more than that, it fed his deeper quest for justice. He wanted to uncover what was hidden, the truth that others tried to bury.

When Jake finally pulled up to the address he had found, he parked his car on the gravel driveway and took a deep breath. The house before him was modest, a weathered structure that had clearly seen better days. The paint was peeling, and the front porch sagged slightly, but there was a certain charm to it—a sense that it had been well-loved over the years.

Jake stepped out of the car, the crunch of gravel under his feet the only sound in the still afternoon. He felt a mix of anticipation and dread as he approached the front door. This was it—the moment that could either break his story wide open or leave him with nothing but dead ends.

He knocked on the door, the sound echoing in the quiet. Time seemed to stretch, each second feeling like an eternity. Just as he was about to knock again, the door creaked open, revealing a small, frail woman. She had a kind face, though it was etched with the lines of age and sorrow. Her hair was white and thin, pulled back into a loose bun, and she wore a simple floral dress that hung loosely on her thin frame.

"Hello," Jake greeted her warmly, mustering a smile despite the tension he felt. "My name is Jake Marlowe. I was hoping to speak with you about Michael Hayes?"

The woman eyed him cautiously, her hand trembling slightly as she gripped the door. "Who are you, exactly?" she asked, her voice wary.

Jake hesitated for a split second, then decided on a lie that he hoped would gain her trust. "I'm a reporter, working on a piece about Michael. I want to make sure he gets the credit he deserves for saving the mayor all those years ago."

The woman's expression softened, and she nodded, seemingly convinced by his words. "Come in," she said, opening the door fully and stepping aside to let him in.

Jake entered the house, immediately struck by how it felt more like a shrine than a home. The living room walls were lined with photographs of Michael Hayes—a man with dark hair and deep-set eyes, his strong jaw and sharp cheekbones. There were pictures of him as a boy, a young man, and then as an adult in his police uniform. The room was filled with a deep sense of loss, every corner speaking of a life that had been lived with intensity and ended in tragedy. The air carried the faint scent of lavender and something else—maybe old wood, or the lingering memory of incense burned long ago.

"Would you like some hot tea?" she offered, her voice gentle as she motioned to the couch.

"Yes, please. Thank you," Jake replied, taking a seat on the worn but comfortable couch.

The woman disappeared into the kitchen, and Jake took the opportunity to glance around the room, absorbing every detail. His eyes landed on a newspaper clipping pinned to a corkboard on the wall. It was a faded article about Amanda Jacobs' death, the headline reading: "Tragic Accident Claims Life of CEO Richard Jacobs' Wife." The clipping was surrounded by other photos and documents, some frayed at the edges.

Jake's gaze shifted to a desk in the corner, its drawers slightly ajar, as if someone had rummaged through them recently. He felt a small thrill of anticipation. This house was more than just a home; it was a place where clues might still be hidden.

The woman returned with two steaming cups of tea, handing one to Jake before settling into an armchair across from him. She blew on her tea softly before taking a sip, her eyes drifting to a photo of Michael in his police uniform.

"So," Jake began carefully, "I was hoping to speak with Michael about his time in the force, and about the work he did to protect the mayor. Is he here?"

The woman's hands trembled slightly, and she set her tea down on the table. "I'm Michael's mother," she said, her voice tinged with sorrow. "Michael... Michael took his own life about ten years ago."

Jake's breath caught in his throat, his heart skipping a beat. He blinked, momentarily stunned. The words hung in the air, heavy and suffocating. He'd come here expecting to find Michael alive. His mind scrambled to adjust to this new, unsettling reality. "I—I'm so sorry," he stammered, trying to regain his composure.

She nodded, her eyes welling with tears as she looked at the photographs that lined the room. "He was a good man. He just... he lost his way after Amanda died."

Jake's mind raced. Amanda. "Amanda?" he asked, trying to piece together the connection. "Do you mean Amanda Jacobs?"

Michael's mother nodded again, her expression pained. "Yes. They grew up together, not really friends at first, but classmates. They were high school sweethearts and nuts about each other; that was before Michael joined the force. Amanda hated the idea of him being a cop, so when he told her he was going to join, she broke up with him. She got married and had a baby with Richard Jacobs not long after. Michael was heartbroken, but he threw himself into his work."

Jake leaned forward, trying to follow the thread of the story. "How did they reconnect?"

The old woman's voice wavered as she spoke, clearly struggling with the memories. "I don't know how they reconnected, but they did. It was about a year before she died. They were together again, at least for a while. But after she passed… Michael was never the same. He wanted to be close to her again, but he started drifting further and further away. I couldn't save him because his heart was so broken."

Tears filled her eyes, and she covered her face with her hands, her shoulders shaking with silent sobs. Jake felt a deep sense of empathy for this woman, who had lost so much, but his mind was also racing with the implications of what he had just learned. Michael and Amanda had been together—reconnected just before her death.

"Mrs. Hayes," Jake began gently, trying to piece together the next question carefully, "do you know if Michael ever mentioned anything about the Jacobs family? Specifically, Richard Jacobs?"

She shook her head, wiping her eyes as she tried to compose herself. "Michael wanted to protect me, so he told me nothing. But I know he was close with Amanda. Richard… I don't know much about him, but Michael never spoke of him directly. He only ever mentioned Amanda."

Jake's eyes drifted to a small, framed photograph on a nearby table. The edges were torn, as if someone had ripped it out of something in haste. He could just make out a woman's hand in the corner—delicate, almost too small to be certain it was a woman's at all. He picked it up, curiosity piqued.

Noticing his interest, Mrs. Hayes reached over and took the photo, turning it over. "I found this in Michael's room after he died," she said softly. "It doesn't make much sense to me, but on the back, it says, 'Remember our deal, Michael.' I've kept it, hoping it would somehow explain why he left us. I don't know who wrote it, or what it means, but maybe… maybe you can make sense of it."

Jake took the photo, his fingers brushing against the faded ink. His pulse quickened as he read the words. The note was vague, but something about it felt significant, like a whisper of a secret waiting to be uncovered.

"Thank you," he said, pocketing the photograph. "I promise I'll do everything I can to find out what happened to Michael, and why."

Mrs. Hayes nodded, her eyes filled with a gratitude that only deepened Jake's resolve. Though Michael was gone, Jake had still stumbled upon something far bigger than he had anticipated. Amanda's death, Michael's connection to the Jacobs family, and the possibility of a secret deal—it all pointed to a web of secrets that Richard Jacobs might be desperate to keep buried.

As he left the house, Jake couldn't shake the feeling that he was standing on the edge of something huge, something that could expose the dark underbelly of one of the state's most powerful families. He felt a surge of excitement but also a familiar flicker of fear. This was his chance to prove himself again, to show that his instincts were still sharp and his dedication to the truth unwavering.

But going up against Richard Jacobs could mean risking everything. As the sun set, the sky ablaze with fiery reds and oranges, Jake knew one thing for sure: Michael Hayes' story wasn't over. The truth was out there, and he was more determined than ever to find it, no matter the cost.

[FLASHBACK]

The rain pounded against the windows of Michael Hayes' small, dimly lit apartment, the sound creating a steady rhythm that matched the rapid beating of his heart. The room was sparsely furnished, with only a worn couch, a coffee table cluttered with case files, and a few personal items that hinted at the life of a man devoted to his work. The walls, once painted a cheery yellow, were now faded and peeling, the apartment bearing the marks of neglect as Michael had thrown himself into his job, trying to forget the life he could have had.

Michael sat on the edge of the couch, his hands clasped together tightly as he waited. His thoughts raced, filled with a mix of anticipation and dread. He hadn't seen Amanda in five years—not since she had walked out of his life without explanation, leaving him with nothing but memories of what they once had. He had tried to move on, but she had never really left his heart. And now, after all these years, she was coming to him.

A knock on the door startled him out of his thoughts. He stood, his heart pounding even harder as he crossed the room. With a deep breath, he reached for the doorknob and opened it, and there she was—Amanda, standing in the doorway, soaked from the rain, her dark hair plastered to her face, her eyes wide with a mix of fear and desperation.

"Amanda," Michael breathed, the name slipping from his lips like a prayer.

Amanda stepped inside, her body trembling as she looked up at him. The years had been kind to her, but there was a new hardness in her eyes, a weariness that hadn't been there before. She had changed, and so had he, but the connection between them was still as strong as ever. The tension was palpable, the air between them charged with unspoken words.

"Michael," she whispered, her voice trembling as she reached out to touch his arm. The warmth of his skin beneath her fingers sent a shiver through her, grounding her in the moment. She had imagined this reunion countless times, but now that it was happening, she found herself overwhelmed with emotion.

Without thinking, Michael pulled her into his arms, holding her close as if afraid she might disappear again. The feel of her body against his was almost too much to bear. He had longed for this moment, and yet he was terrified of what it meant.

They stood there for what felt like an eternity, simply holding each other as the rain continued to pour outside. Finally, Amanda pulled back just enough to look up at him, her eyes glistening with unshed tears. "I'm sorry," she whispered, her voice breaking. "I'm so sorry, Michael."

He shook his head, gently brushing a strand of wet hair away from her face. "Why did you come here, Amanda?" he asked softly, though he wasn't sure he wanted to know the answer. The pain of the past still lingered, but so did the love he had never been able to let go.

Amanda hesitated, her gaze dropping to the floor as she tried to find the words. "I came because… I need your help. I don't know where else to turn."

Michael's brow furrowed, concern lacing his features. "What's going on? Is it Richard?"

At the mention of her husband's name, Amanda flinched, a haunted look crossing her face. "Yes," she admitted, her voice barely audible. "I've seen things, Michael. Things I can't unsee. I'm afraid… for myself and for Lacy."

"What kind of things?" Micheal asked.

Amanda took a deep breath, her hands tightening into fists at her sides. "I saw him beat a man nearly to death. He didn't even flinch, Michael. He… he enjoyed it. And that's just the beginning. There's so much more. Richard is involved in things I can't even begin to explain—money laundering, drug trafficking, murder. I didn't realize how deep it went until it was too late."

Michael's heart sank as he listened. He had always suspected that Richard Jacobs was more than just a wealthy businessman, but hearing it confirmed by Amanda was a punch to the gut. "Why didn't you come to me sooner?" he asked, his voice thick with emotion.

Amanda shook her head, tears spilling down her cheeks. "I thought I could protect Lacy by staying with him. I thought if I kept my head down, he would leave us alone. But I was wrong. And now... now I'm afraid it's too late."

"It's not too late," Michael said firmly, his hand cupping her cheek as he looked into her eyes. "We can take him down, Amanda. But I need your help. I need you to get evidence—anything that can link him to these crimes. Can you do that?"

Amanda hesitated, the fear in her heart warring with the need to protect her daughter. But as she looked into Michael's eyes, she felt a glimmer of hope, something she hadn't felt in a long time. She nodded, determination filling her chest. "I'll do it. I'll get whatever you need. I just want Lacy to be safe."

A silence fell between them, heavy with the weight of the past and the uncertainty of the future. But in that moment, something shifted. The years of separation, the pain and regret—they all faded away as they looked at each other, two people who had once been everything to each other, now finding themselves back in each other's arms.

Without another word, Michael pulled Amanda closer, his lips capturing hers in a kiss that was filled with years of longing and unspoken promises. The kiss was desperate, hungry, as if they were both trying to make up for all the time they had lost. Amanda responded with equal fervor, her hands tangling in his hair as she pressed herself against him, wanting nothing more than to be close to him again.

They kissed like that for what felt like an eternity, the world outside forgotten as they lost themselves in each other. The intensity of their emotions, the raw need they both felt, was almost overwhelming. It was as if they were trying to reclaim something that had been stolen from them—something they had never stopped wanting.

When they finally pulled apart, they were both breathless, their foreheads resting against each other as they tried to steady their racing hearts. "One day," Michael whispered against her lips, "we'll be free. I promise you, Amanda. We'll be free, and we'll be together."

Tears welled up in Amanda's eyes as she nodded, her heart aching with the weight of his words. "I want that too," she whispered back, her voice breaking. "More than anything."

But as they stood there, wrapped in each other's arms, reality began to seep back in. They both knew that their road to freedom would be long and dangerous. Richard Jacobs was not a man to be trifled with, and the risks were greater than they could imagine.

Michael led her to the bedroom, where they made love with a desperation that came from years of separation and the knowledge that this might be the last time they could be together like this. Their connection was as strong as ever, the love they had shared still burning bright despite everything that had happened. They held onto each other like lifelines, each of them finding solace in the other's arms.

Afterward, they lay in each other's arms, the room filled with the soft sound of their breathing. Michael held Amanda close, his fingers tracing patterns on her bare skin as he listened to her heart beating against his chest. It was a moment of peace in a world that had been anything but peaceful for a long time.

"I need to tell you something," Amanda said quietly, her voice trembling with the weight of the words.

Michael looked down at her, concern filling his gaze. "What is it?"

Amanda took a deep breath, her heart pounding in her chest. "Lacy… she's your daughter, Michael."

Michael stared at her, his mind struggling to process what she had just said. "What?"

Amanda's eyes filled with tears as she continued. "I wasn't sure at first. When I found out I was pregnant, I had just broken up with you and started seeing Richard. I didn't know who the father was. But when Lacy was three, I did a DNA test. She's yours, Michael."

Michael felt a surge of emotions—shock, disbelief, and then an overwhelming sense of love and protectiveness. "She's mine?" he whispered, his voice thick with emotion.

Amanda nodded, tears streaming down her face. "Yes. She's your daughter. I'm sorry I didn't tell you sooner. I thought… I thought I was doing what was best for her, giving her a life with Richard. But I was wrong."

Michael pulled her into his arms, pressing a kiss to her forehead. "You don't have to apologize. You were trying to protect her. But now… now we're going to protect her together."

They held each other tightly, both knowing that their lives were about to change in ways they couldn't even begin to imagine. But for the first time in years, they had hope. And that hope was enough to keep them going.

As they lay there, wrapped in each other's arms, Michael made a silent vow to himself. He would do whatever it took to bring Richard Jacobs down. He would protect Amanda and Lacy, no matter the cost. Because now, more than ever, he knew what he was fighting for.

They drifted off to sleep, holding onto each other as if they were the only things keeping each other afloat. The storm raged on outside, but inside, they had found a brief moment of peace—a peace that they both knew would be hard to come by in the days to come. But for now, it was enough.

Present Day: Paige's Penthouse Apartment

Paige's penthouse apartment was nothing short of stunning. Perched high above the city, the space was a perfect blend of elegance and modernity, with floor-to-ceiling windows offering breathtaking views of the skyline. The living room was furnished with sleek, contemporary pieces in shades of cream and gray, accented by bold pops of color in the form of abstract art on the walls and vibrant throw pillows scattered across the plush sectional sofa. A glass coffee table sat at the center of the room, adorned with a few carefully chosen coffee table books and a vase of fresh white roses.

The open floor plan connected the living room to a state-of-the-art kitchen with marble countertops, high-end appliances, and an island that doubled as a breakfast bar. Everything about the space spoke to Paige's impeccable taste and success—she had worked hard to get here, and it showed.

But it was Paige's closet that truly took Lacy's breath away. It was more like a mini-boutique than a traditional closet, complete with rows of neatly organized designer shoes, racks of perfectly arranged dresses, and drawers filled with accessories. The closet was equipped with smart technology, allowing Paige to adjust the lighting and even rotate the racks to easily access her extensive wardrobe. The walls were a soft blush color, adding a touch of femininity to the luxurious space.

Lacy sat on a velvet ottoman, watching as Paige tried on dresses for the night. "I'm looking for something that doesn't scream 'campaign manager' tonight," Paige said with a grin, rifling through the hangers. "Something that says, 'I'm here to have fun.'"

The first dress Paige tried on was a sleek, black satin slip dress. It hugged her curves in all the right places, with thin spaghetti straps and a thigh-high slit that added a touch of daring. The dress shimmered subtly under the lights, making her look effortlessly elegant and a little dangerous.

"What do you think?" Paige asked, striking a pose.

Lacy tilted her head, considering. "It's gorgeous, but it still feels a bit too… serious? Maybe something a little more playful?"

Paige nodded, slipping out of the black dress and pulling another one from the rack. The second dress was a deep emerald green with a plunging neckline and a cinched waist that flared out into a flowy, mid-thigh skirt. The fabric was light and airy, with a slight sheen that caught the light as Paige twirled in front of the mirror.

"This one's definitely more fun," Paige said, her eyes bright as she admired the way the dress moved.

Lacy smiled. "That's more like it. It's flirty but still classy."

Paige grinned, but she wasn't done yet. "One more," she said, disappearing into the closet and emerging with a third dress. This one was a bold red, with off-the-shoulder sleeves and a body-hugging fit that highlighted her hourglass figure. The fabric was a luxurious velvet, rich and vibrant, with a slit that ran daringly up one leg.

Paige slipped into the dress, adjusting it in front of the mirror. "This one," she said, her voice full of satisfaction. "This is the one."

Lacy nodded in approval. "You look incredible, that dress screams YOU."

Paige turned to face Lacy, a playful smile tugging at the corners of her lips. "I'm hoping to find someone who can make me scream something tonight," she joked, winking.

Lacy burst out laughing, feeling a warmth in her chest that she hadn't felt in a long time. This was what real friendship felt like—light, fun, and completely genuine. "Well, if you don't, they're missing out," Lacy teased back.

As Paige moved to check her reflection in the mirror one last time, Lacy's eyes caught a small box sitting on one of the shelves. The label on the box read "Fendi Heels," but when Lacy curiously opened it, she found something entirely different—vibrators and a variety of other sex toys neatly arranged inside.

Paige turned around just in time to see Lacy's raised eyebrow and the box in her hands. Her cheeks flushed a bright pink, and she let out a shy laugh as she quickly took the box from Lacy. "Oops," she said, trying to play it off.

Lacy laughed, unbothered. "Girl, please. We're grown. You should see the bottom drawer of my dresser."

Paige's embarrassment melted away, replaced by a shared laugh that made the moment even more fun. "Touché," Paige said, grinning.

As they continued to get ready, Lacy decided that she was going to let loose tonight. She wasn't just the governor-in-the-making tonight; she was a woman who deserved to have fun, too. She slipped into a short, fitted black skirt that hugged her hips just right, paired with a silky white blouse that she left slightly unbuttoned at the top. She completed the look with strappy black heels that showed off her perfectly pedicured white toenails.

Paige eyed her approvingly. "Lacy, you look amazing. I'm loving this side of you."

Lacy smiled, feeling a surge of excitement. "Thanks. I figured if it's a party, I'm going to dress like it's a party. Besides, you're not the only one who could use a good time."

The two women finished getting ready, applying the final touches to their makeup and slipping on their heels. As they stood in front of the mirror, side by side, they both felt a sense of anticipation. Tonight wasn't just about politics or campaigning—it was about letting go and enjoying life, if only for a little while.

"Ready to go?" Paige asked, her eyes gleaming with excitement.

"Let's do it," Lacy replied, her smile wide and genuine.

As they left Paige's penthouse and headed to Richard's party, Lacy felt a lightness in her step that had been missing for a long time. Tonight, she wasn't the governor or the candidate—she was just a woman at a party, ready to enjoy herself. And she was determined to make the most of it.

Richard Jacobs' 65th birthday party was the kind of event that only the truly powerful could pull off. Held in the grand ballroom of one of the city's most luxurious hotels, the room was a dazzling display of opulence and wealth. Crystal chandeliers hung from the high, intricately carved ceilings, casting a warm, golden light over the scene below. The air was filled with the soft hum of live jazz music, blending with the clink of champagne glasses and the murmur of conversation from the elite guests who filled the room. The scent of expensive perfume mingled with the aroma of gourmet hors d'oeuvres being passed around on silver trays by impeccably dressed waiters.

Everywhere Lacy looked, she saw familiar faces—the kind of people who moved in and out of society's upper circles with ease.

Politicians, CEOs, and a few well-known media personalities were in attendance, dressed in upscale but relaxed attire. The men wore tailored suits with open collars, their jackets casually slung over the backs of chairs or folded neatly across their arms. The women opted for stylish cocktail dresses or sleek pantsuits, the fabrics flowing and comfortable rather than structured or fussy.

The vibe was effortless sophistication, indicating a confident restraint that hinted at real power. Lacy made her way through the crowd, her eyes scanning the room until she spotted her father. Richard was at the center of it all, the very picture of a powerful man enjoying his moment in the spotlight. He was dressed in a perfectly fitted black tuxedo, a crisp white shirt underneath, and a black bow tie that added to his distinguished appearance. His silver hair was neatly combed back, and his eyes, sharp and observant, crinkled at the corners as he laughed with a group of high-profile guests.

"Dad!" Lacy called out, breaking through the throng of people.

Richard turned at the sound of her voice, and his face lit up with a genuine smile. "Lacy, my darling!" he exclaimed, opening his arms as she approached. She stepped into his embrace, wrapping her arms around him and smelling the familiar, comforting scent of his cologne.

"Happy birthday," Lacy said warmly, pulling back to look at him. "You look great."

"So do you," Richard replied, his eyes filled with pride. "I'm so happy you're here."

The warmth in his voice made Lacy's heart swell, and for a moment, the pressures of her campaign and her responsibilities melted away. Tonight, she wasn't the candidate for governor—she was just a daughter celebrating her father's birthday.

The night progressed, and Lacy allowed herself to relax. She had a few drinks, enjoying the rich taste of the champagne that flowed freely. For once, there were no cameras, no reporters, and no campaign talk— just laughter, conversation, and a rare sense of freedom. It was a much-needed reprieve, a moment to breathe and just be herself.

She was in the middle of a conversation with a family friend when she saw him—Ben, entering the room. He looked incredibly handsome. His long, thick, black hair was down, cascading over his shoulders in soft curls that framed his strong jawline. He wore a charcoal gray suit that fit him perfectly, accentuating his broad shoulders and tall frame. There was something effortlessly handsome about him, a kind of quiet confidence that drew her attention immediately.

Feeling a bit bolder from the champagne, Lacy walked over to him, a smile tugging at her lips. "Ben," she greeted him warmly. "I'm glad you could make it."

Ben turned to face her, his breath catching slightly at the sight of Lacy. She looked stunning in a sleek, form-fitting outfit that highlighted her figure, her hair cascading in loose waves over her shoulders. She was sexy, confident, and completely at ease—seeing her like this, so carefree, left him momentarily speechless.

"I wouldn't miss it," Ben finally managed to say, his voice a bit huskier than usual. He quickly recovered, with a teasing smile.

"You know, you could have brought a plus one. Abby, maybe?" Lacy added.

At the mention of Abby, Ben's expression tightened, and he shook his head. "Abby's not a factor in my life anymore," he said firmly, his tone leaving no room for doubt. He needed Lacy to know that—though he wasn't entirely sure why it mattered so much to him.

Lacy gave him a friendly smile, reaching out to touch his elbow in a gesture that felt both intimate and comforting. "I see. Well, I'm glad you're here, Ben. It's nice to see you outside of work for a change."

As she spoke, Richard watched the interaction from across the room, his eyes narrowing slightly. There was something about the way Lacy and Ben were standing together, the way their body language spoke of an unspoken connection. To an outsider, it might have looked like friendly banter, but to Richard, it conveyed something more—something he didn't like.

The night continued, with the party in full swing. Lacy floated from conversation to conversation, but she couldn't help but feel a slight tension lingering in the air. She noticed her father watching her a few times, a look of contemplation on his face. She dismissed it at first, thinking he was just observing the party, but when she found herself alone for a moment, Richard approached her, his expression serious.

"Lacy," Richard began, his voice low and stern, almost scolding. "Remind me again. Who is that young man you were talking to?"

Lacy blinked in surprise at the sudden change in her father's mood. "Ben? He's my speechwriter, Dad. You've met him before. He's a....... trusted colleague."

Richard's gaze was intense as he looked down at her. "I don't like it," he said bluntly. "He's not the kind of man you need to get close to. He's.....not for you."

Before Lacy could respond, Ben returned with a glass of water for her, sensing the tension. He handed her the glass, his eyes flicking between her and Richard, his guard immediately going up as he sensed Richard's disapproval.

Richard forced a tight, polite smile, nodding curtly at Ben. "If you'll excuse me, Lacy, Benjamin," he said, his tone clipped as he turned and walked away.

Lacy was mortified, feeling the weight of the awkward encounter. "I'm sorry about that," she began, but Ben shook his head, cutting her off with a reassuring smile.

"We can't apologize for our parents," Ben said softly, his eyes meeting hers with understanding. "It's okay."

Lacy returned his smile, though she still felt a bit shaken by the exchange. "I think I'm going to head back to the office to grab a few things. I'm working from home tomorrow."

Ben nodded, sensing that she needed a moment away from the party. "I'll come with you," he offered. "It's getting late anyway."

They left the party together, slipping out without saying goodbye to Richard. The drive to the office was quiet, both of them lost in their thoughts. When they arrived, Lacy went straight to her desk to gather her things while Ben waited near the door, the weight of the evening settling heavily on both of them.

As they prepared to leave, they were suddenly confronted by a figure emerging from the shadows—Jake Marlowe, the persistent reporter from the State Tribune. His eyes were sharp and determined, his presence an unwelcome intrusion.

"Senator Jacobs!" Jake called out, his voice cutting through the silence. "Does your father know anything about your mother's death? Or about Officer Michael Hayes? Do you care to comment on your father's business or your involvement?" Lacy froze, the questions hitting her like a physical blow. Before she could respond, Ben stepped between them, his expression darkening as he glared at Jake. "Back the fuck up," Ben growled, his voice low and threatening—a side of him Lacy had never seen before.

Jake took a step back, startled by the intensity in Ben's voice, but the questions hung in the air, impossible to ignore. Lacy's mind flashed back to the last conversation she'd had with her mother, the memory almost too painful to bear. She felt a cold knot of fear tightening in her chest, the words of the reporter stirring something deep and unresolved within her.

Ben managed to push Jake off, his protective instincts kicking in as he turned to Lacy, concern etched on his face. "Are you okay?" he asked, his voice softer now.

Lacy nodded, though she was anything but okay. Her thoughts were racing, her heart pounding as the implications of Jake's questions began to sink in. "I need to talk to my father," she said quietly, her voice trembling with the weight of her decision.

Ben, ever the gentleman, insisted on seeing her back to her apartment. The drive was silent, and when they arrived, Ben walked her to the door, making sure she was safe before leaving. "If you need anything, call me," he said, his voice full of concern.

Lacy nodded, but as soon as the door closed behind her, she felt the full weight of everything crashing down on her. She wasn't okay—far from it. Her mind was reeling, the questions about her mother's death, the memories of her last words, and the suspicion surrounding her father all swirling together in a chaotic storm.

Tomorrow, she would confront her father. She needed answers—answers that she was no longer willing to ignore. But tonight, all she could do was try to calm the storm inside her, knowing that her life might never be the same once she learned the truth. Now that the adrenaline had faded, a quieter regret settled in. She'd bolted so fast she hadn't even looked back at Ben—hadn't said thank you, hadn't lingered like she always secretly wanted to. She had hope this would give them another moment to themselves but alas it was another missed opportunity.

The late afternoon sun filtered through the tall windows of Richard Jacobs' home office, casting long shadows across the room. Lacy sat in one of the plush armchairs facing her father's desk, her hands clasped tightly in her lap. She had come here for answers, but the events of the previous night left her feeling more unsettled than ever. Taking a deep breath, she broke the silence.

"Dad," she began, her voice steady but tinged with unease, "there's something I need to tell you."

Richard looked up from the papers he was reviewing, his expression shifting from focused to concerned. "What is it, Lacy?"

She hesitated, gathering her thoughts. "Last night, after the party, I went back to the office to grab a few things. And... this reporter came out of nowhere. He started asking questions about Mom and Michael Hayes. It was intense, and I would have been scared, but Ben was there."

At the mention of Ben, Richard's expression tightened, his jaw clenching ever so slightly. "Ben," he repeated, almost as if testing the name. "Always around, isn't he?"

Lacy frowned, feeling the familiar tension rise between them. "Dad, he's just my campaign worker. We work well together, that's all."

Richard leaned back in his chair, studying her. "Is that all it is? Because the way he looks at you—"

"What do you mean? Never mind," Lacy interrupted, her frustration bubbling up. "He's a good guy. He cares about the campaign."

"Maybe," Richard conceded, but his eyes remained sharp. "But you have to be careful, Lacy. I've seen what happens when people get too close."

"What are you saying?" Lacy's voice was firmer now, her gaze locking onto his. "Do you think I can't handle myself?"

Richard held her gaze for a long moment before sighing. "I'm saying this because I know how these things go. Feelings get messy. People get hurt."

Lacy could feel the irritation gnawing at her, but she pushed it aside. "I appreciate your concern, but I'm fine. I just... I need to know more about Mom. About what happened."

Richard's expression shifted slightly, his brows knitting together. "Why now?" he asked quietly, almost cautiously.

"Because I've been hearing things," Lacy replied, leaning forward. "And I know you've always tried to protect me, but I'm not a child anymore. I deserve to know the truth. Especially if journalists are going to be harassing me about it."

Richard's lips tightened. He seemed to consider his words carefully, as if weighing what to say next. "Your mother... she was complicated," he began, his voice low. "But she loved you. I want you to understand that, no matter what else you hear."

Lacy watched him closely, noting the slight tremor in his hands. "What do you mean, 'no matter what else'?" she pressed.

Richard hesitated, then sighed heavily, as if the weight of years was finally catching up with him. "There were things… things between her and Michael Hayes that you don't know about."

Lacy's heart pounded in her chest, but she kept her voice steady. "Like what?"

Richard swallowed, his Adam's apple bobbing slightly. "They had an affair. For a few months. I found out, but we… we tried to work through it."

The room seemed to shrink around Lacy, the air heavy. "And?" she whispered, her voice strained.

Richard's gaze flicked away for a moment—just a flicker, but enough for Lacy to catch. "She told him it was over. That night, she invited him to the house to end things for good. She was so afraid of how he would take the news… I should have listened."

Lacy's instincts flared. "Wait," she said, frowning. "Mom invited him over? Why would she do that if she wanted to end it?"

Richard blinked, caught off guard. "She… she wanted to do it in person. To make it clear."

Lacy felt a chill run down her spine. "But you said before that she was scared of him, that he was becoming erratic…"

"She was scared," Richard insisted quickly, almost too quickly. "But she also felt guilty. She wanted to face him, to end it right."

Lacy felt a knot tighten in her stomach. "And you were okay with that?" she challenged. "Letting her meet him alone, knowing he was dangerous?"

Richard's face hardened for a split second, then softened again. "I didn't know until it was too late," he murmured, his voice breaking. "I couldn't let her go to his place. That seemed even more dangerous… I didn't know he had planned to—," his voice broke.

Lacy's eyes narrowed. "But you were home, weren't you? You said you found them—"

Richard's expression darkened, his voice firm. "I found them afterward, Lacy. I tried to stop him, but… it was too late."

She could feel her heart pounding in her ears, the pieces not fitting together. "And Michael? He just disappeared after that?"

Richard's eyes held hers for a beat too long. "He ran," he replied. "I guess he knew he'd go to prison for what he did, especially since everyone thought he was a hero."

Lacy nodded slowly, still trying to process everything. There was something that didn't sit right, a small, nagging feeling at the back of her mind. "So, why not tell me all this before?" she asked, her tone more measured. "Why the accident story?"

Richard leaned in, his face close to hers, his eyes intense. "Because I didn't want you burdened with that kind of truth," he whispered. "I didn't want you to hate her… or me."

Lacy studied his face, searching for any cracks in the facade. "And now?" she asked softly. "Why tell me now?"

Richard paused, then smiled softly, his eyes still locked onto hers. "Because you asked, and you're strong enough to know now."

He reached out and took her hands, squeezing them just a bit too tightly. "I wanted to protect you, Lacy. Always. But you've grown up, and you deserve to know everything."

Lacy swallowed hard, still not entirely convinced but sensing she wouldn't get more from him today. She nodded slowly. "Okay. Thank you… for telling me."

Richard's face brightened slightly, a hint of relief crossing his features. "Good. Now, let's forget about this for a while. Focus on your campaign, on your future. You've got a lot ahead of you."

Lacy nodded, feeling a mix of emotions churning inside her. "I should get going," she said quietly. "I have a lot to think about."

Richard nodded, standing up with her. "Of course. But Lacy, remember—be careful who you trust. Even those who seem closest to you."

Lacy felt a cold shiver run down her spine, but she forced a smile. "I will, Dad. I promise."

As she turned to leave, Richard's voice stopped her. "And, Lacy… let's have Ben over for dinner soon," he said casually, but there was something in his tone that made her pause. "You know, because you and he have gotten so close…at work."

Lacy's smile tightened, her mind racing. "Sure," she replied, her voice light but guarded. "We'll see."

As she left the room, she felt a mixture of relief and unease. Something was still off, still unsaid. But she'd find out. In her own time.

Richard sat in the dimly lit study, the soft glow of a single desk lamp casting deep shadows across his sharp features. The rest of the house was silent. But Richard's mind was far from restful. He leaned back in his leather chair, steepling his fingers, eyes narrowing as he considered his next move.

With a measured breath, he reached for the vintage rotary phone on his desk—an old-fashioned piece, but one he trusted for its discretion. He dialed a number he knew by heart, listening to the quiet hum of the line as it connected, the steady pulse of his heartbeat ticking off the seconds.

After a few rings, a familiar voice answered. "Yes, Richard?"

Richard's tone was calm, but there was an edge to it, a hint of steel. "It's time we had a conversation about your employee."

There was a brief pause, then a knowing sigh from the other end. "Which one?"

"Jake Marlowe," Richard replied, letting the name hang in the air for a moment, dripping with disdain. "He's been sticking his nose where it doesn't belong. I need you to rein him in before he causes any more trouble."

A soft chuckle came through the line. "Ah, Marlowe. I've been hearing about his antics. Ambitious, but reckless."

"Ambition is one thing," Richard cut in, his voice hardening, "but recklessness like this… it's a line that shouldn't be crossed. Make it clear to him that he's playing a dangerous game. I want him to understand exactly who he's dealing with."

The man on the other end—a powerful media mogul who owned the State Tribune—paused, considering. When he spoke again, his tone was serious. "Consider it done, Richard. I'll have a word with him."

"Good," Richard replied, leaning back in his chair, his fingers tapping rhythmically on the desk. "And arrange a meeting between us. I'd like to see this Marlowe character for myself."

There was a beat of silence, then the man agreed, "Of course. I'll make the arrangements."

Richard ended the call with a click, setting the receiver down with deliberate care. He allowed himself a small, satisfied smile as he sat back, his eyes narrowing in thought. The pieces were moving into place. Jake Marlowe thought he could poke around without consequence, but Richard had seen men like him before—hungry for a story, blind to the dangers lurking in the shadows.

He glanced at the corner of his desk, where a faded photograph of Amanda lay beneath a stack of papers. For a moment, a flicker of something—regret? fear?—crossed his face. Then it was gone, replaced by a look of cold determination. He wouldn't let Marlowe unravel everything he'd worked so hard to bury. Not again.

Richard's fingers tightened around the armrests of his chair, his mind already racing through the possibilities. This would be a delicate game, but he'd played it many times before. He knew how to deal with men who didn't know when to stop asking questions.

As he turned the lamp down low, the room grew darker, the shadows deepening. The game was in motion now, and Richard intended to win. Whatever the cost.

CHAPTER 10

The following morning, the newsroom of the State Tribune buzzed with the usual energy. Phones rang, keyboards clicked, and the low murmur of reporters discussing their stories filled the air. But in the office of Claire Morgan, the editor-in-chief, the atmosphere was anything but calm.

Claire stood behind her desk, her eyes blazing with anger as she glared at Jake Marlowe, who was seated in front of her. His appearance was disheveled—dark circles under his eyes, his shirt wrinkled from a long night spent chasing leads. But it wasn't his appearance that had Claire fuming; it was his reckless behavior.

"You trespassed on private property," Claire began, her voice rising with each word. "You harassed citizens, and to top it off, you confronted a woman running for governor—all on a hunch that you can't even fucking prove!"

Jake opened his mouth to defend himself, but Claire cut him off, slamming her palm down on the desk for emphasis. "If it were up to me, you'd be fired, Jake. You've crossed every line there is, and for what? A story that isn't even fully baked?"

Jake's face flushed with a mix of frustration and defiance. "Claire, I'm telling you, there's something here. Richard Jacobs is involved in something big—something that could bring him down. We're talking about corruption, murder, maybe even more. We can't just ignore this."

Claire narrowed her eyes at him, her jaw clenched in anger. "You're chasing ghosts, Jake. And you're putting this entire paper at risk. Do you have any idea the kind of power Richard Jacobs wields? You think you can just waltz onto his property and start making accusations?"

Jake's shoulders slumped slightly, the weight of her words settling over him. "I know I took risks, but—"

"But nothing!" Claire snapped, cutting him off again. She took a deep breath, trying to regain her composure. "Luckily for you," she said, her tone softer but still laced with frustration, "Richard Jacobs wants to take a meeting with you."

Jake's eyes widened in surprise. "What?"

Claire leaned forward, fixing him with a stern look. "You heard me. He's requested a meeting with you. So, good luck, Jake. Because after that stunt you pulled, you're going to need it."

Jake sat there, stunned, as the reality of the situation began to sink in. This wasn't just about a story anymore—this was about going head-to-head with one of the most powerful men in the state. He had no idea what Richard Jacobs wanted to discuss, but he knew one thing for certain: he was walking into the lion's den, and there was no turning back.

"Do you understand me, Jake?" Claire asked, her voice low and serious. "This is your last chance. If you blow this, it's over. Do you get that?"

Jake nodded slowly, his mind already racing with the possibilities of what the meeting might entail. "I get it," he said, his voice steady despite the turmoil inside him. "I won't blow it."

Claire held his gaze for a long moment, then finally nodded, her expression softening just a fraction. "Good. Now get out of my office and clean yourself up. You look like shit."

Jake stood up, his resolve hardening as he turned and left Claire's office. The door closed behind him with a soft click, but the tension lingered in the air. He knew he was in over his head, but the stakes were too high to back down now.

As he walked back to his desk, he couldn't shake the feeling that this meeting with Richard Jacobs was going to be a turning point—either the breakthrough he needed or the end of his career. And either way, he had no choice but to face it head-on.

CHAPTER 11

The mood in the campaign office was tense, the air thick with urgency as everyone gathered in the conference room. The usual hum of activity had quieted, replaced by the focused, almost palpable energy of a team preparing for battle. Lacy stood at the head of the table, flanked by Paige, Chloe, and her father, Richard. The rest of the spin team sat around the table, each member tapping away on laptops, flipping through papers, or murmuring strategies to one another.

The reason for the tension was displayed on the large screen at the front of the room—a vicious attack ad launched by her opponent, William Harding. The ad was slick, well-produced, and designed to cut deep. It began with a montage of images: Lacy at various campaign events, shaking hands, smiling at the camera, and giving speeches. But the voiceover was anything but flattering.

"Lacy Jacobs—what does she know about family values?" the voice sneered. The screen shifted to show images of Lacy alone, emphasizing her unmarried status. "Unmarried, no children—how can she possibly understand the challenges of working families?"

The ad continued, flashing through her history in politics, taking jabs at her "lack of executive experience" and branding her a "flip-flopper," showing clips of past speeches where her stance appeared to change on key issues. The final image was of Harding himself, surrounded by his picture-perfect family, smiling confidently at the camera.

"When it comes to leading our state, we need someone who embodies true family values, who understands the needs of our communities. Lacy Jacobs is not that person."

As the ad ended, the room was silent for a moment, the weight of the attack settling over them like a dark cloud. Richard was the first to break the silence, his voice sharp and commanding.

"We need to hit him back," he declared, his eyes blazing with determination. "He's attacking your personal life, Lacy. We can't let him get away with that. We need to remind voters of his flaws, his poor voting record, his terrible policies."

Paige nodded in agreement, already scribbling notes on a legal pad. "He's gone personal, and we should respond in kind. Let's dig into his past, his family life. We'll find something we can use against him."

The spin team quickly jumped into brainstorming mode, throwing out ideas for a retaliatory ad. The atmosphere was charged, everyone speaking at once, the room buzzing with the sound of strategies being formed, scrapped, and reformed in rapid succession.

But as the ideas flew, Lacy glanced at Ben, who was standing near the back of the room, arms crossed, his expression thoughtful. She could see the wheels turning in his mind, and when their eyes met, she knew he was thinking the same thing she was. He stepped forward, cutting through the chatter with a calm but firm voice.

"Or," Ben began, his tone measured, "we could take the high road. Let's show the voters that we're above this kind of mudslinging. Let's run an updated ad that highlights Lacy's strengths—her dedication to families, her work on community programs, and the clear, consistent vision she has for this state."

Richard, who had been nodding along with the others, suddenly turned to Ben, his expression hardening. His eyes narrowed just a fraction, his gaze lingering on Ben for a beat too long. "We're not paying you to run this campaign, Ben," he said curtly, his voice carrying an edge of finality. "We're running an attack ad. We're going after Harding's voting record and policies, and that's final."

Ben's jaw tightened, frustration flickering in his eyes as Richard's words hung in the air. He gave Lacy a look, one that was equal parts resignation and something deeper, then turned and left the room without another word.

Lacy watched him go, feeling a pang of guilt and frustration. She turned to her father, hesitating for a moment. "Dad, maybe Ben has a point. We don't want to stoop to—"

Richard's smile was tight, almost patronizing, as he cut her off. "Lacy, I've been in this game a long time. You can't win by being soft. I know what I'm doing."

He paused, and a flicker of something unreadable crossed his face. "Besides," he added lightly, "we have to consider all possibilities, right? Including the loyalties of the people around you."

Lacy's frown deepened, her frustration bubbling beneath the surface. But before she could argue, Richard turned his attention back to the rest of the room, effectively dismissing her. "Let's move forward," he commanded.

Feeling dismissed, Lacy hurried after Ben, slipping out of the conference room and heading down the hall to find him.

She found him in one of the smaller, empty offices, standing by the window with his back to the door. The tension in his posture was unmistakable, his hands clenched into fists at his sides. Lacy closed the door behind her, needing to give them both a moment of privacy.

"Ben," she began softly, but before she could say more, he turned to face her, his eyes flashing with a mix of anger and something else— something raw and intense.

"He can't run your life, Lacy," Ben said, his voice low, edged with frustration. "He can't run your campaign like you're some puppet on a string. You're a grown woman, and you need to act like it."

Lacy's heart pounded as his words struck a nerve. "I know that, Ben," she shot back, her voice rising despite the need to keep quiet.

"But it's not that simple. He's my father. He's always been there for me, guiding me, protecting me—"

"Guiding you?" Ben interrupted, his tone incredulous. "Or controlling you? You're capable of making your own decisions, Lacy. But every time he snaps his fingers, you fall in line like you don't have a choice."

Lacy felt a surge of anger rising in her chest, the heat of it making her blood boil. "You don't understand, Ben. You don't know what it's like to have the weight of all this on your shoulders. The expectations, the legacy—"

"Maybe I don't," Ben admitted, his voice softening, but only slightly. "But I do know that you're stronger than you give yourself credit for. And I know that you can't keep letting him dictate your life."

The intensity between them crackled like electricity, the air in the room thick with unspoken tension. Lacy took a step closer to him, her eyes locked onto his. "Why do you care so much, Ben? Why does it matter to you?"

The question hung in the air, the silence that followed it heavy and charged. Ben's expression shifted, his frustration giving way to something deeper, more vulnerable. "Because I care about this campaign and… I care about you, Lacy," he said quietly, the words slipping out before he could stop them.

Lacy's breath caught in her throat, the truth in his words hitting her like a freight train. She had felt it too, for so long—this pull between them, this undeniable connection that went beyond work, beyond friendship. It was something more, something she had tried to ignore, to deny, but now… now it was out in the open, and there was no turning back.

Without thinking, she closed the distance between them, her hand reaching up to cup his face as she kissed him. The moment their lips met, it was as if the dam broke, all the tension, the frustration, the unspoken feelings between them pouring out in that one kiss. It was fierce, passionate, a collision of desire and emotion that neither of them could contain.

Ben's arms wrapped around her, pulling her against him, the heat of his body searing through her clothes. The kiss deepened, his tongue sweeping against hers, demanding more, giving more. Lacy moaned softly into his mouth, her hands gripping his shoulders as she pressed closer, feeling the solid strength of him against her.

Just as quickly as the kiss began, it was interrupted by a sharp knock on the door, echoing through the small room like a shot. Lacy and Ben flew apart, their breaths coming in short, ragged gasps as they stared at each other, wide-eyed and flushed. The knock came again, and this time a voice accompanied it.

"Lacy?" Chloe's voice called from the other side of the door. "We need you back in the conference room."

Lacy swallowed hard, her mind racing as she tried to collect herself. She looked at Ben, who was still breathing heavily, his dark eyes filled with something she couldn't quite name. "I have to go," she whispered, her voice trembling.

Ben nodded, his jaw tight as he took a step back, giving her space to compose herself. "Go," he said softly, his voice rough. "I'll talk to you later."

Lacy hesitated for a moment, torn between the need to stay and the responsibility pulling her back to the conference room. But there was no time to dwell on it. She straightened her clothes, ran a hand through her hair to smooth it, and opened the door.

Chloe stood there, a look of impatience on her face. "They're waiting for you," she said briskly.

Lacy nodded, glancing back at Ben one last time before hurrying out of the room. As she walked down the hall, her heart still racing, she knew that everything had changed in that one moment. The kiss, the feelings that had surfaced—they couldn't be ignored any longer.

But for now, she had a campaign to win. And whatever was happening between her and Ben would have to wait, at least for a little while.

The city was quiet as Lacy sat curled up on her couch later that evening, the soft glow of a single lamp illuminating the room. The night was still, with only the occasional hum of traffic drifting up from the streets below. In her lap, her journal lay open, the pages filled with her neat, flowing handwriting. She held a pen loosely in her hand, her mind racing as she tried to capture every detail of the day, every fleeting thought and feeling.

But her mind kept circling back to one moment, one memory that had dominated her thoughts since it happened: the kiss with Ben.

Lacy took a deep breath and began writing, her pen moving quickly across the page. She described the way his eyes had darkened with desire, the way his voice had taken on that commanding edge that both thrilled and unnerved her. She wrote about the way his lips had felt against hers—soft and insistent, as if he couldn't get enough of her. She detailed the way his hands had gripped her body, pulling her closer until she could feel every inch of him pressed against her.

As she wrote, Lacy felt a warmth spread through her, a mix of excitement and longing that she hadn't felt in a long time. The memory of his touch, the way his strong hands had explored her body, sent a shiver down her spine. She remembered the way his kiss had deepened, how she had melted into him, completely losing herself in the moment.

And then there was that moment—the evidence of his desire pressing against her stomach. The thought of it made her pulse quicken, her curiosity piqued. What would it be like to let go completely, to explore this thing between them without holding back? It was a dangerous line of thinking, one that could complicate everything, but in that moment, Lacy didn't care.

She was about to reach for her phone, her fingers itching to text Ben, when her phone rang, the sudden sound startling her out of her thoughts. She glanced at the screen and saw her father's name flash across it. For a moment, she hesitated, the memory of their earlier conversation still fresh in her mind. But she couldn't ignore his call, so she sighed and answered.

"Hello, Dad," Lacy greeted, her voice steady despite the whirlwind of emotions she was feeling.

"Lacy, I just wanted to check in on you," Richard's voice came through the line, warm and reassuring. "I know it's been a long day."

Lacy smiled faintly, trying to push thoughts of Ben to the back of her mind. "Yeah, it has. But I'm fine, just going over my talking points for tomorrow's event."

Richard chuckled softly. "Good. It's an important event—getting those young voters engaged. Make sure you're well-prepared."

"I will, Dad," Lacy promised, though her mind was far from the event at Greenbrier University. All she could think about was Ben—how he had left before she returned from lunch, how she hadn't had a chance to see him or talk to him since their kiss. She wondered if he was thinking about it too, if he felt the same way she did.

As Richard continued to talk about the importance of staying focused and on-message, Lacy found herself nodding along, offering the occasional "uh-huh" and "of course." But her thoughts kept drifting back to Ben, to the way he had looked at her, the way he had touched her. She wanted to know if he was feeling the same pull, the same undeniable connection.

When the call ended, Lacy set her phone down and stared at it for a moment, her heart still racing. She was about to text Ben again when she stopped herself, unsure of what she would even say. How do you put into words what had happened between them? How do you explain the intensity of that kiss, the way it had changed everything?

She closed her journal, setting it aside as she leaned back against the couch, her mind still whirling. She wanted to talk to Ben, to see him, but she also knew that crossing that line could complicate everything. Yet, despite all the reasons not to, she couldn't shake the feeling that whatever was between them was real, that it deserved to be explored.

Meanwhile, across town, Ben stood under the hot spray of the shower, his hands braced against the tiled wall as the water cascaded over him. The steam filled the small bathroom, enveloping him in a soothing warmth, but his mind was far from relaxed. He couldn't stop thinking about Lacy—about the way she had kissed him, the way she had felt in his arms.

Ben tilted his head back, letting the water run over his face as he replayed the kiss in his mind. He could still taste her on his lips, feel the softness of her body pressed against his. The kiss had been more than just a release of pent-up tension; it had been electric, charged with a desire he hadn't felt in a long time.

He remembered the way her hands had gripped his shoulders, the way she had pressed closer, as if she couldn't get enough of him. He had felt the same way—overwhelmed by the need to touch her, to claim her, to explore every inch of her body. His heart had pounded in his chest, his blood rushing through his veins as he lost himself in the kiss, in her.

Ben let out a low groan, his frustration building as he thought about how the kiss had ended—abruptly, with a knock on the door. Chloe's interruption had jolted them both back to reality, and he hadn't had a chance to talk to Lacy since. He wondered if she was thinking about him now, if she was as caught up in the memory of the kiss as he was.

He tried to focus on the task ahead—the event at Greenbrier University, the talking points they had discussed—but his mind kept drifting back to Lacy, to the way her body had felt against his, the way her lips had moved with his in perfect sync. He couldn't shake the feeling that this was the beginning of something, that their connection was more than just a fleeting moment of passion.

Ben turned off the shower, stepping out into the cool air of the bathroom. He grabbed a towel, drying off quickly as he tried to push thoughts of Lacy to the back of his mind. But as he got dressed and prepared for bed, he couldn't help but wonder what she was thinking, if she was as conflicted as he was.

He knew that crossing that line with Lacy could change everything, but he also knew that it might be worth the risk. There was something undeniable between them, something that had been simmering beneath the surface for a long time. And now that it was out in the open, he wasn't sure he could go back to pretending it wasn't there.

As he climbed into bed, Ben grabbed his phone from the nightstand, staring at Lacy's name in his contacts. His thumb hovered over the screen, debating whether to text her or leave it for another day. But before he could make a decision, he set the phone down with a sigh.

Tomorrow, he told himself. Tomorrow, he would see her again, and maybe they could talk about what had happened. For now, all he could do was try to get some sleep and prepare for whatever the next day would bring. But as he closed his eyes, the memory of their kiss lingered, a tantalizing reminder of what could be.

The next morning, the team arrived at Greenbrier University, where the atmosphere buzzed with anticipation. Lacy and her team were led to a private waiting area—spacious yet simple, with a few chairs, a long table strewn with papers and laptops, and a coffee station in the corner. Motivational posters decorated the otherwise bare walls, and the hum of campus life outside added to the tension inside.

Paige was focused, running through last-minute details with Lacy. "Remember, Lacy, no matter what Harding says or does today, stay out of the fray. He's going to try to bait you, but we're not stooping to his level."

Lacy nodded, her expression determined. "I won't let him get to me," she promised, her resolve clear in her voice. But even as she said it, her eyes flickered around the room, searching for Ben.

When he walked in, her heart skipped a beat. He looked composed and confident, but the sight of him reminded her of everything she'd been trying to push aside. Lacy felt a rush of emotions—desire, confusion, and something deeper she wasn't ready to name. She quickly reminded herself of the stakes. She was running for governor; she couldn't afford to get distracted by a kiss, no matter how much it had affected her.

Lacy had resolved to put it behind her. She would tell Ben that nothing could happen between them, apologize if she had led him on, and move forward as professionals. But Ben had other ideas. He'd spent the night thinking about her, about their kiss, and he was done pretending it didn't matter. He wanted Lacy, and he was determined to let her know.

Their eyes met across the room, the tension between them palpable. Ben walked to the doorway of the smaller dressing room off the main area, his expression unreadable. Lacy's heart raced—she knew she couldn't avoid this conversation any longer.

"Everyone, could you give us a moment?" Lacy asked, her voice calm and firm. "I need to go over this speech one last time with Ben." Her team nodded and filed out of the room. Once they were alone, Lacy closed the door and turned to Ben, trying to steel herself.

Ben opened his mouth to speak, but Lacy quickly moved across the room, putting as much distance between them as possible. "Ben, I'm running for governor," she began, her voice a little too fast, a little too strained. "The kiss—it was just a mixture of stress and emotions running high. I don't want to lead you on, but we have to stop this. It can't happen."

Despite her words, the lack of conviction in her tone was obvious. Ben could hear it, and so could she. A slow, mischievous smile spread across his face as he took a step closer, closing the gap she had tried to create.

Before Lacy could protest, Ben was in front of her, his presence overwhelming. He reached out, cupping her face in his hands, his touch gentle. "Are you sure?" he asked, his voice low and filled with intent.

"No," Lacy replied, staring deep into his eyes and seeing the same longing reflected back at her.

Then, without giving her a chance to speak again, he kissed her. It was a kiss that left no room for doubt, filled with the same fervor and passion as before, but this time it was charged with a determination that made Lacy's knees buckle.

Lacy gasped into the kiss, her hands instinctively gripping his shoulders as Ben backed her up against the wall. The intensity of it took her breath away, and she felt what little resolve she had left crumbling. Ben's hands slid down her sides, finding the hem of her skirt and hiking it up as he pulled her leg around his waist, pressing her closer.

The heat between them was electric, a current of desire that coursed through them, making it impossible to think of anything but each other. Lacy's mind raced, every part of her telling her to stop, to pull away, but her body betrayed her. She kissed him back with the same fervor, her body responding to his in ways she couldn't control.

Ben's lips trailed down her neck, his breath hot against her skin as his hands roamed over her, igniting every nerve. Lacy moaned softly, the sound muffled by his mouth as he claimed hers again, the intensity building with every second. She was on the verge of surrender, ready to give in to the desire that had been simmering between them for so long.

But just as she was about to lose herself completely, Lacy's sense of duty broke through the haze of passion. With a shaky breath, she pulled away, disentangling herself from him and stepping back on unsteady legs.

Ben let her go, though the intensity in his gaze hadn't dimmed. He watched her, a knowing smirk playing on his lips. "As you wish, Senator Jacobs," he said with a wink, his tone both teasing and respectful as he backed away.

Lacy's heart pounded in her chest as she watched him walk out of the room, the door clicking shut behind him. She leaned against the wall, trying to catch her breath, her mind spinning. She had barely managed to stop herself, but the memory of his touch, his kiss, lingered, making it hard to think of anything else.

When it was time for her to take the stage, Lacy was the picture of composure. She delivered her speech with passion and grace, ignoring the jabs Harding threw her way. The audience was captivated, inspired by her words, and by the time she was done, the applause was deafening.

But as successful as the event was, Lacy couldn't shake the memory of what had happened with Ben. Every time she saw him, her pulse quickened, her mind replaying their heated encounter in the dressing room. She had thought she could forget about the kiss, but now she realized that wasn't going to be possible.

The day eventually wound down, Lacy remained poised and focused, pushing aside the turmoil inside her to project the strength her campaign needed. But when it was finally over and they were back at the hotel, the weight of everything she had been holding back crashed over her.

****

Richard sat behind his massive oak desk, his sharp eyes fixed on the man across from him. The air in the office was thick with tension. The room was elegantly appointed, with rich, dark wood paneling and plush leather furniture, the kind of office that screamed power and control. Large windows offered a sweeping view of the city skyline, but today, they only served as a reminder of the vast empire Richard had built—and the secrets buried deep within it.

Jake Marlowe, the young, tenacious reporter from the State Tribune, was seated in one of the leather chairs opposite Richard. His appearance was disheveled, as if he hadn't slept in days—his shirt slightly wrinkled, dark circles under his eyes. But his gaze was unwavering, a determined glint in his eye as he looked at Richard, unafraid.

"Mr. Marlowe," Richard began, his voice cold and measured, "I'm curious as to why you've taken such an interest in my daughter. You've been harassing her, asking about Michael Hayes—poking your nose where it doesn't belong. Why?"

Jake didn't flinch. He leaned forward slightly, meeting Richard's gaze with equal intensity. "If you've got nothing to hide, Mr. Jacobs, why are you calling this meeting?" His tone was calm, but the challenge in his words was clear.

Richard's eyes narrowed, his jaw tightening for just a moment before he spoke again. "I assume you're here because you think there's a story," he said, his voice smooth and controlled. "But let me assure you—there isn't one."

"Then why was the story buried?" Jake pressed, his voice growing more insistent. "Why did Michael Hayes quit the force right after your wife died? What are you trying to hide, Mr. Jacobs?"

Richard's expression remained impassive, though the tension in the room seemed to thicken. "Michael Hayes was a good man, but he made a mistake—a mistake that cost my wife her life. I buried the story to protect my daughter, Lacy. She didn't need to see her mother's name dragged through the mud. And Hayes… he couldn't live with what he'd done. That's why he quit, I suppose."

Jake's eyes narrowed as he studied Richard, sensing the rehearsed nature of his words. "You're telling me you covered up your wife's affair to protect your daughter?"

Richard leaned back in his chair, his gaze steady and unyielding. "Yes. And I'm telling you this not as a businessman, but as a father. You're chasing ghosts, Mr. Marlowe. There is no story here. I called this meeting to tell you to stay away from Lacy. She doesn't need to be dragged into your baseless investigations."

Richard's fingers tapped against the desk, just once, before going still. "Mr. Marlowe," he said, the slightest edge to his voice, "you're wasting my time chasing them."

Jake held his gaze for a moment longer, then nodded slowly. "Okay," he said finally, his tone almost too agreeable. He stood up as if to leave, gathering his things with deliberate slowness. But just as he reached the door, he paused, turning back to face Richard.

"There is one more thing," Jake added, his voice casual but with an undercurrent of something sharper. "I was looking into some of your businesses, you know, doing my due diligence. And I noticed something interesting. Multiple shell companies, all tied back to you."

Richard's expression remained stoic, but there was a flicker of something in his eyes—annoyance, perhaps, or impatience. "I run many businesses, Mr. Marlowe. That's not exactly a revelation."

Jake took a step closer, his voice lowering as he continued. "These companies—most of them don't seem to do any real business. They exist on paper, sure, but there's no real activity, no employees that I could verify. It's almost as if they're just there to move money around... and obscure its origin."

Richard's fingers tightened slightly on the edge of his desk, but his voice remained steady. "You're grasping at straws, Marlowe. Shell companies are a legitimate business practice, used for asset protection and privacy. There's nothing illegal about it."

"Then there's the matter of your employees," Jake continued, undeterred. "I cross-referenced the names on your payroll with public records, checked their social media profiles. A lot of them don't seem to exist. Fake names, ghost employees—it's almost like you're inflating your payroll to justify high expenses."

Richard's expression hardened, the mask of polite indifference slipping just slightly. "Your half-baked theories are just that—theories. And not very good ones, at that. I have more pressing business matters to attend to than entertaining your baseless accusations. This meeting is over, Mr. Marlowe."

Jake held his ground for a moment, letting the tension simmer between them. He could feel the intensity in Richard's gaze, the faint twitch in his jaw. Jake knew he had rattled the man, even if just a little.

He had planted seeds of doubt, questions that Richard couldn't dismiss so easily.

"Thank you for your time," Jake said finally, his tone respectful, with an edge that hinted at the battle to come. He turned and left the office, the door closing with a soft click behind him.

Richard watched him go, his eyes narrowing as the door shut. He leaned back in his chair, steepling his fingers as he considered the reporter's words. Jake Marlowe was getting too close, asking questions that could unravel everything if he wasn't careful.

But Richard was not a man easily rattled. He had dealt with threats before, and he would deal with this one too. With a slow, deliberate movement, he picked up his phone and made a call.

"We have a problem," he said into the receiver, his voice cold and controlled. "Take care of it. And I need you to retrieve something for me."

Later that night, Jake Marlowe's modest one-bedroom apartment was dark and quiet, the only light coming from the faint glow of the streetlamp outside. It was a cluttered mess of papers, notebooks, and containers of half-eaten takeout. The small space was filled with the scent of stale coffee and the faint, lingering aroma of the last meal he had hurriedly consumed while poring over his notes. His laptop sat on the kitchen table, the screen glowing faintly with the documents he had been working on before exhaustion had finally overtaken him.

Outside, in the shadows of the hallway, two figures moved with calculated precision. Dressed in dark clothing, their faces obscured by black ski masks, they approached Jake's door with the quiet confidence of men who had done this before. The taller of the two expertly picked the lock, the click of the tumblers barely audible in the stillness of the night.

The door swung open silently, and the men slipped inside, their footsteps soft on the worn carpet. The taller man, clearly the leader, motioned to his partner to check the apartment. The second man moved swiftly, sweeping through the small space, ensuring that they were alone. When he returned, he nodded once, indicating that the coast was clear.

Jake was fast asleep on the couch, a blanket haphazardly draped over him. He was unaware of the danger lurking in his home, his breathing steady and peaceful, as if he hadn't a care in the world. But his dreams were about to be shattered.

The taller man approached the couch, pulling out a suppressed handgun from inside his jacket. The cold metal gleamed faintly in the dim light as he raised it, aiming it directly at Jake's chest. The other man moved to the kitchen table, where Jake's laptop was still open. He connected a small device to the laptop's USB port, and within seconds, the hard drive began to erase itself, the data disappearing into the void.

The leader hesitated for just a moment, his finger resting on the trigger. He glanced at his partner, a slight nod exchanged between them—an unspoken understanding. They had done this many times before, and they knew who they were doing it for. Then, with a soft, almost inaudible sound, he pulled the trigger.

The bullet hit Jake square in the chest, the impact jolting him awake in a split second of shock and pain. He gasped, his eyes flying open, his body convulsing as blood began to pour from the wound, soaking through his shirt and pooling on the couch beneath him.

He tried to move, to scream, but the pain was overwhelming, his vision blurring as his body struggled to stay conscious. The last thing he saw was the two men standing over him, their faces hidden, their expressions cold and detached.

Satisfied that Jake was neutralized, the taller man gestured to his partner. "Find it," he ordered, his voice a low hiss.

The second man nodded and began rifling through the clutter on the kitchen table—papers, notebooks, and folders scattering to the floor as he searched. He opened drawers, flipped through files, and finally reached into Jake's jacket, which was draped over a chair. His fingers brushed against something crumpled—a napkin with a photo tucked inside.

He pulled it out, examining the photo of Michael Hayes with a confused frown. "This is what he wants?" the man muttered, turning the photo over. On the back, there was a handwritten note, something scrawled quickly and urgently.

"Why does the boss want this so bad?" the man asked, glancing at his partner, his brow furrowed.

The taller man shot him a hard look, his eyes cold and unyielding. "Who cares?" he replied, his tone sharp. "We're not paid to ask questions. We've got what we came for. Let's go."

He pocketed the photo and then the two men moved swiftly, erasing any signs of their presence. The second man unplugged the device from the laptop, the screen going dark as the hard drive finished erasing. They left no trace behind, slipping out of the apartment as silently as they had entered. The door clicked shut behind them, the sound echoing in the otherwise silent apartment.

CHAPTER 12

The campaign office buzzed with activity as the team prepared for their next stop: Ashland, Virginia. The briefing was in full swing, with Paige at the helm, emphasizing the importance of connecting with small-town voters. "These voters matter," she stressed, pacing in front of the room. "They may be fewer in number, but they're loyal. Winning their support could tip the scales in our favor."

Lacy sat at the table, nodding along as Paige spoke, but her attention kept drifting to Ben. They had been keeping their distance since the kiss, trying to maintain the professional boundary Lacy insisted on. But despite her best efforts, she couldn't ignore the way his gaze seemed to burn into her every time their eyes met. It was an intense, mischievous look that seemed to say, 'you can pretend you don't want this, but I know better'. And the truth was, she did want it—desperately. But she forced herself to focus on the campaign instead.

The next stop was a mobile clinic, a joint effort between the campaign and local healthcare providers to bring medical services to rural communities. It was an important cause for both Ben and Lacy, and she felt a renewed sense of purpose as they discussed the logistics.

After the meeting, Lacy found herself alone with Ben in one of the smaller offices. The energy in the room shifted the moment the door clicked shut, leaving an air thick with unspoken tension. She hesitated, her fingers brushing against the edge of the desk before deciding to break the silence.

"I can't wait to see your hometown," she said, her tone light but carefully measured, trying to steer the moment into safer territory.

Ben's lips curved into a slow smile, one that held just enough edge to make her pulse quicken. "I'm excited for you to see it, Senator Jacobs," he replied, the deliberate formality sharp as a jab.

Lacy rolled her eyes. "Really? Senator? Are you going to stay mad at me forever?"

Ben shook his head, his smile softening, though the intensity in his gaze didn't waver. "Mad? I'm not mad, Senator. I just want you to admit—even to yourself—that you want this." He stepped closer, his voice dipping lower. "And if I can't kiss you, then I won't be calling you Lacy. It's easier to keep things professional that way."

Her breath hitched, but she forced herself to keep her composure. "We can be friends," she offered, her voice carrying a thread of hope, though the uncertainty in her own words betrayed her.

Ben chuckled, a sound as warm as it was exasperated. He tilted his head slightly, studying her. "We could be friends," he said, stepping closer until the space between them all but disappeared. His voice dropped, each word deliberate. "But that's really not what you want, is it, Senator?"

Lacy felt her heart pound as his presence loomed, close and consuming. She swallowed hard, the air around her suddenly charged. "Yes, it is," she whispered, though the words barely made it past her lips.

Ben leaned in just slightly, enough that she felt the heat of him, his lips hovering close enough to brush hers. Lacy leaned in, almost pressing her lips to his. "See?" he murmured, his tone teasing, challenging. Then, just as quickly, he stepped back, giving her the space to breathe even though the tension didn't leave.

"But," he added smoothly, "it would go a long way toward us being friends if you'd agree to meet my grandmother. She's a big fan."

Lacy blinked, caught off guard. "Right... your grandmother?"

Ben gave a lazy shrug, though his grin didn't fade. "I told her you were busy, but she insisted I at least ask. She's got a soft spot for you Senator, apparently."

She hesitated, debating her next move. Frustration warred with curiosity, but beneath it all was something softer—a flicker of intrigue. Finally, she squared her shoulders. "Fine," she said, her tone decisive.

Ben arched an eyebrow. "Fine?"

"Yes, I'll do it," Lacy replied, the words firmer now.

Ben's grin faltered briefly, replaced by a flicker of disbelief. "Seriously?"

"Seriously."

"Really? Why?"

She took a breath, her voice tinged with something that felt almost daring. "Because I want us to be friends, and this will give me a chance to get a lay of the land. Besides, it's 4:30 now—plenty of time to make the trip. Let's go."

She turned on her heel, heading toward the door. But when she reached it, she stopped, realizing Ben hadn't moved. She glanced back over her shoulder, raising an eyebrow. "What? Are you scared?"

Ben laughed quietly, shaking his head as he followed her out. "Not scared," he said, his grin returning with full force. "Let's go."

The drive out to the county where Ben grew up was quiet, the scenery changing from urban sprawl to rolling fields and dense woods. Lacy had intended to stay awake, but the stress of the day caught up with her, and she dozed off as the car hummed along the country roads. When she woke up, it was to the sound of Ben's deep voice gently rousing her. As her eyes fluttered open, she felt a rush of warmth that had nothing to do with the blanket draped over her lap. She realized, with a mixture of comfort and fear, how easy it was to just be herself around Ben—no pretense, no carefully crafted words. It felt so good, so natural, that it scared her. Especially now, during one of the biggest challenges of her life, when letting someone in felt both like the sweetest gift and the riskiest gamble.

And yet, as she met Ben's gaze, she couldn't deny the way her heart seemed to settle, as if some part of her knew this was exactly where she was supposed to be.

"Lacy," he said softly, "we're here."

She blinked awake, rubbing her eyes as she sat up. The car had pulled up to a charming, old-fashioned house with a wraparound porch, surrounded by large oak trees draped in Spanish moss. The air was crisp and clean, a welcome change from the city, and the stars above shone brighter than she had ever seen.

"This is Nonnie's place?" Lacy asked, still groggy but intrigued.

Ben nodded, smiling as he helped her out of the car. "Yep. She's probably been cooking up a storm since I called."

As they walked up to the house, the door swung open, and an elderly woman with a warm smile stepped out to greet them. Nonnie was in her late seventies but had the energy of someone much younger. Her silver hair was pulled back in a neat bun, and she wore a floral apron over her dress.

"Benji!" she exclaimed, pulling Ben into a hug as soon as he reached the porch. "And you must be Lacy," she added, turning to Lacy with a smile. "I've heard so much about you."

"It's so nice to meet you, Ms. Di———------" Lacy replied, returning the hug warmly.

"You stop that. It's Nonnie. And come on in, both of you. Dinner's ready," Nonnie said, ushering them inside.

The meal Nonnie had prepared was nothing short of extraordinary. The kitchen table was covered with dishes. There was homemade lasagna, the pasta sheets layered with rich, meaty sauce and gooey homemade mozzarella, a crisp Caesar salad with homemade dressing, and warm, buttery garlic bread that practically melted in Lacy's mouth.

For dessert, Nonnie had made tiramisu, the layers of coffee-soaked ladyfingers and mascarpone cheese dusted with cocoa powder. The meal was simple, but each bite was packed with flavor, and Lacy found herself savoring every mouthful.

As they ate, the conversation flowed easily. Nonnie was full of stories about Ben's childhood, and Lacy found herself laughing more than she had in weeks. Ben, for his part, seemed relaxed and happy, his usual guarded demeanor softened by the presence of his grandmother. They talked about the campaign, the upcoming event, and Ben's hometown. Nonnie was clearly proud of her grandson, and she didn't hide her approval of Lacy either.

After dinner, they moved to the porch, where they sat under the stars with cups of tea and coffee. The night was cool, and the air was filled with the sounds of crickets and the occasional owl hooting in the distance. Lacy marveled at the sight of the stars, so bright and clear away from the city lights.

As they sat there, Nonnie leaned in close to Ben, nudging him playfully. "You know, Benji, I really like her," she whispered. "You should think about holding on to this one."

Ben laughed, shaking his head. "Nonnie, she's my boss."

Nonnie waved a hand dismissively. "I've seen the way you look at her, Benji. It's not just business."

Lacy, lost in the stars, was jolted back to reality when Nonnie called her name, "Lacy, I'm so glad you came."

Lacy felt her smile widen at Nonnie's words. She loved the older woman's warmth and frankness, and the way she seemed so at ease in her own skin. When Nonnie handed her the beautifully crocheted afghan, calling it the "baby maker," Lacy burst into genuine laughter, the kind that came from deep within her.

"This has been in our family for generations," Nonnie explained, her eyes twinkling with mischief. "We call it the 'baby maker' because it always seems to bring about the next generation." She winked as she handed it to Lacy, who accepted it with a beaming smile, partly because she could see Ben turning crimson beside her.

Ben quickly took the blanket from Lacy and placed it firmly back into his grandmother's hands, his voice rushed. "Okay, thank you, Nonnie. Good night."

Nonnie laughed softly, a knowing look in her eyes. "It also works when the grandmother prays over it," she said, not bothering to look back as she shuffled toward her room.

Ben chuckled and shook his head, clearly exasperated. Lacy, enjoying his embarrassment, decided to tease him a bit. "Ben, your Nonnie was trying to give me a gift. How rude of you," she said, adopting a mockingly prim tone.

Ben's expression shifted suddenly, his eyes darkening, and his voice dropped to a low, teasing murmur as he leaned in close. "If you want to have my baby, all you have to do is ask, Senator Jacobs."

Lacy felt her breath catch, a flush creeping up her neck as she bit her lower lip. Ben's gaze held hers for a moment, something electric passing between them. Then, just as quickly, his smile turned playful and sweet again. He chuckled and winked, breaking the tension. "Thought so. Now come on. I have to lock up, then we can go."

Lacy couldn't help but grin as they headed out, the blanket exchange leaving a warm, amused glow between them. Then Ben chuckled.

When Ben returned, he offered to drive her to the nearest hotel outside of town.

"That sounds fine," Lacy agreed, but then she added with a mischievous smile, "But I'd like to see your apartment first. I have this picture in my head of what it looks like, and I want to see if I'm right."

Ben's smile faltered for a brief moment, surprise flashing in his eyes, but then he chuckled. "Alright, let's go."

As they walked to the car, Lacy felt a flutter of nerves in her stomach. This was different—going to his apartment wasn't just about seeing where he lived. It was about stepping deeper into his world, the parts of him he kept private. Why do I want to know so much? she wondered. She told herself it was to find something, anything, that would make these feelings disappear. Something about him she didn't like. Find a flaw, Lacy, she thought. Find a reason to pull back before you fall too hard.

The closer they got to his apartment, the more she realized how much she wanted to know everything about him, to see if what she felt was just a passing crush or something more. As they pulled up to his place, she could feel the tension building, the anticipation growing with every step.

Ben's apartment was small and cozy, with a comfortable bachelor pad vibe. The walls were a warm shade of beige, and the furniture was practical but stylish— a coffee table made of reclaimed wood, and a flat-screen TV mounted on the wall. There were a few personal touches here and there—a framed photo of Ben and Nonnie on the mantel, a collection of vinyl records in a corner, free weights next to them, and a guitar leaning against the wall.

Lacy was pleasantly surprised. "This is nicer than I expected," she admitted with a grin.

Ben smirked, clearly amused. "Glad you approve."

He ducked into another room, searching for the old photo albums Nonnie had mentioned. Meanwhile, Lacy began to look around, her curiosity piqued. She tried a few drawers, but one wouldn't budge. It was locked.

Ben returned, holding a stack of albums. "Is this where you hide the embarrassing baby pictures?" she teased, nodding toward the locked drawer.

Ben chuckled, shaking his head. "No, but that drawer is none of your business."

Lacy laughed, but as she eyed the photo albums in his hands, her curiosity only grew. Without a second thought, she snatched one from the pile and flipped it open. "Let's see what secrets these hold, then," she said playfully.

Ben rolled his eyes but didn't stop her. "Go ahead, just don't say I didn't warn you," he replied, settling down on the couch beside her.

As Lacy turned the pages, she came across a photo of a chubby-cheeked baby Ben, all curls and big brown eyes, cradled in Nonnie's arms. "Aww, look at you! Benji, you were adorable—and those cheeks!" she giggled, nudging him with her elbow.

Ben groaned, a blush creeping up his neck. "I think we can skip the baby commentary."

But Lacy was relentless. "And who is this handsome little man?" she continued, pointing to another picture of toddler Ben with his parents and Nonnie, all smiles under a bright blue sky. "Your family looks so happy here. Your dad had quite the eye for photography. Look at how he captured the town… it looks so lively, so full of charm."

Ben softened, leaning closer to look at the photo. "Yeah, Dad loved taking pictures around town."

Lacy lingered on a photo of the local diner, its vintage sign bright against the morning light. "I want to see all of this," she said, her voice more earnest now. "Show me the town through your eyes, Ben. Tomorrow. Just you and me."

Ben's smile widened, his eyes bright with a mix of surprise and delight. "You sure you're up for a small-town adventure, Senator Jacobs?" he teased, his voice gentle.

Lacy grinned back, her tone playful but sincere. "Absolutely. I'm always up for a challenge… and maybe I'll find something about you I don't like," she added, half-joking, half-curious.

Ben's eyes twinkled with amusement. "Good luck with that," he said, his voice warm. "But I'd be happy to show you around."

As they left the apartment, heading back to the hotel, Lacy felt a shift between them—something new, something real. The tension that had been simmering for weeks felt less like a barrier and more like a door opening. And for the first time, Lacy felt ready to see what lay beyond it.

Lacy couldn't help the flutter of excitement in her chest as she got ready for the day. Today wasn't about politics, speeches, or the pressures of the campaign—it was a day to explore Ben's hometown, a glimpse into the world he had grown up in. A chance to see the place that made him this man whose aura drew her in.

The next morning when Ben arrived to pick her up from the hotel, she felt more at ease than she had in months. Dressed in a light yellow, halter, floral sundress that complimented her glowing mahogany brown skin, she let her naturally curly hair fall freely around her shoulders. Her smile was radiant, and she noticed the way Ben's eyes lingered on her as she walked up to him.

Ben, in turn, was dressed casually in a gray T-shirt and jeans, his usual buttoned-up demeanor replaced by something more relaxed and genuine. As they set off for the day, the warmth of the sun bathed them in a soft glow, and Lacy felt like she was stepping into a different world—a world that was Ben's.

Their first stop was the local diner, a cozy little place that looked like it hadn't changed in decades. The smell of freshly brewed coffee and sizzling bacon greeted them as they walked through the door. The diner's walls were adorned with framed photos of the town's history, and the booths were filled with regulars who greeted Ben warmly as if he had never left. Lacy couldn't help but smile as they were ushered to a booth by Gladys, a sprightly older woman who had been serving at the diner for as long as Ben could remember.

"Benny, it's so good to see you!" Gladys exclaimed, giving him a warm hug. "And who's this beautiful young lady?"

"This is Lacy," Ben introduced, his smile widening as he looked at her. "She's here to see the sights."

"Well, aren't you lucky to have Ben as your guide," Gladys said with a wink. "He knows all the best spots. Now, what can I get you two for breakfast?"

They ordered a hearty breakfast of pancakes, eggs, bacon, and biscuits with gravy, and as they ate, Ben introduced Lacy to everyone who walked by. She met all the "grandmas" of the town—each one eager to chat with her, sharing stories about Ben's childhood, much to his chagrin.

While they were eating, Ben leaned closer to Lacy and said, "I've always wanted to bring you here, before they shut it down."

Lacy raised an eyebrow, playfully batting her eyelashes. "Oh, really? You think about taking me places?"

Ben rolled his eyes, a smile tugging at his lips.

Lacy giggled, and they both laughed together, drawing a few knowing looks from the older women nearby. In that simple moment, she felt more at ease than she had in a long time. As the laughter died down, Lacy made a mental note to remember this place for an idea. These were the kinds of businesses that needed support, and she found herself appreciating the town even more.

As they continued their journey through Ben's hometown, Lacy felt the pull between them growing stronger, but this time, she didn't mind at all.

After breakfast, Ben and Lacy continued their walk down the main street, each step carrying them deeper into the fabric of Ben's past. Their next stop was the local library, where Nonnie had worked for many years. It was a quaint building, the kind where the scent of old books mingled with the comforting aroma of fresh coffee from a small café inside. The shelves were packed tightly with books that seemed to have a life of their own, each spine a different color, a different story.

Mrs. Porter, the elderly librarian, greeted them with a warm smile as they walked in. "Well, if it isn't Benjamin Carter! And who might this lovely lady be?"

"This is Senator Jacobs," Ben introduced, his voice tinged with affection that he hoped wasn't too obvious.

"Call me Lacy, please. It's a pleasure to meet you, Mrs. Porter," Lacy said, shaking her hand. She couldn't help but notice the twinkle in the older woman's eye as she looked between the two of them.

"Now, Ben, you know you can't come in here without saying hello to Nonnie's old chair," Mrs. Porter said, pointing to a cozy armchair by the window. "She used to spend hours there, reading and telling stories to the kids."

Ben grinned and led Lacy over to the armchair. It was well-worn, its cushions softened by years of use, and it had a comforting presence. Lacy touched the fabric, feeling a pang of envy for the warmth and closeness that Ben and his grandmother shared.

"You know," Lacy began softly, "I think I could see why Nonnie loved this spot so much. There's something special about it."

Ben nodded. "She always said this chair had the best light in the house. She'd sit here and read me stories about faraway places. It's where I first dreamed of going somewhere, of being something."

Lacy looked up at him, caught in the earnestness of his gaze. "And now look at you," she said gently. "You've been all those places, done all those things."

Ben chuckled. "Yeah, but I think this little town had everything I ever needed."

There was a beat of silence as they stood there, their eyes locked. Lacy felt the tension between them, but it wasn't uncomfortable. It was more like a shared understanding, a moment of recognition that neither could deny.

Their next stop was the hardware store where Ben had worked during high school. The store was filled with the scent of wood and oil, the aisles lined with tools, nails, and everything else you might need for a small-town project. The owner, Mr. Thompson, a gruff but kind-hearted man, clapped Ben on the back as they walked in.

"Ben, good to see you, son," Mr. Thompson greeted. "And who's this young lady you've brought with you?"

Lacy introduced herself with a bright smile, and they spent a few minutes chatting with Mr. Thompson about the town, the campaign, and how much things had changed—and stayed the same—over the years. As they spoke, Lacy couldn't help but notice how Ben interacted with everyone with such ease, such familiarity.

She leaned over and whispered, "You're like the hometown hero here, Ben."

He shrugged, a bit embarrassed. "Small town. People talk."

"Well," Lacy teased, "I'm surprised you don't have a statue out front. Something with a cape, perhaps?"

Ben laughed, the sound deep and genuine. "Don't give them any ideas. Nonnie might just start a campaign for it."

As they made their way out, Ben's phone buzzed with an incoming video call. He glanced at the screen, recognizing the names: Daniel, Josh, Sam, and Tony.

He answered with a laugh, holding up a finger to Lacy, signaling it would only take a second. "Hey guys, behave. Remember, my boss is with me."

Daniel's voice came booming through the phone, "The hot one in the pantsuits!" The group erupted in laughter.

Ben rolled his eyes, but turned the phone toward Lacy, who grinned and waved. "Sorry, boys, no pantsuits today."

Josh smirked, "Ben, you better bring her to poker night. Let's see if she's got any game."

Ben tried to decline, but Lacy was quick to interject. "Oh, I'll come, but only if you're ready to lose," she shot back, her eyes twinkling with challenge.

The guys cheered, and Sam said, "That's the spirit! We'll see you tonight then. Better bring your A-game, Ben."

When the call ended, Ben shook his head, a mix of embarrassment and amusement on his face. "You're really going to come to poker night?"

Lacy nodded, her smile wide. "Absolutely. You think I can't hold my own?"

Ben chuckled. "Oh, I know you can. But they don't. Should be fun."

The rest of the day was spent back at Nonnie's house, pouring over old photo albums and sharing stories. Ben's friends' words still lingered in Lacy's mind, and she found herself sneaking glances at Ben whenever she thought he wasn't looking. She felt that familiar flutter of excitement, but also a sense of peace she hadn't known she needed.

Nonnie was in high spirits, her laughter infectious as she recounted tales from Ben's childhood. One story involved a very young Ben trying to "fix" her old car with a toy hammer, and another about him sneaking off to read at the library or play sports with all the neighborhood boys. Lacy listened with rapt attention, feeling more connected to Ben with each anecdote.

At one point, Nonnie paused, looking between Ben and Lacy with a knowing smile. "You know, Benji was always a good boy, but he could be stubborn," she said with a twinkle in her eye. "Reminds me of someone else I know."

Ben groaned. "Oh, come on, Nonnie. I think it's time for you to get some rest."

Nonnie laughed but didn't press further. As she stood, she touched Lacy's arm. "It's good to see him smiling like this," she whispered. "Thank you."

As the evening wound down, Lacy and Ben found themselves alone on the porch once again. The sun was setting, casting a warm, golden glow over everything. Lacy turned to Ben, her expression thoughtful.

"Thank you for today," she said quietly. "I think I needed this more than I realized."

Ben nodded, his gaze steady. "So did I."

There was a beat, a charged silence that hung between them. Lacy felt her heart racing, a blend of nervousness and anticipation. She wanted to say something more, to explore the connection that had been building all day, but instead, she simply smiled and looked away, taking a deep breath of the cool, fresh air.

Ben sensed the shift, the unspoken words between them. "Tomorrow… we'll make more memories," he said softly, almost a promise.

Lacy nodded. "Yeah, I'd like that."

They sat there, side by side, as the last light faded, feeling the closeness in the quiet, the pull between them undeniable. And for the first time, Lacy didn't want to run from it. Not anymore. And that was the scariest part of all.

Ben knocked on the door of Sam's house, his knuckles tapping lightly against the wood. Lacy stood beside him, adjusting her dress and feeling a flutter of nerves. She was supposed to meet Sam and all of Ben's childhood friends. These people were very important to him and she wanted to make a good first impression.

The door opened a crack, and Sam's face appeared, his eyes wide and his expression slightly panicked. He stepped out onto the porch, closing the door behind him with a hurried whisper.

"Hey, so… uh, small change of plans," Sam said, glancing nervously over his shoulder.

Ben raised an eyebrow, a grin already forming. "What's going on, Sam?"

Sam lowered his voice, leaning in closer. "My wife found out Lacy was coming… and, well, she's a huge fan. And then she told a few family members, and they told a few more… and now half the family's here, plus some of the guys from poker night. I just wanted to give you a heads-up, Lacy. It's kind of turned into a full-blown party."

Ben's eyes widened with amusement. "We could head back to the hotel," he suggested to Lacy, his tone light.

But Lacy shook her head, a smile spreading across her face. "No, I want to meet everyone. Let's do this."

Ben chuckled and nodded. "Alright, let's go make some new friends."

They walked through the door into a scene bursting with life. The backyard was packed with people—children darting around, dodging adults who were swaying to the rhythm of a lively R&B tune playing from a portable speaker. The scent of barbecue filled the air, rich and smoky, mixed with the sweeter notes of baked goods cooling on a table.

Lacy took in the scene with delight. There was a grill in the corner, manned by Sam's father-in-law, who was expertly flipping burgers and ribs. The sizzle of meat hit the grill, sending up plumes of smoke and the tantalizing aroma of spices. Someone was pouring cold lemonade and Hennessy into red cups, the ice clinking as it hit the glass.

Sam's wife, Michelle, came rushing over, her face lit with excitement. "Lacy Jacobs! I'm Michelle, Sam's wife. I can't tell you what an honor this is!" She pulled Lacy into a warm hug, then turned to the crowd. "Everyone, Lacy's here!"

A chorus of cheers went up, and Lacy found herself enveloped in a whirlwind of introductions. There were the poker buddies—Daniel, Josh, and Tony—all grinning like kids caught in a prank. The wives and girlfriends hovered nearby, welcoming her with warm smiles and friendly chatter. The energy was contagious, and Lacy felt her heart swell as she moved through the crowd.

She made her way over to where Ben was, now holding an infant—a little boy with big, curious eyes. Ben was making funny faces at the baby, who giggled and clapped his tiny hands. Lacy watched Ben, her gaze softening as she saw the tenderness in his expression, the way he interacted so naturally with the child. She didn't care who noticed her staring. She felt a pull in her chest—a deep, undeniable warmth.

Unlike the donor parties or campaign events, this wasn't about proving herself or convincing anyone of her worth. Here, she was among people who believed in her, supported her, reassured her. They encouraged her with every smile, every nod. She felt her heart expand, filling with something genuine and beautiful.

As the night wore on, **Sam's great-aunt Luellen**—sharp-eyed and elegant in a bright yellow dress—caught Lacy's eye and beckoned her over.

Lacy approached, feeling an immediate respect for the woman, who was seated regally in a wicker chair. Aunt Luellen's voice was strong, and her hands trembled slightly as she reached out for Lacy's.

"I waited a long time to vote, child," Aunt Luellen said, her voice warm but firm, filled with the weight of years. "An even longer time to vote for someone who looks like me. You are a hope I've carried in my heart for so many years."

Lacy felt tears welling up, a lump forming in her throat. She grasped Aunt Luellen's hands, feeling their warmth, the roughness of age. "Thank you," Lacy whispered, her voice choked with emotion. "That means more than I can say."

Aunt Luellen smiled, her eyes twinkling. "Governor Lacy Jacobs," she said with a sassy tone and grin. "Amen?"

A chorus of "Amen!" rang out from the crowd, and Lacy couldn't hold back her tears. She laughed, overwhelmed by the moment, feeling it wrap around her like a blanket of love and support.

"Thank you," she said, her voice full of gratitude. "Thank you for believing in me."

The night was perfect, filled with joy, unity, and a sense of shared purpose. As the party began to wind down, Lacy found herself in the kitchen, helping put away leftovers, while Michelle, along with the other wives and girlfriends, teased her about Ben.

"So… are you and Ben?" Michelle started, her eyebrows wiggling.

Lacy smiled, trying to hide her blush. "We're just… colleagues," she replied, though her eyes drifted over to where Ben stood outside, deep in conversation with Sam.

Ben was standing on the back porch with Sam, who had just sent Michelle back inside with a kiss. Sam turned to Ben, a knowing look in his eye.

"So… you got feelings for her?" Sam asked, getting straight to the point.

Ben hesitated, trying to find the right words. "It doesn't matter," he finally said, his voice low. "She's my boss, and she's running for governor. It's complicated."

Sam shook his head, a smile playing on his lips. "Nah, man, it does matter. The two of you… I don't even know how to describe it, but there's something there. And if there is something, see it through—whatever that means. Don't let fear hold you back."

Ben stared out into the night for a moment, considering Sam's words. Finally, he nodded, a slow smile spreading across his face. "You might be right."

Sam clapped Ben on the shoulder. "Of course I'm right. Now go on, get out of here. You and Lacy have a busy few days ahead."

Back inside, Lacy joined Ben, and they were invited back by everyone, assured they'd always have a place there. As they left, Lacy grinned and called back, "Next time, I'm taking all your money at poker night!"

The whole group laughed, and Ben playfully rolled his eyes. They headed out, stopping by Ben's apartment to grab a few things before heading back to the hotel.

Lacy's mind raced as she wandered around Ben's apartment, her fingers grazing over the framed photos and well-worn books. She couldn't stop thinking about his teasing words from earlier: "If you want my baby, Senator Jacobs, all you have to do is ask."

Her heart thudded in her chest. A mixture of fear and desire washed over her, the kind that left her breathless, on the edge of something exhilarating and terrifying. She'd been afraid to get to know Ben, worried that with every story, every look, every touch, she'd find more reasons to care about him—reasons she couldn't afford. But now, she realized, she hadn't found a single thing to dislike.

When Ben emerged from his bedroom, tossing a few clothes into a bag, he caught her watching him. There was something intense in her gaze, a vulnerability she wasn't used to feeling, and for a moment, she hesitated. But then, without another thought, she closed the distance between them.

"I don't care about anything else right now, Ben," she whispered, her voice low and steady, filled with something she couldn't name. "I want you."

Without another word, she closed the distance between them and kissed him.

Ben's lips were warm against hers, and for a second, he seemed caught off guard. His hands instinctively found her waist, pulling her closer, and for a few moments, he kissed her back with a passion that sent a thrill through her body. She could feel his heart pounding in sync with hers, his breath hot against her skin. She deepened the kiss, pressing herself closer, trying to convey everything she couldn't say in words.

But then she felt a hesitation in his kiss, a pause that made her pull back slightly to search his eyes. Ben's expression was conflicted, his gaze filled with longing but also something else... something that made her chest tighten with fear.

He pulled away slowly, his hands slipping from her waist, his breath ragged. "Lacy," he murmured, his voice hoarse. He looked at her, his dark eyes searching hers, and for a moment she saw the battle raging within him. "I can't... I just can't keep doing this."

"What?" Lacy whispered, her voice breaking. "What do you mean?"

He took a step back, running a hand through his hair, frustration etched into every line of his face. "I mean... I can't keep going back and forth like this. I've done it before—this push and pull, this uncertainty. With Abby... God, with Abby, it was always this way, and it nearly tore me apart. I can't go through that again."

Lacy's heart sank. She had thought they were finally on the same page, that they were both feeling the same pull, the same connection. But now... now his words felt like ice water poured over her hopes.

"So... what was that kiss?" she asked, her voice small and hurt. "Was that a goodbye?"

Ben shook his head, his voice pained but firm. "No, Lacy... I don't know if it's.... I just... I need to know you're sure. I need to know this is something real for you, not just some... escape or a moment of weakness. I can't keep getting pulled in, only to be pushed away when you decide it's too much or too messy. I've been there before. I can't do it again."

Lacy felt tears prick at the corners of her eyes, a mix of frustration, confusion, and heartbreak. "I thought... I thought we were on the same page," she whispered, her voice barely holding steady.

Ben's gaze softened for a moment, but there was still a guarded look in his eyes, as if he was steeling himself against what he had to say next. "Maybe we were... for a moment. But the reality is, we never will be. You know why? Because you'll always choose him. Your father. And he'll always find a way to come between us."

Lacy's heart clenched, his words cutting deep. "That's not fair," she murmured, her voice small, laced with hurt.

Ben let out a bitter laugh. "Fair? Lacy, you can't even stand up to him when it comes to what you want. And I know you want me, but not enough to fight for it. And I'm not going to spend my life fighting a battle I've already lost."

Lacy stared at him, stunned, the sting of his words spreading like a wound she couldn't hide. She felt herself crumbling inside but forced herself to stand tall. "I didn't realize you had so little faith in me… or in us."

Ben's face softened, but the hurt remained in his eyes. "It's not about faith, Lacy. It's about reality. And the reality is, I'll always be worried that when shit gets real you won't stick around or that you don't even really know what you want."

The weight of his words hit her like a punch to the gut. She felt her throat tighten, her heart breaking open. "I understand," she whispered, though her voice cracked on the words. She turned quickly, trying to swallow the lump in her throat. "I… I'm gonna take an Uber back."

Ben's expression flickered with concern, but he held his ground. "Lacy, let me drive you," he offered, a hint of desperation in his voice. But the hesitation was there, and that was all it took for her to pull back completely.

"No, thanks," she replied, her voice stronger now, almost brittle. She was already moving toward the door, her back straight, shoulders squared, even as her vision blurred with unshed tears. "I'll be fine. I'll… I'll see you tomorrow."

She didn't look back as she hurried out, her tears finally spilling over the moment she was outside his apartment, the cool night air hitting her skin like a wake-up call. She had thought, for just a moment, that maybe this was the beginning of something real. But now… now it felt like an ending she hadn't seen coming.

Inside, Ben stood in the silence of his apartment, watching the door slowly close. His chest was tight, his heart pounding with a mix of regret and a strange, hollow ache. He knew he could have said something, anything to keep her there… but he hadn't. He couldn't.

And as the quiet settled in, he wondered if he had just let the best thing in his life slip through his fingers.

CHAPTER 13

The tension in the campaign office had been building for weeks, like a storm cloud ready to burst. Lacy had done everything she could to avoid being alone with Ben, throwing herself into the campaign with laser focus. The mobile clinics were a success, and her new ads—a clever mix of poise and toughness—were resonating with voters. Lacy was doing what she did best: winning.

But she was also doing something she wasn't proud of—she was icing Ben out. She made him directly report to Jason, ensuring they didn't have to interact as much. She stopped asking for his opinion on anything that wasn't strictly business, and whenever they happened to be in the same room, she found an excuse to leave.

Ben noticed every brush-off, every sidelong glance, every casual avoidance. He understood she was upset, but this? This was more than he'd expected. He felt the distance like a raw wound, and it was starting to mess with his head. He was frustrated, he was angry, and for the first time since he joined the campaign, he felt like just a speechwriter—a replaceable cog in the machine.

The final straw came when Jason called in sick, and Lacy sent an intern with her notes for Ben to read over. He was supposed to help her draft a critical speech, but instead, she sent someone else. His patience snapped.

Ben stormed through the office, his jaw clenched. He needed to talk to her, face to face. He needed to understand what the hell was going on. He spotted Lacy down the hall, disappearing into the supply closet.

Perfect.

He marched over, barely pausing to knock before pushing the door open, almost slamming it shut behind him. Lacy jumped, startled, a box of Post-it notes in her hand.

"Really, Lacy?" Ben seethed, his voice low but filled with anger. "You can't even be bothered to meet with me about my job?"

Lacy's eyes narrowed, and she set the box down with a deliberate motion. "Don't you take that tone with me," she shot back, her voice equally hushed but sharp. "I'm your boss, remember?"

Ben scoffed, stepping closer. "Oh, trust me, I remember. How could I forget when you've made it so damn clear these last few weeks?"

Lacy crossed her arms over her chest, her posture defensive, her eyes flashing. "I'm doing what's best for this campaign, Ben. You know that."

"Bullshit," Ben hissed. "This isn't about the campaign, and you know it. This is about you avoiding me like the damn plague."

Ben's eyes were intense, locked onto Lacy's with a mixture of anger and frustration. His voice was low, barely more than a whisper, but there was a sharp edge to it. "You think this is just about your notes, Lacy? About me being some speechwriter you can toss aside when it suits you?"

Lacy glared back, her own voice equally hushed but filled with heat. "You think I'm tossing you aside? I'm trying to keep things professional, Ben! This is a campaign, not some... soap opera."

Ben's mouth tightened, his frustration boiling over. "Oh, that's rich, coming from you. Professional? You've been avoiding me since the night at my apartment. I've been in campaigns before, Lacy. I know what it looks like when someone's trying to keep things professional, and this isn't it."

Lacy felt her chest tighten, her pulse quickening. "Maybe I just didn't want to make things more complicated than they already are. Did you think of that?"

Ben took a step closer, his eyes flashing. "Complicated? I didn't make it complicated. You did! The moment you pulled away... the moment you decided your dad's approval mattered more than what you felt—"

"Don't you dare bring my father into this," Lacy snapped, her voice quivering with restrained anger. "This has nothing to do with him."

Ben laughed, but there was no humor in it. "Of course it does, Lacy. It always does with you. Everything comes back to Richard Jacobs, doesn't it? Every choice, every step... You act like you're this fearless woman, but you're still afraid to piss off Daddy."

Her face flushed with shame and fury. "HOW DARE YOU. I am not afraid of him!" she hissed, stepping closer, their bodies almost touching now. "And what about you comparing me to your ex every chance you get as if things are completely different. There is so much at stake with this election—my family and my career—so fucking forgive me for being a little scared of that!"

"I'm not comparing you to her," Ben shot back, his voice cracking slightly. "But you're doing the same damn thing she did—pushing me away when things get too real, when things get complicated. You think I don't know what's at stake for you?!?"

Lacy's eyes flashed with hurt. "You don't! You don't know what it's like for me! To have to balance this campaign, my father, and... and you. I never expected this! Expected YOU!!" she says, gesturing wildly at Ben, on the verge of tears

Ben's jaw tightened, his voice quieter now but still filled with frustration. "And you think I did!?!?"

Their words hung in the air, heavy and charged. Their breaths were quick and shallow as they stared at each other. Lacy's chest heaved with emotion, her hands clenched at her sides. She felt like she was standing on the edge of a cliff, staring down into the unknown.

For a long, tense moment, neither of them moved, their eyes locked, their faces inches apart. Then, as if pulled by a magnetic force they couldn't resist, Lacy surged forward, her lips crashing into Ben's.

The kiss was instant, born of anger, frustration, and something deeper that had been simmering between them for too long. Ben hesitated for a second, his body rigid with the conflict of wanting her and knowing he shouldn't, but then he gave in. His arms wrapped around her waist, pulling her closer, his mouth moving against hers with a hunger that matched her own.

Lacy's hands gripped the front of his shirt, her fingers twisting into the fabric as if holding on for dear life. The heat of his body seeped through the thin material, his scent—clean and woodsy—filling her senses. She felt the roughness of his stubble against her cheek, the press of his chest against hers, the electric thrill of his hands on her back.

She tasted the lingering hint of cinnamon from his breath, felt the vibration of a low growl in his throat as he deepened the kiss. Her mind went blank, everything else—her father, Abby, the campaign—fading away, replaced by the intensity of this moment, this feeling, this connection.

The kiss turned fierce and demanding as if they could pour all the emotion between them into this one act. Lacy responded instantly, her hands tangling in his hair, pulling him closer as if she needed him to be as close as possible. The taste of him, the heat of his body pressed against hers—it was overwhelming, intoxicating.

Ben's hands roamed over her body, pulling her against him with a desperate need, as if the closeness wasn't enough. The scent of her perfume, light and floral, mixed with the faint smell of paper and ink from the supplies around them, creating a heady mixture that made his head spin. Lacy's fingers fumbled with his belt, their movements hurried, frantic, as if they couldn't get close enough, fast enough.

He lifted her, pressing her against the wall of the small closet, his body fitting perfectly against hers. Lacy's breath hitched, her legs wrapping around his waist as she felt his fingers slide beneath her skirt, the roughness of his touch sending shivers down her spine. She bit back a moan, the sheer intensity of it all nearly overwhelming her. She could feel his breath on her neck, hot and fast, his lips brushing against her skin in a way that made her entire body tingle with anticipation.

Ben's fingers found her, slipping inside with a skillful ease that made Lacy's breath catch in her throat. She ground against his hand, her body instinctively moving to match the rhythm he set, the pleasure building rapidly, almost too rapidly. Her back arched against the wall, her fingers digging into his shoulders as she tried to stay quiet, the sound of their heavy breathing filling the small space.

Before she could even think, Ben was inside her, his thrusts deep and intense, each one sending shockwaves through her. The sensation was agonizingly good, each stroke pushing her closer to the edge, making her want to scream his name. But she couldn't, not here, not now. Ben seemed to sense this, his lips curving into a wicked smile as he pushed her to the brink of madness.

"You wanna scream?" he asked, his voice dark and teasing, almost daring her.

Lacy bit her lip, trying to hold back, but the need was too great, the pleasure too intense. In one swift movement, Ben ripped her panties off, the sound of the fabric tearing echoing in the small closet. He shoved them into her mouth, effectively silencing her, her eyes widening with a mixture of surprise and arousal.

Ben didn't stop, didn't let up. He fucked her harder and harder, his movements almost punishing in their intensity, each thrust sending a wave of pleasure crashing through her. Lacy's hips moved against his, meeting him stroke for stroke, the sensation of him filling her completely driving her to the edge. The taste of her own panties in her mouth, the silkiness of the fabric against her tongue, added another layer of sensation, pushing her closer and closer to the brink.

And then, with a final, deep thrust, they both climaxed together, the intensity of it almost too much to bear. Lacy's entire body shook, her legs tightening around Ben as she rode out the waves of pleasure, her eyes rolling back in her head. Ben held her close, his breathing ragged, his heart pounding in his chest as the aftershocks of his own orgasm pulsed through him.

For a few moments, they just stayed like that, Lacy sitting there with Ben still inside her, their bodies pressed together, the weight of what they'd just done settling over them. Slowly, they began to untangle, the reality of their situation creeping back in. Lacy slid off him, her legs shaky, as she stood up, fixing her emerald green pencil skirt and cream-colored top, her fingers trembling slightly as she tried to smooth her hair back into place.

Ben watched her, his breath still coming in heavy gasps as he adjusted his pants, his eyes never leaving her. He could see the tension in her shoulders, the way she deliberately avoided looking at him. But there was no denying what had just happened between them, no going back from it.

Lacy took a few steps towards the door, her back to Ben, her hand on the doorknob. She paused, just for a moment, before turning back to him, her expression unreadable. "1877 La Salle Ave. The Towers, apartment 1901. Be there around 7:30," she said, her voice steady, but her eyes flashing with a mixture of both satisfaction and lingering desire. "And bring dinner."

She gave him a small, almost teasing smile, a wink that was both playful and charged with the promise of more to come, before turning on her heel and walking out of the closet, leaving Ben standing there, his heart pounding, her torn panties in his hand, and a grin slowly spreading across his face.

Richard Jacobs sat in his darkened home office, the only light coming from the flickering flames in the fireplace. His eyes were fixed on the photograph in his hands, his fingers absentmindedly twirling it around. It was a picture of Michael Hayes, the one he had taken from Jake Marlowe's apartment. The photograph was old and slightly faded,

Michael's young face looking directly into the camera with a serious expression. There was something haunting in his eyes—a mix of determination and vulnerability that Richard couldn't shake.

Richard's face hardened as he stared at it, memories he had buried for years clawing their way back to the surface. His grip tightened on the photo, bending it slightly at the edges. He hated that face. Hated the way it looked at him, even from a simple photograph. But he couldn't stop looking.

His mind slipped back to that night—the night everything changed.

Flashback: The Last Night

The sound of Amanda's screams echoed in Richard's ears as he stumbled back, his hands shaking. The smell of gunpowder and blood hung thick in the air. Amanda lay crumpled on the floor of his office, her eyes wide open, lifeless, staring up at the ceiling. His breath came in short, ragged bursts as he stared at her, his heart pounding in his chest.

It had all happened so fast. Too fast.

Michael Hayes stood in front of him, his gun still raised, his face twisted in a mask of shock and horror. "Amanda!" Michael shouted, his voice breaking, his hand trembling as he stared at the woman he had loved.

Richard's voice was cold and sharp, cutting through the haze of the moment. "What did you do, Michael? What the hell did you do?"

Michael's hand shook violently, his knuckles white around the grip of the gun. "No... no, this was you, Richard," he stammered. "You shot her."

Richard's own gun was still hot in his hand, the weight of it suddenly feeling like a lead brick. He knew the truth, but he also knew how to twist it. "I shot to protect myself, Hayes," Richard hissed, "from a crazed man with a gun who shot my wife because he was obsessed and wouldn't leave her alone."

Michael's face contorted with rage as he his gun at Richard's head. "Don't lie! You know why she was here—why she ended it with you!"

"Because of you," Richard replied coldly, his lips curling into a sneer. "Because you poisoned her mind. But it doesn't matter now, does it? She's dead, Michael… and it's your fault."

Michael's gaze shifted down to Amanda's body, his face crumbling. Tears began to well in his eyes, and for a moment, he seemed to lose all strength. His hand lowered slightly, his breath coming out in desperate, ragged sobs. "Amanda… no… no…"

Richard seized the moment, stepping closer, his voice lowering to a menacing growl. "Get out of my house, Michael. Now."

But Michael didn't move. His eyes darted back to Richard, and the anger returned, sharper this time. "No… I'm not leaving without her," he whispered. "I'm taking my daughter with me. I'm taking Lacy."

Richard felt a jolt of shock course through him, but he kept his face neutral, his mind racing. Lacy. He'd suspected it for years, but Amanda had denied it vehemently. Yet here was Michael, the fool, revealing the truth in his grief.

Richard's voice was steady, but his words dripped with cold venom. "Lacy is not your daughter, Michael. She's mine. She always has been."

Michael shook his head. "No… you know she's mine. Amanda told me everything. I'm taking her, Richard. I'm taking her away from you."

Richard stepped closer, his gun still in his hand but pointed down. His voice was low, filled with threat. "You do that, and I will pin this whole thing on you. The world will know you killed Amanda. Lacy will only ever know you as the man who murdered her mother."

Michael's face contorted in anguish. "You son of a bitch," he spat, his voice trembling with a mixture of fear and fury.

Richard leaned in, his voice calm, almost soothing. "Run, Michael. Leave this town. If you care about her at all, you'll disappear. I will care for Lacy as if she is my own. But if you stay here or try to come back for Lacy… you will lose everything. I promise you that."

Michael's grip on his gun loosened, his face a mixture of despair and defeat. He knew he was trapped, caught between the truth and the lies Richard could spin into something so much worse.

Slowly, Michael nodded, lowering his weapon. "I'll go," he whispered, his voice hollow. "But she'll never be yours, Richard. She'll never be yours."

Richard watched as Michael turned and walked out of the office, his steps slow, heavy with grief and rage. He stayed perfectly still, his gun still held tight, waiting until he heard the sound of Michael's car roaring to life in the driveway. He exhaled slowly, his mind already racing with the steps he would take to make sure no one ever questioned what had happened that night.

Present Day

Richard blinked, his fingers tightening around the edges of the photo until the corners crumpled beneath his grip. His heart hammered in his chest, but his face remained cold, as if carved from stone. Slowly, he set the photo down, forcing the flood of memories back into the dark recesses of his mind where they belonged.

Michael Hayes was gone. Amanda was gone. And Lacy… she was his. She would always be his.

He stuffed the photograph into the drawer beneath his desk, his legs shifting to conceal the movement. The drawer slid shut with a soft scrape, and for a brief moment, his fingers lingered on the handle, as if reluctant to let go of the past. The office door swung open, breaking the moment. Richard's expression was composed in an instant.

A tall man entered, his sleek black suit blending into the dim shadows of the room. His eyes flickered toward Richard, catching the subtle shift in posture, but he made no comment. Instead, he slid into one of the chairs across from the desk, his movements smooth, practiced.

"Sorry to interrupt," the man said, his tone easy and familiar. His smirk flashed briefly in the low light. "Just thought you'd want an update on the latest developments."

Richard leaned back in his chair, his fingers steepling as he observed the man. "Go on," he said, voice cool, betraying nothing.

"The contractors are locked in," the man continued, settling in as if they had all the time in the world. "Deals are solid. They're ready to move as soon as we give the word."

A flicker of satisfaction crossed Richard's features. "Good. Very good."

The man hesitated, a faint smile playing on his lips as he leaned forward slightly. "You know," he began, his voice dropping, "when Lacy wins this election, you'll have the entire state in your hands. Every district. Every official." He paused, letting the weight of those words settle in the air. "No one will dare cross you."

Richard's gaze hardened, his expression shifting into something sharper, darker. He leaned forward, elbows resting on the desk as a slow, calculating smile spread across his face. "When Lacy is governor," he said, his voice a low rasp, "the state will be locked down. Everything in place. Every piece where it needs to be. Make sure you keep the drive protected."

The man nodded, his own smile widening to mirror Richard's. But then Richard's expression turned colder, his eyes gleaming with a hunger that stretched beyond mere political power.

"And when she's president..." Richard's voice dropped to a chilling whisper, his words soaked with ambition. "The world will follow."

The man's grin matched his in darkness. "To the future, then," he said, producing a small silver flask from his jacket. He poured a dark amber liquid into two crystal glasses, the rich color glowing in the muted light.

Richard took one of the glasses without breaking eye contact, raising it slightly. Their gazes locked, and they clinked their glasses together in a soft chime that reverberated ominously through the room.

"To the future," Richard echoed, his tone cold and controlled. They drank, the sharp burn of whiskey cutting down their throats, but neither man flinched. They set their glasses down with a soft clink.

The man leaned back, his smirk returning. "Everything's going as planned. Well," he paused, the smirk fading into something more serious. "Almost everything."

Richard's eyes narrowed, his smile evaporating. "Almost?"

The man shifted in his seat, pulling his jacket tighter around him. "There's a problem with one of the holdouts. Dmitri Ivanov. When we took over his territory, you gave him the same choice you gave the others—die behind your family name or join you. He chose neither."

Richard's fingers drummed lightly on the desk, his expression unchanging. "And now?"

"He's making noise. Rallying the old guard, trying to stir up what's left of his crew." The man's voice dropped, his tone serious now. "If we don't handle him, he'll become a liability."

Richard leaned back, his gaze calculating, cold. "Ivanov..." he mused quietly. "He's always been too proud to know when he's beaten."

The man nodded. "So, what do you want me to do?"

Richard's eyes flickered toward the chessboard on the far end of his desk, the pieces carefully arranged mid-game. His fingers brushed the queen's piece, the symbol of control, power, and strategy. His lips curled into a slow, deliberate smile as he stared down at the board.

"Handle it," Richard said softly, the menace barely veiled in his voice. "And make sure the rest of them understand—I will not tolerate freelancers."

The man gave a single nod, understanding the command beneath the surface. "Consider it done."

A satisfied glint returned to Richard's eyes. He stood, walking over to the large window that overlooked the city skyline. "Good," he murmured, his gaze distant as the weight of his growing empire pressed against his shoulders like a crown.

The man stood as well, giving Richard a final glance before turning toward the door. He paused for a brief moment. "Ivanov won't be a problem for long."

Richard didn't respond, his gaze fixed on the horizon. After a long beat of silence, he spoke again, his voice soft but deadly clear. "Make sure of it."

The man nodded and slipped out the door, leaving Richard alone in the office, the shadows lengthening across the room. Richard stood by the window for a long moment, staring out into the city he was so carefully stitching together.

Soon, he thought, a smile curling at the corners of his lips. Very soon.

Ben arrived at the Towers just before 7:30, carrying a takeout bag filled with Thai food from a small, hole-in-the-wall restaurant they both loved. The spicy aroma of chili, lemongrass, and coconut milk had filled his car on the way over, and now it clung to his clothes, mingling with the faint scent of jasmine that lingered in the hallway outside her apartment. He stood there for a moment, trying to calm the pounding in his chest, his mind consumed with thoughts of her— her taste, her touch, the unrestrained heat that had flared between them in the closet. Now, he was here, and there was no turning back.

He knocked on the door, the sound echoing slightly in the quiet hallway. After a moment, he heard the soft click of the lock, and the door swung open to reveal Lacy standing there, her presence almost taking his breath away. She was wearing an emerald green nightie that stopped just above her thighs, the silk fabric skimming her curves, accentuating the length of her legs. Over it, she wore a matching robe, tied loosely at her waist, the deep green color making her skin look like warm honey in the soft light spilling from her apartment. Her dark hair hung in loose waves around her shoulders, and the subtle scent of shea butter clung to her, sweet and rich, like something you wanted to taste.

Her eyes sparkled with a mix of mischief and desire as she looked him over, noticing the way his gaze traveled from her face to the hem of her nightie. "Right on time," she murmured, her voice low and teasing. She stepped aside, letting him in, the silk of her robe brushing against his arm as he passed by, leaving a trail of warmth in its wake.

Ben entered, the spicy scent of the Thai food blending with the smell of her skin, creating a heady mixture that made his head spin. The apartment was sleek and modern, with a breathtaking view of the city through the floor-to-ceiling windows. But his attention was entirely on her. Lacy closed the door behind him with a soft click, her eyes never leaving his.

"What did you bring?" she asked, tilting her head slightly, her lips curving into a small smile.

"Pad Thai, green curry, and those spring rolls you like," he replied.

She raised an eyebrow, amused. "Mmmmm, that sounds delicious."

Ben took a step closer, his eyes locked on hers, a grin tugging at his lips. "Yes, it does."

Lacy turned and walked toward the kitchen, her hips swaying slightly, the silk of her nightie clinging to her as she moved. Ben followed, unable to tear his eyes away. She set the bag down on the counter, opening it and peeking inside, the fragrant spices of the food filling the air.

He stepped up behind her, so close that he could feel the warmth radiating from her body. His hand reached around her, fingers brushing hers as he helped her open the container. She didn't pull away; instead, she leaned back slightly, pressing her back into his chest. He couldn't resist leaning down, his lips brushing against the back of her neck.

She shivered at his touch but didn't move, didn't speak. "Hungry?" she asked, her voice just above a whisper, her breath catching slightly.

"Starving," he murmured against her skin, his hands sliding to her waist, pulling her back against him more firmly.

Lacy turned in his arms, her smile widening. She placed her palms flat against his chest, feeling the rapid thud of his heartbeat under her touch. "Good," she whispered, her voice thick with anticipation.

Ben's breath hitched, and in one swift motion, he cupped her face and kissed her hard, tasting the lingering sweetness of her shea butter lip balm mixed with the faint traces of wine. She responded instantly, her arms wrapping around his neck, pulling him closer. The kiss was a collision of need and desire, filled with all the frustration and tension that had built up between them over the past few months.

He pushed her back against the kitchen island, the cool granite contrasting with the heat of their bodies. Lacy's fingers tangled in his hair, tugging him closer as his hands slipped beneath her robe, feeling the smooth silk of her nightie and the warm skin beneath it. She arched into his touch, her breath hot against his cheek as she whispered, "Don't stop."

Ben grinned against her lips, his hands moving to the sash of her robe, pulling it loose with one quick tug. The robe fell open, revealing the full curve of her breasts, the delicate lace trim of her nightie, and he felt his pulse quicken. His hands roamed over her body, caressing the soft fabric, feeling the heat of her skin beneath. She moaned softly, her nails digging into his shoulders as he dipped his head, kissing along her collarbone, tasting the slight saltiness of her skin mixed with the warm, nutty scent.

Her head fell back, a soft moan escaping her lips as his tongue trailed down her throat, his hands sliding to her waist, gripping her tighter. "Ben," she gasped, her voice a breathy plea, and he felt a jolt of desire run through him, straight to his core.

He lifted her onto the counter, his hips fitting perfectly between her legs as she pulled him closer, her body arching to meet his. The silk of her nightie slid up her thighs, exposing more of her skin to his touch, and he felt the soft brush of her inner thighs against his hands. His mouth found hers again, a fierce, demanding kiss that tasted like wine and spice, and something uniquely her.

Lacy's fingers found the hem of his shirt, tugging it up and over his head, her touch feverish, impatient. He could feel the cool air against his skin, followed by the warmth of her hands as she explored his chest, tracing the lines of his muscles with her fingertips. He groaned, his hands sliding beneath her nightie, feeling the smooth, silky skin of her thighs, his fingers brushing higher, making her breath hitch.

Lacy gasped against his mouth as Ben's fingers slid inside her, his touch deliberate and demanding. Her hips bucked forward instinctively, a moan slipping past her lips as she felt his fingers curl, finding that perfect spot that made her entire body tremble. He moved with a confidence and skill that sent electric sparks of pleasure through her, making her toes curl against the cool granite countertop.

She dug her nails into his back, urging him on, her breath coming in quick, ragged gasps. The scent of her mingled with the sharper, spicier notes of the Thai food, filling the air around them with a heady mix that made everything feel more intense, more vivid. Her legs tightened around his waist, pulling him closer as she whispered his name, her voice thick with need.

Ben's thumb circled her clit, slow and teasing, making her body arch off the counter as he held her steady with his free hand.

"Y-Yes," she stammered, her head falling back, her eyes fluttering shut. "Don't stop… please don't stop."

He began to move faster, his fingers thrusting deeper, matching the rhythm of his thumb's movements. He could feel her tightening around him, her breath coming in shorter, more frantic gasps, and he knew she was close. He pressed his thumb harder against her clit, increasing the pressure just enough to send her right to the edge.

Lacy's hands flew to his shoulders, gripping him tightly as she came undone around him, her body shuddering with the force of her climax.

She let out a low, keening cry, her nails digging into his skin, her thighs trembling against his hips. Ben watched her, mesmerized, feeling the way her body clenched around his fingers, the way her breath caught in her throat.

He withdrew his fingers, making her whimper at the sudden loss, only to slide his hands up her thighs and hook them around his waist. She barely had time to catch her breath before he positioned himself at her entrance and, pausing for a brief moment, slid his other hand to his back pocket, pulling out a condom. He grinned at her as he ripped the packet open, her eyes dark with anticipation as she watched him roll it on with practiced ease.

With one smooth, powerful motion, Ben thrust into her, stretching her, filling her completely. Lacy's head snapped back, her mouth opening in a silent scream as pleasure rushed through her, sharp and overwhelming.

Her legs tightened around his waist, pulling him deeper, her body craving more.

Ben's grin widened as he felt Lacy's body arch against him, her moans spurring him on. His hands gripped her waist, pulling her closer until there was no space left between them. The soft, silky fabric of her nightie bunched around her hips, her skin warm and smooth under his palms. He could feel the beat of her heart, quick and frantic, matching the rhythm of his own.

He kissed his way down her chest, trailing his lips over the swell of her breasts, flicking his tongue over her nipples as she gasped, her body trembling under his touch. "Ben… oh, God…" Her voice was a low, breathless moan, her hands tangled in his hair, pulling him closer, needing more of him.

He thrust into her again, harder this time, and Lacy's head fell back, a guttural moan escaping her lips. Her body clung to his, her nails dragging down his back as she matched his rhythm, each thrust sending waves of pleasure crashing through her. She felt him everywhere—inside her, around her, the solid strength of his body pressing against hers. The sensation was dizzying, every inch of her skin alive with need.

"Ben," she whimpered, her breath coming in ragged gasps as the heat between them built to a fever pitch. His hands gripped her hips tighter, pulling her closer, and with each thrust, he could feel her tightening around him, her body trembling on the edge.

He growled low in his throat, his lips finding her neck, biting down gently as he whispered, "Come for me, Lacy. Now."

His words sent a shudder through her, and she obeyed, her body giving in to the overwhelming pleasure. Her climax hit her hard, and she cried out, her entire body convulsing in his arms. Her thighs trembled around his waist, her nails leaving marks on his back as she clung to him, riding out the intense wave of sensation.

Ben followed her over the edge moments later, his grip on her tightening as he buried himself deep inside her one last time, his body tensing as he came, his breath hot and heavy against her skin. His release was powerful, intense, the culmination of everything that had built between them.

For a moment, there was nothing but the sound of their ragged breathing, the pounding of their hearts, and the warmth of their bodies pressed together, trembling and slick with sweat. Slowly, their breathing steadied, and Ben leaned back slightly.

Afterward, he lifted his head, his forehead resting against hers, their eyes meeting in the dim light of the kitchen. Lacy's smile was soft, a little dazed, but filled with a warmth that made Ben's heart pound even harder.

She touched his cheek, her thumb brushing against his stubble. "That was… wow," she whispered, a breathy laugh escaping her lips. Ben chuckled, his thumb tracing lazy circles on her hip.

"Yeah… definitely wow," he agreed, his voice low and rough. She leaned forward, capturing his lips in a slow, tender kiss, tasting him, savoring the moment. "We should… eat before the food gets cold," she murmured against his lips, a hint of playfulness in her tone.

Ben grinned. "You should go pee first," he teased, brushing his thumb over the piercing one last time, sending a small shiver through her. "While I set the table."

Lacy laughed softly, swatting his hand away. "Fine, fine. I'll freshen up," she said, sliding off the counter with a delicious ache in her body, her legs still a bit unsteady. She walked toward the bathroom, the green silk of her nightie swishing around her thighs, leaving Ben watching her go, a deep warmth settling in his chest. As she disappeared into the bathroom, Ben busied himself in the kitchen, setting out plates, pouring wine, and arranging the food.

By the time Lacy returned, her hair brushed, face fresh, and the nightie adjusted back into place, he had transformed the kitchen into a cozy dining spot. "Looks good," she said with a soft smile, taking a seat and smoothing the fabric of her nightie over her thighs. She looked over at Ben, sliding a glass of wine her way. They ate quietly at first, letting the comfortable silence stretch between them, the spicy, rich flavors of the Thai food mingling with the memories of what they'd just shared. But as the meal continued, Lacy set down her fork, her gaze turning serious. "So… what do we do about this?" she asked, her voice soft but steady.

Ben leaned back in his chair, considering her words. "We keep it quiet," he replied. "For now, at least. Until after the election."

Lacy nodded, biting her lip. "Agreed."

They sat in silence for a moment, letting the weight of their decision settle. Then Lacy smiled, her eyes sparkling again. "We can do this," she said, her voice filled with quiet determination. "We just have to be smart."

Ben reached across the table, squeezing her hand. "We will be. And after the election… we figure out the rest."

A slow smile spread across her face as she nodded in agreement. They cleaned up after dinner, working together seamlessly, sharing small touches and quiet laughter as they moved around the kitchen.

Once the dishes were done, Lacy grabbed a couple of wine glasses and led Ben toward the bedroom.

"Since we're supposed to keep things low-key," she said with a grin, "how about we watch a show?"

Ben raised an eyebrow. "What are we watching?"

Lacy's grin widened as she grabbed the remote and settled onto the bed, patting the spot next to her. "Narcos," she said with a smirk. "I've been saving it for a while. Seemed like a good time to start."

Ben chuckled, slipping out of his jeans and joining her in bed, wearing only his boxers. "Narcos, huh? I'm down. Though I've gotta admit, I might get distracted."

Lacy laughed, leaning into him as she pulled up the third episode. "We'll see how long you last."

They snuggled under the covers, Lacy resting her head on Ben's shoulder as the opening credits rolled. The room was dimly lit, warm and cozy, and despite the tension that had been brewing all evening, everything now felt peaceful.

As the episode played on, Ben wrapped his arm around Lacy, pulling her closer, and she relaxed into him, her fingers absently tracing patterns on his chest. The show's drama unfolded on the screen, but their attention drifted, content just to be close to each other.

By the time they reached the next episode, Lacy's eyelids were growing heavy. She stifled a yawn, snuggling deeper into Ben's side. "Think I'm about to fall asleep," she murmured, her voice drowsy.

Ben kissed the top of her head, his voice soft and warm. "That's okay. I'm not going anywhere."

Lacy smiled, her breath evening out as sleep slowly claimed her. Ben kept watching the show for a while longer, but eventually, his own eyes began to droop. He turned off the TV, pulling the covers up around them as they both drifted off, wrapped up in each other, with the promise of more nights like this to come.

Lacy woke to the soft light of morning filtering through the curtains, the bed beside her empty but still warm. She blinked, slowly coming to her senses, her hand instinctively reaching out to the spot where Ben had been, only to find it vacant. A faint smile tugged at her lips as she stretched, the pleasant ache from the night before reminding her of everything they had shared. The rich, buttery scent of something delicious wafted through the apartment, filling the air with the unmistakable aroma of freshly brewed coffee and what smelled like pancakes. The house was quiet, but the warmth of Ben's presence lingered, wrapping around her like a comforting blanket.

She slipped out of bed, her nightie falling softly against her thighs, and reached for the robe she had discarded the night before. Wrapping it around herself, she padded barefoot down the hallway, following the mouthwatering aroma to the kitchen.

When she entered, she saw Ben at the stove, his back to her, expertly flipping an omelette in one pan while French toast sizzled in another. He was dressed in only his boxers and a simple white T-shirt, his hair slightly tousled from sleep. The sight made Lacy's heart skip a beat, a feeling of warmth and contentment spreading through her.

As if sensing her presence, Ben turned, a wide smile spreading across his face as soon as he saw her. "Good morning, beautiful," he said, his voice soft and filled with affection.

Lacy's smile mirrored his as she walked over to him, standing on her toes to press a quick kiss to his lips. For just a moment, she allowed herself to push away the doubts about what this was or what it could be. Right now, she was just a girl, and he was just a guy who had spent the night and was now making her breakfast. Nothing more, nothing less.

"This all looks so good," Lacy said, glancing over the array of food he'd prepared. There were golden-brown French toast slices, fluffy omelette filled with vegetables and cheese, and a side of crispy bacon. She raised an eyebrow playfully. "But it's just the two of us. This is a lot of food, don't you think?"

Ben chuckled, shaking his head. "You only think it's a lot because you consider coffee a meal," he teased, his voice taking on a lovingly commanding tone. "Go sit down. I'll make you a plate."

Lacy laughed softly, appreciating the care he was putting into this simple moment. She did as he said, taking a seat at the small dining table, the warmth from the kitchen wrapping around her like a cozy blanket. She watched him move with ease and confidence, feeling a surge of affection for this man who could make her feel so cared for with just a few simple gestures.

When Ben brought the plates over, the food looked even better up close, and the aroma was irresistible. They began eating, the conversation light and easy. As they enjoyed their meal, Ben suddenly looked at her with a mischievous glint in his eye.

"So," he said casually, his tone laced with playful curiosity, "you're really into some kinky stuff, huh?"

Lacy nearly choked on her bite of French toast, coughing slightly as she laughed. "Whatever do you mean?" she responded, trying to sound demure but failing miserably as her cheeks flushed.

Ben leaned closer, his eyes darkening with amusement and something more as he kissed her, his lips lingering on hers for just a moment. "I was just thinking about how you let me fuck you with your panties in your mouth in the supply closet," he whispered against her lips, his voice low and teasing.

Lacy's blush deepened, but she couldn't help the smile that tugged at her lips. "I may have certain... how you say... desires," she admitted, her voice light but tinged with a hint of coyness.

They both laughed, the sound filling the kitchen with warmth and ease. But then Ben's expression softened, a more serious look in his eyes as he took her hand in his. "I hope one day you'll share them all with me," he said quietly, his voice sincere.

Lacy's heart fluttered at his words, and she felt a rush of emotion she hadn't expected. "Maybe I will," she replied softly, her smile returning as she leaned in to kiss him gently on the forehead.

They finished their breakfast, the conversation shifting back to lighter topics as they cleaned up together, laughing and joking as they washed the dishes, the two of them falling into an easy rhythm that felt natural, right.

After the kitchen was clean, they showered together, the intimacy of the morning extending into the warm spray of water. Lacy felt a deep sense of comfort in the way Ben's hands moved over her skin, the tenderness in his touch contrasting with the playful banter that continued between them. It was easy, being with him, and for once, she didn't overthink it. She just let herself enjoy the moment.

Once they were dressed, Lacy had her personal shopper deliver some clothes for Ben, and he couldn't resist making a joke about "how the other half lives," which made Lacy laugh out loud.

As they settled back into the living room, Ben asked her what she had been up to lately. Lacy's face lit up with excitement as she began to tell him about a secret project she had been working on, inspired by her time in his hometown. She laid out her plan to promote small businesses in rural towns across the state, using her social media to highlight local shops and creating a small business directory on the state's website. She explained how she was planning to launch this initiative at Gladys's Diner in two weeks, hoping to drum up business for the beloved local spot before moving on to Sal's.

Ben listened intently, clearly impressed but not at all surprised by her intelligence and passion. When she finished, he leaned in and kissed her, a deep, lingering kiss filled with admiration. "Lacy, that's amazing. You should be so proud of what you're doing."

She blushed slightly, her heart swelling with pride and something more as she kissed him back. "Thank you," she murmured against his lips, feeling a connection between them that went beyond the physical.

They spent the rest of the morning cuddled up on the couch, watching a movie and enjoying each other's company. But eventually, Ben had to leave to check on Nonnie. He promised he'd call when he got back home, and Lacy nodded, feeling a pang of sadness as she walked him to the door.

After he left, Lacy invited Paige over to talk about her small business initiative. Paige loved the idea, and they spent the rest of the day working through the logistics, refining the plan, and brainstorming ways to make the launch a success.

Later that evening, after Paige had left, Lacy decided to take a long, relaxing bath. She poured Epsom salts and bubble bath into the steaming water, letting the warm, fragrant water soothe her muscles as she sank into the tub. She closed her eyes, her thoughts drifting back to Ben and the way he had made her feel that morning.

Just then, her phone rang, and she smiled when she saw Ben's name on the screen. "Hey, Lacy. You busy?" his voice came through, warm and familiar.

"No, just in the tub," she replied, her smile widening.

His voice took on a sultry tone. "Then I called at the right time. What are you wearing?" he joked, his voice teasing.

Lacy laughed, the sound bubbling up naturally. "A scuba suit," she responded playfully.

"Mmm," Ben replied with a chuckle, "I bet you look hot in that."

They both laughed, the conversation flowing easily as they talked about their days. It was comfortable, the kind of back-and-forth that felt like second nature, like they'd been doing this forever. After a while, they said their goodnights, Ben reminding her to get some rest since she had an early interview the next morning.

Lacy hung up the phone, still smiling, and floated on air as she dried off and got ready for bed. As she slid under the covers, she couldn't help but notice that her pillow still smelled faintly of Ben, a mix of soap and something uniquely him. She hugged the pillow close, feeling a sense of contentment wash over her as she closed her eyes.

Sleep came quickly, and as she drifted off, her thoughts were filled with images of Ben—his smile, his laugh, the way he had held her that morning, making her feel safe and cherished. She fell asleep with a peaceful smile on her lips, feeling more content than she had in a long time, already looking forward to the next time she would see him.

CHAPTER 14

The hospital room was heavy with the sterile scent of antiseptic and the steady beeping of the machines surrounding Jake Marlowe's bed. The room was dimly lit, the only light coming from the soft glow of a bedside lamp. Mary and Thomas Marlowe sat beside their son, holding onto his hands, their faces pale and etched with grief.

Jake lay there, his chest rising and falling with the mechanical breaths of the ventilator, his face still, almost peaceful. His mother's fingers trembled as she brushed a strand of hair from his forehead, her other hand clutching his lifeless fingers with a desperate grip. She had been praying for a miracle, but now… now the doctors had told her there was no hope left.

A doctor entered, his expression somber, and nodded to Thomas. "It's time," he said softly, his voice filled with the gravity of what was about to happen. "Are you ready?"

Mary's breath caught in her throat, her eyes filling with tears that blurred her vision. She nodded, even though every fiber of her being screamed no. Thomas squeezed her hand, his own eyes brimming with unshed tears, his face a mask of stoic pain. "We're ready," he whispered, his voice raw.

The doctor reached over and switched off the machine, the steady beep fading into an unbearable silence. Mary felt her heart break open in her chest, the reality of what was happening hitting her like a wave.

She clung to Jake's hand, her tears spilling freely now, as if trying to hold onto him for just a few moments longer.

The room was filled with a stillness that felt like it could crush them all. Finally, the doctor placed a hand on Jake's chest, listening with a stethoscope before speaking the words Mary had dreaded: "Time of death… 3:47 p.m."

A wail tore from Mary's throat, a sound so raw and primal that it seemed to come from the very depths of her soul. "No! No, no, no!" she sobbed, collapsing against Jake's bed, her shoulders shaking with grief. "My baby boy… my baby boy…"

Thomas wrapped his arms around her, trying to steady her, his own tears finally spilling over. "Mary… please," he whispered, though his voice cracked with his own anguish.

A detective, standing just outside the door, hesitated before stepping inside. Detective Harris, a seasoned officer with deep lines etched into his face from years on the job, cleared his throat. "Mr. and Mrs. Marlowe," he began, his voice gentle but firm. "I'm so sorry for your loss. I wanted to let you know… we've done everything we can, but… we haven't been able to find anything. The case has gone cold."

Mary's head whipped around, her eyes blazing with fury and grief. "Cold?" she repeated, her voice rising. "Cold? He was murdered, and you—" her voice broke into a scream, "you've done nothing!"

Detective Harris shifted uneasily on his feet, glancing down at the floor before meeting Mary's eyes. Her outburst had left him momentarily stunned, but he knew he needed to explain.

"Mrs. Marlowe, I know how this looks," he began, his voice strained. "We've swept the scene more than once. We spoke to every potential witness in the block, combed through hours of surveillance footage, and checked every angle we could. But… there's just nothing new, no leads, nothing we can use to move forward."

Mary's face contorted with anger and disbelief. "Nothing?" she repeated, her voice incredulous. "You're telling me that my son—my son, who was a good man, a reporter just doing his job—was shot in his own home, and you found nothing?"

Harris felt the weight of her accusation. "I understand your frustration, ma'am. I do. But these things… they're not always simple." He swallowed hard, trying to find the right words. "We canvassed the neighborhood. No one saw anything out of the ordinary, and there were no signs of forced entry. Whoever did this was careful. They knew what they were doing. They left no prints, no evidence… and no witnesses who could give us a clear description."

Mary shook her head, her hands trembling. "Then what about the footage? You said there were cameras… why can't you find anything?"

Harris sighed, rubbing the back of his neck. "The cameras outside the building… they were tampered with. Whoever did this had cut the feed. All we got was a brief clip of two men in masks entering the building. It's not enough to make an ID. And the hallway cameras… they didn't catch anything useful either. The footage was corrupted."

"That's it?" Mary's voice cracked, her anger turning to despair. "You've given up?"

Thomas, his voice thick with emotion, spoke up, trying to keep his composure. "Detective, there's got to be something. We can't just… let this go."

Harris sighed deeply, sensing the desperation in Thomas's voice. "I promise you, we're not giving up," he replied, his tone softening. "But we're at a standstill. With no new evidence, we have nothing to build a case on. We've done everything we can with the resources we have. Unless something changes, we don't have enough to keep this active."

Mary's face crumpled, her voice rising to a near scream. "No! No, that's not enough! My son was murdered, and you're telling me it's just going to end like this? You're just going to close the file and move on?"

She lunged forward, her fists pounding on Detective Harris's chest, each word punctuated by a sharp, angry hit. "Do something! Do something! My baby boy is dead!"

Harris stepped back, raising his hands defensively, but his face showed nothing but empathy and exhaustion. "Mrs. Marlowe, please... I'm so sorry. I wish there was more we could do."

Thomas quickly moved in, wrapping his arms around Mary, pulling her away from the detective. "Mary, please... come on," he whispered, trying to soothe her, his own eyes brimming with tears. "We have to go. There's nothing more they can do right now."

Mary collapsed against her husband, sobbing uncontrollably, her voice breaking with grief. "My baby boy... Jake... he didn't deserve this... he didn't deserve any of this..."

Her wails echoed through the sterile hallway of the hospital, piercing and raw, filled with a pain that seemed too much for her body to contain.

Harris watched, his heart heavy, feeling the weight of his own inadequacy. He had seen this pain before, this kind of heartbreak. But this... this was different. Jake Marlowe had been digging, asking dangerous questions, poking around where few dared to tread. And now, the trail had gone cold, and he had no answers for a mother whose life had just been shattered.

Mary's cries gradually softened, her energy spent, her body trembling against Thomas's. The detective waited, wanting to offer something—anything—to give her hope. But all he had were empty hands and a case that seemed to slip further from his grasp with every passing day.

"I'm sorry," he repeated, his voice thick. "I truly am."

Mary's eyes lifted, a fiery determination cutting through her grief. "Then find whoever did this," she spat, her voice hoarse. "Find them, or I will. You hear me? I will."

Thomas nodded, holding his wife tighter, as if he could shield her from the harshness of the world. But he knew there was no shield, no protection from the reality that had invaded their lives. They were alone now—except for the memory of their son, and the desperate need to see his killer brought to justice.

CHAPTER 15

The campaign bus rolled into Ashland, Virginia, Ben's hometown, greeted by what seemed like the entire population, with the mayor leading the welcoming committee. The air buzzed with excitement, everyone eager to see their town featured on the news. Even Gladys, the beloved diner owner, was beaming with pride at the thought of her little place making it onto TV. The warm reception filled the air with a palpable energy, and the sight of familiar faces made Ben's heart swell with pride.

As the bus doors opened, Lacy stepped out, greeted by cheers and applause. Nonnie was there, along with Ben's friends from high school, Ben was holding Sam's niece, a chubby-cheeked baby girl who was all smiles. When Lacy reached them, Ben passed the baby to her. The little girl immediately reached out, touching Lacy's face with her tiny hands, and Lacy's heart melted. She smiled down at the baby, her warmth evident in her eyes. The crowd collectively sighed, and the moment was captured perfectly by the photographers, a picture-perfect moment that would soon be all over social media.

After finishing her greetings, Lacy handed the baby back to Ben and made her way to the hotel conference room to meet with her staff. She was all business now, preparing them for the days ahead. The room buzzed with focused energy as she went over the plan, assigning tasks and ensuring everyone was ready for the busy schedule. But as Lacy spoke, Ben's eyes never left her. He watched her with a mix of admiration and desire, every word she spoke only intensifying the pull he felt towards her.

It had been a few days since they last saw each other, and even longer since they had been together in the way he craved. Ben had gone ahead to his hometown to talk to everyone and rally support, proving he was more than just a speechwriter as he handled some logistics as well. But now, being so close to her again, the anticipation was driving him wild.

As the meeting wrapped up, Lacy dismissed everyone with tasks to complete. Before leaving, she gave Ben a sly smile and a wink, disappearing towards her room. Ben's heart raced—he knew that look. As he made his way to his own room, he couldn't stop thinking about her, the way she moved, the way she looked at him. But as soon as he entered his room, he knew he had to see her.

Lacy had barely closed the door behind her when she heard a knock. Her heart pounded, knowing exactly who it was. She opened the door to find Ben standing there, his eyes dark with desire. They barely had time to shut the door before they were all over each other, their kisses intense, their hands roaming desperately as if trying to make up for the time apart.

Ben backed her against the wall, his lips never leaving hers, his voice low and commanding. "Don't ever be gone that long again," he growled, his eyes burning with intensity.

"Yes, sir," Lacy breathed, her response sending a shiver of arousal down his spine. Ben growled, even more turned on by her words, and their kisses deepened, their bodies pressing against each other in a fevered need.

But then Lacy pulled back slightly, her breath coming in ragged gasps. "We can't right now," she panted, even as she continued to kiss him, unable to stop herself. "We only have about ten minutes."

Ben knew she was right, but that didn't stop him from trailing kisses down her neck, his hands gripping her hips. "Fine," he finally relented, his voice rough with frustration and need. "But tonight, I'm taking you back to my place, and I'm going to tie you to my bed and fuck you in every way I can think of until the sun comes up."

Lacy's eyes flashed with excitement, and she pulled him into another searing kiss. "You promise?" she whispered against his lips.

Ben smiled wickedly, his eyes dark with desire. "I swear, baby."

They finally pulled apart, both of them breathing heavily, trying to regain some semblance of control. Lacy gave him a quick kiss on the cheek before walking towards the door. But before she left, she turned back to him, a mischievous smile playing on her lips. "I prefer handcuffs and rope to zip ties," she said, her voice teasing yet full of promise.

Ben stared at her, slightly shocked but undeniably excited by the possibilities her words conjured up. She winked at him before slipping out of the room, leaving him standing there, mind racing with anticipation and excitement for what the night would bring.

As she walked down the hallway, Lacy couldn't help but smile to herself, her heart pounding with excitement. She had always been careful, always in control, but with Ben, she found herself wanting to let go, to explore the depths of her desires. And she knew tonight would be the night they both pushed those boundaries together.

Ben went back to his room and couldn't stop thinking about Lacy's parting words. His mind filled with images of her, tied up and at his mercy, the anticipation almost too much to bear. He smiled to himself, knowing that tonight would be unforgettable.

The day at Gladys's Diner began with a bright sun hanging in the sky, casting a golden glow over the small town. The diner, a staple of the community for decades, had never seen such a buzz of activity. News cameras were set up outside, reporters eagerly awaiting Lacy's arrival, while the townspeople, from excited children to elderly grandmothers, filled every booth and counter stool, the smell of freshly brewed coffee and sizzling bacon wafting through the air. The diner, with its nostalgic nod to simpler times, today was the center of something new and important.

Lacy stepped out of the campaign bus, her heels clicking softly against the pavement as she was greeted by a wave of applause. She was dressed in a tailored cream suit, her hair swept back into a sleek ponytail, exuding confidence and poise. But it wasn't just her appearance that commanded attention—it was the way she carried herself, the way she moved through the crowd with genuine warmth, stopping to shake hands and share smiles with the people she was there to serve.

Inside the diner, the air was thick with the comforting smell of freshly baked biscuits, and the hum of conversation filled the room. Lacy made her way to Gladys, who stood behind the counter, her face beaming with pride. Gladys was a stout woman with a kind face, her apron stained with the evidence of years spent serving up meals to the town. As Lacy approached, Gladys wiped her hands on her apron and opened her arms wide.

"Well, look at you, Miss Lacy," Gladys said, pulling her into a warm hug. "You brought the whole town out today!"

Lacy laughed, the sound genuine and light. "Looks like it, Gladys. But I think it's your cooking that really brought them here."

The older woman chuckled, her eyes twinkling with amusement. "Maybe so, maybe so. But we all know who they came to see."

The day unfolded with Lacy moving from table to table, meeting everyone from retired teachers to young parents with babies on their hips. The grandmothers, a group of sharp-tongued, quick-witted women who had known Ben since he was a little boy, were especially eager to speak with her. They laughed with her, sharing stories of the town's history, and some even brought tears to her eyes as they spoke of their hopes and concerns for the future.

"I just want to know that my grandchildren will have a good life here," one of the grandmothers said, her voice trembling slightly. "That they'll have opportunities and not have to leave town to find work."

Lacy took the woman's hand, squeezing it gently. "That's exactly why I'm here. We're going to make sure this town, and others like it, thrive. Small businesses, local jobs, better education—those are my priorities."

As the day went on, Lacy felt a sense of pride swelling within her. She had always been driven, always known what she wanted to achieve, but today, surrounded by people who were genuinely excited about what she was doing, she felt like she had truly found her voice. She was no longer just her father's daughter, or just a candidate; she was a leader, someone who could make real change.

By the time lunch was served, the diner was buzzing with activity. Plates of fried chicken, collard greens, and mac and cheese were passed around, and Lacy made sure to sit down with Gladys for a few moments, posing for pictures with the woman who had been such a pillar of the community.

"This has been such a wonderful day, Lacy," Gladys said, her voice full of emotion. "I can't thank you enough for bringing all this attention to my little diner."

Lacy shook her head, her smile warm and genuine. "No thanks necessary. It's always a pleasure to serve where I'm needed, Gladys." She paused, her eyes twinkling with mischief. "But if you want to give me that sweet potato pie recipe, I wouldn't say no."

Gladys laughed heartily, shaking her head. "Now that's a family secret, Miss Lacy. Can't be giving that away."

They both laughed, the sound blending with the chatter and clinking of dishes around them, a moment of pure, simple joy. The day was winding down, but the energy in the diner was still high as people continued to enjoy the food and each other's company.

As Lacy stood to greet more people, she found herself surrounded by the grandmothers once again. They were full of questions, their curiosity endless and their tone loving but persistent.

"Now, Lacy, honey, when are you going to settle down?" one of them asked, her eyes twinkling with mischief.

"And how come you're so thin? You need to eat more, baby. You can't keep a man being all skin and bones!" another chimed in, poking her gently in the side.

Lacy laughed, holding up her hands in mock surrender. "One question at a time, ladies! I'm working on it, I promise."

Nonnie stepped in at that moment, hands on her hips, her voice playful and firm. "Leave her alone, you nosy old hens! Give the girl some room to breathe!"

The grandmothers burst into laughter, their eyes crinkling with delight. But before Lacy could catch her breath, Ben appeared, making his way through the crowd. The grandmothers turned their attention to him, their faces lighting up as they showered him with affection.

"Oh, Ben! You're looking as handsome as ever," one of the women said, patting his cheek.

"We were so sorry to hear about you and Abby," another added, her voice filled with sympathy. "But you know, we all have beautiful granddaughters…"

Before Ben could respond, a few of them started hinting at their single granddaughters, asking if he was interested in being introduced. Lacy, who had been listening with amusement, turned around to look at Ben, curiosity piqued.

Nonnie, who hadn't missed the exchange, smiled slightly but said nothing, her eyes flicking between Ben and Lacy with knowing amusement.

Ben, however, kept his cool, offering the grandmothers a charming smile. "That's very kind of you," he said, his tone smooth, "but I already have my eye on someone."

The grandmothers erupted in excited whispers, pressing him for names and details, but Ben just winked, playing coy. "We're not ready for the world to know… yet. But one day, I'll be proud to bring her here and introduce her to everyone."

The grandmothers sighed and cooed, clearly delighted by his words. Nonnie leaned into Lacy, her voice low enough for only Lacy to hear. "I was always rooting for you two," she said, her tone filled with affection.

Lacy turned to her, slightly embarrassed but touched by the sentiment. "Grandmas always know more than you think," she whispered back, a shy smile tugging at her lips.

Nonnie's eyes softened, and she squeezed Lacy's hand. "You make my Benji so happy," she said, her voice tender.

Lacy's heart warmed at the words, and she hugged Nonnie tightly, feeling a deep sense of gratitude and connection to the woman who had always been like a second mother to Ben.

As the day wrapped up, the sun began to dip low in the sky, casting long shadows over the diner. The event had been a resounding success, and Lacy couldn't have been more proud of what she and her team had accomplished. They had brought attention to the town, lifted spirits, and most importantly, shown the people here that they mattered.

Back at the hotel, the team gathered in the lobby to unwind. Ben's friends had joined them, and as Paige and Lacy walked in, Tony, one of Ben's old friends, immediately noticed Paige. He shot Ben a look, his grin wide. "Who's that?" he whispered.

Ben chuckled, shaking his head. "Leave it alone, Tony. She'd have you for breakfast."

Tony, undeterred, smirked. "I'd gladly return the favor." He made his way over to Paige, who looked him up and down with a critical eye.

"You look clean enough," Paige said, her tone teasing but with a hint of approval. "Sure, why not."

As they walked off, Lacy chuckled, shaking her head. "I'm going to my room and passing out," she announced, though a secret smile played on her lips as she thought about her actual plans for the evening.

The group chatted for a bit longer, each eventually heading off in different directions. Lacy returned to her room, the events of the day playing in her mind. She felt exhilarated and fulfilled but also ready for a different kind of excitement. She freshened up with a quick shower, letting the warm water relax her muscles, before slipping into something far less professional—a one-piece red top that hugged her curves, a black skirt with a daring slit up the side, black knee-high boots, and an overcoat. She felt a thrill as she looked at herself in the mirror, anticipation building.

With a final glance in the mirror, she snuck out the back door of the hotel where Ben was waiting, leaning against his car. His eyes darkened with desire as he took in her appearance, his jaw tightening.

"You look so good, baby," he said, his voice low and filled with admiration. He loved calling her that, and she loved hearing it.

Lacy smiled, her own voice teasing. "You don't look half bad yourself."

Ben wasted no time, opening the car door for her before quickly sliding in behind the wheel. The drive to his apartment was quick but careful, both of them eager but restrained, the tension between them palpable.

As soon as they arrived, Ben rushed her inside, their hands and lips already exploring, the promise of the night ahead thick in the air. The door closed behind them, sealing them off from the world, leaving only the two of them to fulfill the promises they had made earlier that day.

The tension between them was palpable, an electric charge that had been building all day. Lacy reached out, tugging Ben toward her, their bodies colliding with a desperate need. Their lips met in a deep, passionate kiss, their tongues tangling as if they were starved for each other's touch. Ben's hands roamed over her body, pulling her close, the firmness of his grip unmistakably possessive.

Lacy broke the kiss, her breath coming in short gasps as she looked up at him with a teasing smile. "You better have been talking about me earlier today," she murmured, her eyes searching his.

Ben chuckled, his thumb brushing over her lower lip as he leaned in close, his breath hot against her ear. "And only you," he whispered, his voice thick with desire. He pulled her closer, his grip tightening, leaving no doubt in her mind.

Her smile turned sultry, her tone dripping with longing as she responded, "You don't share me with anyone else."

"Good," Ben growled, his voice deep and filled with promise. "Because I have promises to keep." He kissed her again, slower this time, savoring the taste of her, the softness of her lips. As they kissed, his hands moved to her coat, unbuttoning it with deliberate slowness, the anticipation in the air making every second feel like an eternity.

Ben had been thinking about her nipples all week, the piercings that had captivated his imagination, and daydreaming just wasn't cutting it anymore. As he slipped her coat off her shoulders, his eyes caught sight of her hard nipples, the metal peeking through the thin fabric of her shirt. He felt a surge of desire so intense it made him dizzy.

With a low, hungry growl, Ben bent down, sliding the fabric away to expose one perfect breast. He wasted no time, his mouth closing over her nipple, his tongue flicking the metal, the sensation sending a jolt of pleasure through Lacy's body. She moaned, her hands gripping his shoulders as he sucked and licked, each tug of his lips making her wetter, more desperate for him.

Ben kissed his way back up to her mouth, his eyes dark with desire, pupils blown wide. "What's your safe word?" he asked, his voice rough with need,

"Mercy," Lacy breathed, her voice trembling with anticipation.

"Use it if you need it," Ben said, his tone commanding yet tender. He kissed her again, deep and possessive, as he walked them to the bedroom, each step filled with unspoken promises.

Once inside, Ben stayed dressed but stripped Lacy completely, his hands slow and deliberate, each piece of clothing removed with reverence. He admired her naked body, the way her skin glowed in the dim light, the way her chest rose and fell with each shaky breath. She was perfection to him, and he was going to worship her the way she deserved.

Ben tied her wrists and ankles to the four corners of the bed, the soft ropes holding her securely in place. He watched her, eyes filled with lust and a deep, unspoken longing. The sight of her spread out before him, vulnerable and trusting, made his desire for her grow stronger.

Kneeling on the bed, Ben spread her knees, his fingers tracing the inside of her thighs, kissing his way up her smooth skin, taking his time, enjoying every inch of her. When he finally reached her lips again, he kissed her with a renewed hunger, his hands sliding up her sides, making her shiver with anticipation.

"Lacy," he whispered, his voice thick with need, his eyes locked onto hers. "Do you trust me?"

"Yes," she breathed, her voice filled with certainty.

"Yes what?" he asked, his eyes drunk with lust and his tone demanding but not harsh.

"Yes…sir," Lacy replied her voice laced with overwhelming need.

Ben kissed her deeply, his hands moving over her body, caressing, exploring, as if he wanted to memorize every curve, every dip of her flesh. He kissed and sucked at her neck, trailing his tongue down to her collarbone, then lower, his mouth worshiping her breasts, lingering at her nipples his tongue playing with the silver barbell , drawing out her moans as he licked and sucked.

He moved further down, his lips pressing kisses to her stomach, her hips, until he was between her legs, his breath hot against her sensitive skin. Lacy's breath hitched, her body tensing in anticipation. Ben looked up at her, his eyes dark with desire. He lowered his mouth to her, his tongue flicking out to taste her, the first touch sending a shudder of pleasure through her.

Ben took his time, licking and sucking at her clit, his tongue working her with slow, deliberate strokes. Lacy moaned, her hips bucking, but the ropes held her in place, leaving her at his mercy. The sensation was overwhelming, her body trembling as Ben teased her, his fingers joining in, sliding inside her, finding that perfect spot that made her see stars.

Lacy was panting, on the verge of begging for release, but Ben wasn't done with her yet. "Patience," he murmured, his voice a soft command as he pulled back, reaching for the toy he had prepared. He turned it on, the soft hum filling the room as he pressed it to her clit, the vibrations making her gasp, her body arching off the bed as the pleasure built to unbearable levels.

Ben watched her, his eyes filled with lust as she got wetter, her juices coating his fingers, dripping down to the bed. He kissed her thighs, working his way back up to her mouth, his lips claiming hers in a deep, possessive kiss. "It's okay, baby," he whispered against her lips, his voice, a low growl. "Let go."

Lacy couldn't hold back any longer. The tension snapped, and she came hard, her body convulsing, a loud, desperate moan ripping from her throat as the orgasm crashed over her. Ben was there, holding her, his mouth on her, cleaning up the mess he had made, every kiss a promise kept.

As she came down from her high, Ben untied her ankles, slipping out of his clothes with a quick, practiced motion. Before she had fully recovered, he was sliding inside her, agonizingly slow, filling her completely, the sensation so intense it took her breath away. Ben moved slowly at first, savoring the feeling of being inside her, the way her body clenched around him, the heat, the wetness, everything he had been dreaming about.

His strokes became more deliberate, harder, as he watched Lacy, her eyes half-lidded, her lips parted in a silent moan. He increased his pace, driving her mad with need, her hands gripping the sheets as he pounded into her. She was close again, the pleasure building rapidly, and when she finally came, it hit her like a freight train, her entire body shaking with the force of it.

As Ben slid out of her, the absence of him left Lacy momentarily gasping for air, her body aching with the sudden emptiness. But before she could even gather her thoughts, he moved with an almost primal urgency, releasing her ankles and flipping her onto her knees with a rough but controlled force. The cool air of the room barely touched her skin before Ben was behind her again, his large hands gripping her waist firmly, positioning her exactly how he wanted.

Without hesitation, he thrust deep inside her, his movements powerful and unrelenting. Each stroke was long, deliberate, and precise, hitting her core with such intensity that Lacy's moans turned into desperate, breathless screams. The sensation was overwhelming, her body trembling under the force of his possession.

"Fuck!" she cried out, her voice high and desperate, her entire body shaking with the need for release.

Ben growled low in his throat, his voice rough with desire as he tightened his grip on her hips, pulling her back onto him with each thrust. The sound of their bodies colliding filled the room, mingling with Lacy's increasingly frantic moans.

"Cum for me," he commanded, his tone leaving no room for disobedience.

The words alone were enough to push her over the edge. Lacy's body convulsed as another powerful orgasm tore through her, her cries echoing through the room as the pleasure overtook her. Ben wasn't gentle—his teeth sank into her shoulder, the sharp sting of pain only heightening the intensity of her release. The combination of pain and pleasure was exquisite, overwhelming, and it pushed her into a realm of sensation she had never experienced before.

But Ben wasn't done. He could feel the shivers still running through her body as she came down from her orgasm, but he needed more, craved more of her. In one swift movement, he repositioned them again, pulling her on top of him as he laid back, guiding her down onto him.

Lacy's mind was blank, her thoughts consumed by the need for more of him. She braced herself against his chest, her legs shaking as she slowly started to ride him, her body still trembling from the aftershocks of her orgasm. But the need inside her was insatiable, driving her to keep going, to take him deeper, to feel him fill her completely.

Ben's hands gripped her hips, guiding her movements, helping her find the rhythm. He watched her, his eyes dark with lust and possessiveness as she rode him, her movements shaky but determined. Every time she slid down onto him, he felt her tighten around him, her wetness coating him, making it impossible to hold back.

"Fuck, baby," he groaned, his voice thick with need. "You feel so fucking good."

Lacy whimpered at his words, her body responding to the filthy praise, her movements becoming more urgent. She could feel the pleasure building inside her again, each thrust pushing her closer to the edge. Ben's hands moved up her body, his fingers finding her nipples, twisting and tugging at the piercings, making her jerk with him still deep inside her.

She was close again, her body teetering on the edge of another orgasm, her legs starting to shake uncontrollably. Ben could feel it too—the way she tightened around him, the way her breath hitched with each thrust. He reached up, his hand wrapping around her throat in a possessive grip, pulling her down to meet his eyes.

"Don't fucking stop," he growled, his tone commanding and dark with need. "Keep riding me."

Lacy obeyed, her body moving on instinct, her vision blurring as the pleasure became almost unbearable. The feel of his hand around her throat, the way he filled her so completely, was too much, but she couldn't stop, didn't want to stop. She needed to cum again, to feel that sweet release that only he could give her.

"Please, sir," she begged, her voice a desperate plea. "Please let me cum."

Ben was close to the edge himself, the sight of her above him, completely at his mercy, driving him wild. His grip on her throat tightened slightly, his hips thrusting up to meet her, pushing her even closer.

"Cum with me," he demanded, his voice rough and filled with possessive need.

The command was all it took. They exploded together, the orgasm hitting them both with a force that left them breathless. Lacy's body shook violently, her cries filling the room as she came hard, her muscles clenching around him, milking him as he spilled inside her. The pleasure was so intense it left her vision blurry, her mind blank, and all she could feel was him—inside her, around her, completely overwhelming her senses.

Ben held her close, his hands still possessively on her hips as they rode out the waves of pleasure together, their bodies trembling from the intensity of it all. When the last tremors subsided, he slowly untied her wrists, pulling her down to lay on top of him, their bodies still connected, their breathing heavy and ragged.

"You were amazing tonight," Ben murmured, his voice soft and full of pride as he held her close, his lips pressing gentle kisses to her hair, her forehead, her lips.

Lacy curled up next to him, her fingers tracing the line of his jaw, stroking his facial hair as they lay together, the aftershocks of their pleasure still rippling through them. She felt a deep sense of contentment, of being completely and utterly fulfilled, not just physically but emotionally as well.

Ben got up briefly, returning with an apple and a bottle of water, his eyes tender as he handed them to her. The simple act of care touched something deep inside her, a warmth spreading through her chest.

"Come on," he urged gently, "if you can't eat, at least drink some water."

Lacy smiled, the gesture filling her with warmth. She took a sip of the water, her body still trembling slightly from the aftershocks of their shared pleasure. Letting go of control was something she rarely allowed herself to do, but with Ben, it felt natural, safe. Outside the bedroom, she was always the one making decisions, planning ahead, cautious about every step, but here, in his arms, she could surrender completely.

Ben watched her with a tender gaze, his heart swelling with affection as she sipped the water. He knew how strong and capable she was, how much she carried on her shoulders every day, and it filled him with pride and a fierce protective instinct to be the one she trusted enough to let go with.

Lacy finished the water, setting the bottle on the nightstand as she snuggled back into Ben's embrace. She felt a sense of peace, of safety, that she rarely allowed herself to feel. In Ben's arms, she was free to be vulnerable, to let someone else take the reins, and it was a freedom she cherished.

As she drifted off to sleep, her body exhausted and completely sated, she felt so safe, so seen, and yet still delightfully wicked. All the things she loved, wrapped up in one perfect night.

Ben held her close, his heart swelling with a feeling he had been trying to deny for too long. He watched her, the way she softened in sleep, her lips slightly parted, her breaths slow and even. He had been thinking about her all day, the campaign barely a distraction from the thoughts of her that consumed him. And now, here tonight, in the aftermath of their intense connection, he finally admitted to himself what he had been fighting: he was falling for Lacy.

She was a match for him in so many ways, her strength, her vulnerability, her fire, and her tenderness. As he drifted off to sleep, the realization settled deep in his chest, a warm, undeniable truth. He didn't have to wait for the campaign to be over to know that what they had was real, and it was only the beginning.

The early morning light filtered softly through the trees as Ben and Lacy made their way to his car, the air crisp and fresh, a stark contrast to the heat they had generated the night before. The town was still sleeping, the streets quiet, allowing them the cover they needed to sneak her back to the hotel. Ben opened the car door for her, his touch lingering on her arm as she slid into the passenger seat. They were both smiling, a shared secret hanging between them, adding a new layer of intimacy to their already complex relationship.

As Ben started the car and pulled out onto the road, the silence between them was comfortable, charged with the remnants of the night's passion and the sweetness of their connection. Lacy couldn't stop herself from sneaking glances at him, her heart fluttering at the sight of his tousled hair, his strong hands gripping the steering wheel, the way his lips curled into a smile every time their eyes met.

They pulled up to the back entrance of the hotel, the soft glow of dawn just beginning to lighten the sky. Ben put the car in park but didn't turn off the engine. Instead, he leaned over, cupping her face with one hand, and kissed her deeply, their mouths moving together in a slow, lazy rhythm that was as much about savoring each other as it was about the kiss itself.

Lacy moaned softly against his lips, her hands sliding up to thread through his hair, pulling him closer. The taste of him, the feel of his lips on hers, made it hard to remember that she had to leave, that they couldn't linger here forever.

After what felt like an eternity and yet no time at all, Lacy reluctantly pulled back, her breath coming in soft, shallow pants. She bit her lower lip, looking at him with a mix of longing and resignation.

"Seriously this time, Ben, I have to go," she whispered, her voice filled with regret.

Ben smiled a lazy, satisfied grin that made her heart skip a beat. He leaned in, pressing a soft kiss to the tip of her nose. "Knock 'em dead today, baby," he murmured, his voice warm and full of affection.

Lacy couldn't help but smile back, giving him one last quick kiss before slipping out of the car. She moved quickly but quietly, using the early hour to her advantage as she made her way to the back door of the hotel. The hallways were dimly lit, the silence only broken by the soft hum of the hotel's heating system, a comforting background noise as she navigated the familiar route to her room.

She reached her door, relief washing over her as she realized she had made it back without being noticed. Her fingers wrapped around the doorknob, ready to slip inside when a voice, smooth and teasing, cut through the darkness.

"Walk of shame, are we, Madame Governor?"

Lacy's heart skipped a beat as she whipped around, eyes wide. Paige was sitting casually at the small desk in the corner of the room, her silhouette outlined by the faint light streaming in through the curtains. Paige's dark skin gleamed softly in the low light, her posture relaxed yet unmistakably confident, her sharp, gorgeous features highlighted by the hint of a smirk playing on her full lips.

"How did you get in here?" Lacy asked, her voice barely above a whisper as she stepped inside and closed the door behind her, her mind racing to come up with an excuse, anything to deflect from the obvious.

Paige arched an eyebrow, clearly unimpressed by the deflection. "Don't change the subject," she replied smoothly, her tone light but carrying an undercurrent of amusement. "Look at you," she continued, her smirk widening as her eyes roved over Lacy's rumpled clothes and tousled hair. "You're one hot mama. Late night donor gala?"

Lacy opened her mouth to protest, to come up with some sort of plausible lie, but her brain seemed to short-circuit, leaving her standing there, speechless. Finally, she just sighed, running a hand through her tangled hair. "Okay, Paige, what do you know?"

Paige's eyes gleamed with mischief, but there was no malice in her gaze, only the warmth of a friend who had caught onto something exciting. "Nothing concrete," she admitted with a shrug, "but I have lots of theories." She leaned back in the chair, crossing her legs as she fixed Lacy with an expectant look.

Lacy took a deep breath, knowing there was no way out of this without coming clean. Paige was far too sharp, and besides, Lacy had come to trust her new friend's judgment and discretion. So, she started from the beginning, telling Paige everything from the first stolen kiss to the passionate night they had just shared.

Paige listened intently, her expression shifting between shock, excitement, and genuine happiness for her friend. When Lacy finished, Paige let out a long, slow breath, a grin spreading across her face.

"Well, damn, Lacy," Paige said, shaking her head in amazement. "You've been holding out on me. And here I was, thinking I'd have to work to keep you relaxed on this campaign. You've made my job way too easy."

Lacy couldn't help but laugh, the tension easing from her shoulders. "So now you're going to give me a hard time about sleeping with the staff, huh?"

Paige's grin turned wicked, but her eyes sparkled with affection. "Oh, absolutely. But seriously, I'm happy for you. You've seemed more content lately, more… at ease. And it's not just me who's noticed. Voters have, too. They've picked up on the shift in your confidence, the way you carry yourself. It's like you're not as uptight anymore, and I guess we know why." Paige winked, her tone playful, but there was a serious edge beneath her words.

Lacy blushed, the warmth of Paige's words settling into her chest. "I didn't realize it was that obvious."

Paige leaned forward, resting her elbows on her knees, her expression turning more serious. "It's obvious to those of us who know you, and that's a good thing. But Lacy, you need to figure out if this is the real thing. If it is, we're going to need a timeline, a plan for how to go public. We can't risk this blowing up in our faces, especially not with the campaign in full swing."

Lacy nodded, her mind already racing with possibilities, concerns, and the deep, undeniable feelings she has for Ben. "I know," she said softly, her voice carrying the weight of the decision she knew she had to make.

Paige stood up, crossing the room to give Lacy a tight hug. "Whatever happens, I'm here for you," she said, her voice filled with sincerity. "Just be careful, and don't rush into anything. You've got a lot on the line, but you deserve to be happy, too."

Lacy hugged her back, the warmth of Paige's embrace grounding her in the moment. "Thanks, Paige," she whispered, grateful for the unwavering support.

Paige pulled back, giving Lacy a reassuring smile before heading for the door. "I'll go get everything ready for today. You take a moment, get your head straight, and then we'll tackle the press like the badass team we are."

Lacy nodded, watching as Paige left the room, the door clicking softly shut behind her. The room was quiet again, the only sound her own breathing as she stood there, alone with her thoughts.

She leaned against the desk, her mind spinning as she thought about Ben. She wished it was just the incredible, mind-blowing sex that had her heart racing every time she thought about him. But it wasn't. It was the way he looked at her, the way he made her laugh, the way she sought his opinion on everything, even when she didn't need to. It was the warmth in his smile, the strength in his arms when he held her close, the easy way he fit into her life, making her feel seen, understood, and cherished.

A small, frustrated sigh escaped her lips as she rubbed her temples, trying to make sense of the swirl of emotions inside her. She wished she didn't care so much, that she didn't think about him constantly, didn't crave his touch, his voice, his presence. She wished she could brush it off as a simple fling, a distraction during a stressful campaign. But deep down, she knew that wasn't true.

Was it really her wishing that? Or was it her father's voice, echoing in her mind, warning her that she couldn't have it all—success and love, ambition and happiness? She had spent so long listening to that voice, letting it shape her decisions, her life, but now, with Ben, she found herself questioning it, wondering if maybe, just maybe, she could have it all.

Lacy shook her head, pushing those thoughts aside as she got dressed, slipping into her usual business attire. She had a long day ahead of her, and there was no room for distractions, no matter how tempting they might be. But as she fastened the last button on her blouse and straightened her skirt, she knew two things with absolute certainty: she was falling for Ben, and the prospect of it terrified her.

With a deep breath, Lacy left her room, her heels clicking softly against the carpet as she made her way to meet Paige and prepare for the day ahead. She knew she had to keep her focus, to stay sharp, but as she walked down the hallway, the thought of Ben lingered at the edge of her mind, a constant, irresistible pull that she couldn't quite shake. And despite the fear, despite the uncertainty, she couldn't help but smile, a small, secret smile that spoke of the depth of her feelings and the hope that maybe, just maybe, they could make this work.

CHAPTER 16

4 Months Later….

The office was buzzing with excitement, a rare feeling in a place usually defined by its relentless pace and political maneuvering. It was Friday, and everyone was in a celebratory mood for two reasons: Ben's birthday and Lacy's recent climb in the polls. Just a single point gained, but that point felt like a lifeline, pulling her campaign within 1 point of her opponent. Victory was in sight, and for now, that was enough to bring smiles to faces usually fixed in furrowed concentration.

The campaign staff gathered around a long table decorated with a mishmash of birthday balloons, colorful streamers, and a cake with the words "Happy Birthday, Ben!" scrawled in bright blue icing. Lacy stood at the edge of the group, clapping along with everyone else, keeping her expression neutral but warm. Her eyes discreetly trailed Ben as he stood at the center of it all, laughing with an easy, unguarded joy that seemed to light up the room. She fought the urge to smile too broadly, to step too close. Here, she was Senator Jacobs, and there were lines to maintain.

As the office sang "Happy Birthday" off-key but with enthusiasm, Ben leaned over to blow out the candles. His eyes met Lacy's for a fleeting moment—a private smile exchanged just for them—before she quickly looked away, her expression smoothing back into something more neutral, more professional. But she couldn't help the tiny thrill running through her. It had been a few months since they'd started seeing each other, and those quiet moments they shared—the laughter over silly TV shows, the smell of something sweet baking in the oven, the feel of his hand in hers as they read side by side—made her feel alive, unguarded.

When the song ended and the cake was cut, Lacy slipped away from the crowd, sneaking off to her office. She shut the door softly behind her and sank into her chair, fingers already moving toward the stack of papers on her desk. There was still so much to do—press releases to approve, a fundraising speech to finalize. She clicked her pen and got to work, the muffled noise of the party fading behind the door.

A soft knock interrupted her rhythm. The door creaked open, and Ben peeked in, a mischievous grin lighting up his face.

"Excuse me, ma'am," he teased in a low voice, "but there's a decree from the birthday boy: no work allowed on my birthday."

Lacy tried to hide her smile. "Is that so?" she replied, leaning back in her chair and folding her arms across her chest.

Ben stepped in, closing the door behind him. "Yep, I'm afraid it's non-negotiable," he said, moving around the desk to lean against it, crossing his arms with a mock-serious expression. "So... you got any campaign stuff this weekend?"

Lacy raised a brow. "I've got an interview tomorrow morning. Why?"

He hesitated for a moment, that playful glint in his eyes softening into something more sincere. "I was thinking… me and my friends are going camping this weekend to celebrate. The wives will be there, too. We'll probably get drunk, have a contest to see who's the best fisherman—you know, the usual." He paused, watching her closely. "What do you say?"

Lacy laughed softly. "Sounds like a blast."

Ben's grin widened. "I'm glad you think so, because… I want you to come with me."

Her smile faltered for just a second, caught off guard by the invitation. Camping with Ben and his friends? That felt like a new step—uncharted territory. Before she could respond, the door swung open again, and Paige walked in, whispering loudly, "Everybody decent?"

Ben's eyebrows shot up in surprise, but Lacy waved a hand, suppressing a smile. "Paige knows about us."

Paige nodded with exaggerated enthusiasm. "Oh yeah, Lacy tells me everything. And by the way, good for you," she added with a wink.

Lacy gave her a mock warning look, though there was something subtly possessive in her look. "Alright, alright. Now, what were you two talking about?"

Ben quickly explained the camping trip, and Paige's usual playful expression shifted into something more serious. Her eyes flicked between them before she turned to Lacy. "Can I talk to Ben alone for a second?"

Lacy blinked, a little thrown. "Of course," she said, slipping out of the office and closing the door behind her. Curiosity nagged at her as she lingered in the hallway, her ear almost pressed to the door.

Inside, Paige wasted no time. She didn't sit, didn't soften her tone. "Do you care about her?" she asked bluntly, eyes narrowing as she studied Ben's reaction.

Ben straightened, the playful air around him fading. "Yes. Of course, I do."

Paige crossed her arms, her expression unyielding. "But do you understand what that means? This isn't just about liking her, Ben. Lacy's not some small-town girl with an easy life. Her world is brutal— faster, louder, and a hell of a lot meaner than you're used to." She paused, letting the weight of her words settle. "She's lived in it her whole life. She knows how to survive in it. Do you?"

Ben's jaw tightened. "I'm not scared of her world."

Paige raised an eyebrow, unimpressed. "Really? Because it's not just political rallies and campaign stops. It's missing anniversaries, it's being publicly dragged through the mud because she wore the wrong dress or didn't smile enough during an interview. It's tabloids calling her every name under the sun and, by the way, they'll come for you too. You think you're ready for people calling you the dumb pretty boy who lucked into a life of money and power? A simp?"

Ben's face darkened, but he didn't back down. "I'm not worried about what people say."

"You should be," Paige shot back, her voice sharp. "Because it's relentless. Every misstep, every moment that you're not perfect, they'll be waiting. They'll tear at you, pick you apart. And guess what? Lacy's not going to be there to comfort you all the time. She'll be on the front lines, fighting battles you can't even begin to understand. Can you handle that? Can you really handle being second in line? Because that's what it's going to be. She's going to miss dinners; she's going to miss you sometimes because the job will always come first. Can you live with that?"

Ben was silent for a moment, his confidence shaken as Paige's words sunk in. She watched him, arms still folded, her expression unreadable.

Ben didn't break eye contact. "You know what made me realize Lacy was the one I could really see a future with?" he asked, his voice strong and steady. "She said something to me once: I want to make people's lives better. I want to embody leadership that uplifts and serves communities. Because if service is beneath you, leadership is beyond you." He paused, letting the weight of his words settle between them. "That was the moment I knew she was going to be president one day. And I remember thinking, If I get to be the person she confides in, the one she opens up to, I'll consider myself the luckiest man alive. One day I will help write her State of the Union speech and sit beside her as she delivers it. Lacy is someone special and I know that. And I want to be the person who makes sure she never forgets that."

Paige blinked, surprised by his conviction, but said nothing, so Ben continued, his voice resolute. "I'm not worried about the noise, Paige. I'm not scared of the tabloids or the missed anniversaries. I know what I'm signing up for."

Paige stood there, arms still folded, studying him closely. "What about when it gets ugly?" she pressed, her tone still hard but quieter now. "When she's too exhausted to even talk to you? When the world chews her up and spits her out?"

Ben didn't hesitate. "Then I'll be there. I'll be there to hold her. When she cries, I'll wipe her tears, and when the world's too loud, I'll make sure we come home and laugh. Because that's what we do. We fight for each other. We love each other. And that's what matters. The rest? It's just noise."

For a long moment, Paige said nothing. She stared at him, her eyes searching his face for any sign of doubt. But there was none. Ben met her gaze, unwavering.

Finally, she let out a breath, shaking her head, a small, reluctant smile creeping onto her face. "Damn," she muttered, almost to herself. "That's a hell of a speech."

Ben just nodded, his expression still serious. "It's not just a speech, Paige. It's the truth."

Paige unfolded her arms, the tension in her stance easing just a fraction. "Alright," she said quietly. "I can see you've thought about this." She pointed a finger at him, though her tone was softer now. "But understand this, Ben: if you ever break her heart, I'll make sure you regret it… ways your life will never recover from, m'kay?"

Ben gave her a firm nod. "You won't have to worry about that."

Paige stared at him for a few more seconds, then finally, she relented. "Alright, we'll see." She moved to the door, opening it to find Lacy lingering outside, clearly pretending not to have been eavesdropping.

"Come back in," Paige called, her usual teasing tone creeping back as she tapped something on her phone. "You can have her Saturday at 11:30, but she's mine again by Monday at 7:30 sharp. And no visible marks, Ben. None. I'm not explaining hickeys to the press."

The next morning, Lacy sat in the passenger seat of Ben's camper, her fingers tapping rhythmically against her thigh as they drove along the winding, tree-lined road. The crisp morning air filled her lungs, clearing away the usual campaign stress. This was new territory for her, in more ways than one. The men she'd dated before Ben were all predictable—polished and perfect on paper, but completely devoid of spontaneity. Ben was different. He made her laugh until her sides hurt, challenged her, surprised her. And now she was about to spend a weekend camping with him and his friends—a world she'd never pictured herself in.

Ben glanced over at her, noticing the quiet but constant tapping of her fingers. "You sure you're not nervous?" he teased, a grin lighting up his face. He reached over, intertwining his fingers with hers.

Lacy smirked, shaking her head. "Nope. I'm good. But I'll tell you this right now—I'm not touching anything slimy."

Ben raised an eyebrow, amusement glinting in his eyes. "Oh, really?"

"Really," Lacy replied, her voice firm with a playful edge. "I'll catch a fish, sure. But don't expect me to touch a dead one, or clean it, or whatever else you people do out here." She scrunched her nose at the thought, fighting a smile.

Ben laughed, his deep, easy laugh that always seemed to disarm her. "Okay, princess," he said, lifting her hand and pressing a soft kiss to her knuckles. "I'll handle the slimy stuff. You just sit back, look pretty, and catch the biggest fish of the day."

Lacy rolled her eyes, but the flutter in her chest was undeniable. "Deal," she said, squeezing his hand.

They drove in comfortable silence for a few more miles, the trees growing thicker as they neared the campsite. The air smelled fresh, untouched by city life, and for the first time in a long time, Lacy felt a sense of peace. She turned her head to look at Ben, wondering how this rough-around-the-edges, small-town guy had managed to get under her skin in ways no one else had. It wasn't just the laughter or the way he made her feel relaxed—it was the way he saw her. Really saw her. Beyond the senator, beyond the polished exterior she had to maintain every day.

When they arrived at the campsite, a wide clearing surrounded by tall pines and oaks, the crisp scent of pine needles and fresh earth filled the air. The sound of a babbling brook added a serene backdrop as Ben parked the camper.

Sam and Michelle arrived just minutes later, followed by Daniel and Mila, then Josh and Bria, then Tony and Samrya. Everyone greeted each other warmly, and Lacy found herself instantly welcomed into the group, their camaraderie easy and familiar.

Ben and the guys immediately got to work setting up the tents and unloading the gear. Meanwhile, Lacy joined the women as they started on the fire. Michelle cracked open a beer and handed it to Lacy, while Mila offered her a glass of wine.

Lacy hesitated for a second before taking the beer. "When in Rome, right?" she said with a grin, taking a sip.

Samrya grinned. "You're gonna fit right in."

As they worked on the fire, the conversation quickly turned to Lacy. "So," Mila asked with a mischievous glint in her eyes, "how'd you and Ben meet? Was it like one of those political dramas where the senator falls for the regular guy?"

Lacy laughed, shaking her head. "Something like that. We met during an interview, actually. I needed a speechwriter for my campaign, and Ben was one of the candidates." She shot a glance at him across the campsite. "I hired him on the spot. Couldn't let anyone else have him."

The women laughed, and Michelle raised an eyebrow. "I bet! Was it just professional at first?"

Lacy shrugged, grinning. "We tried to keep it that way, but it didn't last long. There was just… something about him. From the first day, he wasn't intimidated by the whole 'senator' thing, and that's rare."

Bria leaned in with a grin. "So, how long before you realized it wasn't just work?"

"Longer than you'd think," Lacy admitted, taking a sip of her beer. "I mean, everyone in the office was gossiping about us, but we kept it professional as long as we could."

Mila's eyes gleamed with curiosity. "But you had to know, right? There had to be something."

Lacy blushed slightly, thinking back. "Yeah, I think I did. He made this terrible joke during the interview. I laughed, and I remember thinking, 'I like this guy'."

The women burst into laughter again, and Bria raised her glass to Lacy. "Sounds like he's the one who charmed you."

Lacy grinned. "He definitely did. But I wasn't the only one. You should've seen how the rest of the office reacted when Ben walked in. He was the talk of the town."

Michelle smirked. "I can imagine. I mean, come on, look at him!" She nodded toward Ben, who was helping Sam and Josh set up the tents, his easy confidence and laughter filling the air.

Mila tilted her head. "But he's not just good looks. He's got depth. We've all seen how much he cares about you, Lacy. He's different when you're around."

Lacy's heart fluttered at the words, and she glanced back at Ben, who caught her eye and gave her a wink that made her stomach flip. She smiled softly. "Yeah… he's definitely something special."

Mila grinned, sipping her wine. "Okay, but we need more than that. What's he like as a boyfriend?"

Lacy hesitated for a second, but the warmth of the group made it easy to open up. "He's… thoughtful. In ways that catch me off guard.

Like, one minute we're working on a speech, and the next he's making me laugh so hard I forget what I'm stressed about. He's always finding little ways to surprise me."

Michelle smiled softly. "He's in love with you. You know that, right?"

Lacy's chest tightened slightly, the words 'he's in love with you' hanging in the air. It was something neither she nor Ben had said out loud yet. They both knew those words would take things to another level, make everything feel more real, and maybe a little scary. But she could feel it. They both could.

Trying to keep the moment light, Lacy shrugged with a playful smile. "I think I'm lucky he puts up with me."

Bria leaned forward, her smile warm. "I think you're both pretty lucky."

Finally, the group set out toward the lake, laughter echoing through the trees as the men carried the fishing rods and coolers, already bantering about who would catch the biggest fish. The women trailed behind, exchanging amused glances, knowing this was more about the guys showing off than anything else.

"Alright, ladies," Sam called out, grinning. "No pressure, but the real competition starts now. Hope you're ready to lose."

Mila rolled her eyes, nudging Lacy with a smirk. "They always get like this. Just wait. The trash talk gets worse the more beers they drink."

Ben wrapped an arm around Lacy's waist as they reached the shore, pulling her close. "You sure you're ready for this, princess? Don't want you getting overwhelmed by my skills," he teased, his voice low and playful.

Lacy raised an eyebrow. "Oh, I'm ready. As long as you remember our deal."

Ben chuckled, leaning down to kiss the top of her head. "But of course. But I'll still be catching the biggest fish."

They all spread out along the shore, the sunlight sparkling on the water as they set up their lines. The men were already deep in competition mode, standing near each other and tossing back drinks as they cast their lines, the air filled with lighthearted jabs.

Josh cast his line with a flourish. "I hope you guys are ready to bow down to the fishing king," he said, puffing out his chest.

Sam scoffed, taking a swig of his beer. "Yeah, right. The only thing you're catching is a cold. I've got this in the bag."

Ben, standing next to Lacy, chuckled. "You're all in for a surprise."

The women gathered nearby, chatting and sipping their drinks, watching the men get more animated as the tipsiness settled in. The first few catches were small, tiny fish that barely put up a fight. Tony held up one no bigger than his hand, laughing.

"Look at this monster! You all better be scared now!" he joked, holding the fish up like a trophy.

Mila snorted. "If that's what we're up against, we've got this in the bag."

As the afternoon wore on, the fish started getting bigger, and the competition heated up. One by one, the men caught fish, each of them claiming theirs was the biggest, their trash talk escalating with every cast.

"I've got the biggest one, no question," Sam declared, reeling in a decent-sized bass. "This is it. The winner."

Josh rolled his eyes. "In your dreams, man. Mine's at least a pound heavier."

Ben leaned down to Lacy, grinning. "You ready to show them how it's done, princess?"

Lacy nodded, feeling the thrill of the challenge. She cast her line, steady and focused. Within minutes, she felt a strong tug. She steadied herself, reeling it in slowly. A few moments later, she pulled out a sizable fish—bigger than any caught so far.

The group erupted in cheers and laughter.

"Holy shit!" Sam said, inspecting the fish with exaggerated seriousness. "I think we've got a winner, folks."

Ben beamed with pride, tossing his fishing rod aside as he lifted Lacy off her feet, spinning her around. "That's my girl!" he laughed, his voice full of excitement. He kissed her, the thrill of the moment making it all the sweeter. "Not bad, princess."

Lacy giggled, her arms wrapped around his neck. "Not bad? I think I deserve a prize for that," she teased, twisting her hips playfully.

Ben moaned low, his eyes darkening slightly as he leaned in closer. "Oh, you'll get your prize," he whispered, his voice a little rougher. "But first, make sure you eat enough at dinner tonight."

Lacy raised an eyebrow, confused. "Why?"

Ben's grin turned wicked as he kissed her, biting her lower lip gently. "Because you're gonna need all your strength tonight."

Lacy felt a flush of heat run through her at his words, her heart racing as he set her back down. The laughter and cheers from the group faded into the background for a moment as she looked into Ben's eyes, a mixture of anticipation and excitement swirling between them.

They weighed the fish back at camp, and it turned out Lacy's catch was the biggest—by four ounces. The group groaned, playfully conceding defeat as Ben lifted Lacy up once more, kissing her again in celebration.

"Not bad, princess," he teased, his lips brushing her ear.

As the day turned to evening, everyone gathered around the campfire. The scent of grilled sausages and vegetables filled the air as the flames crackled, casting a warm glow over their faces. The group settled into comfortable conversations, laughing and sharing stories, the easy camaraderie continuing into the night.

Ben and Lacy sat on a blanket near the fire, his arms wrapped around her as she nestled into him, feeling his steady breath against her back. The fire flickered softly, and the stars began to dot the sky, the cool night air a perfect contrast to the warmth of the fire.

Across the fire, Sam and Michelle exchanged a look, watching Ben and Lacy from a distance. Sam leaned closer to his wife, his voice soft. "Look at them. He's happier than I've ever seen him."

Michelle nodded, her gaze soft. "She's good for him. I think they're good for each other."

Ben and Lacy sat in comfortable silence, the crackling fire and the murmur of the group creating a peaceful backdrop. Ben's hand traced soft circles on Lacy's arm as they sat together, and without a word, he began kissing her shoulder, moving slowly up to her neck. Lacy closed her eyes, leaning into him, feeling the softness of his lips and the warmth of his breath.

"Ready to call it a night?" she whispered, her voice gentle, her body relaxing against his.

Ben's lips curved into a smile against her skin. "Yeah, let's head back."

They stood, saying their goodnights to the group. The others waved them off, still laughing and chatting around the fire as Ben and Lacy made their way back to the camper. Inside, the world seemed to shrink down to just the two of them, the full moon casting soft light through the small window.

The air inside the camper was thick with warmth and the scent of the forest outside mingled with the woodsy musk of Ben. Lacy stood in front of the small bathroom mirror, the steam from their shared shower swirling around her, leaving her skin glistening and her hair damp. Ben leaned against the wall, his gaze steady, intense, locked on her every move.

"Slower," Ben murmured, his voice a low rumble that sent a shiver down Lacy's spine. "I love watching you."

A slow smile tugged at Lacy's lips as she let the towel fall deliberately, drawing the fabric over her breasts, down her torso, and along the curve of her hips, before tossing it aside. The heat of his stare was palpable, like a caress against her skin.

Ben's eyes darkened with hunger, his tongue darting out to wet his lips as he stepped forward. "Kneel," he ordered softly.

Without hesitation, Lacy sank to her knees on the plush rug at the foot of the bed, her hands resting delicately on her thighs, her gaze lifted to meet his. Anticipation throbbed in the air between them, thick and electric.

"What's your safe word?" Ben asked, his voice gentle but firm.

"Mercy," Lacy whispered, her pulse quickening as she said it, feeling the delicious tension coil tighter in her belly.

Ben nodded, his fingers grazing her cheek before trailing down her neck. "Give me your hands."

Lacy lifted her hands to him, and with slow, deliberate movements, Ben wrapped a thick blue rope around her wrists, binding them together with expert precision. The rough texture of the rope against her skin heightened her awareness of every sensation, every tiny shift in the atmosphere. Once her hands were tied, Ben stood her up, gently guiding her to the edge of the bed.

Bending her over the bed, her breasts pressing into the cool sheets, Lacy felt the weight of Ben's gaze roaming over her naked form. He reached into a drawer, pulling out a small candle and lighting it. The soft flicker of the flame cast shadows across the walls, dancing like silent promises of what was to come.

At first, Lacy was unsure of what he intended until she felt the first few drops of hot wax land on her ass, the sensation sharp but surprisingly arousing. She gasped, her breath hitching as Ben rubbed the heated wax into her skin, massaging the warmth deep into her flesh. The blend of pain and pleasure sent shockwaves through her body, her mind buzzing with want.

"You like the way that feels baby?" Ben's voice was rich with satisfaction, his fingers teasing the heated skin where the wax had dripped. Lacy could only moan in response, her legs trembling slightly as he dripped more wax down the small of her back, watching with dark fascination as she flinched and then moaned again deeper this time.

Ben blew out the candle, the soft puff of air breaking the momentary silence. He knelt behind her, his mouth pressing hot, open-mouthed kisses to her inner thighs, working his way up until his lips found the most sensitive part of her, his tongue diving into her folds with expert ease. Lacy cried out, her hips bucking against his face as his tongue worked in slow, tantalizing circles, drawing out every moan, every gasp she had.

"Please, sir… let me come," she begged breathlessly, her voice trembling, her wrists straining slightly against the bindings as her body spiraled toward the edge.

"Not yet, baby," Ben growled, the vibrations of his voice sending shivers straight to her core. He teased her, pulling her just to the brink before pulling back, licking and sucking, his fingers digging into her hips as she writhed beneath him.

When he finally allowed her release, Lacy's world exploded into white-hot pleasure. She trembled, her breath coming in ragged gasps as she came hard, her moans filling the small space of the camper. Ben wasted no time, positioning himself behind her and sliding into her with one rough thrust, his erection stretching her in the most exquisite way.

The pace he set was relentless, his hips slamming into hers as he fucked her from behind, the slap of skin against skin filling the air. "You feel so good," he groaned, gripping her hips tighter, driving into her with a raw, primal need. Lacy's body responded to him instinctively, pushing back, matching him thrust for thrust as the fire inside her built again.

"Come for me, baby," Ben commanded, his voice dark and possessive.

Her body was shaking as she neared the edge again. With one final, powerful thrust, Ben pushed her over, and Lacy screamed as her orgasm ripped through her, the intensity leaving her breathless and trembling.

Ben turned her over swiftly, his lips crashing into hers as he kissed her deeply, his hands working quickly to untie her wrists, but only to bind them again—this time behind her back. He blindfolded her, the loss of sight amplifying every touch, every whisper of his breath on her skin. She was completely at his mercy, and the thrill of it sent a fresh wave of arousal through her.

Ben lit the candle once more, and this time, he dripped the wax all over her body. Lacy's back arched as the hot droplets landed on her breasts, her nipples, and her stomach, each drop sending tiny shocks of pleasure-pain through her. The sensation was unbearable, but in the best way, and when Ben rubbed the cooling wax into her skin, it turned to oil, slick and warm.

He massaged her, his strong hands roaming over every inch of her body, kneading the tension out of her muscles as he whispered filthy, possessive things in her ear, each word making her wetter, needier.

"I'm going to fuck you again," Ben growled, his voice low and full of promise. " Until you scream my name."

And he did. He grabbed her hips, positioning himself between her legs as he thrust into her again, his pace rough and animalistic. Lacy's body was a live wire, every nerve ending on fire as he fucked her hard, his hands gripping her so tightly she knew there would be marks. But she didn't care. She wanted it all—the pain, the pleasure, the intensity of it, of him.

Ben lifted her off the bed, holding her against him as he thrust up into her, using his strength to move her up and down his length. Lacy's hands were still bound behind her, her body completely at his mercy as he used her, his grunts of pleasure mixing with her breathless moans.

"Sir... sir, please... I'm going to come," Lacy gasped, her body shuddering with the force of her impending orgasm.

"Do it, baby. Come for me," Ben groaned, his fingers sliding down to play with her clit. The moment he touched her, Lacy shattered, her orgasm crashing over her in waves, her body shaking uncontrollably as she screamed his name.

Ben followed her over the edge, his release filling her as he came with a guttural moan, his hips jerking as he thrust into her one last time.

Panting, Ben laid her back on the bed and lowered himself between her legs, his mouth hot and eager as he licked up her juices, tasting her, prolonging her pleasure. Lacy came again, softer this time, her body trembling as the overstimulation sent her into a blissful haze.

"Mercy," she whispered, her voice soft and spent.

Ben immediately stopped, untying her wrists and disposing of the condom before pulling her into his arms, his fingers brushing gently through her hair. "You okay, baby?" he asked, his voice tender now.

Lacy smiled, her body still tingling with aftershocks. "Yeah... I am, I promise," she replied softly. "Will you hold me?"

"Always," Ben whispered, wrapping his arms around her tightly, holding her close as they drifted off to sleep, the moonlight casting soft shadows over their entwined bodies.

The soft morning light crept through the small camper window, casting a warm glow across the bed. Lacy stirred, the gentle rise and fall of Ben's chest beneath her a soothing rhythm. She nestled closer, her head resting against him, savoring the peaceful moment.

Then her phone rang.

Lacy groaned, rolling over to dig through her jeans on the floor. Pulling out her phone, she squinted at the screen, blinking to clear her still-sleepy eyes.

Dad.

Her heart skipped a beat, a wave of irritation washing over her. She cleared her throat before answering, trying to sound alert. "Hey, Dad," she mumbled.

Richard's voice was sharp, cutting through the quiet of the camper. "Where are you?"

Lacy sat up, glancing at the sleeping figure beside her. "I'm, uh, scouting a location for an upcoming event," she lied, trying to keep her voice steady. "Just trying to get ahead on some campaign stuff."

There was a pause on the other end, thick with suspicion. "At this hour? You sound like you just woke up." His tone was more probing now, clearly doubting her words.

Lacy swallowed, glancing around the camper as she scrambled for something more convincing. "Yeah, it's been a long week, so I caught up on sleep out here before I hit the ground running. You know how these things go."

There was a long pause. "I'm sure," Richard said, his voice laced with skepticism. "It's funny. You're always busy with campaign stuff when I ask about your personal life."

Lacy's pulse quickened. He was digging. He knows something.

"I'm always busy with campaign stuff, Dad. That's the nature of running for office."

"Uh-huh." Richard's voice was low, sharp. "I'm just making sure you're not mixing business with pleasure. There are plenty of distractions when you're running for governor—don't forget why you're in this."

Lacy clenched her jaw, feeling her frustration rise. "I haven't forgotten. I know exactly why I'm doing this."

Richard was quiet for a moment, as if weighing his next words. Then, in a tone that was almost too casual, he said, "I also remembered we never got around to that dinner I invited Ben to. Funny how that keeps getting delayed."

Lacy's stomach tightened, her heartbeat quickening as she realized what he was hinting at. He's fishing. He didn't know she was with Ben, but he was definitely suspicious. "Yeah, well, Ben's been really busy. We've both been swamped."

Richard's voice sharpened again. "Too busy to meet the man whose daughter he's working for? I don't buy it, Lacy."

Lacy closed her eyes, gripping the phone tighter. "Look, Dad, I don't have time for this right now. I'll schedule dinner when things calm down, okay?"

"That's what you said the last three times," Richard said coolly. "I'm not asking anymore, Lacy. I expect him at dinner this week."

Lacy felt the walls closing in. "Fine," she snapped, her patience wearing thin. "I'll talk to him."

"Good," Richard said, his voice firm. "I'll see you both soon."

She hung up, tossing the phone aside as she let out a frustrated breath. She didn't have the energy to deal with her father right now—especially not with him sniffing around about Ben.

Ben stirred beside her, blinking awake as he stretched, his hand reaching out to pull her back down beside him. "Everything okay?" he asked, his voice still groggy.

Lacy sighed, lying back down next to him but staring up at the ceiling. "My dad. He's pushing for that dinner with you again. He's... suspicious about something. I think he knows I'm not exactly on a campaign trip right now."

Ben frowned, propping himself up on his elbow. "Suspicious? Like, about us?"

Lacy shrugged. "I don't know. He didn't say it outright, but he's definitely pushing harder. He said we've been dodging the dinner too many times, and he's not going to let it slide anymore."

Ben ran a hand through his hair, clearly not thrilled with the idea. "You think he knows about us?"

"I think he suspects something," Lacy said, her voice soft. "But it doesn't matter. He's demanding we come to dinner, and he's not taking no for an answer this time."

Ben sighed, resting his hand on her arm. "I've got to be honest, Lacy... I'm not exactly eager to have dinner with your dad. Especially if he's already suspicious."

Lacy turned to face him, her hand brushing his cheek. "I get it. I've been trying to avoid this for a reason. My dad's intense, and he's going to make you feel like you're under a microscope the whole time. I've been protecting us from that."

Ben was quiet for a moment, his eyes searching hers. "But if we have to do it to get him off our backs, I'm in," he said finally. "I'll deal with it. For you."

Lacy's heart softened, and she leaned in, kissing him gently. "Thank you. I just don't want him getting into your head. He has a way of doing that."

Ben kissed her back, his hand sliding into her hair as he pulled her closer. "Don't worry. He won't get in my head. I've got you, and that's all I need to know."

They kissed again, lingering this time, trying to savor the peace before the reality of Richard's demands crept back in. When they finally pulled apart, Lacy smiled, her forehead resting against his.

"We'll get through it," she said softly. "Let's just enjoy the rest of the trip for now, okay? No more worrying about my dad."

Ben smiled, brushing his lips against hers once more. "Okay. Let's make the most of it."

Lacy sighed in relief, grateful for the small reprieve. For now, the weekend was still theirs, and she was determined to hold on to it.

The day unfolded with more laughter and lighthearted moments as they spent time fishing, cooking, and swapping stories around the campfire. The group's camaraderie helped Lacy relax, and she and Ben managed to push the tension from the morning aside, enjoying the easy pace of the day.

As the evening settled in, Lacy found herself curled up next to Ben by the fire, his arm wrapped around her. The warmth of the flames, the soft murmur of voices, and the cool breeze off the lake created a serene backdrop for the night. Every so often, Lacy caught Ben's gaze, and they shared a quiet smile, silently promising that no matter what awaited them with Richard, they were in it together.

For now, the night was theirs, and Lacy was determined to hold onto it for as long as possible.

Monday Morning

Lacy stepped into her office, feeling lighter than she had in weeks. The weekend had been exactly what she needed—laughing with Ben and his friends, the calm of the outdoors, and even catching a fish. As she set her bag down, the door creaked open and in sauntered Paige, a mischievous grin plastered on her face.

Paige immediately narrowed her eyes, circling Lacy like a detective on the prowl. "Alright, let's see... any hickeys to report?" she teased, inspecting Lacy's neck with mock seriousness.

Lacy rolled her eyes, but she couldn't help the smile that tugged at her lips. "Paige, stop it," she said, swatting at her. "It was an amazing trip, okay? I love Ben's friends, and yes, I even caught a fish. So you can stop playing mother hen now."

Paige crossed her arms, grinning. "Oh, I'll stop, but only because you came back in one piece. Seriously, I'm glad you had fun."

Before Lacy could respond, the door opened again, and Chloe stepped in, her expression curious. "What's going on in here? I couldn't find you all weekend, Lacy."

Lacy straightened up, adjusting some papers on her desk. "I needed some time away. A little reset before the final push of the campaign. Paige okayed it."

Paige nodded, folding her arms with a mock-authoritative air. "Yup, I gave her permission. She's allowed to be human once in a while."

Chloe looked between them, raising an eyebrow. "Well, your dad was looking for you. He called me Saturday, said he was worried."

Lacy's smile faltered. She glanced at Chloe, her voice tighter than she intended. "Why is my father calling you?"

Chloe shrugged. "He couldn't reach you, so he called me. Asked if I knew where you were."

Lacy's stomach twisted at the thought of her father digging around again. But she pushed the irritation down, refusing to let it show. "Well, I'm fine. Thanks for checking in," she said, brushing off the matter and turning back to her desk. "Let's just focus on the next couple of weeks. We've got a lot to do before the final campaign push."

Chloe nodded, though Lacy could feel her watching, maybe still suspicious. But for now, the matter was dropped, and the three of them spent the rest of the morning preparing for the busy weeks ahead. There were speeches to finalize, events to plan, and press releases to approve. The day flew by in a whirlwind of meetings, but Lacy's mind kept wandering back to that call with her father. Something about it felt off, but she forced herself to focus. There were bigger things at play right now.

Lacy arrived at the State House for a briefing, her thoughts still tangled in the logistics of the campaign, but she was determined to keep her head clear. As she stepped into her office, Lena, her chief of staff, was waiting for her with a tablet in hand.

"Good afternoon, Senator," Lena said briskly, her tone all business. "We're set for the veto session briefing. I've outlined the key points for you to review."

Lacy smiled, appreciating Lena's no-nonsense efficiency. "Thanks, Lena. You're a lifesaver."

"Always," Lena replied with a small smirk before handing over the tablet. "Let me know if you need anything else. I'll be right outside."

Lacy watched as Lena left the room, the door clicking softly behind her. She sank into her chair, letting out a breath she hadn't realized she was holding. The room fell quiet, and for the first time that day, Lacy allowed herself a moment to just... think.

The campaign. Ben. Her father. Everything felt like it was moving so fast. She stared out the window, the weight of all her responsibilities pressing down on her chest. How had her life gotten so tangled?

Suddenly, a commotion outside her office broke her train of thought. Raised voices. Lacy stood, moving toward the door just as it opened to reveal Lena, who was trying to block a distraught woman from coming in.

"Senator Jacobs can't talk right now," Lena was saying, trying to remain professional as the woman grew more agitated.

Lacy stepped forward, placing a hand on Lena's arm. "It's okay, Lena. Let her in."

The woman, disheveled and clearly upset, stepped into the office, wringing her hands nervously. Her eyes were red and swollen, as if she'd been crying for days. Lacy motioned for her to sit.

"I'm sorry to just show up like this," the woman said, her voice shaky. "But I didn't know what else to do. No one's helping me."

Lacy sat across from her, offering a calm but concerned look. "What's your name?"

"Mary Marlowe. I live in your district," the woman replied, her voice thick with grief. "My son, Jake... he was a reporter at the State Tribune. He was killed a few months ago."

Lacy's heart skipped a beat. She vaguely remembered hearing about the incident, a robbery gone wrong. "I'm very sorry for your loss, Mary," Lacy said quietly. "What did the police say?"

" They're saying it was a random robbery," Mary's voice trembled, her fingers twisting in her lap. "But I don't believe it. Jake wasn't some random target."

Lacy frowned, trying to recall more details about the case. Jake Marlowe. The name rang a bell, but she couldn't quite place his face. He'd never been someone she'd interacted with much, but she knew he'd been persistent—always digging deeper, pushing for stories others might shy away from.

"They said it was a robbery gone bad," Mary continued, her voice growing more desperate. "But they're not investigating it properly. His computer was wiped clean, but not stolen. His things were gone through, but nothing valuable was taken. It doesn't make sense. And now the police won't listen to me. They won't even look into it."

Lacy leaned forward, her brows furrowing. "They wiped his computer?"

Mary nodded, her eyes filling with tears. "Everything was gone. Jake had been working on something big, I just know it. He kept telling me he was onto something. But now... it's all been erased. Like it never existed."

Lacy's mind raced. "Do you know what he was working on?"

Mary swallowed hard, reaching into her bag and pulling out a small sticky note. "I don't know for sure, but I found this among his things." She handed Lacy the note. On it was a name and an address: Michael Hayes.

"Michael Hayes?" Lacy repeated, frowning. The name tugged at the edges of her memory, but she couldn't place it.

Mary nodded, wiping at her eyes. "Jake had been meeting with him, I think. He didn't tell me much, but he mentioned the name once or twice. I think this Hayes person knows something. I went to the police, but they just brushed me off. Please, Senator... I need your help."

Lacy stared at the sticky note in her hand, her pulse quickening. Something about this didn't sit right. A robbery that didn't add up, a reporter working on a big story, and a name she couldn't quite place. Michael Hayes.

"Mary," Lacy said softly, folding the note in her hand. "I'll look into this. I can't promise anything, but I'll do what I can."

Mary's face crumpled in relief, her hands shaking as she clasped them together. "Thank you," she whispered. "Thank you so much."

Lacy nodded, though her mind was already spinning with possibilities. As Mary left the office, Lacy sat back in her chair, staring at the note in her hand. Something about Jake's death wasn't right. And the name Michael Hayes felt like the first clue in a much bigger story.

Alone in her office, Lacy sat back in her chair, staring at the sticky note in her hand. The name Michael Hayes nagged at her, tugging at her memory like a loose thread she couldn't quite pull free. She grabbed her laptop, typing the name into the search bar.

A flood of results appeared. Several names popped up, but it wasn't until she clicked through a few pages that she landed on an image—a man's face staring back at her. Lacy's breath caught in her throat. He looked so familiar. Dark hair, square jaw, a quiet intensity in his eyes. But why couldn't she place him? She felt a strange sense of recognition, like she had met him before, or at least seen him in passing. But where?

Shaking her head, she minimized the window and pulled up another search: Jake Marlowe. The results loaded quickly, and when his picture appeared on the screen, Lacy froze.

The same reporter who had approached her months ago, outside her campaign headquarters on that cold, rainy night. His questions had been relentless—pressing her for details about her mother's death, something she had rarely spoken about publicly. His persistence had unsettled her then, but now... now he was dead.

Lacy's heart raced, her mind spinning as memories flooded back. She had brushed him off that night, assuming he was another reporter digging up old wounds for a headline. But what if he hadn't been? What if he'd been onto something?

Her fingers hovered over the keyboard, thoughts swirling in her head. Why had Jake been asking about her mother? What had he been working on? And how was Michael Hayes connected to all of this?

A darker, more troubling thought began to creep into the edges of her mind: Did her father have anything to do with this? She shuddered, pushing the thought away, but it lingered like a shadow she couldn't shake. Had her dismissal of Jake that night somehow contributed to his death? If she had listened, would he still be alive?

Her chest tightened, guilt and fear intertwining as the questions piled up, threatening to overwhelm her. The clock ticked in the quiet room, but Lacy didn't notice how much time had passed. She was consumed by the web of connections forming in her mind, a web that seemed to grow darker with every new revelation.

Suddenly, the door creaked open. Lena stepped in, glancing at her watch. "Senator, it's time to go."

Lacy blinked, startled. "What?" She looked at the clock and realized how late it had gotten. Hours had slipped by, lost in her thoughts.

"You've been sitting here a while," Lena observed, her voice careful. "Everything alright?"

Lacy hesitated, feeling the weight of the sticky note still in her hand. She nodded slowly, forcing a smile. "Yeah, I'm fine. Just... shaken up by that woman earlier. It's a lot to take in."

Lena gave her a sympathetic look but didn't press further. "If you need anything, let me know," she said before leaving the room.

Lacy nodded, though her mind was miles away. She spent the rest of the evening trying to focus, but the questions wouldn't leave her alone. All night, she kept wondering how all of this was connected, and whether her father—or her actions—had played a role in Jake Marlowe's death.

She couldn't shake the feeling that this was just the beginning of something much darker. And this time, she wasn't sure if she was ready for the answers.

Thursday Night: Dinner at the Jacobs Estate

The dining room of the Jacobs estate was as grand as ever—high ceilings, dark oak furniture, and large, gilded portraits of past generations lining the walls. The flickering glow from the chandelier cast a golden hue over the long mahogany table, adorned with fine china and crystal glasses. Lacy sat across from her father, feeling the weight of the evening pressing down on her.

The meal had been prepared by Richard's private chef, each dish an exquisite display of culinary mastery. Grilled lamb chops, delicately seasoned with rosemary and thyme, rested on a bed of roasted vegetables. Beside them were truffle mashed potatoes and a rich red wine reduction. The air smelled of savory herbs, garlic, and decadence, but despite the beauty of the meal, Lacy's appetite had all but disappeared.

Richard sat at the head of the table, cutting into his lamb with meticulous precision, his movements slow and deliberate. Every so often, his eyes flicked toward Ben, who was seated next to Lacy, answering Richard's questions with polite enthusiasm. But the way Richard asked them—the thinly veiled disinterest in his tone—made it clear he wasn't really listening.

"So, Ben," Richard said, taking a sip of his wine, "what exactly does a speechwriter like you do when the Senator is off campaigning? Are you... sitting around, waiting for instructions? Or are you more proactive?"

Ben smiled tightly, sensing the edge beneath Richard's question. "Well, I'm always working on drafts, revising messages based on the latest polling, and adjusting for new developments. It's all about staying ahead of the curve."

Richard hummed, nodding as though considering Ben's response, but his eyes didn't leave his plate. "Hmm, ahead of the curve. That's important, isn't it? Knowing what's coming before it happens." He glanced up, his gaze resting on Lacy for a brief moment before returning to Ben. "Staying prepared is half the battle."

Lacy forced a smile, sensing the tension building. "Ben's been incredible on the campaign," she interjected, hoping to lighten the mood. "He's always got the right words ready when I need them."

Richard's lips curled into a faint smile, but it didn't reach his eyes. "I'm sure he does." He leaned back in his chair, wiping the corner of his mouth with his napkin. "I'm curious, Ben. What do you think about this next phase of Lacy's career? Governor's quite a jump. A lot more responsibility. And, of course, more eyes on her."

Ben met Richard's gaze with steady composure. "I think Lacy's more than ready. She's always been driven to serve people, to make a real difference. That's what makes her such a strong leader."

Richard raised an eyebrow, his smile widening, though there was something almost predatory in the way he looked at Ben now. "Driven. Yes, Lacy's always been driven." He shifted his gaze to Lacy, holding her eyes for a beat longer than necessary. "You've always known where your loyalties lie, haven't you, sweetheart?"

Lacy's heart skipped a beat. The way he said it—calm, but with an edge, like a threat cloaked in affection. She forced herself to maintain her composure, her fingers gripping her wine glass a little tighter. "Of course, Dad. Everything I do is for the people of this state."

"Is it?" Richard's tone was soft, but the implication hit her like a stone. He cut another piece of lamb, his knife scraping against the plate. "It's good to stay loyal, especially in times like these. Too many distractions can lead to... problems."

Lacy's stomach tightened, the cryptic nature of his words swirling in her mind. Was he hinting at something? Did he know about her suspicions—or worse, about her time with Ben? The thought sent a cold shiver down her spine. She glanced at Ben, who seemed unfazed by the conversation, though she could sense he was picking up on the tension too.

Lacy tried to keep things light, laughing softly as she reached for the mashed potatoes. "Let's not get too heavy, Dad. We're here to enjoy dinner, not have another strategy meeting."

Richard's smile didn't waver, but his eyes darkened ever so slightly. "Of course. But you know, Lacy, dinner is where the most important strategies are often laid out. It's all about knowing who's sitting at the table—and more importantly, who's not."

As Ben glanced at Lacy, his eyes softened—filled with a quiet admiration that didn't go unnoticed. Lacy felt the warmth of his gaze, a small smile tugging at her lips despite the tension of the evening.

Richard, however, caught the exchange. His eyes narrowed ever so slightly before he spoke, his voice smooth but cold. "You know," Richard began, swirling his wine, "the press can be a real hassle. They can twist anything—turn a smile into a scandal, or a simple handshake into betrayal. Vermin, really. Always chasing stories." He paused, his gaze lingering on Lacy. "But it can get dangerous if they dig too deep."

Lacy's smile faded, her fingers tightening around her wine glass as the weight of his words settled over the table like a storm cloud.

Ben, sensing the tension beneath Richard's words, cleared his throat and shifted the conversation. "This dinner is amazing, by the way. Your chef really knows their craft."

Richard smiled, but there was no warmth in it. "Yes, I make sure only the best work for me. In all areas."

The statement hung in the air, and Lacy couldn't shake the feeling that it was another veiled comment, another sign that Richard was always two steps ahead, pulling strings she wasn't fully aware of.

The conversation drifted, but Richard's eyes seemed to linger on Lacy, as if he were studying her, weighing something unsaid. After a long pause, he spoke again, his voice low and almost conspiratorial.

"You know, Lacy, the press can be a dangerous thing. One wrong word, and they'll spin it however they want. It can get deadly if they're not careful. You've seen it happen. Some people...just disappear."

Lacy's blood ran cold, the words ringing in her ears. She blinked, trying to keep her face neutral, but her mind was reeling. Deadly? Disappear? Was this a coincidence? Or was he referring to Jake

Marlowe, the reporter who had been killed, and whose computer had mysteriously been wiped clean?

Deep down, her doubts were growing. She couldn't shake the feeling that Richard knew far more than he was letting on. And the darker thought lingered, gnawing at her: Did her father have something to do with Jake Marlowe's death? Had her loyalty to him, and her dismissal of Jake that night, somehow led to his death? If she asked him, she knew he would get defensive. She knew she had to find the truth and she had to do it in the shadows.

Dinner continued, but Lacy's mind raced. She kept trying to piece together the clues. Her father's comments, the strange circumstances surrounding Jake's death, the name Michael Hayes. Was it all connected? And if so, what was her father's role in it? Was she, unknowingly, a pawn in one of his larger plans?

As the meal wound down, Richard looked directly at Lacy, his tone casual yet loaded. "I hope you're being careful, Lacy. People in your position can find themselves in... difficult situations if they aren't mindful of who they trust."

Lacy swallowed hard, forcing a smile. "I am, Dad. I always am."

Lisa, her father's housekeeper, came into the dining room, politely signaling the end of dinner. "Senator Jacobs, the car is ready."

Ben rose from his seat, offering a polite nod to Richard. "Thank you for having me, Mr. Jacobs."

Richard barely glanced at him. "Of course."

As they left the estate, walking down the grand steps of her childhood home, Lacy's mind was miles away. She had smiled, laughed, played the part of the dutiful daughter—but inside, she was filled with questions. And the most troubling one of all was the one she kept circling back to: Did Richard know about Jake? And worse... had she unwittingly played a role in his death?

Ben glanced at her as they got into the car. "You okay?"

Lacy forced another smile. "Yeah. Just... shaken up by my dad. He always knows how to push my buttons."

Ben nodded, but Lacy wasn't really present. The rest of the night, her thoughts would remain on her father's cryptic comments, the mystery of Jake Marlowe's death, and the growing suspicion that her father was far more involved than she ever realized.

As Ben and Lacy walked down the grand steps of the estate, Richard stood in the doorway, watching them with a cold, calculating gaze. His expression remained unreadable, but his eyes followed them until they disappeared from sight. Slowly, he pulled out his phone and dialed a number, his voice low and deliberate.

"Get me everything you can find on Benjamin Carter," Richard ordered, his tone dripping with quiet authority. "I want to know who he really is."

He ended the call without waiting for a response, slipping the phone back into his pocket as a faint, knowing smile crossed his lips.

CHAPTER 17

Lacy barely registered the bustling city streets as she drove toward the State Tribune office, her mind lost in a swirl of dark possibilities. Had her father been hinting at something during dinner last night? Was he really capable of murder? The thought gnawed at her. She had always heard rumors about Richard Jacobs—whispers about the way he handled those who crossed him—but she had never believed them. Her father, though not overly affectionate, had always provided for her.

There's no way he did this, she told herself, gripping the steering wheel tighter. But she couldn't shake the creeping doubt that lingered from last night's cryptic conversation. She had to know for sure, for her own peace of mind—and for Mary Marlowe. She owed it to Jake's mother to do her due diligence.

When she arrived at the State Tribune office, Lacy parked outside, taking a deep breath. She didn't know exactly what she was looking for or what questions to ask, but she needed to start somewhere. If anyone had answers about Jake Marlowe, it would be Claire Morgan, the editor-in-chief.

The reception area buzzed with activity as she entered, reporters and staff moving in all directions, the hum of phones ringing and keyboards clacking filling the air. Lacy asked for Claire at the front desk, her voice steady despite the nerves building in her chest. Within minutes, a young assistant led her down a corridor to Claire's office, knocking lightly before stepping aside.

"Come in," Claire's voice called from behind the door.

Lacy pushed the door open, finding Claire Morgan seated behind a large, cluttered desk, surrounded by stacks of papers and drafts. Claire glanced up, her eyes sharp behind her glasses, the air of authority unmistakable.

"Senator Jacobs," Claire said, raising an eyebrow. "This is a surprise. What can I do for you?"

Lacy closed the door behind her and sat down across from Claire, taking a moment to gather her thoughts. "I wanted to talk to you about Jake Marlowe," she said, her voice measured.

Claire's expression didn't change, but there was a flicker of something in her eyes—something that told Lacy she'd struck a nerve. "Jake was a good reporter," Claire replied evenly. "It's a shame what happened to him, but I'm not sure what I can add to that. The police have already investigated."

"I'm not sure they've investigated enough," Lacy said, leaning forward slightly. "His death was ruled a robbery gone wrong, but something doesn't feel right. His computer was wiped, his notes gone. Doesn't that strike you as odd?"

Claire's eyes darkened, and she crossed her arms, her posture suddenly more defensive. "Senator, I run a newsroom. Things get lost, stolen, corrupted. It happens. Jake was passionate about his work, but he also pushed boundaries. Sometimes... people don't like being pushed."

Lacy frowned, the evasion clear in Claire's tone. "Do you know what he was working on before he died?"

"Jake always had several irons in the fire," Claire said with a shrug. "I couldn't keep track of all of them. He was digging into a number of stories, but nothing out of the ordinary."

Lacy wasn't convinced. "But something had to be big enough to warrant his files being erased. That's not typical, Claire."

Claire's gaze sharpened. "I think you're reaching, Senator. The police handled it. Sometimes things just happen—random, tragic things. I suggest you don't dig into this too much. It won't bring him back."

There it was—a subtle warning, but a warning nonetheless. Lacy's pulse quickened. "I'm not here to play politics, Claire. I'm trying to figure out what happened. Jake was asking questions about my mother's death before he was killed. You don't think that's worth looking into?"

Claire's eyes flashed briefly with something Lacy couldn't place— fear, perhaps? Or something deeper? "People ask questions all the time, Senator. This is journalism. You know that as well as anyone."

Lacy sat back, letting the silence hang in the air for a moment before speaking again, her tone more deliberate. "Why are you being so dismissive? Jake's death, the wiped files, it's all too convenient, don't you think?"

Claire's jaw tightened, and for the first time, Lacy saw the cracks in her composure. "Senator Jacobs, I suggest you leave this alone. You're running for governor. You don't need to get tangled in something that could derail everything you've worked for. Jake's death was a tragedy, yes. But poking around in it now won't do you any favors."

Lacy's breath caught. It was more than a warning now—Claire was trying to push her away, to steer her off course. "Are you hiding something, Claire?"

Claire let out a dry laugh. "I'm protecting my newsroom. The Tribune doesn't chase ghosts or conspiracy theories. Jake knew the risks of his job, and sometimes, those risks catch up with you."

Lacy leaned in, her voice low. "Or was Jake digging into something you didn't want him to?"

Claire's expression hardened, the pretense of politeness gone. "You really don't know when to stop, do you? Drop this, Senator. For your sake. For your father's sake."

Lacy froze. The mention of her father, casually dropped into the conversation, sent a chill down her spine. Her stomach turned. "What does my father have to do with this?"

Claire didn't blink. "Nothing. If you're smart, you'll keep it that way."

Lacy stood slowly, her hands shaking as she clenched them into fists. "I'm not going to let this go, Claire. Jake's family deserves the truth."

Claire held her gaze for a long moment, then gave a small, tight smile. "Sometimes the truth isn't worth the cost. Now if you will excuse me."

The words lingered in the air as Lacy turned on her heel and left the office, her heart pounding. She didn't know what Claire was hiding, but one thing was clear: Jake Marlowe's death was no random robbery, and Claire Morgan was protecting something—or someone.

And if her father was involved, Lacy was now more determined than ever to uncover the truth.

The day was clear, the early autumn air crisp with a slight breeze that carried the scent of damp leaves. Lacy stood with her campaign team on the corner of a neighborhood street, the sun casting long shadows over the houses. The group was buzzing with nervous energy, clutching their clipboards and campaign flyers.

Paige stood at the center of it all, commanding attention without needing to raise her voice. She had a natural way of taking control, her sharp eyes scanning the group, assessing them like a general before battle. Lacy could see the intensity in her face, a look that always meant business.

Paige clapped her hands, drawing the group's focus. "Alright, everyone," she started, her voice steady but firm. "This isn't just another canvassing run. Today, we're hitting a key neighborhood— one that's been ignored by other politicians for far too long. We're not here to give speeches or talk *at* people. We're here to listen." She glanced at Lacy, a hint of warmth flickering in her eyes. "Lacy's strength isn't just in her words. It's in the fact that she listens, she cares. We need to make sure every person we meet today sees that."

The volunteers nodded, their confidence growing under Paige's clear direction. She continued, her voice rising slightly with purpose. "I want you to knock on every door with purpose. Let them know we see them. We value them. No one gets skipped, no one's voice goes unheard. Now go make it happen."

With that, Paige began dealing out assignments like cards, her movements efficient and her instructions clear. "Matt, you're with Rachel. Take the east side and work your way toward Fifth. Caroline, you and James hit the north block." She glanced at Lacy, giving her a nod of reassurance. "You and I are working the middle. Let's get this done."

Lacy smiled, feeling a bit of the weight lift from her shoulders as she followed Paige's lead. She was always amazed at how easily Paige could rally people. That's why she's been by my side for so long, Lacy thought. She knows how to cut through the noise and get things done.

The team broke off, and the rhythmic sound of their footsteps echoed down the sidewalks. Lacy tried to immerse herself in the task at hand, the familiar routine of knocking on doors, shaking hands, and talking to constituents. But her mind kept drifting, slipping back to the unsettling conversation with her father the night before.

Paige noticed immediately. As they reached the first house on their list, she gently pulled Lacy aside, her eyes narrowing with concern. "What's going on, Lace? You've been a million miles away all day."

Lacy forced a tight smile, knowing she couldn't exactly tell Paige about the dark thoughts swirling in her mind. "It's nothing. I'm just distracted."

Paige tilted her head, her expression softening as she dropped her voice. "Is it Ben?" she asked, searching Lacy's face. "You can talk to me, you know."

Lacy shook her head, trying to brush it off. "No, trust me, it's not Ben." She hesitated, then started again, her voice more strained than she intended. "It's just my dad. He's been... a lot lately."

Paige's gaze softened, understanding flooding her features. She placed a hand on Lacy's arm, giving her a sympathetic smile. "I get it. Dads can be ugh, right?" She let out a small laugh, though her eyes remained serious. "But I really need you here today, Lacy. These people need to see you, the real you. I know your dad's a lot, but let's focus on what you're good at. You've got this."

Lacy exhaled slowly, grateful for Paige's unwavering support. "Thanks, Paige. I needed that." She straightened up, ready to dive back into work. "Okay, let's go knock on some doors."

With renewed focus, Lacy and Paige moved house to house, knocking on doors, introducing themselves to families, and listening to the concerns of the neighborhood. The scent of freshly cut grass mingled with the distant aroma of someone grilling dinner nearby. Children played in the streets, their laughter a sharp contrast to the heaviness in Lacy's mind.

For a while, the work was steady, routine. Lacy focused on smiling, on engaging with each person they met. But soon, they arrived at a small, weathered house tucked at the end of the block. Lacy knocked, the sound echoing louder than it had at the other homes. A man opened the door, his presence imposing, his face hardened with years of experience. He looked at them through narrowed eyes.

"Hi, I'm Lacy Jacobs, and I'm looking for Imogen Ivanov," Lacy said, her voice steady despite the man's intense gaze.

The man didn't respond immediately. His expression remained cold, but something shifted in his eyes. "What do you want with her?" he asked, his thick Russian accent clear.

Before Lacy could answer, his eyes darkened as if realizing something. His gaze swept over her face, then to her campaign button, finally landing on her last name. "Wait. What did you say your name was?"

"Lacy Jacobs," she repeated, slower this time, an uneasy feeling creeping into her chest.

The man's expression changed instantly. His face drained of color, and his jaw tightened. "Jacobs?" he repeated, the word hanging in the air like a curse. He stared at her, his eyes wide with panic, then anger. "Stay away from me and my family!" he barked suddenly, his voice shaking with fury.

Lacy froze, completely thrown off guard. "I—"

"GET OUT!" he screamed, cursing in rapid Russian as he slammed the door so hard the frame shook. Behind the door, his voice carried, shouting something incomprehensible in Russian as heavy footsteps stomped away from the entrance.

For a moment, everything felt suspended in the air. Paige and the other volunteers exchanged baffled glances, some shrugging it off as an odd encounter. But Lacy stood frozen, her thoughts spiraling.

What the hell just happened? Why had her last name triggered such a visceral reaction? She knew the Ivanovs were connected to the Russian community, but Jacobs wasn't exactly a rare name. Still, the fear in the man's eyes had been unmistakable. And the anger—it was like he knew something about her, something dark.

"Lacy?" Paige's voice cut through the haze, tugging her back to the present. "Come on, we've got more doors to knock on."

Lacy blinked, trying to steady her racing heart. "Yeah, okay," she muttered, but the confusion lingered. The rest of the afternoon passed in a blur. She smiled, answered questions, listened to concerns, but her mind kept drifting back to that door.

Despite the strange encounter, the day rolled on with moments of brightness. At one point, a local news crew showed up, capturing footage of the campaign in action. They interviewed Lacy, who, despite her distractions, easily slipped into her role. She listened intently to the concerns of the neighborhood residents, nodding thoughtfully and promising to address their issues. Several people praised her for showing up in a neighborhood other politicians ignored.

One elderly woman leaned into the microphone and said, "Lacy Jacobs is the first politician to ever come to our street. I don't care what she's running for, she's got my vote."

As the afternoon wore on, a group of teenage boys gathered around Lacy's car, their excitement infectious. One of the boys, wide-eyed with admiration, asked, "Is this ya whip?"

Lacy laughed, handing her keys to one of them. "It sure is. You want to check it out?"

The boy's face lit up as he slid into the driver's seat, his friends crowding around, taking videos and laughing. One of the boys filmed the whole thing, the camera shaking with excitement as he shouted, "Yo, vote for Ms. Jacobs to be governor or whatever, 'cause she got da best whip in the state!"

Lacy burst into laughter, playfully accepting their teenage endorsement, and the news crew caught it all on camera. The impromptu moment with the boys gave her a boost of energy, something to shake off the heaviness that had clung to her all day.

Later that night, Lacy sat on her couch, scrolling through clips from the day's campaign trail. The news segment played on her phone, showing the boys gathered around her car, laughing and recording, their excitement palpable. It was one of the lighter moments of the day, and Lacy let herself smile, grateful for the distraction.

Her phone buzzed, and Ben's name flashed on the screen. She answered, already feeling her heart lift at the sound of his voice.

"I saw you on the news," Ben said, his voice warm with pride. "You looked incredible out there. And those boys—man, you won them over with your car. Teenage vote locked down."

Lacy smiled, sinking deeper into the couch. "They were hilarious. I think the car was the real winner."

Ben chuckled softly. "Nonnie saw it too. She was so proud. We both are. You're killing it out there."

Hearing Ben's voice always had a way of grounding her, of making the chaos of her life feel manageable. They talked for a while, chatting about the campaign, sharing little jokes. For a brief moment, Lacy allowed herself to enjoy the conversation.

Then, Ben made an offhand comment that sent her spiraling. "You know," he teased, "I'm just glad I don't have to see your dad anytime soon. That dinner was... well, let's just say I'm good with not doing that again."

Lacy's smile faltered. The words hit her like a punch to the gut, and suddenly, everything she had been pushing away all day came rushing back. Her father. His cryptic comments. The Russian man's terrified reaction. It all felt connected, but she couldn't make sense of it.

"Yeah, um, I'm really tired, Ben," she said abruptly, her voice tighter than she intended. "I should eat something and head to bed."

Ben hesitated, picking up on the change in her tone. "Hey, you okay?"

"Of course," she lied quickly. "I'll talk to you later. Bye." She hung up before Ben could say anything else, her hands trembling as she set the phone down.

Her mind raced. Is my father a murderer? Did he have something to do with Jake Marlowe's death? Or worse—had he hurt that man or his family today? How many of the dark rumors swirling around Richard Jacobs were true?

Memories swirled in a chaotic tide, dragging her back to high school, to whispers and jokes she had dismissed for years. Boys had teased about dating her. "Don't date Lacy—her dad might kill you." She had always laughed along, rolling her eyes at their dark humor. But now, with a cold pit settling in her stomach, those jokes didn't feel so far-fetched.

And then there was Sal.

Her breath caught as the memories sharpened. Sal had been her first real boyfriend, her first love. They had been inseparable, their late-night phone calls stretching into hours, talking about everything and nothing until one of them finally drifted off. He was the one she had trusted completely, the one who made her heart race every time he smiled at her in the crowded school hallways.

They had talked about the future like they were already living it. College plans, their first apartment, what it would be like to leave behind their small town and build a life together. Sal was the boy she had imagined marrying someday, the boy who made her believe in forever.

She remembered the night they made the decision. Sitting in the bed of his truck under a blanket of stars, Sal had taken her hand, his eyes soft and full of something that made her feel both safe and alive. "Are you sure?" he'd asked, his voice trembling just enough to remind her that he was as nervous as she was.

"Yes," she had whispered, her cheeks burning but her heart steady. "I love you, Sal. I want this to be special. I want it to be us."

For weeks, they had planned every detail—where, when, how they would make it perfect. It wasn't just about sex. It was about them, about solidifying what they already knew in their hearts: that they were meant to be.

But then, just days before it was supposed to happen, Sal had broken up with her.

He hadn't even given her a reason. He'd been cold, distant, his words clipped and rehearsed. "It's not working," he had said, avoiding her eyes as they stood in the empty hallway near her locker. "I think we should see other people."

She'd been devastated, blindsided. The boy who had spent months telling her she was his forever had ended it with a single sentence, walking away without a backward glance.

At the time, she had blamed herself. Had she been too clingy? Too eager? Too naive? The breakup had left her reeling, shattering the trust she had so freely given.

But now, years later, a darker thought crept into her mind, chilling her to the bone. Did my father have something to do with that?

She swallowed hard, her heart pounding in her chest. The timing, the abruptness of it all—it felt wrong now, more than it ever had before. Sal had loved her; she'd been certain of that. So what could have made him change so suddenly, so completely?

The answer slithered into her thoughts, uninvited and unwelcome: Richard Jacobs. Her father had always loomed over her relationships like a silent threat, his name alone enough to inspire fear. She thought of Sal, the boy who had wanted a future with her—until he didn't.

Had he been warned off? Threatened?

Lacy pressed her palms to her temples, trying to steady the whirlwind of emotions and memories. The thought of her father interfering, of him tearing apart something so pure and innocent, left her feeling hollow. And if that was true—if Richard Jacobs had really destroyed her first love—what else had he done?

Her thoughts spiraled further into the dark, the questions multiplying faster than she could answer them. What don't I know?

Her heart raced, her chest tightening with anxiety. Her Apple Watch buzzed with a notification: Heart rate elevated—132 BPM.

She needed to calm down.

Her mother's voice echoed in her mind, soft and steady: When your mind is clear and your heart is steady, you will see the path clearly.

Lacy placed a hand on her chest and another on her stomach, focusing on her breath. Inhaling deeply, exhaling slowly, she began to steady herself. The chaotic thoughts in her head quieted just enough for her to think clearly.

She made a vow to herself: I will find out the truth. I will uncover what my father has done, no matter the cost.

Lacy sat on the edge of her bed, her thoughts still racing, but with a new clarity. She picked up her phone and opened a message to Paige, her fingers hovering over the keyboard for a moment. I need space. Just a little more time to figure this out. She typed quickly, knowing she couldn't give too much away.

"Hey, I'll be in late tomorrow. Can you adjust my schedule? And... don't tell Chloe."

She hit send before she could second-guess herself. The idea of Chloe being so close to her father made her stomach turn. There was something about their growing connection that felt... wrong. Too convenient. Too close. She couldn't afford to trust Chloe right now.

Paige responded almost immediately.

"No problem. I've got it covered. Everything okay?"

Lacy hesitated, then forced a reply: "Yeah, just need to catch up on a few things. Thanks."

Setting her phone down, she exhaled slowly. Tomorrow, she'd start finding answers—away from the prying eyes of her father and anyone else too closely aligned with him. For now, she would let the thoughts fade under the calming rush of the shower and prepare for the next step.

Lacy woke up with a single, burning thought: I need answers. The weight of her suspicions had grown too heavy to ignore, and today, she was going to do something about it. She moved through her morning routine quickly, her mind racing with questions, her heart set on finding the truth.

Dressing in a pair of dark jeans, a cozy cream-colored sweater, and simple white sneakers, Lacy glanced in the mirror. She considered wearing a hat and sunglasses but decided against it—too conspicuous. Instead, she slid on a pair of sleek, oversized sunglasses. They added just enough anonymity without making her look like she was hiding something. She grabbed her keys, her phone, and a resolve she hadn't felt in days, then headed out the door.

The familiar scent of bacon and eggs hit Lacy as she walked into Sal's Diner, the greasy spoon she'd been visiting for years. It was comfort food—familiar, warm, and full of memories. She loved it here and made a point to stop by every few months. The last time had been just a few weeks ago, and Sal had been beaming about the baby, now almost three months old.

Sal Sr. stood behind the counter, chatting with a few regulars, his face lighting up when he saw Lacy approach. "Lacy Jacobs! Always good to see you, my dear."

"Hi, Mr. Salvador," Lacy said, offering him a smile. "Is Sal here today?"

Sal Sr. chuckled, shaking his head. "No, no, he's at home with Marianne and the baby. You should stop by and see them! The boy's growing fast. Trip's already three months old."

"Trip?" Lacy asked, raising an eyebrow.

Sal Sr. grinned proudly. "Salvador the Third. We call him Trip." He wiped his hands on his apron. "I'll let him know you're coming."

Lacy's heart skipped a beat. She hadn't planned to go to their home—just wanted to grab some food and maybe catch Sal for a quick chat. But now, with the invitation open, it felt like an opportunity she couldn't ignore.

Lacy pulled up in front of Sal's house, her hands tightening on the steering wheel as she stared at the quaint, suburban home. Flowers hung from the porch, and the smell of fresh-cut grass mixed with the crisp autumn air. This is the last place she expected to dredge up the past. But here she was.

She rang the doorbell, and after a few moments, the door opened to reveal Sal. He looked the same as ever—tall, broad-shouldered, with the same dark hair and warm green eyes. He greeted her with a tight smile.

"Lacy, hey! You must've heard Trip was born," he said, stepping aside to let her in.

Lacy smiled faintly, the nerves prickling at the back of her neck. "Yeah, your dad told me. Congratulations."

Sal led her into the living room, where baby toys were scattered across the floor and the scent of coffee lingered in the air. Marianne was sitting on the couch, cradling a tiny bundle in her arms. She looked up and smiled brightly at Lacy.

"Lacy! Come in," she said, her voice soft. "You've got to meet our little man."

Lacy approached slowly, her heart tugging as she saw the baby nestled in Marianne's arms. He was small, with wide eyes and chubby cheeks, his tiny fists waving in the air. Marianne gently handed him over, and Lacy took him in her arms, holding him close. The baby smelled like baby powder and warmth, and for a moment, Lacy's chest tightened as she thought of holding her own child one day—raising them in a world that wasn't haunted by corruption and lies.

Marianne excused herself to feed the baby after a few minutes, leaving Lacy and Sal alone in the living room.

They sat in awkward silence for a moment, Sal fiddling with the sleeve of his shirt while Lacy stared at the floor. She hadn't planned this out. She didn't know how to start. But her need for answers outweighed her hesitation.

"Sal," she finally said, breaking the silence. "Why did you break up with me?"

Sal froze, his hand pausing mid-fidget as he looked up at her, his brow furrowed. "Come on, Lacy," he said with a strained chuckle. "That was high school. We were kids. Ancient history."

Lacy shook her head, her gaze intense. "No, Sal. We weren't just kids. We were planning everything. We said 'I love you.' We were going to lose our virginities to each other." She hesitated, then added softly, "I thought we had something real."

Sal ran his hand through his hair, clearly uncomfortable. "Is that what this is about? I didn't sleep with you, and now—"

"Stop," Lacy interrupted, her voice sharp. "You know that's not what this is about." She took a deep breath, trying to calm her nerves.

"I said that to prove a point, Sal. We were serious, and then one day, you just ended it. No warning, no reason."

Sal's face tightened, his hands now fidgeting again. He didn't respond, staring at the coffee table as if it held the answers.

Lacy's patience snapped. "Sal, I need to know why."

He stood abruptly, his body stiff with tension as he paced across the room. "You shouldn't be asking these questions, Lacy. You shouldn't have come here." His voice wavered between anger and fear, his movements erratic as if trying to decide what to do next.

Lacy followed his movements with her eyes, refusing to back down. "Sal, please. If my father threatened you, if he made you break up with me... I need to know. I need to understand."

Sal stopped pacing, his back to her. For a moment, he didn't speak, his shoulders heaving with a deep breath. Then, slowly, he turned to face her, his expression dark and conflicted. "Lacy," he said softly, "it's not just me anymore. It's my family, too. I have a wife. I have a son. I won't put them in danger."

Lacy's heart clenched at his words. She stood and took a step toward him, her voice breaking with emotion. "I just want to stop more families from getting hurt. Someone has died, Sal. And I need to know if you think my father had anything to do with it."

Sal rubbed a hand over his face, his fingers trembling slightly. He looked at her with a mixture of fear and guilt, as though he was balancing on the edge of revealing something terrible. "All I can say," he said, his voice barely above a whisper, "is that your father is not the man you think he is."

Lacy felt a chill run down her spine, her suspicions deepening. "Sal..." she began, but he cut her off.

"You need to go," he said firmly, stepping toward the door and opening it. "It's best if we only see each other at the diner from now on."

Lacy stared at him, her heart pounding in her chest. She had come here for answers, and though Sal hadn't said much, he had said enough. She knew, deep down, that her father was involved in something far darker than she had ever imagined.

She walked toward the door, pausing briefly as she stepped outside. "Thank you, Sal," she said quietly. "You've told me everything I needed to know."

Sal nodded, but his face remained grim as he gently closed the door behind her.

Sitting in the driver's seat, Lacy's hands trembled as she gripped the steering wheel. Her mind raced with everything Sal had said—and hadn't said. He was scared. Of her father. Of what might happen if the truth came out.

Her father isn't the man she thought he was.

Lacy stared out the windshield, her heart heavy with confusion and dread. She had come for clarity, but the only thing she felt now was an even deeper sense of uncertainty. Yet one thing was clear: she was on the right path. The truth was there, hidden in the shadows of her father's power. And she was closer to uncovering it than ever.

With a steadying breath, Lacy started the car and drove away, the weight of Sal's warning lingering in the air as she vowed to keep searching for the truth—no matter what it cost her.

Lacy sat in front of her mirror, staring at her reflection as she pulled her long, straight hair back into a sleek ponytail. Her hands trembled slightly as she smoothed down the flyaways, securing the last piece of her armor—the mask of Senator Jacobs. Today, she wasn't just Lacy, the woman grappling with impossible questions about her father's secrets. She was a political force, polished and poised in an expensive designer suit—a deep navy that contrasted perfectly with her skin. Her heels were tall, sharp, and confident.

But inside, she was screaming. The moment she got home from Sal's, she'd barely made it inside before unleashing a raw, guttural yell into the emptiness of her apartment. She had paced back and forth, hands shaking with the revelation Sal had left her with. Your father isn't the man you think he is. It echoed in her mind, swirling with questions she couldn't yet answer.

But now wasn't the time to fall apart. She had a job to do—a town hall to prepare for, and in less than an hour, a high-stakes interview with Ramona King, a primetime, Emmy award-winning journalist known for her sharp questions and unforgiving interview style. Ramona was relentless, known to push her guests to the edge. It wasn't going to be an easy conversation.

Lacy checked her phone—a text from Paige reminding her the news crews would be there soon to set up. Lacy let out a long breath, steeling herself. She had to focus. Not today. Not here.

The campaign headquarters buzzed with activity as the team prepared for the interview. The hum of voices mixed with the clattering of cameras being set up, the thud of footsteps rushing across the floor, and the quiet tap of keyboards. Lacy moved through the office like a ghost, offering small nods and smiles to the staff but barely hearing what anyone was saying. Paige was doling orders as usual, her voice sharp and commanding, while Chloe managed the media crew, making sure everything was in place for the filming.

"Lacy, we need to go over the talking points for the infrastructure bill," Paige said, stepping into her path, a tablet in hand.

Lacy blinked, her mind momentarily blank as she tried to process what Paige had said. Infrastructure. Roads. Bridges. The usual. "Yeah, sure. Later," she mumbled, brushing past Paige without stopping.

Paige frowned, clearly noticing something was off, but Lacy was already moving away. She couldn't focus on details right now. Not when her mind was still racing with thoughts of Sal and her father.

As she made her way toward her office, Ben appeared in front of her, blocking her path with a concerned expression. "Lacy, wait," he said softly, placing a hand on her arm. His touch was firm, and it stopped her in her tracks.

She looked up at him, her heart twisting at the worry in his eyes. She knew he could see through her, that he sensed something was wrong. But how could she tell him? How could she tell anyone?

"Are you okay?" Ben asked, his voice low and soothing. "You seem... distracted."

Lacy forced a smile. "I'm fine," she lied, her voice too quick, too thin. "I'm just... nervous about the interview. You know how Ramona King is."

Ben raised an eyebrow, clearly not buying it. "You've never been nervous before an interview in your life."

Lacy swallowed, her throat tight. She hated lying to him. He was the one person who truly knew her—the person who saw beyond the polished exterior. But she couldn't let him in. Not with this. Not with everything she didn't even understand herself. So instead, she did the one thing she could think of.

She kissed him.

It was a sudden, impulsive move—breaking the unspoken rule they had about public displays of affection in the office. But in that moment, she needed the comfort, the connection. Her lips pressed against his softly, but with enough urgency that Ben's concern only deepened. He pulled back slightly, his brow furrowed.

"Lacy..." he began, but she shook her head.

"I've got to go," she said, stepping back before he could ask more questions. "We'll talk later."

Without waiting for his response, she turned and walked away, her heels clicking sharply against the floor as she headed toward the dressing room to finish getting ready.

The set was perfectly staged. Lacy sat in a comfortable armchair, the lighting soft and flattering. Ramona King sat opposite her. The newsroom buzz of campaign headquarters had been replaced by a calm professionalism—camera crews adjusting their equipment, makeup artists making final touches, and the low murmur of assistants checking sound levels. The air smelled faintly of coffee and fresh paint, the studio lights humming overhead.

Ramona was poised and intimidating, her dark eyes fixed on Lacy with a sharp, unrelenting focus. She was known for her ability to dig beneath the surface, to push her interviewees until they revealed more than they intended. But Lacy had been through this before. She was practiced. She was prepared.

Focus. She straightened her shoulders, smoothing the fabric of her suit, and met Ramona's gaze with a confident smile.

"Thank you for joining me today, Senator Jacobs," Ramona began, her voice smooth but edged with curiosity. "There's a lot to discuss, so let's dive right in."

Lacy nodded, her mind already in overdrive. "Of course. I'm ready."

The questions started off easy—familiar territory about her platform, her views on healthcare reform, her plans for job creation. Lacy answered them all effortlessly, her voice steady, her words flowing as if she'd rehearsed them a thousand times. She could feel the tension in her body easing slightly as she settled into the rhythm of the interview.

But then, Ramona leaned forward slightly, her eyes narrowing as she shifted gears. "You've spoken a lot about leadership and public service, Senator. But what happens when you're faced with failure? When the policies you've championed don't work the way you've promised? How do you handle being wrong?"

It was a trap. The kind of question designed to trip her up, to make her defensive. But Lacy was ready.

"Failure is part of leadership," Lacy said, her voice calm and measured. "No one is perfect, and no policy is without flaws. But what defines a leader isn't whether they fail—it's how they respond to that failure. I believe in transparency, in accountability. If something doesn't work, we don't hide from it. We address it, we adapt, and we make it better."

Ramona's lips twitched into a small, almost imperceptible smile. She knew Lacy was too polished, too experienced to fall for the trap. But she wasn't finished yet.

"Some would say that politicians are often more concerned with public image than with actual solutions," Ramona said, her voice cutting. "What do you say to voters who feel disillusioned by promises that never seem to come to fruition?"

Lacy smiled slightly, her pulse steady. "I understand that frustration. I really do. And I think it's important for voters to hold their representatives accountable. But I also believe that real change takes time. It takes persistence. It's easy to get cynical, but that's exactly why we need to keep fighting. Because if we give up, nothing changes."

The cameras zoomed in slightly, capturing the intensity in Lacy's expression. She could feel the weight of the room's attention on her, every eye watching her, every microphone capturing her words. She remained calm, unshakeable, as Ramona continued to probe, throwing question after question her way.

But Lacy danced through them all. She knew this game. She knew how to handle the pressure.

When the interview finally wrapped, Lacy could barely remember the last half hour. She had been on autopilot, her responses flowing out of her without conscious thought. The moment she stepped out of the bright lights and back into the dim corridors of her campaign headquarters, the weight of the day hit her like a tidal wave.

She walked through the office, barely acknowledging anyone as she headed for the door. Paige and Chloe were busy analyzing the interview, discussing strategy for the upcoming town hall, but Lacy was already gone in her mind.

Ben caught up with her just as she reached her car. He didn't say anything, just nodded, knowing their usual protocol—making sure no one saw them leave together. He would meet her at her apartment in half an hour, like always. They were careful.

By the time Ben arrived, Lacy was already curled up on the couch, still in her suit, her heels discarded by the door. She looked up at him, her eyes tired, the confident mask she had worn during the interview completely gone.

"Just hold me," she whispered, her voice barely audible.

Ben didn't hesitate. He sat down beside her, pulling her into his arms. He didn't ask any more questions. He didn't need to. He could see it in her eyes, feel it in the way she trembled slightly as she rested her head on his chest. She was fighting something—something deeper than the campaign, deeper than politics.

As he stroked her hair, his mind replayed the words Paige had said to him earlier: "She'll fight battles you'll never know about."

Tonight, he could feel the truth of those words more than ever. And Ben hated that. He hated that Lacy was keeping him in the dark, hated that he couldn't be her shield, her confidant in whatever storm she was weathering.

But he respected her too much to push. Lacy was fiercely independent, and if there was one thing Ben understood, it was that Lacy would only let him in when she was ready. So he held her, his fingers gently stroking her hair, offering her whatever comfort he could.

CHAPTER 18

Lacy woke before the sun had fully risen, her body tensing as she slipped out of bed. The early morning light barely filtered through the curtains, casting the room in a soft, gray glow. Beside her, Ben stirred, his arm reaching out instinctively for her. His half-awake voice was low and groggy, "Lace? Why are you up? It's 6:30... on a Sunday."

She hesitated, glancing down at him, guilt twisting in her stomach. Ben looked at her with soft, sleepy eyes, the kind that made her heart ache. She hated lying to him. He was so kind, so good to her, but for his own safety, she couldn't let him in—not until she knew the truth, not until she knew who she could really trust.

"Just a few quick campaign things," she lied, her voice steady despite the turmoil inside her. "I'll be back soon, and we can have breakfast, maybe spend some time together before you head to Nonnie's."

Ben frowned slightly but nodded, too tired to press her. "Okay," he muttered, closing his eyes again.

Lacy bent down, kissing him softly at first, then more passionately, as if trying to apologize for the deceit she couldn't speak aloud. She felt Ben's arms tighten around her, pulling her closer, but she gently pulled away. "I'll see you soon," she whispered, her breath still catching from the kiss as she slipped out of bed.

Dressed in jeans, a t-shirt, and a fitted leather jacket, her hair loose and slightly tousled, Lacy walked out the door, her mind already on what lay ahead. She wasn't sure what she would find at the house at the end of the street—the one where the man had slammed the door in her face just a few days before. But today, she was determined to find out why her name had sparked such fear in him.

The street was eerily quiet as Lacy parked her car a short distance from the house. The wind had picked up slightly, rustling the leaves and carrying the faint scent of damp earth. She glanced around, checking the windows for any signs of movement, but the house looked deserted, like a place that held its secrets tightly. Too tightly.

Lacy steeled herself, her pulse quickening as she approached the door. Just as she raised her hand to knock, a sudden cold sensation pressed against the back of her head—steel, hard and unforgiving.

"Turn around slowly."

The voice behind her was a woman's, sharp and thick with a Russian accent. The gun pressed firmly against her skull sent a jolt of panic through Lacy, but she forced herself to remain calm. Slowly, deliberately, she turned to face her attacker.

Standing before her was a striking woman—tall and fierce, with sharp cheekbones and icy blue eyes. She held a shotgun, her hands steady, but her eyes betrayed a flicker of recognition.

"Fuck are you doing at my house, bitch?" the woman spat, her English broken, but her meaning crystal clear. Then, as if something clicked, her grip on the gun slackened slightly. Her eyes widened in recognition. "Wait... You are that black lady running for governor. I've seen you on TV."

Lacy swallowed, her heart pounding in her chest. The woman lowered the shotgun, though she kept it in hand, her eyes now more curious than hostile.

"My husband tells me you were here before... with cameras and shit, He says that's why I should have never become a citizen of this shithole country," she said, her voice still guarded. "Don't worry, I won't shoot you. If I kill you, I will most definitely die."

Lacy allowed herself a slow breath, the tension in her body easing only slightly. "I didn't come here to cause trouble. I just want to talk," she said, her voice steady, though her nerves still hummed with the memory of the gun at her head.

The woman smirked. "Talk? Fine. Come inside. Have tea with me."

Imogen Ivanov's home was surprisingly warm and inviting despite the icy reception at the door. The faint smell of freshly brewed tea filled the air, mixing with the scent of old wood and spices. The furniture was modest but comfortable, the walls adorned with family photos and Orthodox icons that glimmered faintly in the dim light.

They sat at the small kitchen table, the shotgun now leaning against the wall, though Imogen's eyes never fully relaxed. She poured two cups of tea, her movements precise and deliberate.

"So, you come to my house because of my husband?" Imogen asked, eyeing Lacy with suspicion. "He is angry. You said your last name, Jacobs. He told me."

Lacy stirred the tea absently, watching the steam rise from the cup. "Yes. When I said my name was Jacobs, he got very upset. I don't understand why, but I want to."

Imogen looked away, her expression hardening. "You are smart woman. You must know."

Lacy leaned forward slightly, her voice soft but insistent. "Please, Imogen. I want to help. I know your husband is afraid of something... of someone. If you tell me why, maybe I can help protect you. Both of you."

Imogen's lips curled into a bitter smile. "Help protect me? Like the police?" she scoffed, shaking her head. "Police say same as you. But your father... your father pays them, too. Why would I trust the daughter of such a man as Richard Jacobs?"

Lacy's heart skipped a beat at the mention of her father, but she didn't let it show. She knew she had to remain calm, calculated. "I'm not my father. I know what people say about him. I know the rumors. But I'm not here as his daughter. I'm here because I want to get justice for you and your family. I can help."

Imogen stared at her, unmoved, her expression cold. But Lacy pushed on, her voice firm. "I'll make you a deal. You answer one question for me, truthfully, and I'll help you take down my father. I'll help you get your justice."

The silence that followed was thick with tension, the air practically vibrating with Imogen's hesitation. She didn't speak at first, her fingers tightening around the handle of her teacup. But Lacy didn't back down.

"Did my father hurt someone in your family, too?'

Imogen's face went pale, her eyes widening in shock. The silence in the room was deafening, broken only by the faint ticking of a clock on the wall. Then, as if the dam had finally broken, Imogen's eyes filled with tears. Her body trembled, and she began to cry, her sobs shaking her thin frame.

Lacy felt her own chest tighten as she reached out, gently pulling Imogen into her arms. The woman resisted for only a moment before collapsing into Lacy's embrace, her sobs muffled against Lacy's shoulder.

"Yes," Imogen whispered through her tears. "Your father... he had them killed. My brother, my cousin... They refused his deal. Whenever he takes new territory from other gangs, he say you can die behind your family name or join me in a new family. They refused him......And now they are dead."

Lacy felt a cold wave of dread wash over her. The confirmation felt like a punch to the gut. Her father had done this. Her father had murdered these men, just like he had probably had Jake Marlowe killed. The truth made her feel sick to her core.

They sat like that for what felt like an eternity, Lacy holding Imogen as she cried, her own mind spinning with the implications. She didn't know what to do, didn't know how to process this. But she knew one thing for sure: her father was even more dangerous than she had ever allowed herself to believe.

Suddenly, they both froze. The sound of heavy footsteps thudded on the wooden floor outside, and Imogen pulled back, her face filled with panic. "You have to go," she whispered urgently, her eyes wide. "If Dimitri finds you here, he will kill you. For revenge."

Lacy stood quickly, her heart racing. Imogen grabbed her arm, practically shoving her toward the back door. "Out the back. Now."

Lacy nodded, her mind still reeling as she hurried through the back door and out into the yard. She glanced back once, locking eyes with Imogen for just a moment before turning and running to her car.

Lacy's hands gripped the steering wheel so tightly her knuckles were white. Her entire body felt numb, her mind swirling with everything she had just learned. Her father had murdered those men. *And she was sure he killed Jake Marlowe, too.* And now, Lacy was caught in the middle of a storm that she had never seen coming.

As she drove through the quiet streets, she realized with terrifying clarity that she didn't know who she could trust anymore. Her own father had done unspeakable things, and she had no idea how deep it all went. She felt cold, detached from everything around her. The streetlights blurred in her vision as tears welled up in her eyes.

Who was her father?

Her chest tightened again as she thought back to all the times people had whispered about him, joked about him in high school, said that dating Lacy Jacobs was a dangerous game because of who her father was. And now, she had to face the possibility that they were right. That he was capable of anything.

She had to get to the bottom of this, no matter what it cost her. But for now, all she could do was go home and figure out her next move.

She wiped the tears from her eyes and took a deep breath, trying to steady her shaking hands. The truth was a heavy weight, but she had to carry it. She had no choice.

Lacy walked into her apartment, the familiar warmth of the space calming her frazzled nerves for a brief moment. The scent of freshly brewed coffee hit her as soon as she stepped inside. She heard the soft clinking of plates in the kitchen and made her way toward the sound, her heart heavy with everything that had transpired that morning.

Ben was in the kitchen, setting down two plates of breakfast—scrambled eggs, toast, and sliced fruit. The simplicity of the meal, the care with which Ben had prepared it, tugged at Lacy's chest. She stood there, watching him, her heart swelling at the sight of him doing something so ordinary and so thoughtful. For a brief moment, all the darkness, all the questions, and fears faded into the background.

He looked up and smiled, his eyes lighting up as they met hers. "Hey, I thought you might be hungry," he said, his voice soft and warm. He picked up the plates and set them down on the table, glancing over his shoulder at her. "Everything okay?"

Lacy forced herself to smile, pushing aside the chaos in her mind. She crossed the room, wrapping her arms around him from behind, pressing her lips softly against his neck. "Everything's perfect," she whispered, and for a moment, she allowed herself to believe it.

Ben turned in her arms, brushing a loose strand of hair behind her ear before pulling her in for a kiss—gentle at first, then deeper, more passionate. The world outside the apartment melted away, leaving only him and the way he made her feel. Safe. Loved. Like everything might still be okay.

When they finally broke apart, Lacy's heart was pounding. "I just want to forget everything," she murmured, her voice barely above a whisper. "Just for a moment."

Ben kissed her forehead, smiling softly. "Then let's do that."

They sat down at the table, their conversation light, filled with laughter that felt both like a relief and a reprieve from the weight Lacy had been carrying. They joked about silly things—old inside jokes, stories from the campaign trail, memories that made her forget, even if just for a little while, the storm brewing inside her.

As they finished eating, Ben glanced at the clock and sighed. "I should head over to Nonnie's soon," he said, standing and gathering their plates.

Lacy smiled at him, standing up to help clear the table. "Tell her I said hi," she said, brushing his arm softly.

Ben leaned down and kissed her one last time before grabbing his coat. "You'll be okay?" he asked, his eyes searching hers for any lingering unease.

Lacy nodded, the smile on her face hiding the turmoil beneath the surface. "I'll be fine," she lied.

He gave her one last look, concern flickering across his face, but he didn't push. With a final nod, he left the apartment, closing the door softly behind him.

The moment Ben was gone, the weight of everything came crashing back down. The silence of the apartment wrapped around her like a shroud, heavy and suffocating. Lacy stood there for a moment, her mind racing with everything she had learned—about her father, about the men he had killed, about the lies that had surrounded her for so long.

The silence became too much. A sob broke free from her chest, and before she knew it, Lacy was crying—deep, gut-wrenching sobs that left her breathless and trembling. Her knees gave way, and she sank to the floor, her body shaking as the tears poured out. Her breaths came in short, ragged gasps as she cried openly, her heart breaking under the weight of it all.

She had held it together for so long, but now, in the quiet of her apartment, with no one to see, she let the grief, the fear, and the betrayal wash over her. Every sob felt like a release, but also a reminder of how much she had lost—how much she still stood to lose.

For twenty-five minutes, she wept—her body hunched over, her hands clutching the floor as if trying to hold on to something solid in a world that felt like it was slipping away. The tears blurred her vision, her breath coming in shallow, uneven bursts.

Finally, when there were no more tears left, Lacy stood, her legs shaky beneath her. She stumbled toward the bathroom, her hands gripping the edge of the sink as she stared at her reflection in the mirror. Her eyes were red and puffy, her cheeks streaked with tears, and her hair was disheveled. She barely recognized the woman staring back at her.

She splashed cold water on her face, the coolness shocking her back to the present. The water dripped from her chin as she looked back into the mirror, her breath steadying, her heartbeat slowing. She felt a strange calm settle over her, the kind that comes when you've cried all you can cry.

Lacy knew what she had to do. There was no more room for doubt, no more time to second-guess. She had to take down Richard Jacobs. Even if it meant sacrificing everything—the campaign, her reputation, even her life. Her father was a murderer. A monster. And she couldn't allow him to keep doing what he was doing.

She placed a hand on her chest, feeling the steady rise and fall of her breath. Her mother's words echoed in her mind, words that had guided her through every trial: "When your mind is clear and your heart is steady, you will see the path before you."

The path was clear now. No matter the cost, she would get justice. She would uncover the truth and protect the people her father had hurt—no matter what it took.

With a deep breath, Lacy dried her face and straightened her shoulders. She texted Paige, her fingers moving quickly across the screen: I'll be in late tomorrow. Change my schedule and don't tell Chloe anything.

As she set her phone down, a wave of exhaustion hit her, but beneath it, a resolve had taken root. Tomorrow, she would start putting the pieces together. Tomorrow, she would get closer to the truth.

The heavy iron gates of the Jacobs estate creaked open, and Lacy drove up the long gravel driveway, her heart pounding in her chest. She had been here countless times before, but never like this—never with a mission to uncover something so dark that it made her question everything she had ever known about her father. The estate was quiet, still as a grave, with Richard out of town for a few more days. Lacy knew this was her only window to search the house without raising suspicion.

The morning sun was just starting to burn away the fog that clung to the grounds, but despite the light, the mansion felt cold and oppressive. She parked her car and stepped out, adjusting her coat against the cool breeze. Lacy stood there for a moment, staring at the house where she had grown up, the place that had once felt safe, familiar. Now it felt like a labyrinth of secrets.

With a deep breath, she walked to the front door, unlocking it with the key code she still had from when she lived here. The door swung open silently, and Lacy stepped inside. The air inside was cool and faintly musty, the scent of leather and old wood mixing with a hint of her father's cologne. The house was as pristine as ever, with not a single item out of place, but to Lacy, it felt like every corner was hiding something. Something dark.

She had no idea what she was looking for, but her gut told her that whatever it was, she would find it here. Years of working as a lawyer had trained her to trust her instincts, and right now, those instincts were screaming at her to search every inch of this place.

Lacy started with her old bedroom. It was untouched, frozen in time from the day she had moved out.: the soft pink wallpaper, the shelves filled with books from her childhood, and the neatly made bed. She stood in the doorway for a moment, her eyes scanning the room for anything out of place. It felt eerily normal, like a room waiting for a girl who no longer existed. She ran her fingers along the edge of the dresser but found nothing unusual. No hidden papers, no secret notes.

The next stop was the library, where her father often entertained guests. The dark mahogany shelves were lined with leather-bound books, meticulously organized. Lacy pulled a few off the shelves at random, flipping through the pages quickly but found nothing except yellowed pages of old novels and legal texts. The scent of aged paper filled the room as she moved to the grand fireplace, running her hands over the mantle, searching for anything that might stand out. But there was nothing.

Finally, she made her way to her father's study.

Her father's study was where she knew she had the best chance of finding something. The room was dark, the heavy curtains pulled back slightly to let in a sliver of morning light. The air was thick with the scent of cigar smoke, even though Richard hadn't smoked in years. His large, imposing desk stood at the center, its surface clean, save for a few neatly stacked papers and a polished brass lamp. Family photos lined the shelves behind the desk—one of Lacy as a child, another of her mother.

Lacy approached the desk cautiously, running her fingers over the polished wood. She tried to open the top drawer, only to find it locked. She tried another drawer. Locked as well. Frustration began to build, but she kept calm. There was always a way in.

Just as she was about to move to another part of the room, her phone buzzed in her pocket, startling her. She fumbled for it, her heart racing, and saw Paige's name flash across the screen.

Lacy quickly stepped into the hallway, answering the call in a whisper. "Hey, what's up?"

Paige's voice was tinged with suspicion. "You tell me. Do you have another lover? I'm happy to work around whatever you need, but clue me in next time, please."

Lacy felt a pang of guilt. "No," she whispered back, trying to sound casual. "I just... I started my period and needed the morning. I'll be in soon."

There was a brief silence on the other end, then Paige sighed. "Okay. But hurry up, Lacy. We have a big day ahead."

"Got it. I'll be there soon," Lacy said quickly, hanging up before Paige could ask more questions. She couldn't risk her finding out what she was really doing.

Lacy returned to her father's desk, her hands now shaking slightly. She crouched down to check the drawers again, this time noticing that one of the smaller ones wasn't locked. Her heart leapt as she carefully pulled it open, her breath catching in her throat.

Inside, there was a small stack of papers—mostly bills and unremarkable correspondence. But tucked beneath them, something caught her eye: a torn photograph. Lacy's fingers trembled as she pulled it out. The photo was of a man—a man who looked strikingly familiar to her, though she couldn't immediately place him.

But it wasn't just the man's face that grabbed her attention. It was the rips in the photograph, jagged and uneven, like something had been violently torn apart. And then, on the back of the photo, in her father's unmistakable handwriting, were the words: "Remember our deal, Michael."

Her blood ran cold.

Michael Hayes. Jake Marlowe's mother had said that Jake was looking into a man named Michael Hayes before he died. This was him. This was the man.

Lacy sat back, staring at the photograph, her mind spinning. Why was this picture torn in such a way that felt so... familiar? And why had her father written those words? What was the deal?

Her thoughts raced as she slipped the photo into her jacket pocket and closed the drawer. She had to get out of there. But before she left, her eyes fell on the family photo of her mother on the desk—the one that had always been there, smiling warmly at her.

Suddenly, it hit her. She had seen this picture before, or the other half at least.

By the time Lacy got home after work, the city had grown quiet. She dropped her keys on the table and made a beeline for the small side table next to her favorite chair, where she kept a photo of her mother. Her hands trembled as she picked it up, staring at the torn edges of the picture.

The photograph of Michael Hayes was in her other hand, and slowly, Lacy brought the two torn edges together.

A perfect match.

Her heart pounded in her chest as she stared at the now-complete photograph. Michael Hayes and her mother. The way they were standing, close, intimate. They clearly knew each other—well.

Her breath came in shallow gasps as she tried to process what this meant. Who was Michael Hayes to her mother? And more importantly, what did this man have to do with her father's shady dealings?

Her mind swirled with questions, but one thing was now certain: Jake Marlowe had been killed for getting too close to this connection. And now, she was too.

Lacy sank into her chair, staring blankly at the torn photograph in her hands. What am I going to do? she thought, her mind spinning. She couldn't call the police. Her father had his hands in every pocket, every institution. She had no one she could fully trust anymore.

Maybe she should go to the press. But who? She thought about Claire Morgan. The editor-in-chief had been evasive last time, but maybe she knew more than she was letting on.

Lacy's heart raced as she made her decision. Tomorrow, she thought, her resolve hardening, I'm going to confront Claire. And this time, I'm getting answers.

She set the photograph down, her breath still shaky as she stood. Walking into the bathroom, she splashed cold water on her face, trying to calm the storm inside her. As the water dripped from her chin, she looked at her reflection in the mirror. Her eyes were bloodshot from stress, her face pale, but her gaze was steady.

She knew what she had to do. This was bigger than politics. Bigger than her career. It was about justice.

And tomorrow, she would begin to unravel the web her father had spun.

****

The morning sun filtered through the skyscrapers, casting long shadows across the city as Lacy strode confidently toward the State Tribune. She was sharply dressed in a fitted black blazer, a crisp white blouse, and tailored pants. Her hair was pulled back into a sleek ponytail, her makeup flawless, every inch of her exuding the polished, formidable presence of a woman who had built her career as a successful lawyer and now was a rising political force.

Today wasn't about campaigning, though. Today was about control. She was done being manipulated, done playing defense.

As she stepped into the building, her heels clicked with precision across the marble floors. The State Tribune newsroom buzzed with the usual morning energy—reporters hunched over desks, phones ringing, editors barking orders from the corners of the room. But all of that faded into background noise as Lacy headed straight toward Claire Morgan's office, her mind focused on the task at hand.

Claire had agreed to meet with her, but the conversation had been clipped. "I only have a few minutes," Claire had said over the phone.

A receptionist tried to stop her as she neared the office, but Lacy waved her off with the kind of authority that brooked no argument. She knocked once on Claire's door before pushing it open and stepping inside.

Claire Morgan looked up from behind her cluttered desk, her sharp eyes narrowing as Lacy entered. The editor-in-chief was as formidable as ever, her presence commanding, despite the weary look on her face. Papers and notebooks were strewn across the surface of her desk, but the most striking thing was the guarded expression Claire wore, as though she already knew why Lacy was there.

"Senator Jacobs," Claire said coolly, gesturing to the chair in front of her. "I only have a few minutes."

Lacy didn't sit. She kept her posture straight, standing just inside the doorway. Her eyes locked onto Claire's. "That's fine," Lacy replied, her voice as sharp as the suit she wore. "This will only take two."

Claire's brow arched, but she said nothing.

Lacy's heart raced, but her exterior was ice cold. She pulled out her phone, glanced at the time, and then met Claire's gaze. "Here's how this is going to go. I have evidence—and witnesses—linking a prominent businessman we both know to multiple wrongdoings, including murder."

Claire's expression didn't falter, but there was a flicker of something—worry? guilt?—in her eyes.

Lacy continued, her voice steady. "I think you're working for him, or at least protecting him. But here's the deal, Claire: You have 24 hours to come forward with what you know. If you don't, I will personally take this to the FBI, and anyone connected to the murder of Jake Marlowe—including you—will be spending an eternity behind bars. The choice is yours."

The silence in the room was thick, the air heavy with tension as Claire stared at her. For the first time, the editor looked unsettled, her fingers twitching as she shifted uncomfortably in her chair. Lacy had struck a nerve, and she knew it.

She glanced at her watch, letting the silence hang for a beat longer. "Look at that," she said, her voice calm but edged with a hint of triumph. "It only took me forty-nine seconds."

With that, she gave Claire one final look—challenging, daring her to make the wrong choice—before turning on her heel and walking out of the office without another word. The sound of her heels echoed through the newsroom as she strode toward the exit, leaving a stunned Claire Morgan in her wake.

The moment Lacy stepped out of the Tribune's office, a surge of adrenaline rushed through her. For the first time in what felt like forever, she was in control. She had been so used to reacting—to Richard's manipulations, to the unfolding chaos around Jake's death, to the growing suspicions about her father—that she had almost forgotten what it felt like to be on the offensive.

But now, the tide had shifted. And with Claire on notice, Lacy had a weapon in her arsenal.

As she climbed into her car and headed back to campaign headquarters, she couldn't help but smile to herself. She'd have to slip back into the Jacobs estate tonight to put the photo back where she found it, but that was a task for later. For now, she had a campaign rally to attend—and a job to do.

Lacy arrived at campaign headquarters with renewed energy. The building buzzed with activity as staffers rushed around, preparing for the upcoming rally. Posters with her face and slogans plastered the walls, volunteers were busy organizing, and Paige stood at the center of it all, directing everyone with military precision.

Lacy stepped inside, her sharp eyes scanning the room, and she felt a momentary rush of pride. This was her team—her people. And despite everything happening in the shadows, this was her purpose.

Paige spotted her, marching over with a clipboard in hand. "You're late," she said, her tone light but firm. "I hope you have a good reason."

Lacy flashed her a grin, but there was steel behind it. "I handled something important this morning. But I'm here now."

Paige nodded, giving her a quick once-over, then turned back to the chaos around them. "Alright, boss, let's get you prepped for the rally."

Lacy slipped into campaign mode easily, falling into the familiar rhythm of speeches, handshakes, and promises. But even as she smiled and greeted supporters, the photograph of Michael Hayes burned in the back of her mind.

Tonight, she'd deal with the photo. Tonight, she'd continue unraveling the web her father had spun.

But for now, she smiled, shook hands, and prepared to fight for the future she had always believed in—even if it meant taking down the man who had raised her.

Later that evening, the dim light from Lacy's desk lamp cast long shadows across the campaign office, making the room feel emptier than it actually was. The hum of the city outside provided a low, constant background noise, but inside, the only sound was the quiet tap-tap of her fingers on the keyboard. It was late, later than she'd normally stay, but with Ben at poker night and the day's whirlwind of events still spinning in her head, Lacy had decided to wrap up a few loose ends before heading home.

The air smelled faintly of the takeout she'd had earlier, the lingering scent of soy sauce and ginger clinging to the room. She pushed her chair back, standing and stretching, feeling the tightness in her shoulders from hours of work. She had been successful earlier that evening—sneaking back into her father's estate, carefully replacing the torn photograph in his desk. No one would suspect a thing. For the first time in days, she felt like she was one step ahead.

A faint sound came from the hallway—the creak of the door opening. Lacy straightened up, glancing toward the entrance, half-expecting to see Chloe or Paige, maybe checking in on her before heading home themselves.

"Chloe?" she called out, her voice echoing slightly in the otherwise quiet office. She waited for a response but heard nothing.

Her fingers paused over her keyboard, her senses suddenly on high alert. There was something about the silence that felt... off. A shadow moved just beyond the doorway, and Lacy's heart skipped a beat.

She stood, her pulse quickening, ready to brush it off when Claire Morgan stepped into the room, her silhouette sharp against the dim light.

Lacy's breath caught in her throat. The faint scent of Claire's perfume. Claire's expression was unreadable, but her posture was tense, her shoulders rigid as if coiled for something.

Lacy's first instinct was smug satisfaction. "Claire," she said, folding her arms across her chest, her voice smooth, "I assume you've come to do the right thing, to help me?"

But Claire didn't smile, didn't offer any words of concession. Instead, her eyes narrowed, and the look on her face sent a cold shiver down Lacy's spine.

"No," Claire said quietly, stepping further into the office, her heels clicking softly on the polished floor. "You're going to help me."

Before Lacy could respond, she saw the glint of something metallic in Claire's hand. Her stomach dropped as the reality of the situation hit her like a punch. Claire wasn't here to talk.

She was holding a gun.

Claire raised the gun and pointed directly at Lacy.

CHAPTER 19

Lacy's pulse hammered in her ears as she felt the cold, hard muzzle of the gun press against her back. Claire—no, not Claire, but someone else—had shoved her into the back of her own car. The driver, an unfamiliar man, didn't even glance her way as he stepped on the gas. The streets outside passed by in a blur, but Lacy barely noticed, her mind reeling with fear, confusion, and something far worse: uncertainty.

"Where are you taking me?" Lacy's voice came out steadier than she expected, but the grip of fear was tightening in her chest. The air in the car felt stifling, her mind swirling with the unknown.

Claire—whoever she really was—kept her eyes forward, her voice cold and cutting. "Shut up."

Lacy swallowed hard, her throat tight. Her heart raced, and her thoughts screamed at her to stay calm, to figure a way out of this. She stared out the window, but it was as though they were driving through a void. Time stretched, distorted, until she had no idea how long they'd been in the car. The city's streets slowly gave way to darker, winding roads, thick woods closing in on either side. The silence in the car was oppressive, suffocating.

When the car finally slowed to a stop, they were deep in the woods, the shadows of trees looming large in the dim moonlight. The driver said nothing as Claire opened the door, yanking Lacy out with the gun still pointed at her side.

"Move," Claire snapped, jabbing the gun harder into Lacy's ribs. Lacy complied, her steps unsteady but her outward composure never wavering. Inside, though, she was unraveling. She had no idea what awaited her, but she knew she had to remain calm. No matter how terrified she felt, she couldn't show it. Not yet.

They trudged through the forest, the damp earth crunching beneath their feet. The air smelled of pine and decaying leaves, sharp and cool in the night. Ahead, a dilapidated old cabin came into view, barely visible in the thick foliage. It looked abandoned, but as they got closer, Lacy noticed faint light seeping through the cracks in the wooden boards. This was no ordinary cabin.

Claire pushed her inside, flipping on a single overhead light. The interior of the cabin was nothing like what Lacy had expected. The walls were plastered with photographs—gruesome crime scenes, mugshots, diagrams, and in the center, a large picture of her father, Richard Jacobs, staring down at her like some kind of omnipresent figure.

Lacy's breath hitched as she took it all in, her mind racing to process what she was seeing. Her father's image loomed large, surrounded by criminals and bloody trails of violence. But the most unnerving part was the clear sense of control in all of it—this was not chaos. This was meticulous. Organized. Planned.

"Sit," Claire ordered, gesturing toward a small wooden table where two cups of steaming coffee waited. Lacy hesitated for a moment, her instincts screaming at her to bolt, to do something, but she forced herself to comply. She sat, keeping her back straight, her face a mask of cold composure.

Claire took a seat across from her, sipping her coffee with an unsettling calm. "Relax," she said, her tone a strange mix of authority and exhaustion. "I'm not going to kill you."

Lacy didn't respond. Her fingers drummed lightly on the wooden table, the tension in her body coiled so tightly she felt she might snap at any moment. The smell of the coffee was sharp in the small room, but Lacy barely noticed it. Her mind was on the pictures, on the ominous layout of what looked like a criminal investigation—but why did her father's face dominate the center of it all?

After a long, measured sip, Claire set her cup down. "Let's cut to the chase. I'm Agent Jennifer Housley, FBI. I've been undercover for years, working with a joint task force to take down your father, Richard Jacobs."

The words struck Lacy like a blow. She fought to keep her expression neutral, but she felt her stomach twist into knots. The sound of her father's name, paired with "FBI," confirmed what she had been fearing: Richard Jacobs wasn't just powerful. He was dangerous.

Housley didn't stop. "We know Mary Marlowe came to you asking questions about her son."

Lacy shifted in her seat anxiously as Agent Housley continued. "I believe Jake was closing in on Richard's operation and Richard put a hit out on him. The police will never find anything. We've been watching him for a long time. He's good. Really good. He's built an empire right under everyone's noses. And you, Lacy, are part of his next move."

Lacy's throat tightened, her mind spinning. "What do you mean?"

Agent Housley leaned forward, her gaze sharp, assessing Lacy's every reaction. "We believe he's using your campaign. You becoming governor will give him control over more than just his business. It'll give him political power—complete control of the Commonwealth. He's been removing his competition for years, starting at the bottom, taking out drug lords and cartel families from the inside. You've been his cover."

Lacy's mouth went dry. The accusations were dizzying. "What are you talking about? I've been trying to help people—clean up the city, protect communities. What does that have to do with him?"

Housley sighed, flipping open a file she'd pulled from her bag. She slid a few photographs across the table. "You think you've been cleaning up the city. But all the while, he's been using you to take out his rivals. While you were on the city council, every time you pushed for more police presence in certain areas, he was making sure those areas belonged to his enemies. He was using you to wipe out the competition, clearing the way for his empire to grow."

Lacy stared at the photos. Familiar streets. Familiar names. Gangs and well-known drug dealers she'd seen dismantled during her time on the city council. But now, with the way Housley framed it, she saw it differently. It wasn't law enforcement protecting the city. It was her father playing chess, moving pieces to gain more control.

Suddenly she felt sick. Staring back at her was a picture of Imogen Ivanov's dead body.

Lacy's breath came in shallow, uneven bursts. She hadn't known Imogen Ivanov well, but the thought of her dead, executed like so many others in her father's world, hit her harder than she expected. It wasn't just a name on a list. Imogen had trusted her, had poured out her pain in those quiet moments over tea. Now, she was gone. Another casualty.

"Was she………executed?" Lacy's voice was a whisper, barely audible, as she struggled to hold back the swell of emotions threatening to break through. Her hands trembled slightly, her nails digging into the soft flesh of her palms.

Housley nodded, her expression grim. "We found her two days ago. It was a message, Lacy. The same kind of hit we've seen before. Her husband's gone underground. We lost our only witness."

Lacy's heart pounded in her chest, the air suddenly thick and suffocating in the dimly lit cabin. The smell of damp wood mingled with the faint aroma of coffee, but the room felt cold now, colder than before. A sharp, bitter taste rose in the back of her throat. How much more was there? How deep did this go?

She felt the weight of the task ahead, the enormity of what she was being asked to do. She had to help. For Imogen. For the countless others who had suffered under her father's unseen hand.

But there was a nagging doubt still clawing at her insides. A sense of unreality, of disbelief.

Lacy straightened in her chair, her voice regaining some of its strength. "How do I know you're telling me the truth about all of this?" Her eyes locked onto Housley's, searching for any sign of deceit. "I mean... my own father has been lying to me for years. How and why should I trust you?"

Agent Housley didn't flinch. She leaned back in her chair, her expression hard but not unkind, and reached into her bag. Slowly, deliberately, she pulled out a thick file and slid it across the table.

"The task force," Housley began, her tone measured, "includes the FBI, DEA, ATF, and Homeland Security. We've been following your father for a long time, and more recently, we've been following you."

Lacy's heart skipped a beat, her pulse quickening as her fingers hesitated over the file. "Following me?" she repeated, her voice laced with suspicion.

Housley didn't blink. "We had to make sure you weren't working with him. That you weren't... complicit in what he's been doing: the drugs, money laundering, racketeering. We are so close and we had to be sure."

Lacy flipped the file open, her eyes scanning the contents—surveillance reports, photos of her coming and going from various campaign events, meetings, her apartment. Each detail meticulously noted, tracked.

And then she saw it. A familiar face. A familiar silhouette.

Benjamin A. Carter.

Her chest tightened. There, in black and white, were photos of her and Ben—months of them. At campaign headquarters, stepping into her apartment, at campaign events, even walking along the street. Together.

Lacy shifted in her seat, trying to keep her face neutral, but she couldn't stop the wave of heat that rushed to her cheeks. "You know about….?" Her voice was quiet, barely more than a whisper.

Housley nodded, her gaze softening just slightly. "We know about the relationship you've been having with Benjamin Carter. But please understand, this isn't about blackmail, Senator. It's about due diligence. We had to be sure."

Lacy scoffed, her emotions a swirling mix of anger, embarrassment, and... something else. "It's your due diligence to watch me fuck my boyfriend?" The word came out sharper than she intended, the first time she'd ever said it out loud. She pushed aside the brief flicker of glee that the label gave her, focusing back on the situation at hand.

Housley held up a hand, her tone apologetic and firm. "We never placed cameras inside your apartment or your bedroom. We didn't invade your privacy to that level. But we did observe your comings and goings, and yes, we know about your relationship with Mr. Carter. You're good at switching up routines—threw a few of our agents off track."

Lacy shot back, "Thanks for the compliment. But if this isn't about blackmail, what is it about?"

"I'm sorry, Lacy. But we had to be sure. Your father's connections run deep, and we couldn't take any chances. And it is to show you that if we wanted to take you down, we would have leaked these photos to the press. But we didn't want that; we wanted to work with you."

Lacy stared at the photos, her mind whirling. She felt exposed, violated, but at the same time, she understood why they had done it. And the fact that they hadn't crossed certain lines gave her the smallest measure of trust. But this wasn't about Ben, or about the surveillance. This was about the bigger picture.

Lacy closed the file with a soft thud, pushing it aside. Her gaze sharpened as she met Housley's eyes again. "What's the plan, then?"

Housley leaned forward, her voice dropping slightly, as if afraid the walls might have ears. "Your father is meticulous. He doesn't leave loose ends. He's been using you—your position—since you were on the city council. Deploying more police in areas where his rivals were posted, dismantling cartels and gangs piece by piece. You looked like the hero. But all the while, he was playing puppet master."

Lacy's stomach churned. "Yes, a fact you have made me abundantly aware of." She could almost hear her father's voice in her head, all those times he'd praised her for her efforts, told her how proud he was of the work she was doing. Now it felt like a lie. A well-orchestrated manipulation.

Housley continued. "When you've shifted your policies, it has left Richard vulnerable. He had to change tactics, and that's why we're closer to taking him down than ever before. But we need your help, Lacy. We need you to plant a bug in his home office."

Lacy's mind was spinning. Her body felt like it was vibrating with the weight of the request, the enormity of what she was being asked to do. "A bug?" she repeated, her voice barely steady. "You want me to spy on him?"

Housley nodded. "We need concrete evidence. Something we can take to court. Something that will stick. He's careful, but with you in his inner circle, we have a chance. You know him. You know his habits. This is the only way to stop him."

Lacy sat back, her heart pounding in her chest. Could she really do this? Could she betray her father like that?

Her thoughts flashed back to Imogen, to the innocent people who had been killed in Richard's rise to power. And then to Ben—her sweet, loving Ben—who had no idea how deep this all went. She couldn't keep lying to him forever. But she also couldn't drag him into this.

Before Lacy could respond, something in her gut twisted. She had to know. "Before I agree to anything," she said, her voice thick with emotion, "I need to know something."

Housley waited, her eyes narrowing.

"What really happened to my mother?" Lacy's voice cracked slightly. She had held this question in for years, pushing it down, accepting her father's carefully curated story. But now, with everything unraveling, she needed the truth.

Housley's expression softened and, for the first time, Lacy saw a flicker of genuine empathy. "There's more to the story than you've been told. We have an agent, deep undercover, who can give you more details when the time is right. But..."

Lacy leaned forward, her heart racing. "Just answer one question.....did my....did he kill my mother?"

The silence that followed was unbearable. Housley's hesitation felt like an eternity.

Finally, she nodded. "Yes."

The word shattered something inside Lacy. She felt the air leave her lungs, her body going cold as if she'd been doused in ice water. Every memory of her mother—every smile, every embrace—was suddenly tainted. She had suspected for so long, but hearing it confirmed... it was like the ground had disappeared beneath her feet.

But she didn't cry. She didn't scream. She didn't break.

Instead, she straightened her spine, pushing all the emotion deep down into that well she'd mastered over the years.

"I'll do it.," she said, her voice cold and resolute.

Later that night when Lacy unlocked the door to her apartment, the heavy weight of the day was still pressing down on her shoulders. She stepped inside, expecting the quiet sanctuary she needed to collect herself. Instead, Ben was waiting for her. His tall figure leaned against the kitchen counter, arms crossed, face tight with frustration. She could feel the tension even before he spoke, the air between them thick with unspoken words.

"Where the hell have you been?" Ben's voice was sharp, edged with a mix of worry and anger. His eyes searched hers, desperate for answers. "We've been texting you all night, calling. Nothing. You just disappear?"

Lacy, still rattled from her meeting with Agent Housley, wasn't in the mood to be interrogated. She dropped her bag onto the floor and sighed, exhaustion seeping into her bones. "Ben, I'm not in the mood for this. Not tonight."

"Yeah? You're never in the mood," he shot back, pushing off the counter, his voice rising.

Lacy snapped, cutting him off before he could finish. "What, Ben? Did I forget to fuck you a seventh time today?" Her words were sharp and cold, a defense mechanism she hadn't meant to unleash but couldn't pull back.

Ben's face hardened, his jaw tightening as the hurt registered in his eyes. "Don't bullshit me, Lacy. You know this isn't about sex. This is about you. You've been pulling away from everything and everyone, and no one can reach you. It's like you're here, but you're not really here. I'm trying to help you, but you keep shutting me out."

Her heart clenched. She could see the pain she was causing, but the fear of pulling him deeper into the dangerous world she was entangled in kept her silent. She knew how much she loved him—God, she knew—but love wasn't enough to keep him safe. And right now, that was her only priority.

Lacy crossed her arms, trying to build a wall around herself, around the pain she didn't want to show. "You don't understand and you could never understand. So I can't do this right now. I can't deal with this… relationship."

Ben's face twisted in frustration. "What do you mean, 'deal with this relationship'? Don't pretend like this is something casual that doesn't matter."

The tension in the room reached its breaking point, both of them standing a foot apart but feeling miles away. Lacy felt the urge to push him, to make him leave, because if he stayed—if he stayed, he'd be in danger.

She looked at him, her eyes cold even as her heart pounded with emotion. "Maybe it doesn't matter…" she said, the words coming out harsher than she intended. But she didn't take them back. She couldn't. "And…. maybe you should just… go now."

For a moment, there was silence. Ben's face went still, his eyes narrowing as the meaning of her words sunk in. The hurt, the betrayal, all of it flashed across his face like lightning. He had tried to be patient, tried to understand, but this was too much. He was done.

"Ok……fine," he said, his voice low and controlled, but there was an edge to it, something dangerous that Lacy had never heard from him before. "If you want me gone so bad, I'll go."

He grabbed his jacket off the back of a chair and headed for the door, his footsteps heavy against the hardwood floor. Lacy watched him, the sound of her pulse drowning out everything else. She didn't think he'd actually leave. Not like this.

But he was.

Her chest tightened, panic rising in her throat as she watched him reach for the door. Tears welled in her eyes, blurring her vision. Before she even realized what she was doing, she was running after him, her hand grabbing his arm, pulling him back.

"Ben!" Her voice cracked, desperation spilling out with every word. He stopped but didn't turn around, his back stiff and unmoving.

Lacy's heart pounded as she moved in front of him, tears streaming down her face. "Please… don't go," she whispered, her voice shaky as she clung to his arm. "I'm sorry. Don't leave. I… I love you. Please don't go."

The words tumbled out, and she felt her whole world crack open. She had never said it before. Never allowed herself to feel it, much less admit it. But now, in a moment where all her world illusions lay shattered, one thing stood before her more real than anything.

Ben's eyes widened, the anger in them melting into shock. For a moment, he just stared at her, his chest rising and falling as he tried to process her words.

"I love you," Lacy repeated, her voice broken but sincere. She stepped closer, her hands trembling as they reached for his face. "Please don't go. I'm sorry."

Ben blinked, his breath catching in his throat. His hands, rough but gentle, came up to cup her face, wiping the tears away with his thumbs. His grip was firm, almost rough, as though he needed to make sure she was real, that the words were real.

"Say it again," he murmured, his voice thick with emotion.

"I love you," Lacy breathed, her lips quivering as she said it again, louder this time. "I love you."

The next thing she knew, Ben's mouth was on hers, kissing her deeply, desperately, as if he was pouring all his frustration, all his hurt, into that one kiss. Lacy kissed him back, her hands clutching the front of his jacket as though it were the only thing keeping her grounded. She tasted salt from her tears, felt the warmth of his breath against her skin. The scent of his cologne—woodsy and familiar—wrapped around her like a cocoon, and for the first time in days, she felt safe.

Lacy's body quivered as Ben's lips crashed against hers, his grip on her waist firm, almost bruising. She clung to him, her nails digging into his shoulders, trying to hold on to something solid, something real amidst the chaos of her world. The taste of him—coffee and something darker—was intoxicating, pulling her under. She gasped into his mouth as he pulled her closer, his hands sliding up her back and then tangling in her hair, tugging just enough to send a spark of pleasure through her spine.

"Say it again," Ben growled against her lips, his voice thick with lust and frustration. His hand cupped her chin, forcing her to look at him. His dark eyes bore into hers, full of an intensity that made her heart race.

"I love you," Lacy breathed, her voice trembling as the words left her mouth again, each one a confession and a plea. Her body ached for him, needed him to consume her, to make everything else disappear.

Ben's lips moved to her neck, biting in a way that left her skin tingling. Lacy moaned, her fingers fumbling with the buckle of his belt, her hands trembling as she tried to unfasten his pants. She needed him now, needed the warmth of his body to drown out the cold reality pressing down on her.

Ben's breath was ragged against her throat as she freed him, his pants falling to the floor. Without hesitation, Lacy dropped to her knees, her hands guiding him into her mouth.

"Fuck." Ben groaned, his hand gripping her hair as she worked her mouth over him.

As Ben's breathing became more ragged, he pulled her up, his lips crashing against hers in a rough, hungry kiss. His hands tore at her clothes, ripping her shirt open and exposing her skin to the cool air of the room. Lacy's breath hitched as her nipples—pierced and aching—were exposed, standing out against the flush of her skin.

"God, I missed you," Ben murmured, his voice hoarse as he pushed her toward the bedroom, his hands never leaving her skin, his fingers trailing over her breasts, down her stomach, making her shiver with anticipation.

When they reached the bed, Ben laid her down, kissing his way down her body, his lips teasing her nipples before his mouth moved lower. Lacy's hips bucked when he reached the heat between her legs, his tongue flicking out to taste her. She moaned, arching her back as pleasure flooded her senses.

"Say it again," Ben demanded, his voice muffled as he kissed her inner thighs.

"I love you," Lacy gasped, her hands gripping the sheets, her body trembling as Ben's tongue delved deeper, sending shockwaves of pleasure through her.

He kissed his way back up her body, his lips brushing against hers as he positioned himself between her legs.

"Ben, I don't want to lose you," she whispered, her eyes locking onto his.

"You won't," Ben promised, his voice low, filled with certainty. He thrust into her without hesitation, filling her completely, his body pressing hers into the mattress. Lacy cried out, her hands gripping his back, nails digging into his skin as he stretched her, claiming her.

"Say it again," Ben growled, his strokes deep and rough, his eyes never leaving hers.

"I love you," Lacy moaned, her voice shaking as her body responded to every thrust, pleasure building inside her, threatening to break her apart.

Ben grabbed her chin roughly, forcing her to look at him. "Look at me," he commanded, his voice dripping with dominance. Lacy's eyes locked onto his, her breath catching in her throat as the intensity of his gaze pulled her under. His dark eyes were filled with lust, with raw need, and it made her feel as though she was losing her grip on control, drowning in him.

His pace didn't slow, each thrust hitting deeper, pushing her closer to the edge. Lacy's body responded, her hips lifting to meet his as her moans filled the room, echoing in the small space.

Ben sat them up, Lacy straddling his lap as she began to ride him. She moved slowly at first, her hips rolling in a steady rhythm, savoring the feel of him deep inside her. But soon, the need overtook her, and she moved faster, her body grinding against his, seeking that release that was just out of reach.

Ben's hands were on her breasts, his mouth sucking her nipples, the sharp tug of his lips sending jolts of pleasure through her. Lacy leaned into him, her fingers tangling in his long, curly hair as another wave of pleasure crashed through her. She moved faster, her hips rocking against him, her breath coming in shallow gasps as she chased her release.

They clung to each other as though their lives depended on it, the connection between them deeper than anything she had ever felt. Ben's hands gripped her hips, guiding her movements, urging her faster, harder.

In one swift movement, Ben turned her over, positioning her on all fours as he thrust back inside her. Lacy gasped, her body trembling as he filled her again, the angle hitting just right. Ben grabbed her hair, pulling her head back as he fucked her from behind, his voice a rough growl in her ear.

"Say it again."

"I love you," Lacy panted, her voice barely audible over the sound of their bodies colliding.

Ben flipped her onto her back again, his body covering hers as he drove into her with renewed intensity. His hand slid around her throat, squeezing just enough to send a thrill through her. Lacy's body was on fire, every nerve alight as he filled her, thrusting deeper, harder.

"Ben," Lacy's voice was breathy, desperate.

Ben slowed, his hand tightening slightly around her throat as he looked into her eyes. His expression was fierce, raw, filled with something she couldn't quite name. "Lacy," he growled, his voice a promise.

"Don't stop," Lacy begged, arching her back, her legs tightening around his waist, pulling him deeper. Ben's hand never left her throat as he thrust harder, his movements rough, and precise, driving her closer to the edge.

As they both neared the brink, their bodies moving in perfect rhythm, Lacy's legs locked around him, holding him in place. She felt the tension building inside her, tighter and tighter, until it finally snapped. She cried out, her body shaking as her orgasm ripped through her, every muscle tightening as she clung to him.

Ben's breath hitched, his thrusts becoming erratic as he reached his own release. "Lacy, I'm..." his voice was strained, a warning.

In that moment, as her body shuddered with release, Lacy's thoughts drifted unbidden to all she had lost. Her mother, stolen too soon. The innocence of her youth, shadowed by her father's ruthless ambition. The quiet moments of peace she once imagined her life would hold. And now, with Ben, all she stood to lose felt like it loomed even closer, a stark reminder of how fragile this happiness was. Part of her, raw and aching, needed to hold on to something—someone—forever.

But Lacy didn't let go, her legs still wrapped tightly around him. "I love you," she whispered, and with that, Ben let go, climaxing deep inside her. His body trembled as he came, his face buried in her neck, his teeth sinking lightly into her skin as they rode out the aftershocks together.

Tears filled her eyes, overwhelmed by the intensity of the moment and the emotions crashing through her. Her lips parted, but no words come—only breath, only a silent prayer to the universe, to fate, to whoever was listening: Don't take him from me. Please. Let love be enough.

Ben looked at her, his own eyes softening as he gently wiped away the tears. "I love you, too," he whispered, pressing a tender kiss to her lips.

They lay there, still connected, their bodies tangled together, the room filled with the quiet sounds of their breathing. After what felt like an eternity, Ben slowly pulled out of her, both of them groaning at the loss of contact. He kissed her forehead softly before slipping out of bed.

"I'm going to get some water. You go pee," he said with a smile.

Lacy laughed softly, the sound a mixture of relief and contentment. She did as he asked, feeling lighter, her body still buzzing from their connection. When she returned, Ben was waiting for her with a glass of water and a cookie. He handed them to her before pulling her into his arms, kissing her forehead again.

"Lacy," his tone was serious now.

She shook her head, placing a finger over his lips. "Please, not right now. Not tonight. I'm so sorry for everything, and I'll tell you all about it tomorrow, but tonight... I just want to be with you. The way I couldn't, because of all the bullshit."

Ben smiled softly, his arms tightening around her. "Okay," he whispered. "I need you to know that whatever it is... you got this. And I got you." She pressed a kiss to his chest—right over his heart—and closed her eyes.

They spent the rest of the night talking until they both drifted off to sleep, tangled in each other's arms, the weight of the world outside their door forgotten for just one night.

The morning light filtered softly through the curtains, casting a warm glow over Lacy's bedroom. She lay in Ben's arms, his breathing slow and steady against her neck. For a brief moment, everything felt right—the weight of the world outside their door forgotten. But as the memories of the previous night crept in, the reality of the danger surrounding them stirred something inside her.

Carefully, she slid out of Ben's embrace, not wanting to wake him. His arm fell limply to the side, and he murmured something in his sleep before settling back into the pillows. Lacy stood for a moment, watching him sleep, her heart aching with the knowledge of what she was about to tell him. But not now, not yet. She needed to give him one last perfect morning before the chaos came rushing back.

Lacy padded quietly to the kitchen, her bare feet cool against the hardwood floor. She set to work making breakfast—something simple and comforting. Eggs, bacon, toast, and freshly brewed coffee filled the air with a rich, savory scent. The soft crackle of the frying pan and the hum of the coffee machine were the only sounds as she moved around the kitchen, her mind still racing but determined to push it aside for just a little while longer.

As she was plating the last of the food, she felt a light kiss on her temple. She turned to Ben, standing there, his hair a tousled mess, his eyes warm with affection. He smiled sleepily at her. "Good morning," he murmured, his voice still thick with sleep.

"Good morning," Lacy replied softly, offering him a small smile in return. She gestured toward the breakfast table. "I made us something to eat."

Ben sat down at the table, looking over the spread. "You didn't have to do this, you know."

"I wanted to," Lacy said, joining him with her own plate. For a few moments, they ate in mostly in silence, exchanging small talk about the food, the weather—anything that felt light, safe, normal. But as they sat there, Lacy could feel the weight of what she needed to tell him pressing down on her, making it harder to breathe.

It was Ben who finally broke the comfortable silence, his fork clinking against the plate as he set it down. "Lacy," he began, his tone more serious now, "I need to know... are you really not happy with us? Is that really why you've been so distant?"

Lacy's heart clenched at the question. She had known this moment would come. The truth had to come out, but how could she tell him everything without shattering the fragile peace they'd created? She looked up, meeting his gaze, and shook her head, the words rushing out before she could stop them.

"No, Ben, it has nothing to do with you. I love you. But—" Her voice caught in her throat as she glanced around the apartment, suddenly suspicious. Could her father have bugged her place? It wouldn't be beyond him. A cold wave of realization hit her, and she knew she couldn't risk it. Not here.

Quickly, she stood up, walking over to the speaker and turning up the music until it was blaring. Ben watched her with confusion, his brow furrowing.

"Lacy, what are you doing?"

She grabbed his hand, pulling him toward the bathroom. "Come shower with me," she said, her voice steady despite the tension in her body.

The water roared to life as the shower started, steam filling the bathroom as they stepped in together. The sound of the music and the water provided a buffer, a wall of noise that made Lacy feel just a little bit safer. She let the hot water cascade over her, taking a deep breath before turning to Ben, her heart pounding in her chest.

"I need to tell you something," Lacy said, her voice barely audible over the rush of the shower. "There's something going on—something bigger than the campaign. I didn't mean to pull away from you, but I was trying to protect you." She hesitated, her hands trembling as she continued telling him all she knew.

Ben's eyes widened in shock. "Holy shit. Lacy, are you serious?"

She nodded, the gravity of the situation settling heavily between them. "I was trying to keep you at a distance because I thought it was the only way to keep you safe. I didn't want you involved in any of this. But now... I don't know what to do. I don't want you caught in the crossfire, especially of something you never saw coming."

Ben stared at her, the water running over his face as he processed her words. He reached out, cupping her face in his hands.

"Ben, I know it's a lot. You can leav—"

"Shut up," he interrupted, his tone firm but tender. He kissed her hard, silencing her protests. "I love you."

Tears welled in Lacy's eyes as she felt the strength of his words, the unwavering conviction in his voice. "But, Ben—"

"No," he said, cutting her off again. "You can't get rid of me. I'm in love with you. It's too late."

She felt her heart swell with emotion, the weight of her fear and guilt momentarily lifting as she looked into his eyes. "I love you," she whispered, her voice cracking.

"I love your stubborn ass," he replied, his forehead resting against hers. "And nothing—nothing—is going to change that."

They stood there, the hot water washing over them, rinsing away the outside world. Slowly, deliberately, they began to wash each other, their movements tender and careful, as if they were trying to cleanse themselves of the chaos that surrounded them. Ben's hands moved gently over her skin, grounding her in the moment, making her feel safe in a way she hadn't felt in days.

For now, there was no danger, no deceit. Just the two of them, standing together, vulnerable and exposed, but somehow stronger for it. Lacy closed her eyes, letting herself be held, letting herself believe that they could face whatever came next as long as they had each other.

As they stepped out of the shower, drying off in comfortable silence, Lacy caught Ben's gaze. There was something new there—something deeper, more intense. She realized that they had crossed a line, reached a new understanding, and with it came a sense of peace she hadn't expected.

They dressed slowly, Ben pulling her into his arms once more before they made their way back to the kitchen. But now, there was something different in the air between them. Something real. Something beautiful.

And as Lacy glanced down, a small, unspoken hope flickered inside her. Maybe last night had given them more than just a moment of solace. Maybe it had given them a future—a future she would fight for with everything she had.

CHAPTER 20

Two Months Later

The bedroom was a sanctuary of opulence, draped in shadows and whispers of moonlight. The massive bed dominated the space, its high, tufted headboard gleaming faintly under the silver wash of the night. A faint breeze rustled the curtains, carrying with it the faint scent of jasmine from the gardens below. The air was thick with the mingling aromas of Richard's cologne—smoky, rich, with a hint of spice—and the musk of their recent intimacy.

Richard lay on his back, one arm bent behind his head, his chest rising and falling in a rhythm that mirrored the tide of his thoughts. Beside him, Chloe nestled into the luxurious sheets, her limbs languid, her skin glowing faintly from the heat of their shared passion. Her hair spilled across the pillow in wild waves, framing her flushed cheeks and contented smile.

For a long moment, neither spoke. The world beyond the estate seemed impossibly far away, leaving only the sounds of their breathing and the distant chirping of crickets.

Chloe sighed softly, breaking the silence, and pushed herself up on one elbow. "I'll be right back," she murmured, her voice warm and unguarded.

Richard nodded absently, his gaze fixed on the canopy overhead. His mind was a storm of calculation and unease, but his expression betrayed nothing.

The en-suite bathroom glowed softly as Chloe turned on the light, its sleek marble surfaces gleaming under the cool illumination. She stepped inside and closed the door partway, pausing to stretch. Her body felt loose and weightless, a pleasant hum still buzzing in her veins.

She used the toilet, the faint trickle of water the only sound in the stillness. Then she moved to the sink, the cool porcelain smooth beneath her fingers as she turned on the tap. The cold water was bracing against her skin as she washed her face, droplets clinging to her cheeks and lashes like tiny jewels.

When she straightened and looked into the mirror, her reflection smiled back—a glow of contentment in her soft brown eyes, a hint of mischief in the curve of her lips. The memory of Richard's hands on her, his whispered words, sent a gentle warmth curling through her chest.

Unbeknownst to her, Richard had risen from the bed the moment the bathroom door clicked shut. He moved with deliberate calm, his broad shoulders casting shadows across the room as he strode to his desk near the window. The faint scent of polished wood and leather surrounded him as he pulled out his phone.

He glanced toward the bathroom door, ajar but hiding Chloe from view, then pressed a number on his screen. His voice, low and sharp, cut through the quiet like a knife. "It's me. Move the drive. Tonight. Take it to the safe place."

The voice on the other end was barely audible, but Richard's expression darkened as he listened. "I don't care what you have to do," he growled, his tone barely restrained. "Just make it happen. No loose ends."

His jaw tightened, and his knuckles whitened against the phone. "You know what's on that drive. If it falls into the wrong hands, we're finished. No mistakes."

As the call ended with a curt click, Richard ran a hand through his hair, his breathing heavier now. His movements were sharp, almost restless, as if the very walls of his sanctuary were closing in on him.

The weight of his empire pressed down on him—crumbling, slipping through his grasp, no matter how tightly he tried to hold on.

He turned back toward the bathroom just as Chloe emerged, her face fresh, her expression radiant with unguarded affection. She paused in the doorway, the soft light behind her outlining her silhouette in a halo-like glow.

"Everything alright?" she asked, tilting her head slightly, her voice tender.

Richard's lips curved into a faint smile, his features softening as he crossed the room to her. He took her hand, drawing her gently back toward the bed. "Yeah," he said, his tone steady. "Everything's fine."

As they settled onto the mattress, Chloe looked at him with wide, trusting eyes, her fingers brushing lightly over his. "You wanted to ask me something?"

Richard hesitated, a flicker of something unreadable in his gaze. Then he reached out, tucking a strand of her hair behind her ear. "There's a favor I need from you," he said, his voice measured, tinged with something deeper—almost vulnerable.

Chloe's smile wavered slightly, her heart quickening. "Do you love me?" she asked, the words slipping out before she could stop them.

For a moment, Richard said nothing, his expression unreadable. Then he leaned in, his hand cupping her cheek as his lips brushed hers in a kiss that was slow, deliberate, and disarming.

"I do," he murmured against her lips, his tone low and seemingly sincere.

Chloe's heart soared, and she smiled as she nestled closer to him, unaware of the storm brewing just beneath the surface of his carefully constructed facade.

Outside, the estate's grounds lay silent under the watchful gaze of the moon, but inside, the shadows seemed to deepen. Richard held Chloe close, his touch gentle yet possessive, his mind already racing ahead to what would come next.

The cabin was nestled deep in the woods, its weathered wood exterior blending seamlessly with the dense trees surrounding it. The scent of pine and damp earth filled the crisp air, and the faint rustling of leaves whispered secrets to no one in particular. Inside, the atmosphere was starkly different—alive with the hum of tension and the soft crackle of a fire in the stone hearth.

Lacy sat cross-legged on an overstuffed armchair that looked older than her. She stared at Agent Housley, who stood leaning against the mantle, arms crossed, wearing her signature blend of combat boots and a don't-mess-with-me attitude.

"So," Lacy began, raising a brow, "kidnapping me again? Really? At least this time you didn't hold me at gunpoint."

Agent Housley smirked, shaking her head. "Don't tempt me. It's still early."

Lacy laughed, a dry, knowing sound. "What now, Agent Housley? If this is about the bug, it's been two months, and all we've got is radio silence." Her tone was casual, but her foot tapped an impatient rhythm against the wooden floor. "You're running out of time, and so am I."

Agent Housley straightened, her eyes sharp as she crossed the room to stand in front of Lacy. "This isn't a waste of time, Lacy. Trust me, what you're about to hear will change everything."

Lacy's skepticism softened just slightly. She sighed and leaned back, her fingers running over the frayed arm of the chair. The fabric was rough, and the motion soothed her fraying nerves. "Alright, I'm listening. Blow my mind."

The cabin door creaked open, and Agent Housley turned, stepping aside. In walked a man who seemed to carry the weight of the world on his shoulders. His presence filled the room like a gust of wind, unrelenting and impossible to ignore.

Lacy's breath caught. "Wait," she said, her voice barely above a whisper.

Michael Hayes stood before her, the very image of a ghost brought back to life. His broad shoulders and rugged features were unmistakable, though his face bore more lines, his hair streaked with gray. His eyes, however, were the same—dark, piercing, and locked onto hers with an intensity that made her skin prickle.

"This is agent Paul Tucker, aka Michael Hayes," Agent Housley said, gesturing toward him with a flourish. "Alive and kicking."

Lacy stood, her movements slow and deliberate, her heart pounding. "Last I heard, you were dead. Jake Marlowe was looking for you; he said you died 10 years ago."

Michael nodded, his jaw tightening. "That's the story I needed people to believe." His voice was deep, steady, and carried the weight of truths long buried.

Lacy crossed her arms, her gaze unwavering. "So what's the truth?"

Michael exhaled, rubbing the back of his neck. "I faked my death to get closer to Richard. Going deep underground was the only way to stay alive and keep gathering intel. He spent years trying to bribe Mayor Blake, but he couldn't, so he tried to get rid of him. Thanks to Amanda, we were able to stop the assassination. Richard knew I would always be on him, so I had to disappear. I've spent years building a cover, embedding my guy in his network, and trying to figure out how to bring him down."

"And now?" Lacy pressed. "What's changed?"

Michael's eyes softened as he looked at her, and for a moment, something unspoken hung in the air. He cleared his throat, forcing himself back into the present. "Thanks to the bug you planted, we've confirmed the existence of a flash drive—Richard's holy grail. Every mafia boss, crooked cop, kingpin, you name it, has this holy grail. A thing they use to keep all their stuff straight with contacts, snitches, etc. Now we've got Richard's and it's got everything: his criminal contacts, blackmail files, the cops and politicians he's bought. Everything."

Lacy's breath hitched. She felt the weight of those words settle in her chest, a cold mix of dread and hope. "So what's the problem? Go get it."

Michael glanced at Agent Housley before answering. "That's the thing. We don't know where it is. Richard trusts only one person with its location—his right-hand man. And all he's told him is that "the secret lies with his mother.""

Lacy frowned, pacing the room. Her boots clicked against the floor, mingling with the distant crackle of the fire. The faint scent of cedar smoke hung in the air, grounding her as her mind raced. "His mother? He never talks about his parents, just that they died when he was young. Wait.....does he mean literally or figuratively?"

"We don't know," Agent Housley admitted. "But we're working on it."

Lacy stopped, turning to face them both. "You'd better work fast. The election's almost here. If I win, Richard's power becomes that much more untouchable. And if you think he's dangerous now, wait until I'm in office and he's still trying to pull strings behind the scenes."

Michael stepped closer, his movements slow and deliberate. "You're right to worry, Lacy. Richard's grip on power is tightening. However, he's getting more paranoid, erratic, and sloppy. He's gonna mess up and when he does, we've got him."

Lacy met his gaze, and for the first time, she saw something in his eyes that made her pause. It wasn't just determination or resolve—it was something deeper, something personal.

"What....why are you staring at me?" she asked, her voice quieter now.

Michael hesitated, his jaw working as he searched for the right words. "Sorry..." He shook his head, forcing a faint smile. "Sorry, you just remind me of ummmmm.......you remind me why I started this in the first place."

Agent Housley stepped in, breaking the moment. "We'll contact you when we know more," she said. "For now, keep your head down and stay focused on the campaign. The distraction is working. Richard's too busy watching you to notice us closing in."

Lacy smirked, her confidence returning. "It's the least I can do for him."

The three of them stood in silence for a moment, the weight of their mission hanging heavy in the air. Outside, a gust of wind rattled the cabin's windows, and the scent of rain mingled with the earthy aroma of the forest.

The cabin door closed behind Lacy, her confident stride disappearing into the shadows of the forest path. The distant crunch of her boots on the gravel faded into silence, leaving the room heavy with unspoken words. Michael stood by the window, staring at the empty trail she'd left behind, his broad shoulders rigid but his expression unguarded.

"She's something else," he murmured, almost to himself. His voice carried a weight that didn't go unnoticed.

Agent Housley leaned against the hearth, crossing her arms. "Yeah, she is. But you already knew that, didn't you?"

Michael's lips twitched into a faint smile, though his eyes remained fixed on the darkness beyond the glass. "The last time I saw her, she couldn't have been more than ten. Pigtails, a gap-toothed grin. She wanted to be an astronaut one day, then a veterinarian the next. She was fearless—always climbing trees, always testing limits." He exhaled sharply, his breath fogging the windowpane. "And now look at her. Fierce. Brilliant. She's got more guts than most people I've ever worked with."

Housley tilted her head, watching him carefully. "Proud of her, huh?"

Michael turned slightly, his expression softening. "Proud doesn't even scratch the surface. She's... everything Amanda hoped she'd be.

More than I ever could've imagined." His voice faltered, the name carrying a tremor of grief and regret.

Housley stepped closer, her boots tapping lightly against the floor. "So, what? You gonna tell her? Drop the 'surprise, I'm your dad' bombshell in the middle of all this?" Her tone was laced with dry humor, but her eyes were sharp.

Michael's jaw tightened, his hand curling into a fist at his side. "She deserves to know," he said firmly. "I've already lost so much time. If she knew—"

"She's got enough on her plate," Housley cut in, her voice steady but not unkind. "She's fighting to keep her head above water in a campaign that could change everything—for her, for Richard, for the entire damn state. You drop this on her now, and it won't help her. It'll distract her, make her question everything when she needs clarity the most."

Michael glanced at her, his dark eyes searching her face. "So, what? I wait? How long? How much longer do I let her think I'm just some ghost from her past?"

"Until the time is right," Housley said simply. She softened her stance, her expression losing some of its usual edge. "Trust me, Michael. She's strong, but even the strongest people can only carry so much. You'll tell her when it helps her, not when it complicates everything."

Michael turned back to the window, the faint outline of his reflection staring back at him. The room was silent except for the low crackle of the fire and the occasional creak of the cabin's walls as the wind pushed against them.

"I just…" He exhaled slowly, his shoulders sagging slightly. "I want her to know she's not alone. That she's got someone in her corner who—" He stopped, his voice catching.

Housley stepped closer, her voice softer now. "She does, Michael. Whether she knows it or not, you're here for her. That's enough for now."

He nodded, though the lines on his face remained etched deep. "She's so much like her mother," he said quietly, his voice thick with emotion. "But she's her own force too. Watching her in there… the way she handled herself. The way she looked at me, straight in the eye, no fear, no hesitation. I don't think I've ever been so damn impressed."

Housley smiled faintly, tapping his shoulder once. "Then let her keep doing what she's doing. You'll get your chance to tell her. And when you do, she'll be ready."

Michael didn't respond immediately, his gaze still fixed on the window. The faint glow of the moon cast long shadows across the forest, the world outside quiet but brimming with tension.

Finally, he turned back toward the room, his expression resigned but resolute. "When the time comes," he said softly, almost to himself.

Housley nodded. "When the time comes," she echoed, her tone leaving no room for doubt.

The fire crackled louder, as if punctuating their exchange, the glow illuminating the room in flickers of warmth. And as the cabin settled into silence, Michael let out a slow breath, holding onto the hope that he'd find the right moment to step out of the shadows and into the light of his daughter's life.

The next morning the water streamed over Lacy's skin, hot enough to leave the glass shower door fogged and the bathroom air heavy with steam. She tilted her head back, letting the steady cascade run through her curls and down her back. The faint scent of lavender from her body wash mingled with the warm humidity, soothing the knots of tension in her muscles—if only for a moment.

Her phone buzzed on the marble counter just as she reached for the loofah. She sighed, turned off the water, and grabbed a towel, wrapping it around herself before padding across the tiled floor. The screen lit up with Ben's name, and despite the chaos swirling in her life, her lips curled into a smile.

"Good morning, stranger," she said, her voice warm as she pressed the phone to her ear.

"I miss you," Ben replied, his tone soft and full of longing.

Lacy leaned against the counter, the cool marble pressing into her back. "Oh yeah!?! What do you miss?" she teased, her lips quirking into a playful grin.

"Your laugh," Ben began, his voice honeyed and sincere. "The way you scrunch your nose when you're about to argue with me. The way you always steal the covers, even though you swear you don't."

Lacy chuckled, a warm flush spreading across her chest. "Keep going."

Ben's voice dropped slightly, his words tinged with mischief. "The way you look in my shirts, the little sigh you make when you're falling asleep…how your skin feels against mine…" His voice dipped lower, turning playful. "And the way you moan my name when—"

"Ben!" Lacy cut him off, laughing but feeling her cheeks flush.

"You asked," he said innocently, the smile evident in his tone.

She rolled her eyes, her grin softening. "It won't be like this forever. Once this election is over, and…" She hesitated, her thoughts briefly darkening. "…….things will be different."

"They will," Ben agreed. "And I'll be right here for you Lacy. Always."

She closed her eyes, clutching the phone tighter. "I love you," she whispered.

"I love you, too," he replied, his voice tender.

A glance at the clock snapped her back to reality. "I have to go, Ben. Big day ahead."

"Go get 'em and I'll see you tonight," he said. "And don't forget to eat."

"I willlllllllll," she teased before hanging up.

At campaign headquarters, the energy was electric. Phones rang incessantly, staffers buzzed between desks, and a dozen conversations blurred into a constant hum. The air was thick with the scent of coffee and freshly printed paper. Posters with Lacy's face and slogans like "A Better Tomorrow Together" lined the walls, alongside charts tracking polling numbers and precinct coverage.

Lacy stepped inside, her heels clicking against the polished floor, and was immediately greeted by Chloe.

"Good morning, Lacy," Chloe said, her tablet in hand. "Here's your schedule for the day."

Before Lacy could respond, Paige appeared, her blazer impeccable and her expression sharp. "We've got a polling dip in some counties in the western part of the state," Paige began, her voice cutting through the chaos. "We need to hit that harder with targeted messaging."

"Let's review the data," Lacy said, already following Paige toward the conference room.

As they walked, Chloe jogged to keep up. "Also, your social media team needs you to approve the latest ads, the donor call is at noon, and you have a call with the mayor this evening."

"And I need your work phone," Chloe added casually, holding out her hand. "IT wants to update your software and change the passwords."

Without hesitation, Lacy handed over her phone. "Don't let them take forever; I need that back."

"Of course," Chloe said with a smile before darting off.

As she walked to the conference room, Lacy looked back at Chloe, searching her face for a sign of something. What? She did not know but something felt strange in the pit of her stomach.

In the conference room, Lacy and Paige dove into strategy, their conversation bouncing back and forth with practiced ease.

"What if we highlight those counties' economic plans?" Lacy suggested.

Paige nodded. "Good, but we should also bring in endorsements from local business leaders. It'll boost credibility."

"Perfect," Lacy said, a grin forming. "Look at us, solving problems before our second coffee."

Paige chuckled. "Dream team."

The day was relentless. Meetings blurred into phone calls, and Lacy's mind raced to keep up with the flood of decisions. By the time Chloe brought lunch—a burrito smothered in sauce, guac, and salsa—Lacy was starving.

The aroma hit her before Chloe even set it down. It was rich, spicy, and immediately overwhelming. Her stomach churned violently.

"Oh no," Lacy whispered, her face paling.

Without warning, she leaned over and vomited into the trash can beside her desk. The acrid taste burned her throat as she heaved again, her body trembling.

"Lacy!" Chloe exclaimed, rushing to her side.

"I'm fine. Just take it away," Lacy begged, waving weakly at the burrito.

Chloe grabbed the food and hurried out, her heels clicking frantically against the floor.

Paige appeared moments later, her expression tight with concern. "Are you okay? Do you need anything?"

Lacy wiped her mouth with a tissue and forced a weak smile. "I'm fine. Just stress. You know how it is."

"Lacy, come on." Paige's voice was firm but tinged with concern as she leaned against the edge of the desk, her arms crossed. The hum of campaign headquarters carried on around them—phones ringing, printers whirring, conversations overlapping in a constant buzz of controlled chaos.

"I'm fine, Paige," Lacy said, her tone clipped as she dabbed at her mouth with a tissue. She could still taste the acrid bitterness of bile, her stomach twisting in rebellion.

"You just threw up twice," Paige countered, arching an eyebrow. "You're pale as hell, and you're brushing this off like it's nothing. Is it the stress? Or… something else?"

Lacy glanced up sharply, her eyes narrowing. "It's stress. The campaign, the election, all of it—it's a lot. That's all."

Paige studied her for a moment, her gaze unwavering. "Is it Ben?"

Lacy let out a dry laugh, shaking her head. "Ben's fine. Ben's great, actually."

"Then what?" Paige pressed. "I'm not trying to pry, but if something's going on—"

"Paige," Lacy interrupted gently, forcing a smile. "I appreciate it, really. But I'm fine. Just overworked. I'll go home, get some rest, and be back at it tomorrow. Okay?"

Paige didn't look convinced, but she sighed and straightened up. "Fine. But keep your phone on, alright? If anything comes up—"

"It's always on," Lacy said, cutting her off again. She grabbed her bag, forcing another smile as she stood. "Go captain the ship. You're doing great."

Paige rolled her eyes but couldn't help the faint grin tugging at her lips. "Get some sleep, Lacy. You look like you need it."

At home, Lacy barely made it through the door before her stomach revolted again. She dropped her bag onto the table and sprinted to the bathroom, her heels clattering against the tiles. She barely had time to grab the edge of the toilet before she heaved, her entire body tensing as the contents of her stomach spilled out.

The acidic burn in her throat was excruciating, and tears stung her eyes as she gagged again. Her hands gripped the cold porcelain, grounding her in the moment even as her head swam.

When it was over, she sat back on the cool tile floor, her breath coming in shallow gasps. The faint scent of lavender air freshener mingled with the sharp, metallic tang of vomit, making her stomach churn again.

"This is just stress," she muttered aloud, her voice hoarse. "It's just stress."

She splashed cold water on her face at the sink, rinsed her mouth out and then opened the cabinet where a small box sat, tucked behind a row of vitamins. She hesitated, her hand hovering for a moment before pulling it out.

A little while later, the grocery store was bustling, a cacophony of chatter, carts rattling over tiled floors, and the occasional crackle of the intercom announcing a sale on produce. Lacy tugged her baseball cap lower and adjusted her sunglasses, her stomach still fragile as she navigated the aisles.

The fluorescent lights felt too bright, making her head ache. The air smelled faintly of citrus from a nearby display of oranges, but it was overpowered by the greasy aroma wafting from the deli. Lacy swallowed hard, her stomach twisting in warning as she hurried past.

She grabbed a carton of chicken noodle soup, a box of crackers, and a bottle of ginger ale. The soup can was cool and smooth in her hand, and the sight of the crackers—plain and unassuming—felt like a lifeline.

The cashier gave her a cursory glance as she scanned the items, the beep of the register oddly soothing in its monotony. Lacy mumbled a thank you, clutching the brown paper bag to her chest as she hurried back to her car.

Back home, she heated the soup and sat at the kitchen counter with a bowl in front of her. The savory aroma should have been comforting, but after a single hesitant sip, her stomach rebelled. She set the spoon down, gripping the edge of the counter as the nausea hit her in waves.

"I can't even keep soup down," she muttered, pushing the bowl away.

Defeated, she shuffled to the couch, wrapping herself in a blanket and sinking into the cushions. The fabric was soft, and she curled up tightly, exhaustion overtaking her.

She woke to the gentle press of lips against her temple and the faint scent of cedar and soap. Lacy blinked, her gaze meeting Ben's warm brown eyes as he crouched beside her, his hand brushing a stray curl from her face.

"Hey," he murmured, his voice soft. "You didn't answer your phone. Thought I'd check in."

Lacy smiled faintly, her heart swelling at the sight of him. She leaned in and kissed him, slow and deliberate, as though trying to memorize the way his lips felt against hers.

Ben pulled back slightly, his brow furrowing. "What was that for?"

Lacy hesitated, her chest tightening as the words bubbled up. "Hold on."

She slipped off the couch, returning moments later with the test. She placed it gently in Ben's hand, her fingers brushing his as she stepped back, searching his face for a reaction.

His eyes widened as he stared at it, realization dawning slowly. "Lacy…"

"I'm pregnant," she said, her voice trembling.

Ben stared at her, his mouth opening slightly as if to speak, but no words came out.

And there, in the quiet, the world seemed to hold its breath.

CHAPTER 21

The kitchen was dimly lit, the warm glow from the under-cabinet lights casting long shadows across the marble countertops. Outside, the city twinkled in the evening, muffled sounds of life filtering through the window. Lacy sat at the table, her hands clasped tightly around a glass of water, her mind racing.

Ben stood near the counter, his arms crossed, his broad shoulders taut with tension. The faint scent of the takeout he had brought lingered in the air, though neither of them had touched it.

"You're going to announce it?" Ben's voice broke the silence, low and measured, though the strain was clear.

Lacy looked up, her lips parted slightly. "Yes," she said simply, her tone quiet but firm.

Ben shook his head, a humorless laugh escaping his lips. "Of course you are. Because why wouldn't you take the biggest news of our lives and turn it into part of your campaign strategy?"

"That's not fair," Lacy shot back, her grip tightening on the glass. The condensation made it slick, cool against her clammy palms. "You think I want to have to do this? That I want to drag this baby into the spotlight?"

"Then why are you doing it?" Ben's voice rose, his frustration finally breaking through. He pushed off the counter and paced a few steps, running a hand through his hair. "This isn't just a campaign move, Lacy. This is our child. And you're talking about it like it's just another angle to play."

"That's not what I'm doing," Lacy said sharply, standing now, her chair scraping loudly against the floor. "This isn't about playing angles. This is about protecting us. If I announce it, if people know… maybe it'll change the way they see me. Maybe they'll think twice about voting for someone who's about to have a baby."

"Do you even hear yourself?" Ben demanded, turning to face her. His dark eyes blazed, their usual warmth replaced with something raw. "You're hoping people won't vote for you. You're willing to sabotage your campaign just to stop your father. Do you even want this baby, or is it just your insurance policy? You and your dad have been locked in this sick little chess match since I met you. And now me and my baby are just pawns in this stupid little game of yours."

The words hit her like a slap, and for a moment, she could only stare at him, her chest rising and falling as she struggled to catch her breath.

"How can you say that?" she whispered, her voice trembling. "You think I don't want this baby? That I don't love this baby already? Or you? That I wanted to decide this alone?" Her voice cracked, but she powered through. "I didn't have a choice, Ben. My father—"

"Stop," Ben interrupted, his hand slicing through the air. "Stop making this about him. This is about us. About this baby. About the life we're creating, not the fight you're trying to win."

Lacy's jaw clenched, her chest heaving as she struggled to hold back tears. "Don't you get it? It's all connected. There's no 'us' without him hanging over everything. I can't escape it. We can't escape it. Unless I do this."

Ben stared at her, his dark eyes blazing. "You're dragging our child into this war, Lacy. And you didn't even think to ask me how I feel about it because you knew it was wrong!"

She recoiled slightly, her voice softening. "I thought you'd understand."

"Understand what?" Ben snapped, his frustration boiling over. "That you're using this baby—the baby we made—as some sort of backup plan? How the hell am I supposed to understand that?"

"Thats not why——-!" Lacy's voice broke, and she gripped the edge of the counter, the cool stone grounding her. Tears streamed down her face, hot and unstoppable. "This baby is the reason I'm fighting, Ben. I'm trying to protect us, to give this child a chance at a life where my father's shadow doesn't touch them."

Ben's shoulders slumped slightly, but his voice still carried an edge. "And what about me? I'm supposed to just stand here, watch you make these decisions without me, and be okay with it?"

"No, I'm so sorry," she whispered, her voice trembling. "I should have talked to you and I don't blame you for being angry. But I'm scared, Ben. I'm scared that if I don't act now, we'll lose everything before we even have it."

Ben exhaled sharply, running a hand through his hair. He turned to her, his eyes softening as the tension began to melt away. "You don't have to do this alone, Lacy. You have me. You've always had me. But me and this baby—we're not your backup plan, your insurance policy or a way out of this madness with your father. What happens if your plan doesn't work? How much of me—or this baby—will you sacrifice to end this war with him?"

She stepped closer to him. Her tears fell freely now, her voice thick with emotion. "You never could be. You and this baby… mean the world to me. I will protect you both no matter what happens now we are a family and that means everything to me. "

Ben's expression softened, and he reached out, his hands cupping her face. "Then don't push me out of this, and stop making life-changing decisions without me. We're in this together. Okay?"

She nodded, her lip trembling. "Okay."

Ben pulled her into his arms, holding her tightly as she buried her face in his chest. His familiar scent wrapped around her like a blanket, soothing her frayed nerves.

"I'm sorry," she whispered, her voice muffled. "I didn't mean to shut you out."

"I know," he murmured, pressing a kiss to the top of her head. "We're going to figure this out. Together. Just hold off on the announcement ... for now."

She pulled back slightly, looking up at him with tear-streaked cheeks and a trembling smile. "Ok.......I love you."

"I love you, too," he said, his voice steady and sure.

For a moment, they simply held each other, the faint hum of the city outside filling the quiet between them. The challenges ahead were daunting, the timing terrible, but in that moment, they were a family—and that was all that mattered.

As they stood there, Ben's emotions surged all at once—joy, fear, and an ache so deep it nearly overwhelmed him. He was going to have a baby with Lacy, the woman he loved more than anything, and that thought filled him with a happiness so profound it made his chest tighten. But it wasn't the right time. Not with her father still looming like a shadow over their lives. Had they unknowingly put another life in danger because of Richard Jacobs?

He tightened his hold on her, as if he could shield her—and their unborn child—from the world.

Ben gently guided Lacy toward the bedroom, his arm wrapped around her waist as she leaned into him, her exhaustion evident in every step. The soft glow of the bedside lamp bathed the room in a warm, amber light, casting long shadows against the walls.

"You need rest," he murmured as he pulled back the covers and helped her settle in. The sheets were cool against her skin, and she sighed as her body sank into the mattress.

"Stay," Lacy whispered, her voice fragile, her fingers curling around his hand as he tucked the blanket around her.

Ben smiled softly, brushing a strand of hair from her face. "I wish I could, but I need to check on Nonnie. She's been having trouble sleeping lately, and you know how she worries when I'm not around."

Lacy's lips trembled, and she nodded, though her grip on his hand tightened briefly. "Call me when you get home?"

"Of course," he promised, leaning down to press a deep, lingering kiss to her lips. His warmth and reassurance flowed into her, grounding her even as her worries loomed.

When he pulled away, he moved to the side of the bed and crouched down. His large, gentle hand rested lightly on her stomach, his fingers splayed as if he were trying to feel the life they had created. He leaned in, pressing a tender kiss to her belly before resting his cheek against it for a moment.

"Hi, baby," he whispered, his voice soft and filled with wonder.

Lacy felt tears sting her eyes as she watched him.

Ben finally stood, leaning down to kiss her forehead. "Get some sleep, okay? I'll call you the second I get home."

"I'll hold you to it," she said, her lips curving into a faint smile.

He gave her one last look, a mix of adoration and resolve, before turning and heading toward the door. As it clicked shut behind him, Lacy closed her eyes, her heart full even as her mind swirled with uncertainty about the road ahead.

The drive to Nonnie's house was quiet, the soft hum of the engine and the occasional buzz of his phone breaking the stillness of the night. Ben had promised Lacy he'd call as soon as he got home, but he was already thinking about texting her just to say one more goodnight.

His phone buzzed on the passenger seat, and he glanced over at the screen. It was a text from Lacy's work phone:

Lacy: Hey, I forgot to ask—could you check out the lot off Fifth and Howard? It's supposed to be the backup venue for next week's rally, and I just want to make sure it's good to go.

Ben frowned. He picked up the phone at the next red light, his thumb hovering over the keyboard. She hadn't mentioned anything about a backup venue earlier. Probably because of the whole baby conversation.

Another buzz came almost immediately. This time, it was from Chloe:

Chloe: Sorry, Ben! Meant to send this earlier. Lacy asked if you could check the warehouse at Fifth and Howard. Just a quick once-over for safety stuff.

Ben stared at the screen, his confusion deepening. He debated calling Lacy, but the texts seemed urgent. Maybe she'd remembered something last minute. Maybe it was just campaign chaos. She needed her rest, so he decided not to call and just quickly do a favor for her.

He sighed and turned the car around, heading toward the address.

The warehouse loomed in the distance, its dark, skeletal frame outlined against the faint glow of the city. The lot around it was empty, overgrown with weeds that swayed in the cool breeze. The faint smell of damp concrete and rust filled the air as Ben pulled into the gravel lot, his tires crunching softly.

He stepped out of the car, his breath clouding in the chill. The warehouse was silent, its windows dark and gaping like empty sockets. He shoved his hands into his jacket pockets and walked closer, his boots scuffing against the uneven ground.

"Chloe?" he called out, though he knew it didn't make sense. She wouldn't be here, not at this hour.

The silence was oppressive, broken only by the faint creak of metal as the wind rattled a loose piece of siding. Ben's gut twisted with unease as he glanced around the lot.

"Hello?" he tried again, his voice echoing faintly in the cavernous space beyond the broken windows.

A sharp sound behind him—a scuffle of gravel. He spun around, heart pounding, but saw nothing.

"What the hell…" he muttered under his breath, turning back toward the building.

Before he could take another step, something hard collided with the back of his head. Pain exploded across his skull, bright and blinding, as the ground seemed to tilt beneath him.

His knees buckled, and he crumpled to the dirt, the world spinning as darkness swallowed him whole.

****

The next morning after not hearing from Ben all night, Lacy pressed her phone to her ear, pacing the length of her kitchen, her heart pounding as the call went straight to voicemail yet again. She hesitated, biting her lip before leaving a message.

"Ben, you better not have run off to Mexico without me," she said, trying to keep her tone light but failing miserably. "You're about to be a dad, remember? Call me back. Please."

She ended the call and stared at her phone, willing it to ring. The apartment was too quiet, the kind of silence that pressed down on her like a weight. She poured herself a cup of coffee but couldn't drink it, the bitter smell turning her already unsettled stomach.

As the morning slipped into afternoon, her worry deepened. Ben never went this long without calling, especially after promising to check in. She called him again, and again it went to voicemail.

By early afternoon, she was pacing furiously, her heart racing as she dialed Nonnie.

"Nonnie, it's Lacy," she said quickly when the older woman picked up. "Have you seen Ben? Did he come by last night?"

Nonnie's voice was hesitant, concerned. "No, honey. I waited up for him, but he never showed. I thought maybe he stayed with you."

Lacy's blood turned cold.

"Is everything alright?" Nonnie asked, her voice laced with worry.

"I'm… I'm not sure," Lacy said, her voice shaking. "I'll call you if I hear from him, okay?"

She hung up before Nonnie could ask any more questions. Panic clawed at her chest as she called Ben's poker buddies, one by one, but none of them had seen or heard from him. Her hands trembled as she set her phone down on the counter.

"I didn't want to involve him," she whispered to herself, her voice cracking. "I was so scared this would happen."

Her thoughts raced, her mind jumping from one terrifying possibility to the next. She needed help, but she couldn't involve just anyone. And then she realized—her work phone. Where was it? She tore through her bag, and rifled through the cushions on her couch, but it was nowhere to be found.

The realization sent a chill down her spine.

By evening, Lacy knew she couldn't do this alone anymore. She drove to campaign headquarters, every shadow on the street making her flinch. Paige was in her office, going over logistics for the next week.

"Lacy?" Paige said when she walked in. "You okay? You look—"

"Not here," Lacy interrupted, her voice low and urgent.

"What?"

"Not here," Lacy repeated, grabbing Paige's arm. "We need to talk. At your place."

Paige blinked, confused but concerned enough not to argue. She packed up quickly, and they headed to Paige's apartment.

Once inside, Lacy locked the door and double-checked the windows before turning to Paige.

"Lacy, what's going on?" Paige asked, crossing her arms. "You're freaking me out."

Lacy took a deep breath, running a hand through her hair. "I'm about to tell you something, and I need you to listen. I need you to trust me."

Paige's eyes narrowed slightly, but she nodded. "Alright. Talk to me."

Lacy hesitated, standing awkwardly in the middle of the living room. She looked down at her hands, which were trembling slightly, and took a deep breath. "I need you to promise you won't freak out."

Paige set her bag down on the kitchen counter and turned to Lacy. "Alright," she said, her tone firm but gentle. "You dragged me out of headquarters, looking like the world's about to end. Talk."

Lacy hesitated, then sat down on the edge of the couch. She didn't hold back—she told Paige everything. About her pregnancy, her father's criminal empire, the FBI investigation, Agent Housley's involvement, and Ben's disappearance. As the words poured out, Paige listened in stunned silence, her face shifting between disbelief and concern.

When Lacy finished, Paige stood abruptly, her palms flat against the table. Her breath came fast as she shook her head, muttering, "Holy shit. Holy shit."

Lacy watched her, her hands trembling in her lap. "I didn't want to drag you into this," she said quietly, her voice breaking.

Paige let out a long breath, ran a hand through her hair, and then surprised Lacy by pulling her into a tight hug. "Damn, bitch," Paige said, her voice muffled against Lacy's shoulder. "You are not making my job any easier, are you?"

A startled laugh bubbled out of Lacy, quickly followed by Paige's chuckle.

"Seriously, though," Paige said, pulling back and gripping Lacy's shoulders. Her tone softened, but her eyes were resolute. "We've got this. Let's figure it out. You said Agent Housley can help. Let's call her and find Ben. We're not doing this alone."

Lacy nodded, her resolve hardening. "Okay. Let's do it."

The air was tense as Lacy, Paige, Agent Housley, and Michael gathered in a dimly lit motel room on the outskirts of the city. The faint hum of a fluorescent light buzzed overhead, its flickering casting unsettling shadows on the faded floral wallpaper. Lacy sat on the edge of the bed, her hands trembling as she recounted everything—Ben's disappearance, her work phone missing, and the horrifying realization that Richard might already be pulling strings.

Michael leaned against the doorframe, his rugged face set in a grim expression. Agent Housley sat at a small table by the window, her fingers steepled as she listened intently, the sharp scent of her faintly mentholated cigarette mixing with the musty air. Paige was perched on a chair near the bed, her eyes darting between everyone as the tension built.

"I didn't know what else to do," Lacy said finally, her voice breaking. "I was so scared to bring him into this. And now—"

"We'll find him," Agent Housley interrupted. She exchanged a glance with Michael, who nodded.

Michael pulled out a laptop and began typing rapidly. "Let's start with his phone," he said, his deep voice cutting through the room. "If it's still on, I can trace it."

"Do it," Agent Housley said, her jaw tight.

The room fell into silence, save for the soft clicks of Michael's keyboard and the distant sound of traffic outside. Lacy could hear her own heartbeat pounding in her ears, her palms damp with sweat as she waited.

"Got it," Michael said after a few tense minutes. He spun the laptop around to show a map with a blinking dot. "It's at the warehouse on Fifth and Howard."

Lacy felt her stomach drop. "Why would he be there?"

Agent Housley stood abruptly, grabbing her jacket. "We need to move."

"Wait," Paige said, holding up a hand. "If his phone is still there, he might not be. It could be a trap."

Michael nodded grimly. "She's right. We need to think this through."

Before anyone could respond, Lacy's personal phone buzzed loudly on the nightstand. Everyone froze.

Lacy picked it up, her hands shaking. The screen displayed an unknown number. She swallowed hard, glancing at the others before answering.

"Hello?"

Richard's voice slid through the line like oil, smooth and cold. "Hello, Lacy."

Her breath caught. "What do you want?"

"What I've always wanted," Richard said, his tone almost amused. "For you to know your place. Stay by the phone, don't do anything stupid, and maybe—just maybe—your lover survives this little misstep."

Lacy's stomach churned, bile rising in her throat. "If you hurt him—"

Richard laughed, low and menacing. "You're not in a position to make threats, sweetheart. Stay by the phone and don't do anything stupid."

The call ended abruptly, leaving the room in stunned silence.

"Son of a bitch," Agent Housley muttered, standing and pacing. "We don't have time for this. He's already playing us."

As the room fell into a tense silence, Agent Housley turned to Michael, her voice low but urgent. "What's the hold-up with Ben's exact location? We have his phone pinging at the warehouse. Shouldn't we have him by now?"

Michael exhaled sharply, his fingers tapping against the laptop. "It's not that simple. Richard's men are pros. They're using a signal scrambler—probably one of the newer, high-tech models that cycles through frequencies. It's keeping Ben's exact location bouncing between false pings. I can pinpoint the general area, but unscrambling the signal could take days."

Housley frowned, her expression darkening as she leaned over his shoulder to glance at the screen. "Days we don't have," she muttered.

Michael's jaw tightened. "I know. But unless we find the device scrambling the signal, it's going to be a hell of a lot harder to track him."

Housley straightened, her gaze steely. "We'll have to assume the worst for now. Richard's too damn smart to leave any loose ends, and we can't rely on time to be on our side."

Michael nodded grimly, his fingers already flying across the keyboard again. "I'll keep working on the trace. If there's even a hint of something solid, I'll find it."

Housley turned to Lacy, who was still clutching her phone, her knuckles white. "We'll get him back," Housley said. "But Richard's playing the long game here. That signal scrambler isn't just to hide him—it's to keep us running in circles. We have to stay ahead of him."

Michael glanced up, his dark eyes meeting Housley's. "And if we don't, Lacy's not the only one Richard will destroy."

The gravity of his words settled over the room, the faint hum of tension growing heavier. Housley crossed her arms, her jaw set in determination. "Then we'll work faster."

Michael closed the laptop with a sharp snap. "We need to sweep your place, Lacy. If he knows this much, he's probably got bugs in your apartment and your offices."

Back at Lacy's apartment, the tension was palpable as Agent Housley and Michael began their sweep. The soft rustle of papers and the faint hum of the electronic detector filled the air. Paige and Lacy sat on the couch, the faint scent of coffee lingering from an abandoned mug on the counter.

"What if he's listening to us right now?" Lacy asked, her voice barely above a whisper.

"He's not anymore," Michael said firmly, pulling a tiny black device from under the coffee table. "But he was. This thing's active. We'll keep looking."

Every drawer, corner, and crevice of the apartment was examined. A faint metallic tang filled the air as more devices were unearthed—a tiny microphone hidden in a lamp, another in the bookshelf. Lacy felt like her skin was crawling, knowing how deeply Richard had invaded her personal space.

Finally, Michael sat down, his face grim. "We've cleared it for now. We need to get these over to TechOps and we need to know what Richard heard in the 72 hours this was recording."

"Good but we don't stop here, we need to sweep the offices, too," Agent Housley said, her eyes flashing with determination. "We're going to find Ben, and end this."

Paige crossed her arms, her voice steady. "So what's the plan?"

Michael glanced at Lacy. "We wait for him to call again. And this time, we'll be ready."

CHAPTER 22

The basement was damp, the walls lined with crumbling bricks and streaks of mold that crawled up toward the low ceiling. A single flickering bulb swung overhead, casting sharp, erratic shadows that danced across the grimy floor. The air was heavy with the scent of mildew and rust, mingled with the faint metallic tang of blood.

Ben was slumped in a wooden chair, his wrists bound tightly behind him, the coarse rope biting into his skin. His head throbbed where he'd been struck, a dull ache radiating from the back of his skull. His lip was split, and he tasted copper as he licked it absently. Despite the pain, his dark eyes burned with defiance, locked on the man standing across the room.

Richard Jacobs leaned casually against a rusted metal table, his suit impeccably tailored and starkly out of place in the dilapidated surroundings. His cold, calculating gaze swept over Ben with a mixture of disdain and amusement, the kind of look a predator might give its cornered prey.

"You don't belong in this world," Richard said finally, his voice low and venomous. "And you're playing a game you don't understand. Lacy deserves better than some… pathetic lapdog sniffing around her heels."

Ben let out a low, bitter laugh, shifting in his chair despite the ropes. "Better, huh? Like a controlling sociopath who manipulates her every move? Yeah, she'd be real lucky to end up like you."

Richard's jaw tightened, but he smiled thinly, stepping closer. "She's my daughter. She doesn't need a weak little boy pretending to be a man."

Ben's lips curled into a smirk, his eyes blazing. "Man enough for Lacy morning, noon, and night," he shot back. "Or at least that's how she takes it."

Richard froze, his nostrils flaring, but Ben pressed on, his voice dripping with mockery. "Yeah, she's got this thing she does when I kiss her neck—makes this little sound, almost a gasp. And don't even get me started on her breasts. Perfect. Full. Soft. Pierced—that was a nice surprise. Couldn't keep my hands off them last night."

"Enough," Richard snapped, his voice icy, but Ben was on a roll.

"And her mouth," Ben continued, his tone turning suggestive. "God, that mouth of hers. It does way more than just give speeches the way she suc———-"

The sharp crack of the pistol's butt connecting with his cheekbone cut him off mid-sentence. Pain exploded across his face, and his head snapped to the side. Blood dripped from the fresh gash, mixing with the dried streaks already smeared on his skin.

Richard loomed over him, his eyes cold and hard as steel. "You've got a big mouth for a man who's one word away from dying," he said, his tone eerily calm.

Ben chuckled, spitting blood onto the floor, and turned his head slowly to meet Richard's gaze. "Then do it," he growled, his voice hoarse but steady. "Kill me. But you'll still have to see me every time you look into the eyes of your grandchild."

Richard's eyes widened, the icy mask slipping for just a moment. "What did you say?"

"You heard me," Ben said, his lips curling into a bloody grin. "Lacy's pregnant. Your daughter is pregnant with my child. And you can kill me, but you'll never escape me. Every time you look at that baby, you'll see me staring back at you."

The silence that followed was suffocating, broken only by the faint hum of the bulb overhead and the distant drip of water somewhere in the shadows.

Richard straightened, his grip tightening on the pistol. His expression was unreadable, his sharp mind clearly working through this new piece of information. For the first time, he seemed truly rattled.

Ben leaned back in his chair, his breathing labored but his eyes defiant. "Go ahead, Jacobs. Prove to Lacy what kind of man you really are."

Richard didn't respond, but the way his jaw clenched and his grip on the gun faltered spoke volumes.

The fluorescent lights buzzed faintly in the campaign headquarters as Michael swept the room with a handheld detector. The small, blinking device emitted periodic beeps, signaling no more bugs as he moved it across the wall-mounted shelves filled with dusty files and old office supplies.

"We're clear," he said gruffly, lowering the device. His dark eyes flicked toward Lacy. "For now."

Lacy stood by the table in the center of the room, her arms crossed tightly over her chest. Paige sat nearby, nervously tapping a pen against her thigh, while Agent Housley leaned against the wall, her gaze sharp and unyielding. The stale air of the basement felt stifling, and the faint scent of mildew clung to everything.

"They were listening, weren't they?" Lacy asked quietly, her voice trembling.

Michael nodded. "Whoever planted those bugs wasn't sloppy. This isn't just surveillance—it's control. But these devices can only record up to 72 hours and from what TechOps said the recordings were from last week. He likely used these bugs because they are less traceable and harder to detect. The good news is Richard probably didn't hear much, the lab said it was just some everyday stuff on it. It's actually just Lacy heard on these but who knows how many times Richard replaced them. I know it's a lot to take in, but try not to worry. We will find them. For now, we need to get back to the motel. In case Richard calls."

The air in the dim motel room was thick with tension as Lacy, Michael, Agent Housley, and Paige sat around the small table, their eyes fixed on Lacy's phone lying in the center. The faint buzz of the fluorescent light overhead and the muffled sounds of traffic outside only heightened the unbearable silence.

Lacy leaned forward, her elbows on her knees, staring at the phone as if willing it to ring. Her chest felt tight, her pulse a relentless drumbeat in her ears. The scent of cheap coffee lingered in the air, mingling with the faint metallic tang of the tools Michael had used during the earlier bug sweep.

Paige broke the silence, her voice low but trembling. "We don't have to wait for him to call. We should be doing something. Anything."

Agent Housley's sharp tone cut through the room. "And run straight into whatever trap he's set? No. We wait."

Michael glanced at Lacy, his rugged face unreadable but his tone steady. "Are you ready for this? Really ready?"

Lacy didn't answer. The weight of their gazes pressed on her, but she couldn't look away from the phone.

Finally, it rang.

Everyone tensed as the shrill sound sliced through the quiet. Lacy snatched it up, her hands trembling as she pressed it to her ear.

"Hello?"

Richard's smooth, menacing voice oozed through the line. "Hello, sweetheart. Did you miss me?"

Lacy's breath hitched, but she forced her voice to remain steady. "Where is he?"

"He's fine," Richard said, his tone almost playful. "For now. I'll make this simple: come alone to the old house on Pine Ridge. No tricks, no backup. You try anything funny, and I'll kill him. Tell anyone where you are going, and I'll kill him."

"Why should I believe that you haven't already killed him?" she demanded, her nails biting into the palm of her free hand. Lacy's chest tightened. "Where's Ben? I want proof of life."

There was a pause, then the sound of rustling fabric. Ben's voice, weak but defiant, came through. "Lacy…"

Tears sprang to her eyes at the sound of him. "Ben! Are you okay? Are you—"

"He's fine," Richard interrupted, his tone laced with amusement. "For now."

Lacy's blood ran cold. "What do you want?"

"Simple," Richard said. "Come alone to the old house on Pine Ridge. No backup, no tricks, or your lover doesn't make it out alive."

The line went dead.

The room erupted into chaos.

"You're not going," Michael said immediately, his voice hard and commanding.

"We'll figure something else out," Agent Housley added, pacing the room with sharp, agitated strides.

Paige stood, her hands raised. "Can we just breathe for a second?"

Lacy slammed her hands on the table, silencing them. "Stop!"

Michael turned to her, his voice lowering but no less firm. "Lacy, listen to me. He's baiting you. This is a trap. You go alone, and he'll kill you both."

"Then what do you suggest?" she shot back, her voice cracking. "That I sit here and wait while he tortures and kills Ben? I can't do that!"

Michael stepped closer, his tone desperate. "You don't have to go. Let us handle this. Let me handle this."

"Because that's worked so well before, hasn't it?" she snapped, tears brimming in her eyes. "You've been hiding from him for years, Michael. Years! And look where we are now."

Agent Housley cut in, her voice sharp. "She's right about one thing—he's expecting her, not us. If we charge in guns blazing, Ben dies."

Michael slammed his fist on the table. "If she goes alone, they both die!"

Lacy took a deep breath, forcing herself to steady. She looked at each of them, her voice trembling but resolute. "This isn't just about Ben. Or me. This is about all of us. All the people Richard has murdered, manipulated, and destroyed. Now I have a chance to stop this. To stop him. This is what leaders do. In the face of adversity, they don't run. They don't hide. They do what must be done to protect as many lives as possible."

The room fell silent, her words hanging heavy in the air.

Michael's face softened, and his shoulders slumped. "Lacy…"

"I have to do this," she said firmly, her voice breaking slightly. "If I don't, then what was all of this for? What's the point?"

****

The old house on Pine Ridge loomed like a ghost in the darkness, its jagged edges cutting into the starless sky. Lacy's boots crunched softly against the overgrown gravel driveway as she approached, the cold night air biting at her skin.

The door creaked open before she touched it, the smell of decay and mildew wafting out like a warning. The faint hum of the wind outside only made the house seem more deathly quiet.

"In here," her father's voice called from somewhere deeper inside.

Her stomach clenched, but she forced herself to step forward, each creaking floorboard beneath her feet a reminder that there was no turning back.

The room she entered was dimly lit by a single bulb, casting harsh shadows across the cracked walls. Ben sat in a chair, his head slumped forward, blood matting the side of his face. Lacy's breath caught as she rushed to him, her knees hitting the grimy floor.

"Ben!" she whispered, her hands cupping his face. "Oh my God. Are you—"

"Lacy." His voice was hoarse but firm. "Don't."

A slow clap echoed through the room. Lacy turned sharply to see her father standing by the far wall, a pistol hanging loosely in his hand.

"Touching," Richard drawled, his smile sharp and cold.

Lacy's blood boiled, but before she could respond, her gaze shifted to the figure standing beside him. Her heart dropped.

"Chloe?"

Chloe crossed her arms, avoiding Lacy's gaze.

"How could—- Why are you doing this?" Lacy demanded, her voice trembling.

Chloe finally looked at her, her expression pained. "Lacy….."

"Relax," Richard interjected, his tone mocking. "She's just a pawn."

And then, without hesitation, he raised the pistol and fired.

The sound was deafening. Blood sprayed across the floor as Chloe crumpled, her body hitting the ground with a haunting thud.

Lacy screamed, scrambling backward as the noxious stench of gunpowder and blood filled her nose.

Richard stepped forward, his expression calm, almost amused. "Now," he said, his voice slicing through the chaos. "Let's talk about family. I hear I'm going to be a grandpa."

CHAPTER 23

Richard paced in front of Lacy, his movements slow and deliberate, his gun dangling carelessly at his side. With one brutal blow, Richard's fist connected with Lacy's jaw, sending her sprawling to the floor. Pain shot through her face, her vision blurring as she hit the hard wooden boards with a sickening thud.

"You're an ungrateful little bitch," he spat. "I gave you everything. I made you who you are, and this is how you repay me? Plotting behind my back, working with my enemies? Being a fucking slut who gets knocked up!"

Lacy tried to push herself up from the floor, but Richard moved quickly, slapping her hard across the face. The sharp crack echoed through the room, and she crumpled back to the ground, her lip split and blood dripping onto the dirty floorboards.

Ben strained against his bonds, his muscles burning as he fought to free himself. "Leave her alone, you piece of shit!" he yelled, his voice raw with rage.

Richard turned to him, his lip curling in disdain. "Stay out of this, boy. This… This is family business."

Richard loomed over Lacy, his face a mask of contempt twisted with a dark kind of triumph. His voice dropped, low and venomous, as he stepped closer, the gun still dangling loosely in his hand.

"Weak," he repeated, his words slicing through the air like a blade. "You've always been weak, Lacy. You think you can stand against me?

You don't have it in you. You never did." He crouched down to her level, his piercing eyes burning with an intensity that made her blood run cold. "Do you know what it takes to win, to hold power in your bare hands? It takes blood, sacrifice, and the kind of resolve you can't even fathom." He snarled, kicking Lacy in the ribs as she lay in a heap on the floor.

He straightened, pacing the room now, his voice rising as he spoke. "By the time I was your age, I had already learned that the hard way. My father was just like you—pathetic, spineless, too weak to do what needed to be done. But worse, he wasn't just weak—he was cruel. A drunk. A monster who would rather break us than protect us."

Richard stopped abruptly, his shoulders tense as his fingers tightened around the gun. "You don't know what it's like to come home from school every day, wondering what kind of mood he'd be in, whether it'd be my face or my mother's he put his hands on that night. He made us small. Powerless. And my mother? She loved him. She kept hoping he'd change, that he'd stop drinking, stop lashing out. She thought she could save him. She was wrong."

Lacy's stomach churned as he continued, his tone shifting between bitterness and raw fury.

"When we finally left, it was like being able to breathe for the first time. We started over. We rebuilt our lives. But then, he came back." Richard's jaw tightened, his voice trembling with a raw edge of anger. "Still a drunk. Still a loser. My mother didn't see it, but I did. He hadn't changed. He never would."

Richard turned abruptly, his eyes narrowing on Lacy. "I made a decision that night. I wouldn't let him hurt her again. I wouldn't let him destroy everything we'd clawed our way back to. So, I took his gun—the one he waved around every time he wanted to scare us— and I put a bullet in his head right here. In this house." he continued unbuttoning his suit jacket.

"Do you think that makes me a monster?" Richard demanded, his voice rising with every word. "Maybe it does. But I saved her. I saved myself. And out of the ashes of that man's failure, I built an empire. I built something no one could take away from me. Something that you've lived off of your entire life, Lacy."

He spun toward her, his boots heavy on the wooden floorboards. "And now you think you can destroy it? Tear down everything I bled for because you've decided you don't like the rules? You ungrateful little bitch."

Richard stepped closer to Ben, his shadow swallowing him. He pointed the gun directly at Ben's face, the metal gleaming under the dim light. "How about we make this simple? You and your bastard child die tonight. No more games. No more pretending you're anything but a liability."

"Don't!" Lacy croaked, struggling to her knees, her vision blurred but her resolve hardening. "Please…"

Richard turned to her, his grin returning, wide and cruel. "Ah, there it is," he sneered. "Begging. Just like your grandfather. Just like every weak fool who thought they could stand in my way. You'll beg, Lacy, and it won't matter. You've already lost." He said cocking the gun.

Lacy's fingers tightened around the cold, solid weight of the chess piece in her pocket. It was the pocket-size queen paperweight she'd grabbed absentmindedly from her desk at campaign headquarters earlier that day.

With every ounce of strength she had, she sprung up and swung the piece at Richard's head.

The dull crack of dense glass meeting bone echoed through the room. Richard stumbled forward, the gun flying from his hand as he let out a pained roar.

Lacy dropped the chess piece and dove for the gun, her heart pounding as her fingers scraped the floorboards. Richard recovered quickly, grabbing her ankle and yanking her backward. She let out a sharp cry as her nails scratched at the floor.

The gun skidded across the room, coming to rest near the wall. Both Lacy and Richard scrambled for it, their bodies colliding as they kicked and clawed at each other.

Richard grabbed her by the hair, yanking her head back as she screamed. "You're pathetic," he snarled, his spit hitting her cheek as he dragged her closer.

Lacy twisted in his grip, her elbow slamming into his ribs. He grunted, momentarily loosening his hold, and she pushed him off, crawling desperately toward the gun.

Before she could reach it, Richard tackled her from behind, his hands wrapping around her throat.

"You've always been a disappointment," he hissed, his grip tightening as her vision blurred. "You were never strong enough. Never smart enough. You'll never be queen."

Lacy clawed at his hands, gasping for air as black spots danced in her vision. Her lungs burned, her body thrashing weakly under his weight.

Suddenly, a loud crack split the air.

Richard froze, his head snapping up.

Ben stood behind him, his face pale and bloodied, a gun trembling in his hands. "Let. Her. Go."

Richard released Lacy, standing slowly with his hands raised, a mocking smile curling his lips. "Well, well," he said, his voice smooth. "Maybe you're not as simple as I thought. But you're still a pathetic little boy."

Richard's smile twisted into a snarl as he moved faster than either of them expected. His hand darted behind his back, producing a second gun. The room seemed to explode as he fired.

The bullet struck Ben's shoulder, the force spinning him to the ground. He cried out, clutching at the wound as blood seeped through his fingers.

Richard stood over him, his chest heaving, a manic gleam in his eyes. He kicked the gun away from Ben's reach and leaned down, pressing the barrel of his pistol against Ben's forehead.

"No more games. This ends now," he said darkly.

The sharp bang of a gunshot filled the air.

Richard's body stiffened, his eyes widening in shock. He stumbled back, his hand going to his side where blood began to bloom across his pristine shirt. He turned slowly, his gaze landing on a woman….it was Agent Housley. His body jerked, a crimson bloom spreading across his chest as he stumbled back, his gun clattering to the floor.

Agent Housley stepped into the doorway, her pistol still raised, her expression icy. "Y'all okay," she said.

Lacy stared at her in shock, nodding as Richard collapsed to the ground, gasping for air.

Ben groaned from where he was slumped on the floor, clutching his shoulder. Lacy snapped out of her daze and rushed to his side, dropping to her knees.

"It's okay," he rasped, his lips curling into a faint smile despite the pain. "Just a scratch."

Tears streamed down her cheeks as she leaned into him, their foreheads touching. "You scared the hell out of me."

"Back at you," he muttered, his free hand brushing her cheek.

They laughed and cried together, clinging to each other as they tried to get to their feet.

The sound of heavy boots pounding against the stairs signaled the arrival of more FBI. Agents swarmed the room, their shouts blending into a chaotic symphony as they secured the area.

Lacy turned toward Agent Housley, who was crouched beside Richard. He lay on his back, his breaths shallow and labored. Blood seeped from the wound in his chest, pooling beneath him.

Richard's eyes fluttered open, locking onto Lacy. His lips curled into a bitter smile as he struggled to speak. "You… forgot everything I taught you," he rasped, his voice barely audible.

Lacy knelt beside him, her expression hard but tinged with sadness. "No," she said softly. "You forgot everything you taught me."

She leaned in closer, her voice firm and unyielding. "The queen holds all the power."

Richard's eyes fluttered shut as the medics arrived, quickly tending to his wounds. Lacy stood slowly, exhaustion weighing her down as she turned to Ben.

"Let's get out of here," she said, her voice barely above a whisper.

Together, they climbed the stairs, leaning on each other for support. The house buzzed with activity as agents searched every corner, their voices echoing through the empty halls.

When they reached the top, Michael was waiting for them. His face was pale, his eyes filled with relief and concern.

"Lacy," he said, stepping forward. "Thank you. We couldn't have done this without you."

Lacy reached into her pocket as the medics worked on Richard, her trembling fingers brushing against the smooth surface of her Apple Watch. She pulled it out and handed it to Agent Housley, her voice unsteady. "This recorded everything," she said. "The whole thing. It should be enough."

Agent Housley took the watch, glancing at the screen before slipping it into her jacket pocket. "You're smarter than you give yourself credit for," she said with a rare flicker of admiration.

The agents moved methodically through the house, their voices clipped as they called out updates. Each room had been swept, each drawer emptied, but there was no sign of the elusive flash drive. Frustration hung heavy in the air, mingling with the faint scent of mildew and old wood. The house seemed to hold its breath, as if it were guarding its secrets.

Lacy stood in the center of the living room, her arms crossed tightly over her chest. Her gaze swept the room, landing on the battered furniture, the peeling wallpaper, and the worn floors scarred by years of neglect. Everything in the house screamed decay—except for the mantle above the fireplace.

She froze, her eyes narrowing. The mantle stood out like a shrine, its surface pristine, with a vase of fresh flowers standing sentinel beside a simple urn. The urn was polished, gleaming faintly in the dim light, an incongruous beacon of care amidst the ruin.

Her heart began to race, her mind spinning as she heard Richard's words echo in her memory: "The secret lies with my mother."

"My secrets lie with my mother," Lacy murmured, almost to herself.

Ben turned to her, his brows knitting in confusion. "What?"

She repeated it louder this time, her voice trembling with realization. "My secrets lie with my mother."

The room fell silent as every head turned to her. The agents exchanged puzzled looks, but Lacy didn't wait for an answer. Her breath quickened as she moved toward the mantle, the weight of her decision pressing down on her shoulders. She reached out, her fingers brushing the smooth surface of the urn.

"Lacy, what are you doing?" Ben asked, his voice low and cautious.

She didn't answer. Her chest tightened as she wrapped her hands around the urn, lifting it with reverent care. She hesitated, her fingers trembling as she cradled the weight of the ashes.

"Forgive me, Grandma," she whispered, her voice thick with emotion.

With a deep breath, she tilted the urn. The ashes spilled out in a soft, cascading plume, a fine gray dust settling over the dark wood of the mantle. The scent of burnt earth filled her nose, mingling with the faint floral fragrance from the fresh flowers.

A small pouch rolled out from the ashes, landing with a dull thud.

The room seemed to freeze.

Lacy dropped the urn onto the mantle and snatched up the pouch, her hands shaking as she opened it. She reached inside and pulled out a small, unassuming flash drive.

"Oh my God," Ben whispered, stepping closer.

"The holy grail," Lacy breathed, holding the drive up for everyone to see.

Michael moved to her side, his expression a mixture of pride and awe. "You found it," he said, his voice almost reverent.

Lacy handed the drive to Agent Housley, her fingers brushing against the cold metal.

"Get it to TechOps," Housley said firmly. "Decrypt it. We need to know everything on there—now."

Housley nodded, her usual stoicism replaced with something almost like respect. "We're on it," she said, turning to bark orders to the agents around her.

Lacy swayed slightly, the adrenaline that had carried her this far suddenly abandoning her. She tried to steady herself, but her vision blurred, and a wave of exhaustion crashed over her.

"I…" she started to say, but the words wouldn't come. Her knees buckled, and the world tilted violently as she collapsed.

"Lacy!" Ben shouted, catching her just before she hit the floor. He cradled her against him, his voice rising in panic. "Lacy, wake up! Stay with me!"

Agent Housley spun around, her sharp voice cutting through the chaos. "Medic! We need a medic now!"

Lacy's eyelids fluttered weakly, her breath shallow as Ben pressed his forehead to hers, his own face pale with fear. "Come on, Lace," he whispered desperately.

The sound of hurried footsteps and shouted orders filled the room as the medics arrived, their gear clattering against the floor. They worked quickly, checking Lacy's vitals and securing her onto a stretcher.

Ben refused to let go of her hand, even as they lifted her. "I'm coming with you," he said fiercely, his voice leaving no room for argument.

"Let's move," one of the medics said, leading the way out.

The first thing Lacy noticed when she opened her eyes was the faint hum of the machines beside her bed. The steady beeping of the heart monitor punctuated the sterile quiet of the hospital room. Harsh fluorescent lights overhead reflected off the pale blue walls, making her squint as her vision adjusted. The faint scent of antiseptic lingered in the air, mingling with the aroma of flowers from a nearby table.

Her body felt heavy, her ribs aching with every shallow breath. She tried to sit up, but a sharp pain in her side made her wince.

"Easy," a familiar voice said softly.

She turned her head to see Ben sitting beside her, his arm in a sling, his face pale but his expression warm. His hand reached out to hers, his thumb brushing gently over her knuckles.

"Hey," he said, his voice low and filled with relief.

"Ben," she croaked, her throat dry. "What… what happened?"

"You collapsed. You've been out for two days," he said, his eyes searching hers. "You scared the hell out of me."

Lacy's mind raced, fragments of the fight with Richard flashing through her memory. "The baby?" she whispered, panic tightening her chest.

"The baby's fine," a voice said from the doorway.

A doctor in scrubs walked in, holding a clipboard. Her expression was kind, but her tone was brisk and professional. "You're lucky. You have a few bruised ribs, mild dehydration, and a concussion, but the baby is perfectly healthy."

Tears filled Lacy's eyes as she exhaled a shaky breath. "Thank God," she whispered.

Ben leaned forward, pressing a kiss to her hand. "See? They are a stubborn little fighter just like their mom."

The doctor smiled faintly, nodding. "You'll need to take it easy for a while, which probably won't happen for the next governor of Virginia, but everybody's vitals look good. I'll check in on you later."

As the doctor left, Lacy looked back at Ben, her gaze lingering on the sling around his shoulder. "You're hurt," she said, her voice trembling.

"Just a flesh wound," he said with a grin, though the dark circles under his eyes betrayed his exhaustion. "I'm fine. You're the one we were worried about."

They sat in silence for a moment, the weight of everything they'd been through settling over them.

"What now?" Lacy asked softly.

Ben shrugged, wincing slightly at the motion. "We keep going. Whether you win or not, we figure it out. Together. Whatever happens, I know you got this and I got you."

Her lips curved into a small smile, but before she could respond, the door opened again. Paige strode in, her expression equal parts relieved and determined.

"You're awake," Paige said, a grin breaking across her face. "Thank God. I've been fending off reporters for two days. The world's obsessed with you right now, and we need to capitalize on it."

Lacy blinked, still trying to process everything. "What do you mean?"

Paige set her bag down and pulled out her tablet, scrolling through headlines. "You're everywhere, Lacy," she said, shaking her head with a mix of disbelief and amusement. "'Senator Jacobs: A Hero's Stand Against Corruption,'" she read aloud, her voice taking on the dramatic tone of a news anchor. "'Future Governor Exposes Crime Boss Father in Daring Showdown.'" She paused, raising an eyebrow as she clicked another link. "'Bravery and Resolve: How Lacy Jacobs Took Down a Criminal Empire.' The press is eating this up."

Paige glanced at Lacy, who was sitting on the couch with a throw pillow clutched tightly against her chest. "They're making you out to be some kind of superhero. You're a regular Wonder Woman, Lace."

Lacy groaned, pressing her fingers to her temples. "I stopped a maniac who also happened to be my father, Paige. That doesn't make me a hero—it makes me a mess."

Paige smirked, plopping down beside her. "A hero who's a mess, then. Still counts."

"Listen," Paige said firmly, pulling up a blank document. "This is your moment. We need to craft a speech for your press conference. You have to set the narrative before anyone else does."

Ben chuckled softly, squeezing Lacy's hand. "No rest for the wicked, huh?"

"Not when you're running for governor," Paige quipped, tossing a pen onto Lacy's bedside table. "I'll be back first thing tomorrow to brainstorm."

"I'm gonna grab you some water and something light to eat," Ben said, gently kissing her forehead and leaving the room.

Paige leaned back, her sharp eyes narrowing as she studied Lacy. "So, are you still going forward with announcing the baby?"

Lacy sat up straighter, smoothing her hands over the throw pillow in her lap. "Yes," she said firmly, her voice steady despite the exhaustion that weighed her down. "I've built my reputation on honesty and transparency. I can't stop now—not when it matters most."

Paige tilted her head, her expression thoughtful as she tapped a finger against her tablet. "Alright," she said slowly. "Then we need to make sure we control this narrative, Lace. We've got one shot to get this right, and I am not letting the media turn this into some soap opera scandal."

Lacy raised an eyebrow. "And how exactly do you plan to do that?"

Paige's lips curved into a knowing smirk. "First off, you and Ben need to get married."

Lacy's jaw dropped. "What?"

"You heard me," Paige said, sitting up and clicking her pen as if she were drafting an invisible to-do list. "I can sell two people who fell in love and built a life together, but not two horny rabbits who couldn't keep their hands off each other during a campaign."

Lacy threw the pillow at her, but Paige caught it with ease, laughing. "I'm serious!" Paige continued, undeterred. "A wedding would show unity. Stability. It's the perfect way to frame this—two people deeply in love, starting a family while committed to building a better Commonwealth."

Lacy shook her head, though a small smile tugged at her lips. "You're insane."

"Thank you," Paige said with a wink. "Next, we schedule interviews. Big ones. I'm talking Ramona King, big."

Lacy blinked, the weight of the name sinking in. "Ramona King? She's brutal, Paige. She doesn't hold back."

"Exactly," Paige said, leaning forward, her excitement palpable. "Which is why you're going to win her over. She's the voice of reason in every living room across the state. If she's on your side, the voters will be, too."

Paige grinned. "But first we'll schedule a joint interview—both of you together. We'll let him gush about you and the baby. Sitting side by side, looking like the picture-perfect power couple. We show them your love, your strength, and your honesty. Ramona will eat it up, and so will her audience."

Lacy hesitated, her fingers twisting in her lap. "And the timing of the baby?"

Paige's expression softened, but her determination remained. "We don't shy away from it," she said firmly. "We own it. We say this wasn't planned, but it's the best surprise of your lives. We emphasize how much you love each other, how you're excited to be parents, and how you're not letting this stop you from doing your job. You're still Lacy Jacobs—unstoppable, driven, and ready to fight for the people of this state."

Lacy stared at her, her throat tight with emotion. "You really think we can spin it that way?"

Paige reached out, squeezing Lacy's hand. "It's not spin, Lace. It's the truth. And if there's one thing you've taught me, it's that the truth—your truth—always wins."

The room fell quiet for a moment, the weight of their conversation settling over them. Outside, the city lights twinkled, their glow casting faint patterns across the walls.

"Thank you," Lacy said softly, her voice barely above a whisper.

Paige squeezed her hand again, her smirk returning. "Don't thank me yet. We still have to make Ben wear a tie on national TV. That might be the hardest part of all."

Lacy laughed, the sound breaking through the tension in the room. It was a small moment, but it was enough to remind her that no matter how daunting the road ahead seemed, she wasn't walking it alone.

"But don't worry about this all yet, the doctor says if your vitals stay good thru the night you will be out of here in the morning and we'll talk more then. Rest and spend some time with Ben because it very well may be the last time you do without all eyes on you two."

And with that, Paige turned on her heels and walked out, texting furiously.

The hospital room was bathed in a soft glow from the late morning sun streaming through the window. The antiseptic scent lingered faintly in the air, mingling with the crisp, clean smell of freshly laundered sheets. Lacy moved carefully, folding the last of her belongings into a small overnight bag. Her ribs still ached, each movement a reminder of the chaos she'd endured, but the thought of leaving filled her with relief.

Ben stood nearby, his arm in a sling, the faint shadow of a bruise still visible along his jaw. Despite his injuries, he moved steadily, packing up her things with a quiet efficiency. The sunlight played across his face, softening the exhaustion etched into his features and highlighting the tenderness in his eyes every time they met hers.

"Almost ready?" he asked, his voice low and warm, a small smile tugging at the corners of his mouth.

"Almost," she replied, her voice lighter than she felt as she bent carefully to zip her bag.

Reaching into the drawer of the bedside table for her last few items, her fingers brushed against something unexpected—small and hard, wrapped in soft velvet. Frowning slightly, she pulled it out, her breath catching as she realized what it was.

The small velvet box felt heavy in her hand, the weight of it almost trembling. She opened it slowly, her heart skipping a beat as the light caught the diamond nestled inside. The ring sparkled like a constellation of stars, its intricate filigree band radiating elegance and history.

"Ben… Did Paige…?" she began, her voice trembling as she turned to him, the words faltering when she saw him.

He was already on one knee beside her, his good hand resting lightly on his bent leg, his dark eyes filled with a mixture of nervousness and love.

"No, Paige didn't," he said softly, his lips curving into a small smile. "This one's all me."

Lacy's breath hitched, her hand going to her chest as the world seemed to still around them.

"Lacy," Ben began, his voice steady but rich with emotion, "from the moment I met you, you turned my world upside down. I walked into that interview thinking it would just be another day, but then there you were—brilliant, determined, absolutely unstoppable. You sat across from me, grilling me with questions, and all I could think was, God help me, I'm already falling for her."

Her lips trembled as she stared down at him, the diamond catching the light like a promise in her hand.

"And then," he continued, his voice deepening, "there was the fundraiser. We danced under those lights, and for the first time in my life, everything else disappeared. It was just you. Your laugh, your smile, the way you looked at me like I mattered. That night, I knew—I was in love with you, completely and irreversibly."

Tears spilled over her cheeks, and she reached out, brushing her fingers against his uninjured hand.

"I've loved you through every challenge, every triumph, every impossible moment. You've shown me what strength really looks like—what it means to love someone so deeply that nothing else matters. And now, here we are. I don't want to spend another day, another second, without knowing you're mine forever."

His voice broke slightly as he took a deep breath, steadying himself. "Lacy Jacobs, you are my partner, my anchor, my whole damn heart. I want to stand beside you for the rest of our lives. I want to be the one who cheers you on, who fights for you, who loves you in every way I can. Will you marry me?"

Her hand flew to her mouth, the words caught somewhere between her heart and her throat as tears streamed down her face. She nodded, her voice a whisper at first, then growing stronger. "Yes! Yes! Oh my God, Ben."

A wide grin broke across his face, his eyes glistening with tears of his own. He slipped the ring onto her trembling finger, the band fitting perfectly, as if it had been made for her alone.

Lacy pulled him into a hug, her arms wrapping around him carefully, mindful of his injured shoulder. She buried her face in his neck, her heart pounding against his.

For a long moment, they stayed like that, wrapped in each other, the world outside the hospital room fading into nothing. The scent of the flowers on the bedside table mingled with the faint citrus of his cologne, grounding her in the perfection of the moment.

"I love you," she whispered into his ear, her voice trembling with emotion.

"I love you, too," he murmured, his lips brushing against her temple. "Forever."

The sunlight warmed the room, illuminating the two of them as they clung to each other, the ring on her finger catching the light—a glimmering testament to the life and love they were about to build together.

Later that night, they settled into Ben's apartment, a cozy space filled with books, soft lighting, and the faint scent of cedar. Boxes from their hospital stay sat by the door, forgotten as they sat together on the couch, reviewing notes for Lacy's upcoming press conference.

"We'll focus on the future," Lacy said, twirling her pen between her fingers. "No dwelling on Richard or what happened at Pine Ridge."

Ben nodded, leaning back against the cushions. "You've got this," he said, his voice warm.

She leaned closer, her hand brushing lightly over his thigh. "You know," she murmured, her voice soft and teasing, "there's one thing I didn't get to say earlier."

"What's that?" he asked, his brow arching.

"Thank you….for everything," she whispered, her lips brushing against his ear.

Lacy sat back slightly, studying him. The shadows played over his strong features, accentuating the faint bruise along his jawline and the exhaustion lingering in his eyes. She reached for his good hand, intertwining their fingers. "Come on," she said, standing and tugging him gently to his feet.

Ben frowned slightly but allowed her to lead him. "Where are we going?"

"To relax," she replied with a coy smile, pulling him toward the bathroom.

The bathroom was small but inviting, with soft gray tiles and a deep, clawfoot tub that gleamed under the warm overhead light. Lacy moved to the sink, opening a cabinet and pulling out a small bottle of eucalyptus bath oil. The crisp, invigorating scent filled the room as she poured a few drops into the tub, letting the steam carry it upward.

Ben leaned against the doorframe, watching her with an amused but curious expression. "You're pampering me now?"

"Someone has to," she said, glancing over her shoulder with a smirk. "You deserve it, and you always take care of me."

He chuckled softly, shaking his head, but the affection in his gaze was unmistakable. "Alright, boss. What's next?"

"Get comfortable," she said, walking over to him and slipping her hands to the buttons of his shirt. Her touch was gentle, her fingers working efficiently to free him of the fabric.

Ben didn't protest. He rarely did when it came to her, not because he was helpless but because, in these moments, surrender felt less like giving up control and more like allowing her to weave something sacred between them. He stood still as she undid each button with deliberate care, her fingers grazing his skin with every movement.

When the shirt finally slipped from his shoulders, it revealed the lean, defined muscle beneath, marred by fading bruises and faint scars from their recent ordeal. Lacy's eyes lingered there for a moment, but instead of pity, they held only quiet appreciation.

Her hands moved slowly to the waistband of his jeans, her fingers deft as she worked them loose. There was something ritualistic in the way she undressed him—each piece of clothing peeled away with purpose, her gaze never leaving his. The cool air kissed his skin, but it was quickly replaced by the warmth of her hands, her touch both soothing and electrifying.

"Sit," she instructed gently, guiding him to the edge of the tub.

Ben obeyed, sinking onto the porcelain rim as the water lapped invitingly behind him. Lacy knelt beside him, her knees pressing into the soft bath mat. She reached for a washcloth, dipping it into the water before wringing it out. The damp cloth was warm as she pressed it against his chest, her strokes slow and deliberate.

The sensation of the washcloth gliding over his skin was a delicate mix of warmth and pressure, the eucalyptus-scented water trailing down in thin rivulets. Ben exhaled deeply, the tension in his shoulders easing under her ministrations.

"Better?" she asked softly, her voice low and intimate, as if she were afraid to disturb the fragile stillness enveloping them.

"Much," he murmured, eyes half-lidded as he watched her work. His good hand came up to brush a few stray strands of hair from her face, his thumb lingering briefly against her cheek.

Her hands moved lower, the washcloth tracing along his abdomen in lazy circles. The heat of the water, combined with the friction of her touch, sent tiny shivers radiating through him, the combination of comfort and desire creating an almost unbearable tension in the air.

When she reached his thighs, her strokes slowed further, becoming more deliberate. She paused, glancing up at him with a mischievous glint in her eyes. "You're awfully quiet," she teased, her tone light but her touch anything but.

Ben's breath caught as her fingers, still damp from the washcloth, brushed against the inside of his thigh. "You're making it hard to concentrate. There is very little blood going to my brain right now," he admitted, his voice roughened by the heat pooling low in his belly.

Lacy giggled, her hand moving higher, the washcloth discarded now as her fingers replaced it. She stroked him gently, the pads of her fingers tracing over his length, drawing a sharp intake of breath from him. His body responded instantly, tension coiling tighter with each deliberate movement.

She didn't rush. Every touch, every caress, was unhurried, meant to prolong the moment. The steam thickened around them, turning the air heady and humid, each breath a little heavier than the last. The faint scent of eucalyptus clung to their skin, mingling with the salty tang of sweat and something uniquely them.

Ben groaned softly, his head tipping back as her pace quickened slightly, his good hand gripping the edge of the tub for support. She watched him, fascinated by the way his body tensed and relaxed under her touch, the way his lips parted with every shaky exhale.

When he finally came, it was with a low, guttural moan, his body shuddering as he found release beneath her hand. Lacy held him through it, her touch gentle as he rode out the waves of pleasure. Afterward, she reached for the washcloth again, wordlessly cleaning him up with the same reverence she had shown earlier.

Ben opened his eyes, finding her gaze steady on his. He gave her a lopsided grin, the kind that always made her heart flutter. "God woman, you're amazing."

Once she had finished, Lacy drained the tub and handed him a fresh towel, helping him dry off before leading him back to the bedroom. The sheets were cool against their skin as they climbed into bed.

Lacy curled into Ben's side, her head resting on his chest as his arm wrapped around her securely. The steady rhythm of his heartbeat echoed in her ear, grounding her in the stillness of the moment. The faint scent of eucalyptus lingered between them, a soft reminder of their earlier intimacy.

"Thank you," Ben whispered, pressing a kiss to the top of her head.

"For what?" she asked, tilting her head to look up at him.

"For being you," he said simply, his voice soft and filled with emotion.

She smiled, her fingers tracing lazy, aimless patterns across his chest. The warmth of his skin beneath her fingertips sent a comforting ripple through her. "Always," she murmured, her lips curving upward.

They lay there in silence for a moment, the weight of the day melting away as they breathed in unison. Outside, the hum of the city carried on, but it felt distant, as though the world outside their apartment didn't exist.

Lacy broke the quiet, her voice a soft murmur. "You know Paige is already drawing up plans for the Ramona King interview."

Ben chuckled, the sound rumbling through his chest. "Of course she is. I bet she's got a whole outline. What we'll say, what we'll wear…"

"Knowing her, probably even how we'll sit," Lacy teased, shifting slightly to look up at him.

Ben grinned, his good hand brushing a stray strand of hair from her face. "She's thorough. But what do you want from it?"

Lacy thought for a moment, her fingers stilling against his chest. "Honesty," she said finally. "I want people to see that we're just… us. Not a perfect politician and her picture-perfect partner. Just two people who fell in love and are trying to figure it out as we go."

Ben smiled, his thumb brushing lightly over her cheek. "I think you'll be amazing."

"We'll be amazing," she corrected gently, leaning in to press a soft kiss to his lips.

When she pulled back, her expression grew contemplative. "And then there's the wedding…"

Ben raised an eyebrow, his grin widening. "What about it?"

"Oh, just that Paige is probably going to insist on something big and dramatic," Lacy said with a laugh. "I can already hear her pitching ideas—'A winery, Lacy, with twinkling lights and a string quartet!'"

Ben laughed, shaking his head. "And what do you want?"

"Honestly?" Lacy said, her voice softening. "Something small. Intimate. Maybe in a garden or a quiet beach. Just close friends and family. I don't want the bells and whistles. Just you."

His hand slid down to intertwine with hers, their fingers fitting together seamlessly. "I like that. Simple. Just us, and the people who matter most."

They fell quiet again, the weight of their words settling comfortably between them. After a few moments, Ben broke the silence, his voice thoughtful. "How many kids do you think we'll have?"

Lacy tilted her head, surprised by the question but warmed by it all the same. "I don't know," she said, her smile growing. "More than one, definitely. Growing up an only child… it's lonely. And if something happens…"

Her voice faltered, but Ben squeezed her hand, grounding her. "I know," he said gently. "I feel the same way."

She looked up at him, her eyes searching his. "How many do you want?"

He grinned, a mischievous glint in his eyes. "Three. Maybe four."

"Four?" she repeated, laughing.

"Why not?" he said, his tone playful. "The more, the merrier. Besides, you'll make a great mom. And you'll have me to help, remember?"

Lacy's laughter softened, her expression growing tender. "You'll be an amazing dad."

His gaze softened, and he kissed her forehead. "Thanks, Lace."

They talked quietly, their conversation weaving through dreams of the future. They imagined family vacations, late-night feedings, school plays, and teenage drama. Each shared thought and whispered hope wrapped around them like a warm cocoon, insulating them from the uncertainty of the world outside.

As the night deepened, their voices grew quieter, their words slower. Lacy nestled closer, her eyes growing heavy. "Ben," she murmured, her voice thick with exhaustion.

"Yeah?" he replied, his own eyelids beginning to droop.

"I love you," she whispered, her words barely audible but filled with meaning.

"I love you, too," he said, his voice soft but resolute.

The two drifted off together, their hands still entwined, their hearts beating as one. The apartment fell silent, save for the faint sounds of their breathing and the city outside. It was a rare, perfect moment—a glimpse of the life they were building together, one filled with love, hope, and an unshakable bond.

The next morning....

The preparation room was quiet except for the faint rustling of papers and the soft hum of the air conditioning. Lacy stood in front of a full-length mirror, smoothing the lapel of her tailored navy blue suit. The deep color contrasted beautifully with her rich skin tone, while a crisp white blouse beneath the blazer added a touch of elegance. Her long hair was pulled back into a sleek low ponytail, and her makeup was understated but flawless—just enough to make her eyes seem even more intense as they reflected in the mirror.

Behind her, Ben sat in a chair, his broad frame relaxed but his dark brown eyes watchful. His white button-up was rolled at the sleeves, his muscular forearms resting on his knees as he absently flexed his fingers in the sling. Despite the casual posture, his presence was grounding, a steadying force as Lacy paced.

Paige was perched on the edge of the desk, her emerald-green blazer a vibrant pop of color against the neutral tones of the room. She was scrolling through her tablet, flipping between notes and schedules with the efficiency of someone who had mastered the art of controlled chaos.

"You know," Paige said, not looking up, "there's still time to soften this announcement if you're worried."

Lacy turned sharply, a small smile tugging at the corner of her lips. "Worried? No. I'm not worried. This is the right move."

Paige raised an eyebrow. "You're about to announce your pregnancy to the entire country, tie it to a massive policy initiative, and then answer questions from a press corps that smells blood for a living. It's okay to admit to a little worry."

Lacy crossed her arms, her smile widening. "It's not worry, Paige. It's focus. If we want change—real change—we have to lead by example. Transparency, honesty, and action. That's the tone we're setting, and I'm not backing down from it."

Paige leaned back, letting out a low whistle. "Alright, then. Just remember, I'm your fixer. You lead; I'll clean up the mess."

Ben stretched, his sling shifting slightly. "You got this. I'm going to grab some water for you," he said to Lacy, who gave him a grateful smile.

Lacy sighed, placing her hand lightly on her stomach, a gesture so subtle it could have been missed. "Can I have a minute alone?"

"Of course," Paige said, standing and straightening her blazer. She gave Lacy a small nod before stepping out of the room.

Lacy sat on the edge of the table, her hands resting protectively over her stomach. She took a deep breath, her voice soft as she spoke to the child growing inside her.

"Hey, baby," she whispered, her tone tender. "This is all for you, you know? No matter what happens, I promise you one thing—I'll always protect you, and I'll always be proud of you. You've already made me stronger than I ever thought I could be."

Her voice caught slightly, but she smiled, a single tear slipping down her cheek.

In the quiet hallway outside the press preparation room, Ben leaned against the wall, the cool surface supporting his broad frame as he absently rolled a water bottle between his fingers. The soft hum of the fluorescent lights overhead filled the stillness, and the faint murmur of voices from the press conference area drifted through the air.

Paige's heels clicked rhythmically against the polished tile as she approached. She stopped a few feet from Ben, studying him for a moment before speaking.

"Alright," she began, her tone playful but tinged with genuine curiosity. "Level with me. How are you really feeling about this whole baby thing?"

Ben looked up at her, his dark brown eyes lighting up as a grin spread across his face. "How am I feeling?" he repeated, his voice low and warm. "I mean, it's terrifying, but in the best way. I can't wait to meet them, to hold them. It's… incredible."

Paige raised an eyebrow, crossing her arms. "Incredible, huh? You say that now, but wait until you're changing diapers at 3 a.m. and covered in spit-up. Still incredible?"

Ben chuckled, shaking his head. "Yep. Still incredible."

Paige tilted her head, her smirk softening into something more thoughtful. "You know, as much as I think childbirth is some wild animal-kingdom nonsense, I've got to admit—you and Lacy are going to be amazing parents. The timing's a bit of a mess. Thank you for that, by the way," she added with a teasing smile. "But honestly, I couldn't pitch a better couple to the press if I tried."

Ben's grin faded slightly, replaced by a more heartfelt expression. "Lacy's going to be such an amazing mom," he said quietly, his voice full of conviction. "She's already so strong, so determined. I've never met anyone like her. And now, I get to build a life with her—a real life, not just moments in her apartment."

Paige rolled her eyes dramatically but couldn't hide her grin. "Oh, sure. I'm so sure you hated all the hot sneaky sex. Poor Ben, suffering through all those romantic candlelit nights of passion."

Ben laughed, a deep, rich sound that echoed faintly down the hallway. "You're something else, you know that?"

"Yep," Paige said with a wink. "But that's why everyone loves me. Now, if you'll excuse me, I've got to go drag your fiancée out of her own head." She gave him a mock salute and disappeared into the preparation room.

Ben remained in the hallway, the smile lingering on his face as his thoughts wandered. Memories of Lacy played in his mind like a reel of his favorite moments: the fire in her eyes when she was deep in a debate, the way her laughter could light up a room, the quiet vulnerability she only shared with him late at night.

He looked down at the water bottle in his hand, his thumb tracing the ridges of the plastic. A warmth spread through his chest, a sense of calm certainty that he hadn't felt in a long time. This was where he was meant to be—with her, for her, building a future together.

The door opened behind him, and Ben looked up.

Lacy stepped out, the heels of her navy pumps clicking softly against the floor. Her navy blue suit hugged her figure perfectly, and the light catching on her silver earrings gave her an almost ethereal glow. Her dark eyes met his, and for a moment, the world around them seemed to fade away.

Ben straightened, his smile widening as he extended his hand.

Lacy hesitated briefly, then slipped her fingers into his. Her touch was warm, grounding, and it sent a shiver of reassurance through him.

"You've got this," Ben whispered, his voice steady and low. "And I've got you."

Lacy's breath caught, her eyes shimmering with unshed tears. "I love you," she murmured, leaning closer to brush her lips softly against his.

"I love you, too," he replied, his voice full of quiet intensity.

Paige appeared in the doorway behind them, clapping her hands together with a grin. "Alright, lovebirds. Enough with the sap—it's showtime."

Lacy smiled, squeezing Ben's hand one last time before letting go. As she squared her shoulders and smoothed her blazer, her confidence seemed to grow with every step toward the press conference room.

Ben watched her go, his heart swelling with pride. She was a force to be reckoned with.

The noise was overwhelming as Lacy stepped onto the stage. The flash of cameras created bursts of light, like a chaotic strobe. Reporters shouted questions, their voices blending into a cacophony of indistinct sound. The room smelled faintly of cologne and coffee, the air charged with energy and anticipation.

Agent Housley and Michael stood off to the side of the stage, their sharp suits and composed expressions radiating authority. Lacy could see the reporters swarming them, notebooks and microphones thrust forward, but Agent Housley held up a hand, signaling them to stop.

One reporter's voice rose above the rest. "Agent Hayes, what was Senator Jacobs' role in the operation?"

Michael adjusted his tie, his expression calm but serious. "Senator Jacobs wasn't just involved—she was instrumental. Her courage and cooperation allowed us to gather critical evidence that ultimately took down one of the most powerful criminal organizations in the state. She's a leader in every sense of the word, and her actions speak volumes about her commitment to justice."

Another reporter chimed in. "What do you think about her campaign, given her family's background?"

Agent Housley stepped in, her tone razor-sharp. "What's relevant here isn't her background but her actions. Senator Jacobs has shown that she doesn't just talk about change—she makes it happen. But why don't you hear it from her yourself?"

The reporters turned as Lacy stepped forward, their voices rising in a frenzy. The room buzzed with tension, the scent of adrenaline practically hanging in the air.

Lacy raised a hand, her posture commanding but graceful. "Good afternoon," she began, her voice calm and steady. The noise subsided instantly.

"Thank you for being here today. I know there are a lot of questions, and I'll address three of them directly. After that, my team and I will handle the rest as we continue our campaign."

She glanced briefly at Ben and Paige, who stood at the edge of the room, their faces a mix of pride and anticipation. Taking a deep breath, Lacy turned back to the audience.

"Let me begin by saying this: I am not my father. His actions were his own, and they do not define me. What defines me is my commitment to serving this state and its people with honesty, integrity, and a vision for a better future. Both my actions and voting records show my commitment to every citizen of this commonwealth."

The room was silent, the weight of her words sinking in.

"In that spirit of honesty," Lacy continued, her voice growing softer but no less firm, "I have a personal announcement to make… I am pregnant."

The room erupted into chaos. Cameras flashed, reporters shouted questions, and the buzz of excitement was deafening. Lacy stood tall, waiting for the noise to subside.

"This is a time for transparency, for truth—things that have been sorely lacking in our politics. My pregnancy doesn't change my ability to lead. It strengthens my resolve to fight for policies that ensure every family in this state has the support they need to thrive."

She launched into her vision for the Parental Bill of Rights, her voice growing more passionate as she outlined her policies: codified parental leave, expanded Medicaid for low-income mothers, gender-affirming birth and lactation specialists, and comprehensive postpartum care.

The reporters listened intently, some scribbling notes furiously, others staring in awe as she painted a bold, inclusive vision for the future.

When she finished, she gestured to the audience. "Three questions. Who's first?"

A reporter stood, clearing her throat. "Senator Jacobs, do you believe your pregnancy will impact your ability to govern effectively if elected?"

Lacy smiled warmly, her gaze steady. "Pregnant people across this country work every single day, contributing to their families and their communities. I will be no different. My ability to lead remains unchanged, and I am more committed than ever to ensuring this commonwealth thrives."

Another reporter raised his hand. "Given your father's crimes, how do you plan to regain the public's trust?"

"I plan to earn it," Lacy said firmly. "Not through words, but through actions. By listening to the people of this state and delivering on the promises I've made as I always have."

The final question came from the back of the room. "Do you think this announcement will hurt your campaign?"

Lacy's smile turned slightly wry. "I think it depends on what you value in a leader. If you want someone who hides behind half-truths and deflects accountability, then maybe it will. But if you want someone who leads with honesty and transparency, someone who's willing to fight for every family in this state no matter how they look, then I think I'm exactly where I need to be. That's all we have time for. Thank you."

The room burst into a frenzy of questions as Lacy stepped back from the podium.

In the hallway, Paige, Ben, and Lacy shared a quiet moment together. Paige wrapped her in a tight hug, her voice soft. "You nailed it."

Ben pulled her close, his lips brushing her temple. "I'm so proud of you."

Lacy smiled, her voice steady but tinged with exhaustion. "Now comes the hard part. One week to go. Let's hit it—and hit it hard."

Ben grinned. "Right after you eat.'

Lacy laughed. "Is this what my life is gonna be? You telling me to eat all the time?"

Ben chuckled. "Yes, always."

They left the building, heading straight for campaign headquarters. When they arrived, the entire team was waiting for her, breaking into cheers and applause the moment she walked through the doors.

Later that evening, Lacy sat alone in her office at campaign headquarters. The room, dimly lit by a single desk lamp, was a refuge of quiet amid the organized chaos of the building. The faint sounds of muffled conversations and ringing phones filtered in through the closed door, but inside, it was still.

Her desk was a cluttered landscape of campaign materials—stacks of policy briefs, drafts of speeches, and notes scribbled in her precise handwriting. A half-empty cup of herbal tea sat forgotten at the edge of the desk, its once-steaming contents now cold and bitter. The faint scent of lavender and chamomile lingered, mingling with the smell of paper and ink.

Lacy leaned back in her chair, her hands resting on her stomach as she gazed at the papers in front of her. But her focus had long since drifted. Her dark eyes, usually sharp and calculating, were distant, clouded with thoughts that refused to be pushed aside.

Her father.

The memory of his blood pooling on the floor haunted her like a ghost. She could still hear the echo of the gunshot, feel the icy fear that had gripped her chest in that moment. Now, he lay in critical condition, teetering on the edge of life and death.

She didn't know how to feel.

A part of her—the daughter who had once adored him, who had looked up to him as a larger-than-life figure—hoped he would survive. Hoped for a chance at redemption, even if it was only for her own sense of closure.

But another part of her, one buried deep and wrapped in layers of guilt, wondered if the world would be better off without him. That thought was sharp, cold, and dangerous, and she didn't dare let it linger.

She exhaled slowly, the breath shaky as it escaped her lips. Her fingers traced absent patterns on the edge of the desk, the polished wood smooth under her touch.

"God, what a mess," she whispered to herself, her voice breaking the silence.

Her gaze shifted to the framed photo sitting on the corner of her desk. It was a picture of her and Ben from her first fundraiser, their smiles wide and carefree. That had been before everything had spiraled, before the weight of her father's shadow had settled over them.

A sharp knock at the door jolted her from her thoughts.

"Come in," she called, straightening in her chair and smoothing her blazer.

The door swung open, and Paige burst in, her tablet in one hand and her phone in the other. The glow from the screen illuminated her face, and her expression was a mix of determination and mild exasperation.

"Okay," Paige began without preamble, "so we've got hospitals to visit, parents to meet, and approximately a thousand calls and texts to sort through. Are you ready for this?"

Lacy blinked, momentarily caught off guard by the whirlwind of energy that was Paige. Then she smiled, the weight of her earlier thoughts lifting slightly.

She stood, smoothing the front of her suit jacket and adjusting her ponytail. "Paige," she said, her tone steady and confident, "I was born ready."

Paige grinned, flipping through her tablet as she gestured toward the door. "You are such a fucking nerd, but good, because we've got a lot of ground to cover. And by a lot, I mean you're basically going to be shaking hands until your wrist gives out."

Lacy chuckled softly, following Paige out of the room. The noise of the bustling headquarters hit her like a wave, the energy buzzing around her as staff members hurried back and forth. But this time, the chaos didn't feel overwhelming. It felt purposeful.

Her father's shadow might still linger, but Lacy knew one thing for certain: her future—and the future she was fighting for—was hers to shape.

CHAPTER 24

Lacy lounged on the sectional in her sleek, modern apartment, her legs tucked under her as she watched the morning political commentary. The skyline stretched beyond the floor-to-ceiling windows, sunlight spilling into the room and bouncing off the glossy white surfaces and polished chrome accents.

On the TV, a panel of pundits was engaged in a heated debate. Lacy's focus was sharp, her fingers idly tracing the edge of a throw pillow as she listened.

"Lacy Jacobs should've spent more time focused on her campaign and less time getting pregnant," said a man on the right, his voice oozing disdain. He adjusted his tie and leaned forward, sneering. "How is she going to lead this state? What's she going to do, ask state leaders to excuse her every time she has to pee during a state dinner?"

The man across from him rolled his eyes so dramatically it could've been a performance. "Seriously?" he snapped. "That's your argument? Let's call this what it is: misogyny. Lacy Jacobs didn't just campaign while pregnant; she also helped take down one of the biggest criminal empires in the state. Being governor? That's going to feel like a vacation."

"Oh, please," he said, waving her off. "Let's not pretend. A pregnant woman isn't fit to lead--"

The screen went black abruptly, cutting off his tirade.

"That's enough of that trash," Ben said, walking into the room with a confident stride. He wore soft navy pajama pants that clung to his muscular frame, and a fitted gray T-shirt that stretched across his broad chest. His dark brown eyes were warm as he held out a green smoothie.

Lacy groaned, her lips curling in mock disgust. "It's green," she said, leaning away from it as though it were radioactive.

"And it's good for you," Ben said, sitting beside her on the sectional and nudging the glass toward her. His tone was playful and insistent. "It's packed with vitamins and minerals that you—" he rested a hand on her belly for emphasis, "—and the baby need."

Lacy crossed her arms, giving him an exaggerated pout. "I'd rather eat dirt. And judging by the smell I'm not far off."

Ben smirked, leaning closer. His voice dropped to a low, seductive whisper, sending a shiver down her spine. "Drink it, and I'll do that thing you like."

Her eyes sparkled mischievously as she reached out, trailing her fingers teasingly down the front of his pajama pants. "That thing?" she asked innocently, her lips curving into a wicked smile.

Ben sucked in a sharp breath, his resolve wavering for a moment as his muscles tensed beneath her touch. "Lacy," he murmured, his voice thick.

She leaned in, her lips brushing against his jaw. "What's the matter?"

For a moment, Ben seemed on the verge of giving in. His hand hovered over her hip, his fingers flexing as though debating whether to pull her closer. But then, with a deep breath, he gently captured her wrist, kissed it and moved her hand away.

"Not until your ribs are healed baby," he said softly, though his tone carried an unmistakable edge of regret. "I love you, and I want you more than anything, but I'm not risking it, no matter how tempting you are right now."

Lacy laughed, leaning back and studying him with an amused grin. "You're no fun."

Ben tilted her chin up with his finger, his dark eyes locking with hers. "No," he murmured, brushing his lips against the corner of her mouth. "I'm crazy about you. And when you're ready—when you're fully healed—I'm going to fold you in half and make sure you never doubt that again."

Heat flushed her cheeks, and her pout turned into a smile as she finally reached for the smoothie. "Deal," she said, taking a sip and grimacing. "But this stuff tastes like lawn clippings."

Ben chuckled, smacking her lightly on the butt as she stood. "Go take your shower, superstar. Your glam squad will be here soon."

Lacy laughed over her shoulder, disappearing into the bathroom as the sound of running water filled the apartment.

An hour later, Lacy emerged from her bedroom, transformed by her team of stylists. Her royal blue dress suit fit her like a glove, the tailored blazer accentuating her figure while still looking professional and elegant. Her silver earrings glinted in the light, and her hair was pulled back into a sleek low ponytail that framed her face perfectly.

Ben, leaning against the kitchen counter with a cup of coffee in hand, looked up and froze. His gaze swept over her, admiration evident in the way his lips curved into a slow, appreciative smile.

"You look incredible," he said, his voice low and sincere.

Lacy smoothed her blazer and tilted her head. "Thanks. Now let's hope the voters think so, too."

"They already do," Ben replied, setting down his coffee and crossing the room to her. He leaned in, pressing a kiss to her forehead. "You've got this, Lacy, and I got you."

She smiled, her confidence bolstered by his unwavering support.

At the neutral event space, Lacy stood beside her opponent, William Harding. The brightly lit room had a polished wooden floor and was adorned with state flags. Cameras were positioned to capture the moment as the two candidates encouraged voters to head to the polls.

"Get out and vote," Lacy said warmly into the camera, her tone genuine and inviting. "Every voice matters, and every vote counts."

Harding nodded stiffly, his smile tight. "Participating in democracy is the most important thing you can do for your Commonwealth."

As the cameras cut, Harding turned to her, lowering his voice. "I'll admit, I'm surprised," he said, his tone dripping with condescension. "Someone in your situation—having a child out of wedlock—still campaigning? I'd have thought you'd be at home, learning how to be a proper mother."

Lacy's smile didn't falter, but her eyes hardened ever so slightly. She extended her hand, her grip firm as she shook his. "Thank you for your concern," she said sweetly. "But a proper mother would never allow someone like you to be elected."

She released his hand and walked away, her heels clicking against the floor, leaving him staring after her, speechless.

****

The campaign headquarters buzzed with restless energy that would stretch into the evening. Phones rang constantly, staff scurried back and forth clutching clipboards and laptops, and the smell of fresh coffee wafted through the air, mingling with the faint tang of stress-induced sweat. Correspondents and volunteers poured in and out, delivering updates from polling stations across the state.

Lacy was at the center of it all, stationed at her desk with a tablet in hand, analyzing precinct data. Her suit was still perfectly pressed, but her heels had been traded for comfortable flats—a small concession to the long hours ahead.

Paige sat nearby, a headset covering one ear as she rattled off instructions to someone on the other end of the line. Her emerald-green blazer was immaculate despite the chaos, and her sharp tone cut through the background noise like a blade.

Ben was in another corner of the room, sleeves rolled up as he reviewed the latest numbers with a group of staffers. Even with his injured arm in a sling, he exuded calm authority, his deep voice a steady presence in the whirlwind of activity.

As the hours ticked by and the sun dipped below the skyline, Lacy caught Ben's eye. He gave her a small, reassuring smile, and she felt a flicker of warmth in her chest despite the weight of the day.

Back at Lacy's apartment…..

The apartment was bathed in the golden glow of evening, the warm light streaming through the floor-to-ceiling windows and casting soft shadows on the sleek, modern furniture. The faint hum of city traffic below mingled with the comforting aroma of chicken soup that wafted from the kitchen.

Lacy stood by the windows, gazing out at the skyline. Her reflection stared back at her in the glass—poised, composed, but carrying the weight of a campaign, her pregnancy, and the emotions of the day. The apartment, usually a sanctuary of calm, felt unusually quiet despite the buzz of activity at campaign headquarters.

Behind her, Nonnie bustled around the kitchen, her floral apron swishing as she ladled the steaming soup into a white bowl. Ben sat on the couch, his dark brown eyes watching Lacy intently, his injured arm resting in its sling. The tension in the air was palpable, but the love between the three of them softened its edges.

"You should eat something," Ben said gently, breaking the silence.

"I'm fine," Lacy replied, her voice distant as she continued to stare out at the city.

Ben frowned, setting down the tablet he'd been using to track polling updates. He stood, his tall frame towering over the couch as he crossed the room with deliberate steps. "You're not fine," he said, his tone firmer now. "Lace, you've barely eaten all day, and you've got hours to go before this is over. Please."

Nonnie appeared from the kitchen, her warm smile breaking the tension. She carried the bowl of soup, the steam curling into the air. "Now, now," she said, handing the bowl to Lacy. "This isn't just any soup, sweetheart. This is magic soup. I made it for Ben's mama when she was pregnant with him, and look how he turned out—big, strong, and stubborn as a mule."

Lacy's lips twitched into a smile despite herself. The tension in her shoulders eased slightly as she turned away from the window to take the bowl, the warmth of it comforting in her hands. "Thank you, Nonnie," she said, sitting on the couch.

"Good girl," Nonnie said with a wink. "Eat up. You need your strength— for the campaign. And for my great-grandbaby."

Lacy took a spoonful, the rich broth warming her from the inside out. The flavors of chicken, herbs, and vegetables blended perfectly, each bite grounding her a little more.

Ben sat beside her, his expression softening as he watched her eat. "See? Not so bad, right?"

She rolled her eyes playfully. "It's good, fine...... Fine, it's amazing."

Nonnie disappeared briefly and returned holding the familiar quilt she had given Lacy months ago. The faded fabric, worn but sturdy, carried generations of memories. She held it out with both hands, her eyes shining with emotion.

"This has been in our family for generations and I told you it always works," Nonnie said, smiling softly, placing the blanket in Lacy's lap. "And now it's time to wrap your new family in it. It's brought us luck every time."

Lacy's throat tightened as she ran her fingers over the stitched patterns, the weight of the fabric feeling like an anchor in her hands. She stood, setting the bowl aside, and pulled Nonnie into a warm hug.

"Thank you," Lacy whispered, her voice thick with emotion.

"Of course," Nonnie said, patting her cheek. "You always have a family now."

After Nonnie left, Ben lingered by the door, his good hand resting on the knob. Lacy remained on the couch, carefully folding the quilt as though it were made of glass.

"You sure you don't want me to stay?" Ben asked, his voice hesitant.

Lacy looked up at him, their eyes meeting. His brows were furrowed, his jaw tight. He was trying to mask his concern, but it was etched into every line of his face.

"You've got campaign stuff to do," she said gently, standing and walking over to him.

Ben shook his head, stepping closer. "And I've also got a fiancée who's pregnant, exhausted, and carrying the weight of an entire commonwealth on her shoulders," he countered, his tone firm. "Lace, I don't want to leave you alone right now."

Her lips curved into a small, reassuring smile as she placed a hand on his chest. "I just need an hour," she said. "I promise I'll be okay. Go back to headquarters. Paige probably needs you to keep her from scaring someone."

Ben let out a soft laugh, the tension in his posture easing slightly. "She can be scary."

"Exactly," Lacy said, leaning up to kiss him softly.

He lingered, his good hand brushing against her cheek as his dark eyes searched hers. "Call me if you need me," he said, his voice low and earnest. "I mean it, Lace. I'll come back in a heartbeat."

"I know," she whispered, her smile turning tender.

Ben leaned down, pressing a lingering kiss to her forehead. "I love you," he murmured.

"I love you, too," she replied, watching as he finally, reluctantly, opened the door and left.

The apartment felt impossibly quiet once Ben was gone. The sound of the door clicking shut echoed through the space, leaving Lacy standing alone in the center of the living room. The sleek, modern furniture glinted faintly under the golden glow of the evening light streaming through the floor-to-ceiling windows. The quilt Nonnie had handed her was still in her hands, the worn fabric soft and comforting beneath her fingertips.

For a moment, she simply stood there, frozen in place. The silence pressed against her, amplifying the emotions she'd been holding back all day: fear, exhaustion, hope, and the bittersweet ache of knowing her life was on the brink of irrevocable change.

She moved slowly to the couch and sat down, the quilt pooling in her lap. Her gaze drifted around the room—her sanctuary. The polished chrome accents, the soft gray couch, and the family photos on the shelves all felt so familiar, yet suddenly so foreign.

Her eyes landed on a small picture frame tucked neatly on the bookshelf. It was a photo of her mother, taken when Lacy was just a baby. Her mother's smile was wide and bright, her eyes full of life as she cradled baby Lacy in her arms.

Lacy reached for the frame with trembling fingers, holding it in both hands as tears welled in her eyes. She traced the outline of her mother's face with her thumb, her vision blurring.

"Hey, Mom," she whispered, her voice thick with emotion. "I know it's been a while since we talked, but… I had to tell you. You're going to be a grandma."

The words hung in the air, and Lacy's throat tightened as the tears spilled over, tracing warm paths down her cheeks. "I wish you were here to meet them," she continued, her voice breaking. "Ben would've loved you. Nonnie, too. And the baby…"

She let out a shaky breath, clutching the photo closer. "I think you'd be proud of me," she murmured. "At least, I hope you would

be. I'm trying so hard to be the kind of woman you taught me to be. Strong, brave, and… loving……..I'm proud of me."

Her shoulders shook as a sob escaped her, and she pressed the photo to her chest, letting the weight of her grief and longing wash over her. She cried for the milestones her mother had missed, for the guidance she still craved, and for the love she wished her mother could give to Ben and their baby. Tears slid down her cheeks as she thought of her father, lying in critical condition. She thought of her mother and the mother she wanted to be. She cried for the girl she had been and the woman she had become, for the sacrifices she had made and the future she was fighting for.

For several minutes, she stayed like that, curled on the couch with the photo clutched tightly in her hands. The release was painful, but it was also healing, as though each tear was carrying away a piece of the burden she'd been carrying.

The release felt good—necessary, even. When the sobs finally subsided, she wiped her face with trembling fingers, breathing deeply to steady herself. Her hand lingered on the frame for a moment longer before she placed the photo back on the shelf, a soft sigh escaping her lips.

She straightened, inhaling deeply as she smoothed her blazer. The emotions still churned inside her, but the edges felt softer now, less jagged. Her gaze fell on the remote control sitting on the coffee table, and a small smile tugged at her lips.

Grabbing it, she scrolled through her playlist until the beat of Megan Thee Stallion's "Anxiety" blasted through the apartment.

For a moment, she just stood there, letting the music wash over her. Then, with a laugh bubbling up from her chest, she started to move. Her body swayed and twerked to the beat, the tension melting away as she lost herself in the rhythm. It was silly, freeing, and exactly what she needed.

By the time the song ended, Lacy was breathless, her chest heaving as she leaned against the back of the couch. A genuine smile spread across her face, her laughter echoing through the space.

She ran a hand over her face, then over her stomach, letting out a deep sigh. "Alright, Mom, little nugget," she whispered, glancing back at the photo and her belly. "Let's finish this."

The energy at campaign headquarters was still electric when Lacy arrived. Staffers buzzed around, their excitement and tension palpable.

Paige met her at the door, her blazer still immaculate despite the long day. Her tablet was in one hand, and her phone was pressed to her ear.

"Hold on," Paige said into the phone before turning to Lacy. "You're still holding on in all the key districts. It's tight, but you pulled ahead in a few unexpected counties. If we can beat him by forty thousand votes, we'll be out of automatic recount range."

Lacy nodded, her jaw tightening as she followed Paige to her office. "Forty thousand. Got it. Where are we focusing next?"

Paige rattled off a few key strategies as they walked, her heels clicking against the polished floors. By the time they reached Lacy's office, the weight of the challenge ahead was clear, but so was the determination in Lacy's eyes.

"We've got this," Lacy said firmly.

Paige gave her a quick smile. "I'll keep you updated. Hang in there. Two-and-a-half hours until polls close across the state."

Three hours passed like a slow drip, each second stretching into eternity as the campaign headquarters buzzed with restless energy. The hum of conversations, the sharp clicks of keyboards, and the faint shuffle of papers filled the space. Outside, the city was a blur of lights and movement, the vibrancy of election night reflected in the glass walls of the building.

Lacy sat at her desk, her tablet displaying a precinct map that blurred before her tired eyes. The smell of coffee lingered in the air, mingling with the sharper tang of adrenaline. Her ribs ached from the long day, a dull reminder of the sacrifices she'd made to get to this moment.

She leaned back, her hands gripping the armrests of her chair, and glanced at the clock on the wall. The seconds ticked by with agonizing precision. Every nerve in her body was taut, every breath shallow as she waited for the final update.

Her office door creaked open, and Paige stepped inside. The usually unflappable emerald blazer slightly wrinkled, and her lips pressed into a thin line. Her face was unreadable, and the sight of it made Lacy's stomach twist.

Lacy stood, her legs feeling unsteady beneath her. Her heart pounded, a deep, rhythmic thrum that seemed to echo in her ears. "Well?" she asked, her voice barely above a whisper.

Paige hesitated, her chest rising and falling as she took a deep breath. Then, slowly, her eyes shimmering with unshed tears.

"The votes are in," Paige said, her voice trembling. She stepped closer, the weight of the moment palpable in the air between them. "It's time, Madame Governor."

THE END

EPILOGUE

Lacy sat behind her large oak desk in the governor's office, the late afternoon sun streaming through the tall windows and casting a warm glow on the room. Papers were spread across the polished surface, and her laptop pinged softly with new emails. She balanced her phone against her ear while typing one-handed, her voice calm but firm as she gave instructions.

"No, I want the final language tightened up before it's sent to the committee," she said, leaning back in her chair. Her cream blazer was draped over the back, her silk blouse slightly wrinkled from a long day.

The door opened, and her chief of staff, Leena, poked her head in. "Governor Jacobs," Leena said with a grin, "you've got three very determined constituents who insist on seeing you."

Lacy raised an eyebrow. "Send them in," she said, hanging up the phone and standing, smoothing her skirt.

The door opened fully, and in walked Ben, holding their eight-month-old son, Noah, in his arms. Beside him, their three-year-old daughter, Layla, skipped in, clutching a piece of paper tightly in her small hands.

"Mama!" Layla cried, running toward Lacy with a wide smile. Her curly hair bounced with each step, and her tiny sneakers squeaked on the hardwood floor.

Lacy's face lit up, the fatigue from her day melting away. She crouched down, holding out her arms. "Hey, baby girl! What have you got there?"

Layla thrust the paper toward her, beaming with pride. "I made a picture for you! It's us, see? That's me, that's Daddy, that's baby Noah, and that's you with a crown because you're the queen!"

Lacy laughed, pulling her daughter into a hug. "It's perfect," she said, examining the colorful scribbles of stick figures and a lopsided crown. "I love it."

Ben walked over, balancing Noah in one arm while carrying the baby bag slung over his shoulder. "Hey, gorgeous," he said, leaning down to kiss Lacy's cheek.

Lacy stood, her hand brushing against his chest as she looked at their son. "And how's my little man?" she cooed, reaching out to tickle Noah's belly.

The baby giggled, his chubby cheeks dimpling as he squirmed in Ben's arms.

"Hold that thought," Ben said, wrinkling his nose.

Lacy laughed as Ben walked to the corner of the office where a small changing table was set up. Layla trailed behind him, chattering excitedly about her day. Lacy leaned against her desk, watching them with a warm smile.

Once the diaper was changed, Ben handed Noah to Lacy, who immediately covered his face with playful kisses. "There's my sweet boy," she said between giggles. Noah squealed with delight, his tiny hands patting her cheeks.

Ben stood behind her, his hand resting on her shoulder as he watched. His dark brown eyes softened, and a slow smile spread across his face. "You're amazing, you know that?"

Lacy turned, still holding Noah, and kissed Ben deeply, her free hand sliding up to the back of his neck. The kiss lingered, full of love and an undercurrent of heat that made Ben chuckle softly when they finally pulled apart.

"Still not tired of me yet," he teased, his voice low.

"Never," Lacy replied with a sly grin.

Ben raised an eyebrow. "So, ready to get back on the campaign trail?"

Lacy sighed dramatically, shifting Noah in her arms. "How could I not, after three years of fighting to pass legislation—"

Ben smirked. "Most of which, by the way, you signed into law."

"Exactly. I'm excited to keep going," Lacy said, handing Noah back to Ben as Layla tugged on her skirt. "And to see Auntie Paige again."

Ben leaned closer, his voice dropping into a teasing murmur. "And I'm excited because I know how freaky you get on the campaign trail."

Lacy playfully smacked his arm. "Benjamin!" she teased, her tone mock-stern.

Ben let out a low, exaggerated moan, "Mmmmm."

Lacy chuckled, shaking her head. "Calm down, you menace," she said, her laughter bubbling up as she tried—and failed—to keep a straight face.

The door opened again, and Michael Hayes walked in. His graying hair was neatly combed, and his sharp suit gave him an air of authority that hadn't dulled despite his retirement. But his stern expression melted the moment Layla turned and spotted him.

"Papa!" she squealed, running toward him.

Michael's face lit up as he knelt and scooped her into his arms. "There's my girl," he said, hugging her tightly. "Did you miss me?"

"Yes! Are we going for ice cream?" Layla asked, her eyes wide with hope.

Michael glanced at Lacy with a raised brow.

Lacy laughed, shaking her head. "Not today. We have to get to Sam's birthday party, remember?"

Layla's lips formed a perfect pout, and Michael joined her, mimicking the expression. "But what about ice cream at the party?" Lacy offered, crossing her arms with an amused grin.

Layla and Michael both broke into cheers. "Deal!" Michael said, standing with Layla still in his arms.

"I'll get the kids in the car," Michael said, ruffling Layla's curls and gently patting Noah's back. "You two can finish whatever governor-y things you need to do."

"Thanks, Dad," Lacy said, her voice softening.

Michael paused, his eyes meeting hers. "You know Lacy, I'm proud of you. Your mother would be, too."

Her chest tightened, and she reached out, squeezing his arm. "Thank you for everything."

Michael nodded, his expression tender. "Always."

As Michael scooped Layla into his arms, his graying hair catching the soft afternoon light, Lacy couldn't help but reflect on how far they'd come. After Richard's death, the connection between her and Michael had grown in ways she never expected.

It hadn't been easy at first—untangling the years of secrecy and betrayal that Richard had sown between them. But Michael had been patient, giving Lacy the time and space she needed to process the truth: that he was her biological father, and that he'd spent years in the shadows trying to protect her.

Their shared grief over her mother had been the first bridge between them. Michael's stories of her—vivid memories of her laugh, her fierce independence, and the way she lit up a room—had become a balm for wounds Lacy hadn't realized were still open. They'd spent countless late nights talking, piecing together fragments of the past and finding solace in the love they both carried for the woman who had shaped them.

When Layla was born, something shifted. Michael had thrown himself into the role of grandfather with an enthusiasm that melted any remaining barriers. He'd been there for every milestone, every scraped knee, and every bedtime story, his presence steady and unwavering. He wasn't just there for Lacy—he was there for her family, anchoring them in a way she hadn't known she needed.

Now, as he held Layla close, her tiny arms wrapped around his neck, Lacy felt a swell of gratitude that caught her off guard.

As soon as the door clicked shut behind them, the tension between Ben and Lacy Carter was electric, thick enough to choke on. His dark eyes bore into hers, a smoldering intensity in them that made her breath hitch. Neither moved, as though frozen in a moment suspended between desire and destruction. The air buzzed, heavy with heat and the faint scent of Lacy's perfume—a sweet, intoxicating blend of jasmine and something darker, spicier—an echo of the woman herself.

Ben's control snapped first. He crossed the room in two long, determined strides, his hands immediately framing her face. He crashed his mouth onto hers, kissing her with a ferocity that bordered on desperation. Their lips collided, hot and frantic, teeth grazing, tongues tangling in a battle for dominance. Lacy gasped into the kiss, her fingers clenching at his shirt, knuckles whitening as she tried—and failed—to hold onto even a shred of resistance.

"Ben, we shouldn't…" she whispered, her voice breathless, trembling—but without any true hesitation.

"Yeah?" he growled, lips dragging down her jawline, stubble scraping her delicate skin, leaving a delicious burn in its wake. "Then tell me to stop." His hands slid down, gripping her waist, fingers digging in just enough to send a shiver rippling through her.

Lacy's head tipped back of its own accord, surrendering her neck to him. Her body betrayed her every rational thought, arching into him as her breath hitched again. "I… I," she admitted, voice barely a whisper. The words fell from her lips like a confession, her nails biting into his chest through the fabric of his shirt as though that alone could ground her.

Ben's lips curled into a wicked smirk against her throat. "Didn't think so." His teeth grazed the sensitive hollow just beneath her ear, earning a soft, broken moan from her that made his pulse race.

Without warning, he lifted her off the ground, her legs instinctively wrapping around his waist as he carried her to the desk. The cool wood pressed against the backs of her thighs as he set her down, his hands sliding up her bare legs beneath her skirt. His touch was fire—rough and insistent—leaving trails of heat wherever his fingers roamed.

The shrill ring of her phone shattered the moment like glass. Lacy groaned, her forehead resting against Ben's as they both caught their breath.

"Saved by the bell," Ben muttered, though his hands still lingered on her hips, his touch reluctant to let her go.

Lacy laughed softly, her fingers brushing the back of his neck. "That's just Leena reminding me we have to go to Sam's birthday party," she said, though her tone was filled with regret.

Ben leaned back, his expression equal parts amused and annoyed. "Sam's birth has been cock-blocking me for years now," he joked, his grin slow and wicked.

Lacy burst out laughing, the tension between them easing slightly. "Come on," she said, sliding off the desk and straightening her skirt. "We need to stop by the house first. I want to change."

Their house stood at the end of a tree-lined driveway, nestled in a grove of ancient oak trees that seemed to stand sentinel over the quiet property. It was a two-story farmhouse with whitewashed siding, a wraparound porch, and shutters painted a deep, inviting navy blue. The porch was adorned with rocking chairs and hanging flower baskets, their blossoms bursting with color in the afternoon sunlight. This was their escape from the grandeur and constant scrutiny of the governor's mansion, a sanctuary where they could shed the weight of politics and simply be a family. The house had welcomed countless guests— friends, neighbors, and community members who had become an extended family. Close to Nonnie's cozy home and surrounded by the tight-knit circle of Ben's childhood friends, the house stood as a testament to a life built on love, trust, and the kind of community that carried them through both triumphs and trials.

"Wait until you see some of the new stuff I added to the house," Ben said as he helped Lacy into the car. His voice carried a hint of pride, the kind that always softened her.

She glanced at him, her gaze trailing over his strong arms and the way his shirt stretched across his chest. A slow, knowing smile curled her lips. "Tell me you did it in the tool belt," she teased.

Ben shot her a sideways grin. "Maybe."

Lacy let out a playful sigh, fanning herself dramatically. "Well, now I definitely need to see these renovations. And later"—she leaned in, her voice dropping to a sultry whisper—"you're putting that belt back on. The kids are at Grandpa's tonight."

Ben chuckled, shaking his head as he started the car. "You really have a thing for that tool belt, huh?"

Lacy smirked. "I have a thing for you in that tool belt."

He reached over, his fingers grazing her thigh. "Careful, Lacy. Keep talking like that, and we might not make it to the house."

Lacy smirked, leaning in just enough that her lips nearly brushed his ear. "You're just gonna have to wait," she murmured, her voice laced with mischief. "I like making you wait."

Ben exhaled a quiet laugh, shaking his head before pulling her in, his hand firm at the nape of her neck. His lips claimed hers in a slow, deliberate kiss—one that left her breathless. When he pulled back, he lingered close, his voice a husky whisper against her skin.

"If you make me wait," he murmured, his lips grazing her ear, "then I'm gonna make you beg."

He winked, his thumb tracing a slow, teasing line along her jaw before he finally let her go.

Lacy swallowed, her pulse thrumming, as they stepped out into the quiet hallway, Lacy adjusted her blazer with a practiced flick of her wrist, smoothing her skirt as they made their way toward the lobby.

She could still feel the lingering heat of Ben's touch, the ghost of his hands on her skin making her heart race anew.

Waiting by the front doors was Layla, standing with her tiny arms crossed and a pout so dramatic it was nearly comical. Beside her, Lacy's father—graying but still sharp-eyed—watched the scene unfold with barely concealed amusement.

"Finally!" Layla exclaimed, her high-pitched voice filled with exaggerated exasperation. "You said it wouldn't take long, but it did! It took forever!!! Can we get ice cream now?"

Ben crouched down to her level, his large hands resting on her little shoulders. His expression softened, melting away as he grinned at his daughter. "Of course, princess. Go with Grandpa, and I'll meet you guys in the car, okay?"

Layla's pout vanished, replaced by an excited squeal. "Yay! Ice cream!" She grabbed her grandpa's hand, already chattering happily as they headed for the exit.

Once they were out of earshot, Ben straightened and turned to Lacy, who had that same devilish grin as he did. He leaned in close, his voice a low murmur meant only for her. "Careful, Madame Governor," he teased, his breath hot against her ear. "Keep this up, and we might just end up with another little Carter running around on the campaign trail"

Lacy arched a brow, lips curling into a wicked smile as she gave him a once-over, eyes gleaming with challenge. She quipped, brushing past him with a sway in her hips that she knew would drive him insane. "Wouldn't be the first time," she winked.

www.ingramcontent.com/pod-product-compliance
Lightning Source LLC
Chambersburg PA
CBHW061039310726
48969CB00004B/1015